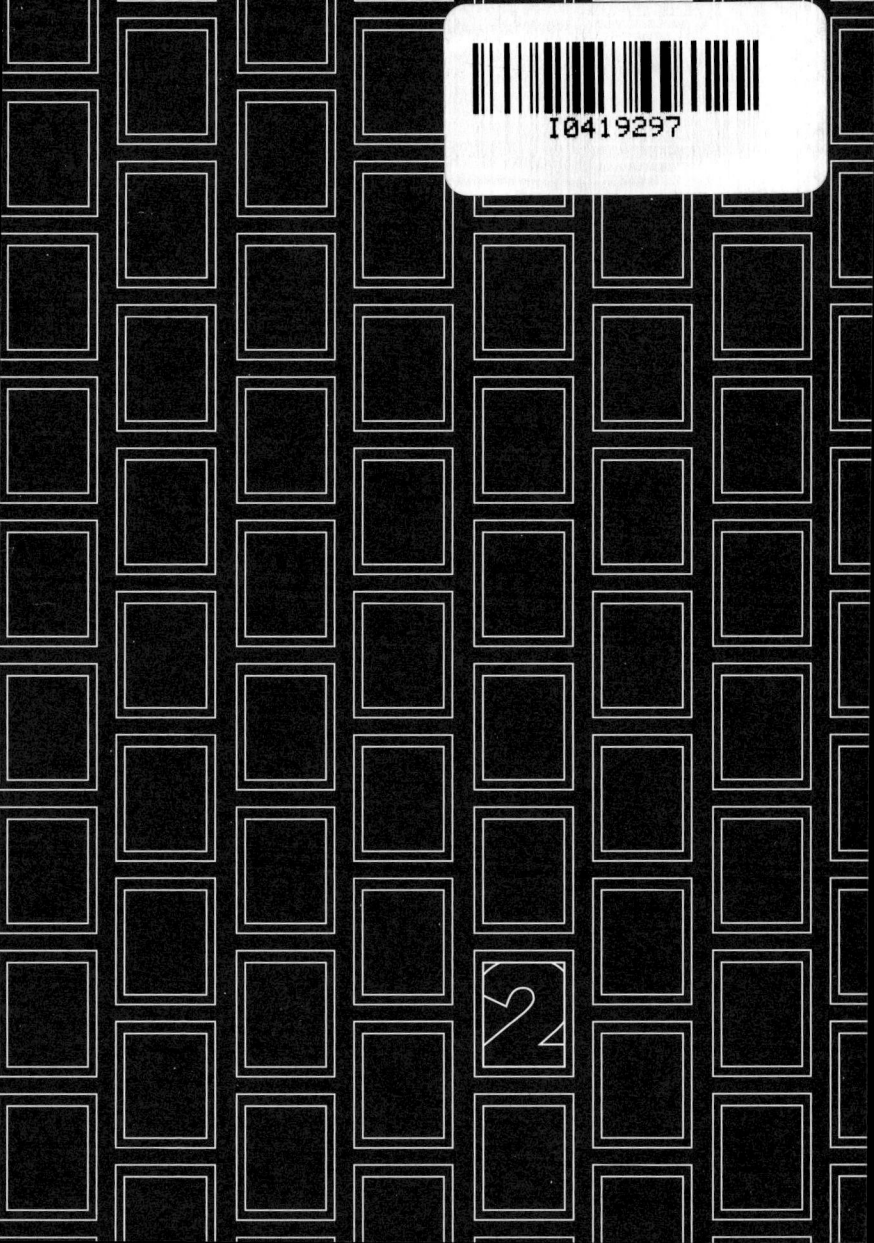
I0419297

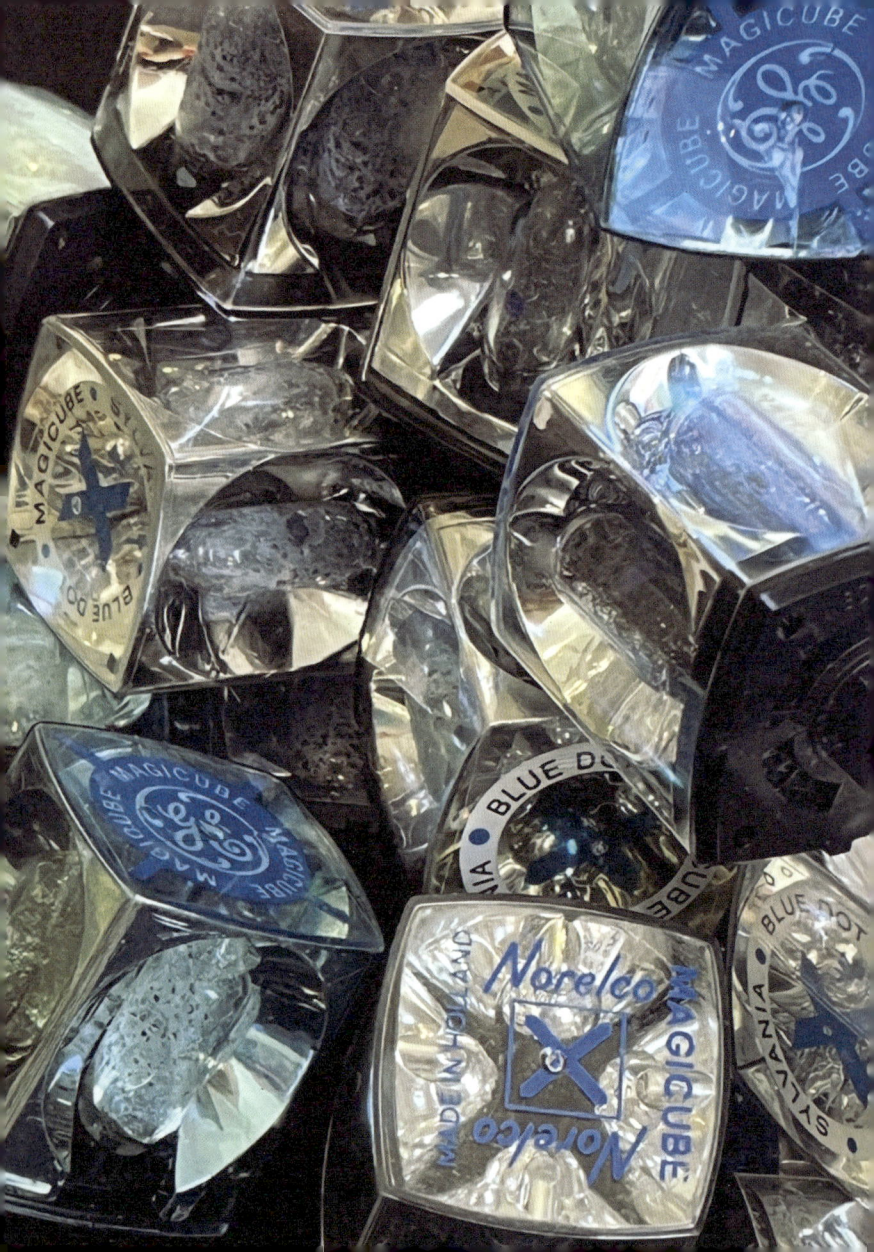

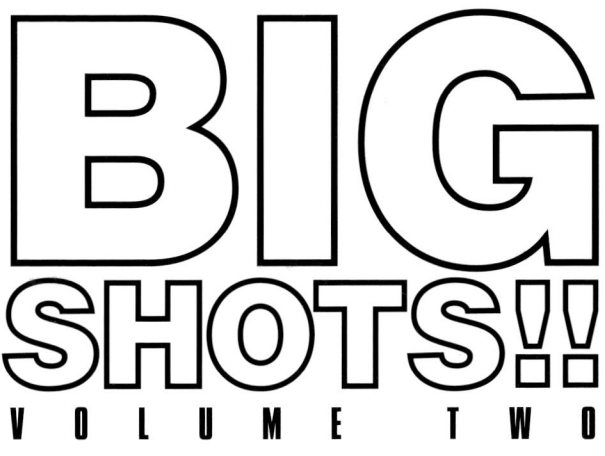

This book is dedicated to my parents, thank you for your unyielding support.

Thank you to everyone who has supported Big Shots! since the beginning, you know who you are, and if you didn't help, it was noted.

Big up to Bill McMullen for working so hard to make this book look so dope.

First published in the United States of America by Blurring Books, LLC
www.blurringbooks.com

All rights reserved. No part of this publication may be reproduced, stored in a retrieval system, or transmitted in any form or by any means, electronic, mechanical, photocopying, recording, or otherwise, without prior consent of the publishers.

Big Shots!! Volume 2

© 2024 Phillip Leeds with foreword by Pharrell Williams

Book design by Bill McMullen

For Blurring Books
Project Manager: Sean M. Johnson
Publisher: DB Burkeman

Brought to you in part by the generous support of
PLEASURES

BTS photographs by Gabrielle Djenné
Pharrell Williams Hong Kong photograph by Elaine 520

Printed in China

2024 2025 2026 2027 / 4 and 3 and 2 and 1 What up?
Library of Congress Control Number: 2016958875
ISBN: 979-8-9861975-8-6

PHILLIP LEEDS

BIG SHOTS!!

VOLUME TWO

Blurring Books

Nothing lasts forever.

I first fell in love with the Polaroid Big Shot camera when I saw Andy Warhol's Red Books exhibit at the Pace/MacGill Gallery in New York during the Spring of 2004. On display was one of Andy's many Big Shot cameras, under glass, looking like a retro-futuristic ray gun blaster. I was already a collector of vintage Polaroid Land cameras and an avid photographer. I was intrigued. The Big Shot looked remarkably different from any other camera I had ever seen and shot a totally different kind of photograph than any of my other cameras. Immediately after seeing the show, I went home and bought my first Big Shot on Ebay for twenty five dollars.

It became my favorite camera.

At the time, I was roaming the earth with rock-n-roll bands as a tour manager. Photography was a hobby of mine. I had zero aspiration to do anything with my photos beyond take them and enjoy them. I loved capturing memories and the nostalgic feeling I got from looking at the photos. I had a road case with a variety of cameras that I traveled with, but it didn't have room to add the Big Shot, which in retrospect was a huge mistake. I should have gotten a new case, as I crossed paths with so many notable people, I regret not having captured their portraits. So the Big Shot stayed home and I took portraits of friends and family who came by the house whenever I was home from tour.

In 2006, I stopped touring and began working in fashion for Billionaire Boys Club, a clothing brand Pharrell Williams (whom I had been touring with) had started. It was here that, unbeknownst to me at the time, my portrait project began to take shape. A lot of notable and notorious folks would come through our showroom in Soho, which became a sort of downtown crossroads of cool, creative people. Most of the time, if I remembered, I would get the Big Shot and take a quick Polaroid when people stopped by.

In these early days of shooting with the Big Shot, the challenge was to find Magicubes, a very specific type of extinct flashbulb that had stopped being produced in the late 1970s. I had to scour eBay and garage sales to keep a steady supply, as the Big Shot doesn't work without a Magicube. Film was abundant, cheap and came in a variety of options. Eventually Polaroid stopped making the film, but luckily Fuji made the FP100 film, which was great. Then, in 2018, Fuji stopped producing the film and that was the beginning of the end. The discontinued film was immediately hoarded by photographers and prices skyrocketed. So with dwindling supply and aging expiration dates, it seems like this project is reaching the end, its natural conclusion.

Like I said, I was not trying to be a photographer, I was not trying to be an author, I was just doing me and ended up hitting an unexpected curve in the road that took me down this way… I'll keep shooting, taking chances with over priced expired film until there is no more… maybe find another camera that gives me this satisfaction.

Nothing lasts forever.

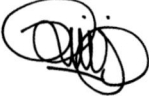

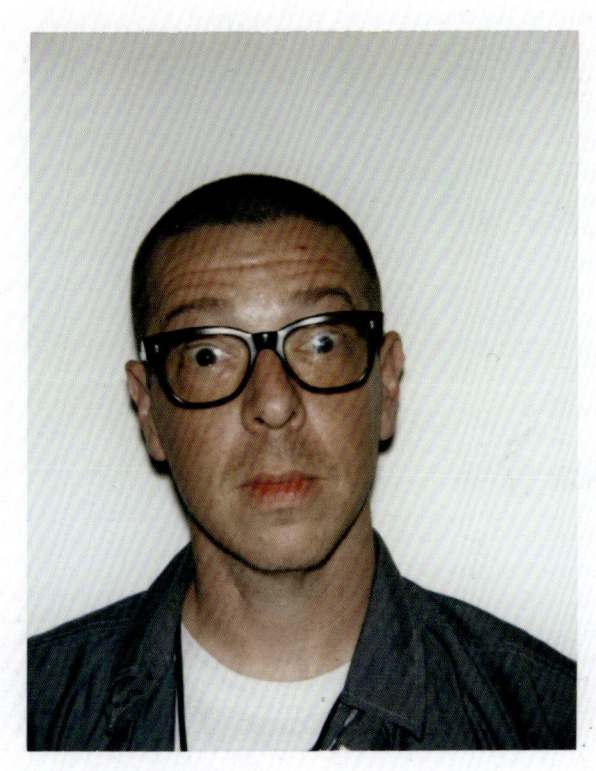

PHILLIP LEEDS, PHOTOGRAPHED BY JR

A few months ago in Hong Kong, I saw an installation with a huge wall of hundreds of Phillip's portraits from his first book. Some of those photos are going on two decades old, but seeing them immediately transported me back to that time and place. It's incredible how a photograph has the power to evoke such strong emotions and memories.

While I personally tend to focus on the future, I deeply respect those who have the ability to curate and appreciate the past. These portraits serve as a testament to the importance of preserving history and cherishing the faces that shape our lives.

Phillip, It's great to see your passion for a medium like film/Polaroid photography not let up. In a world where we all take thousands of photos on our phones that we rarely look at again, it's refreshing to see a book like this.

I'm super proud of you, Phillip.

Blessings and congratulations on another book, brother...

- Pharrell Williams, Paris, March 2024

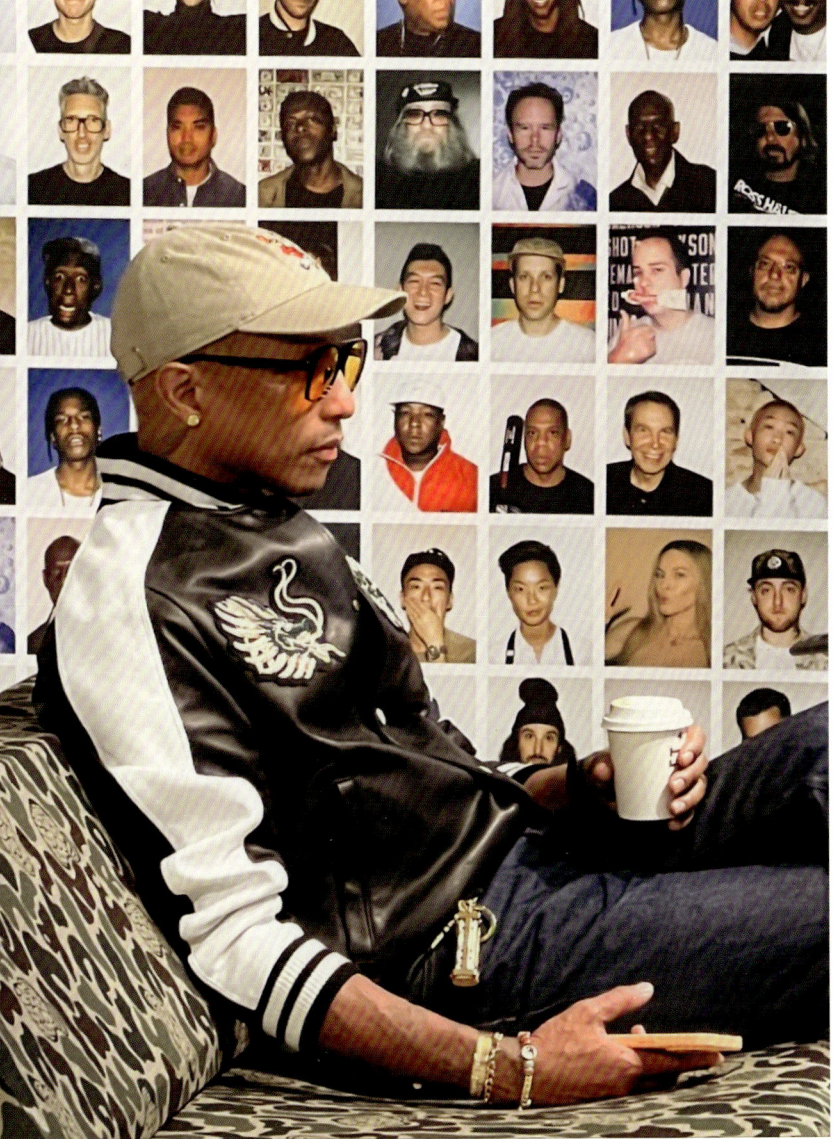

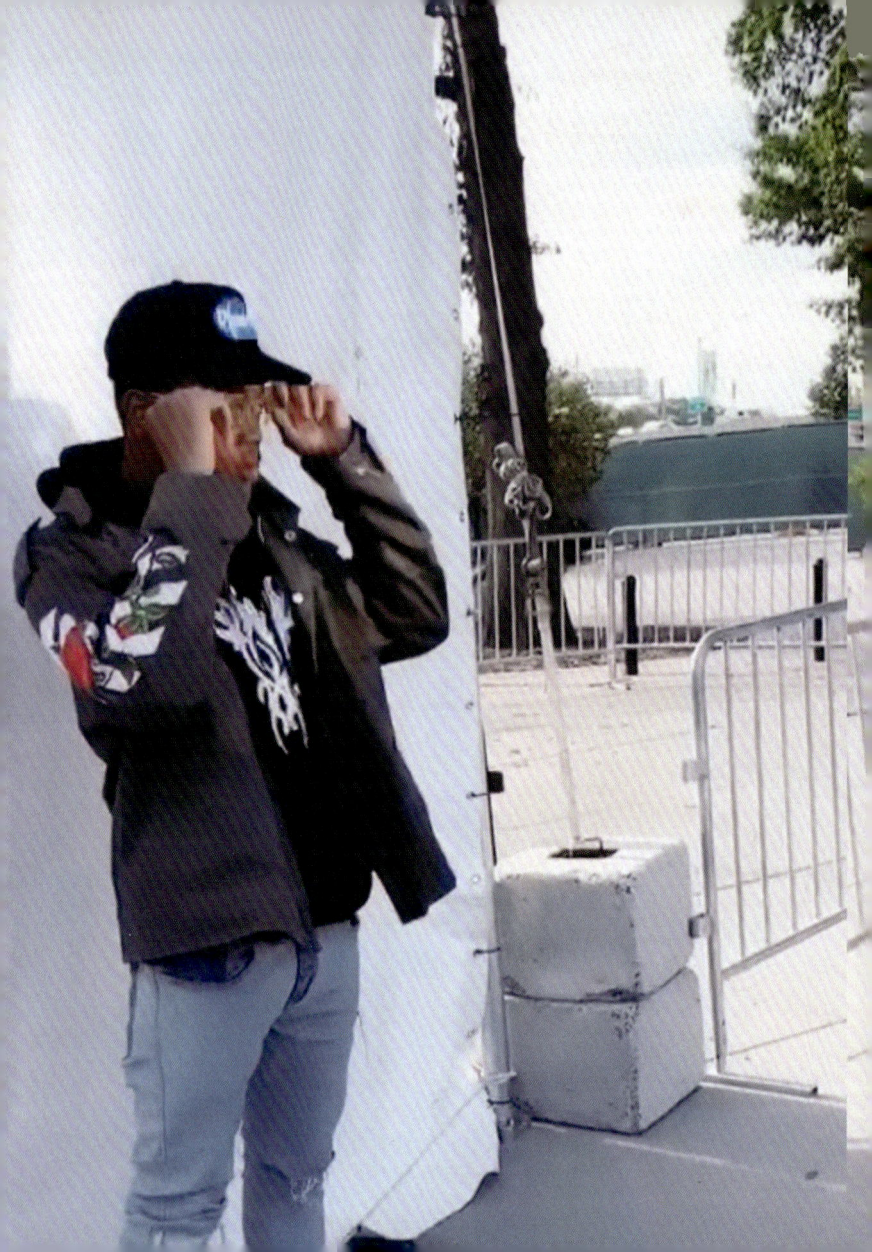

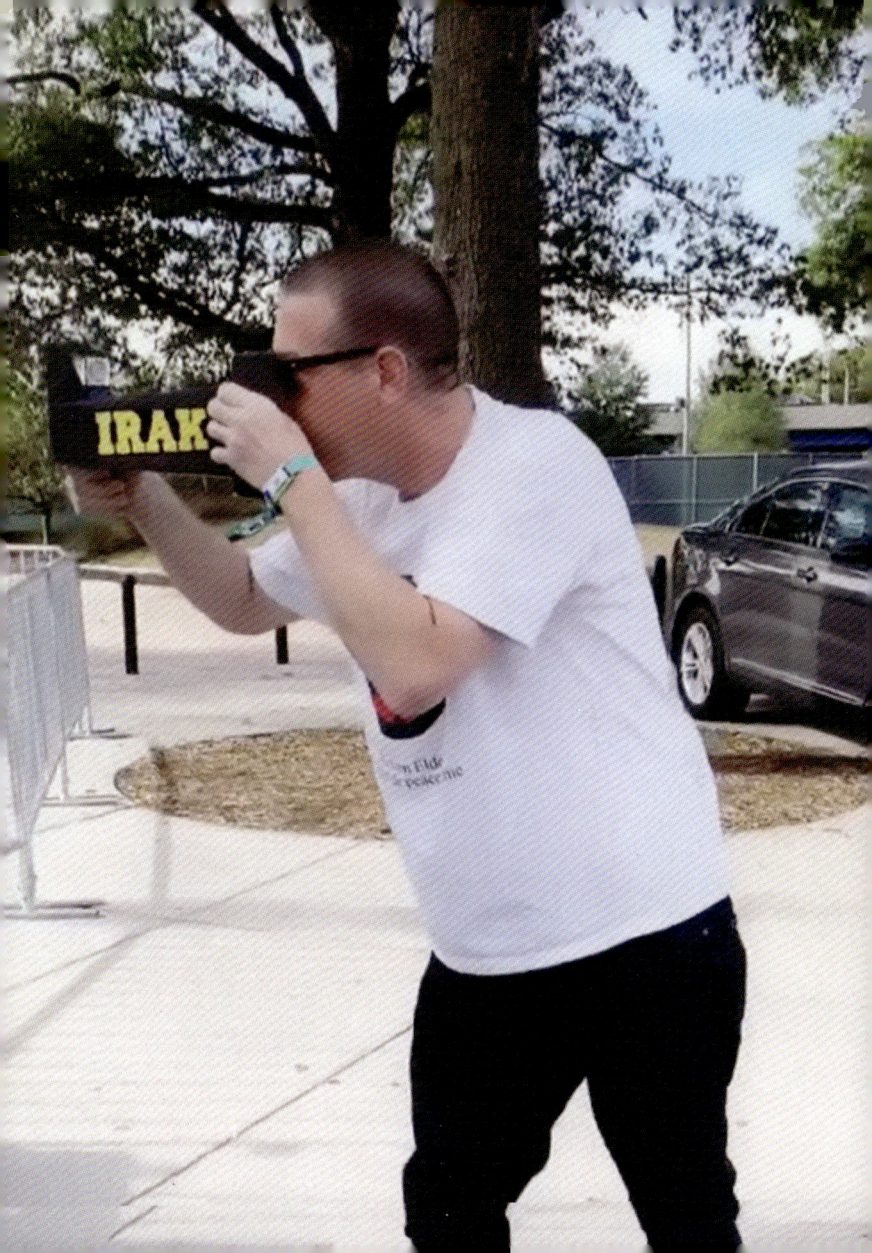

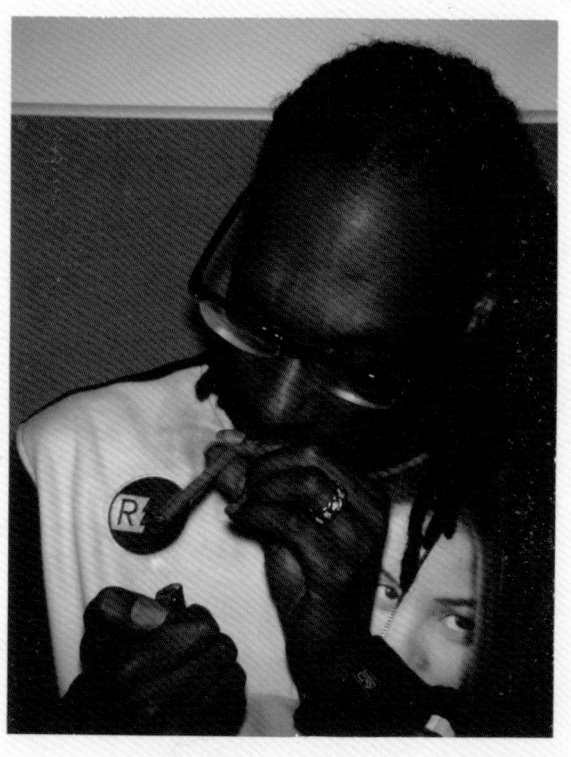

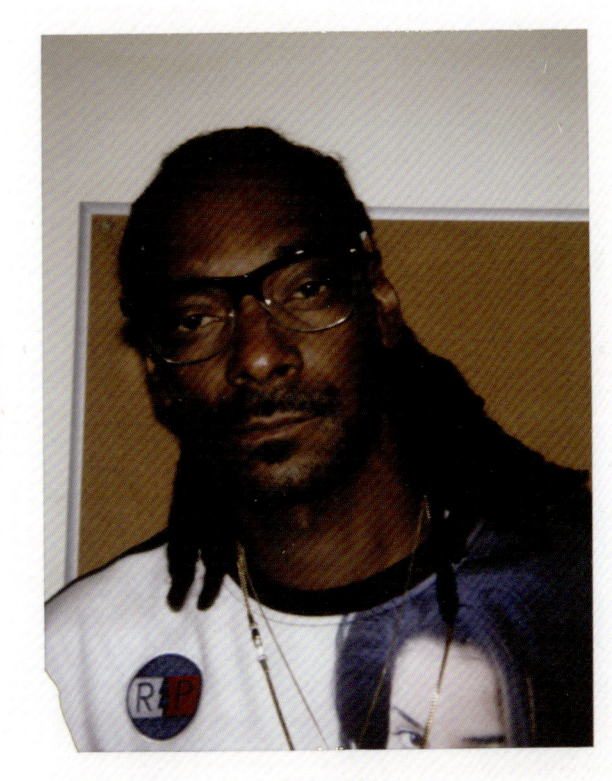

SNOOP DOGG

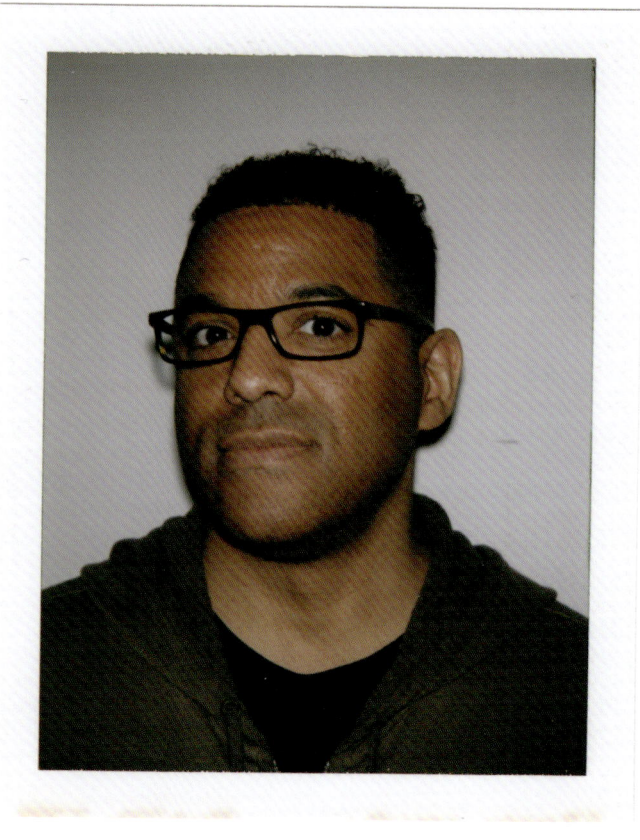

STRO ELLIOT

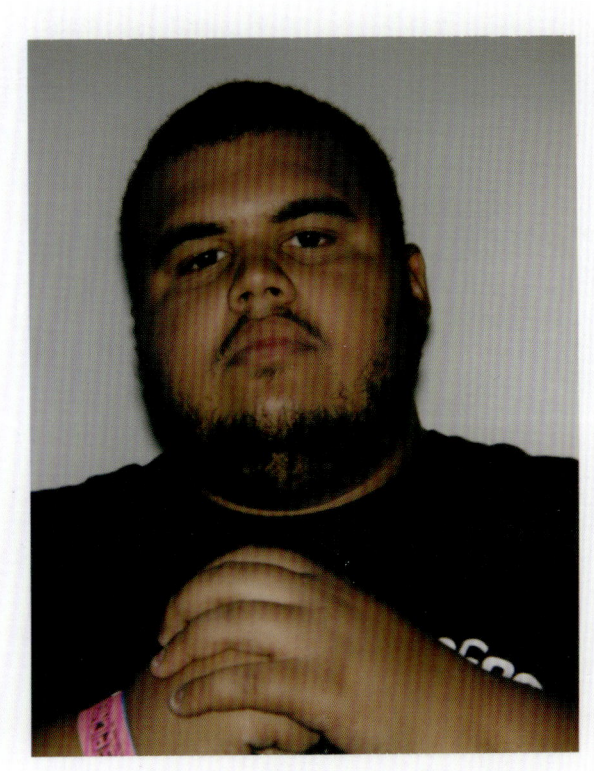

1000WORD$

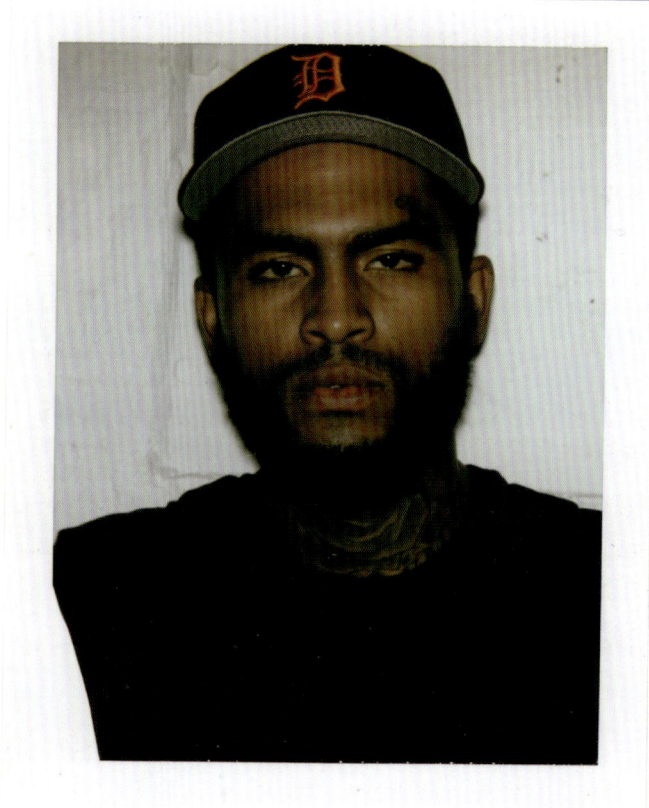

DAVE EAST

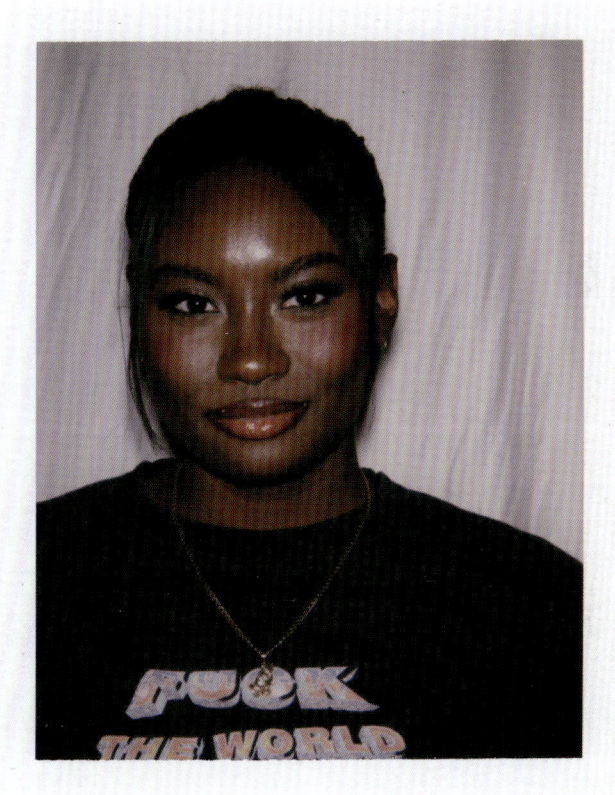

BREANNA CELESTIN

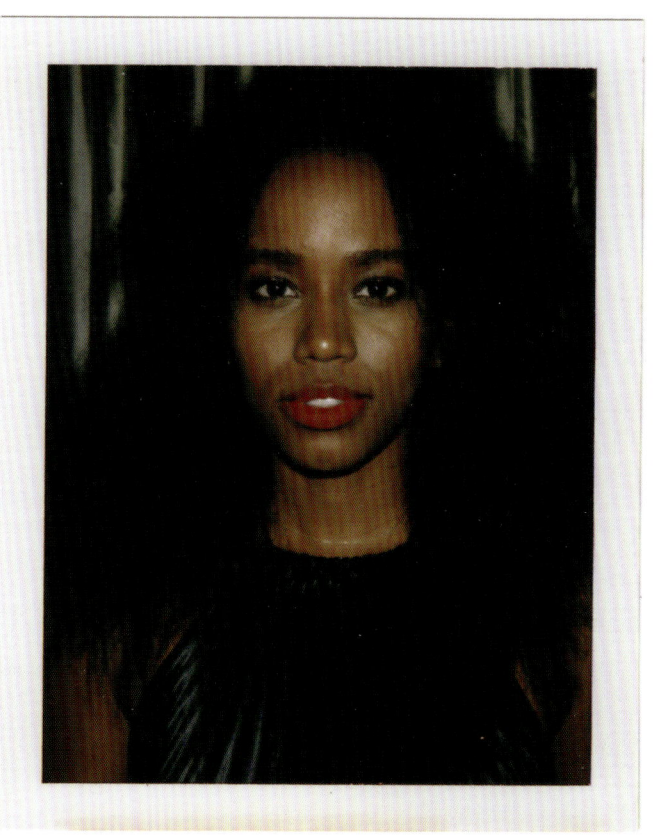

TIFFANY LIGHTY

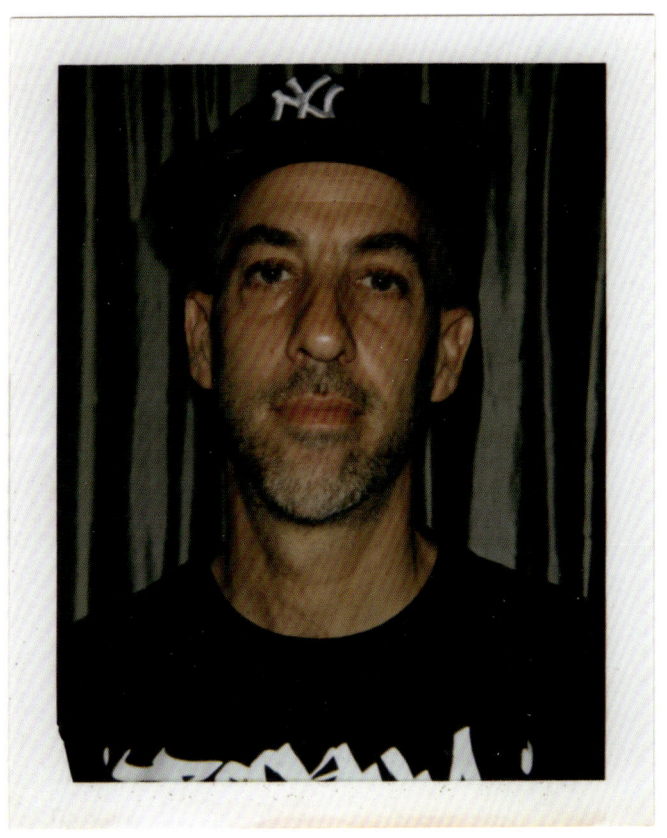

MATTY C

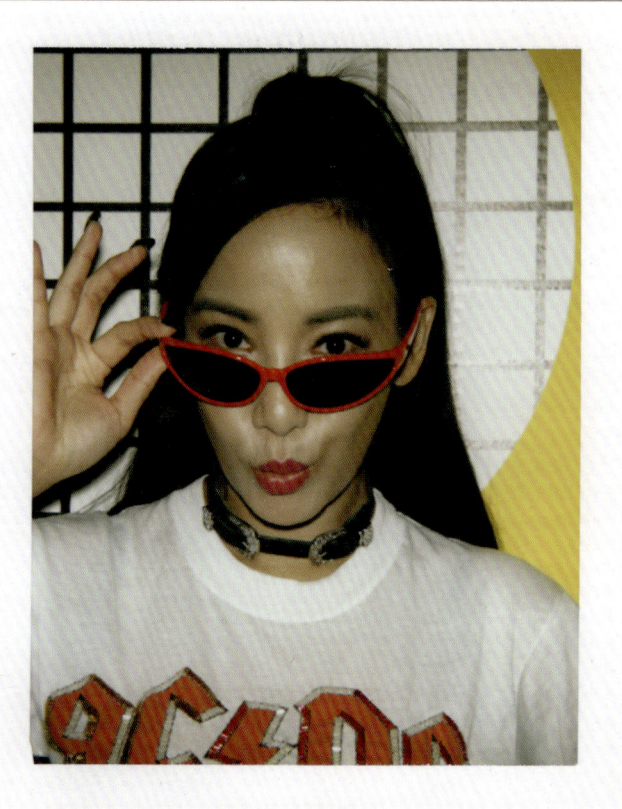

FIONA XIE

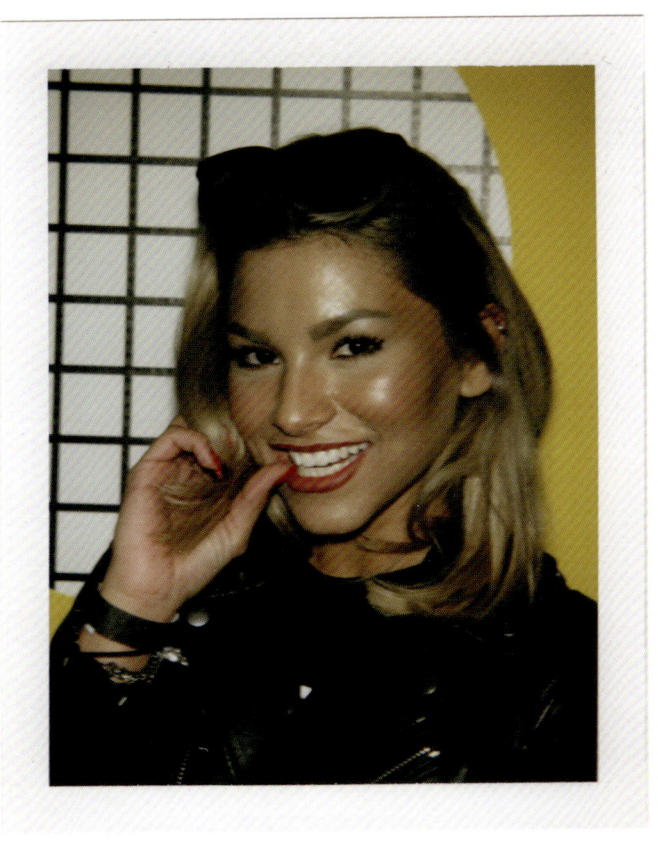

TABITHA NAUSER

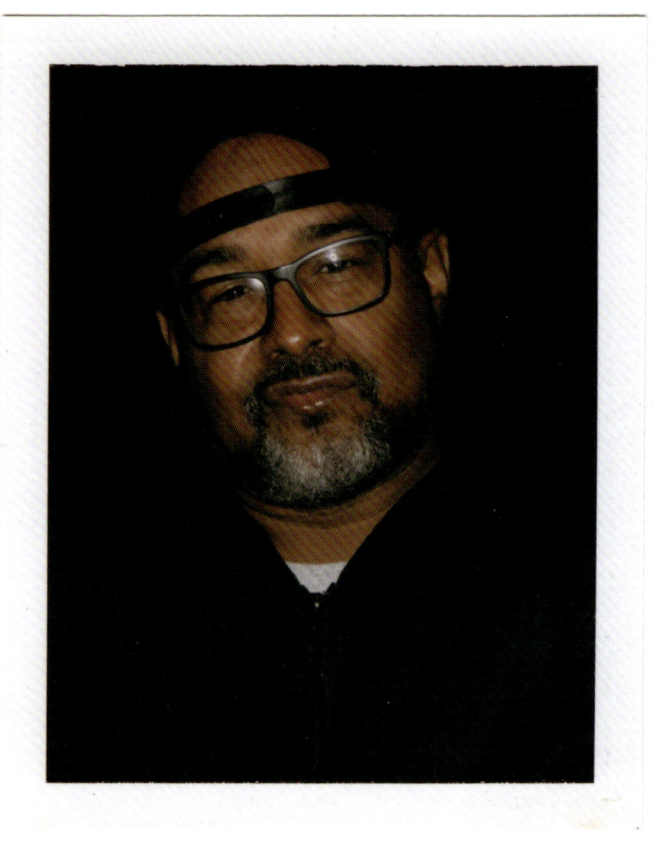

SKILLZ

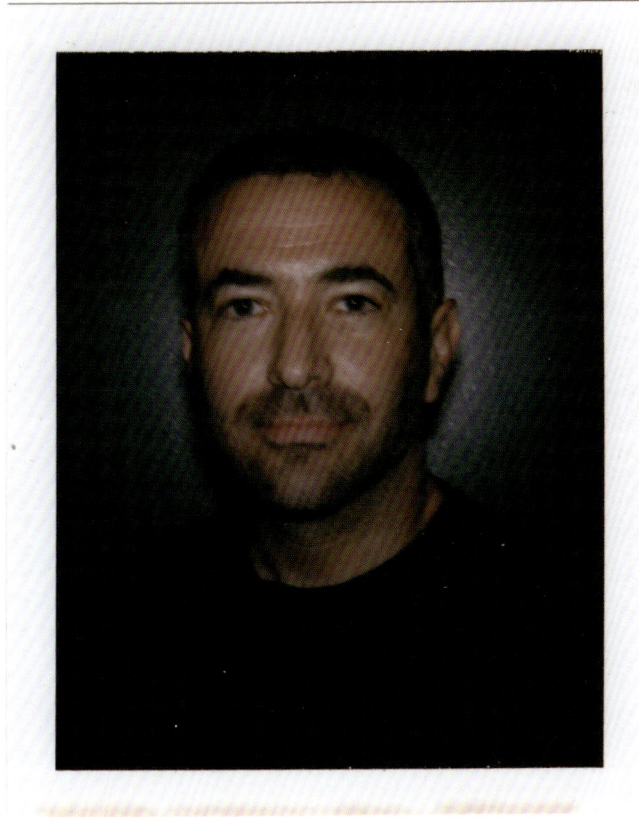

ARI MELBER

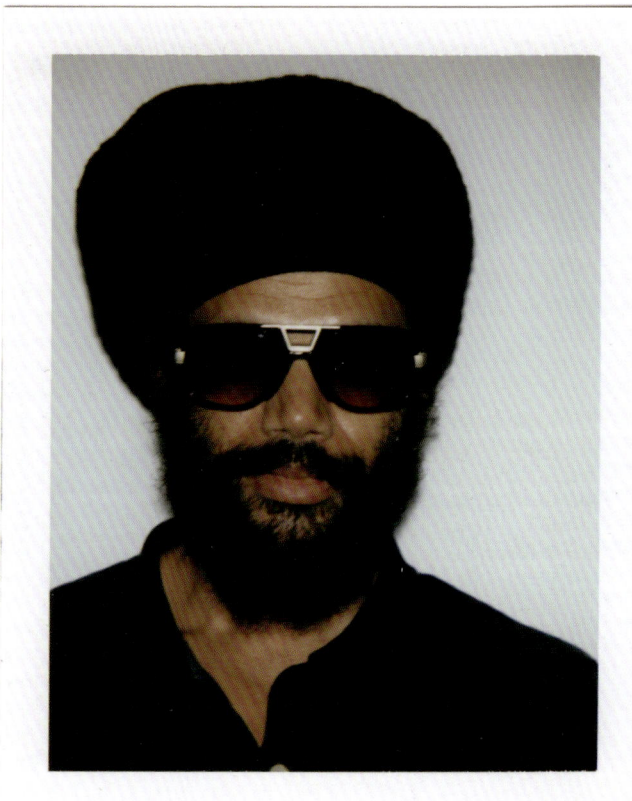

MARTEI KORLEY

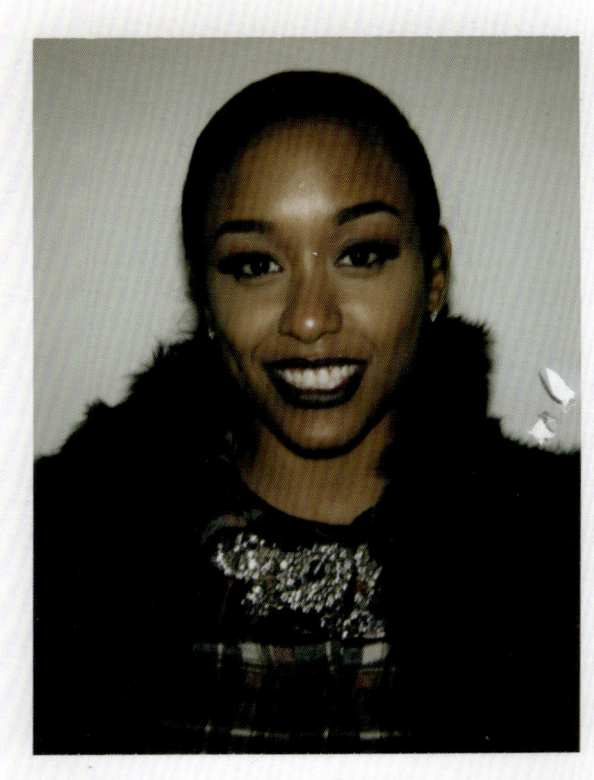

KABRIAH ASHA

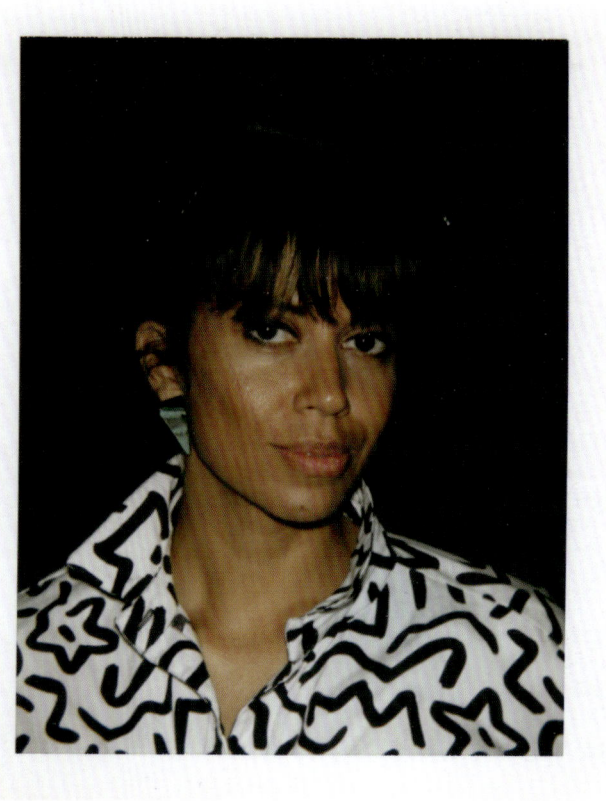

NATASHA DIGGS

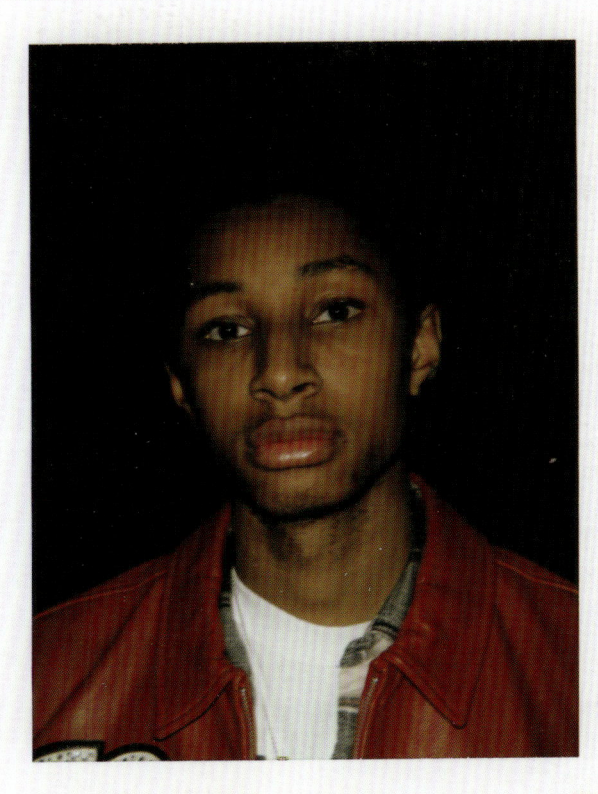

NASIR "NOTE" MARCATO

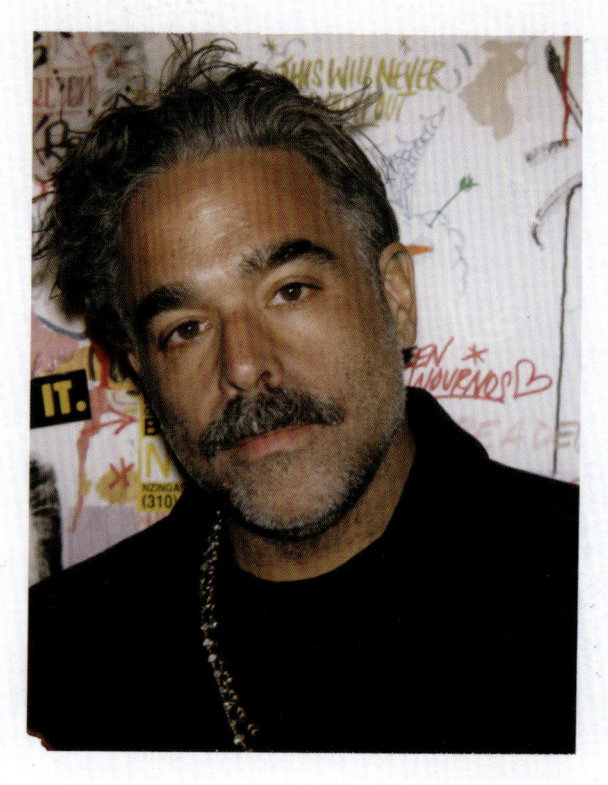

ALEX 2TONE

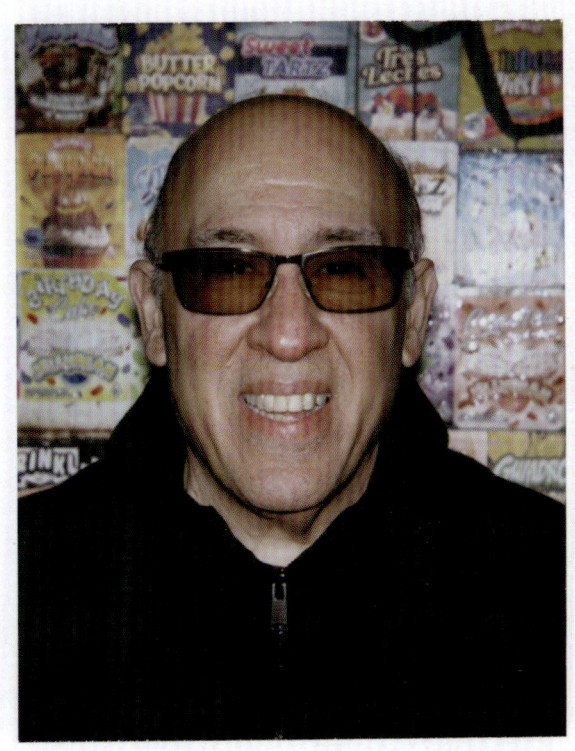

ROB GRUBMAN

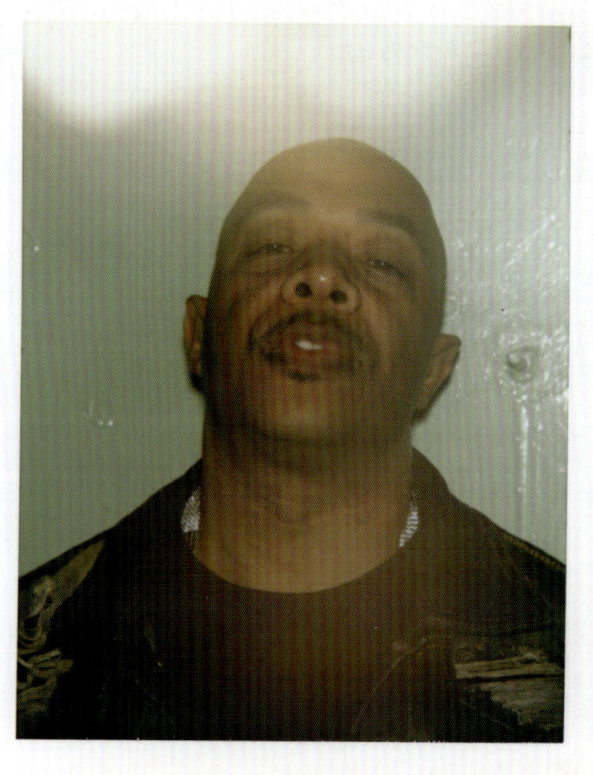

U-GOD

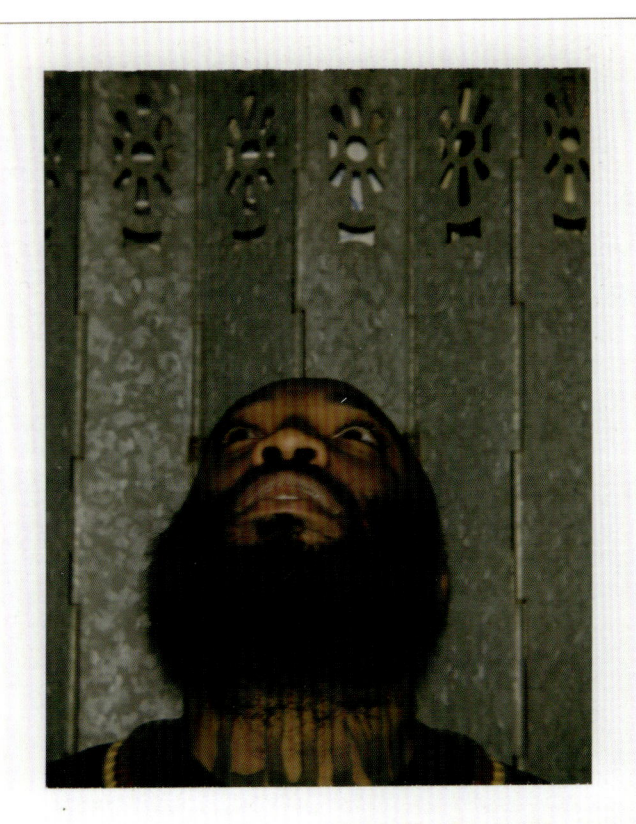

YOUNGLORD

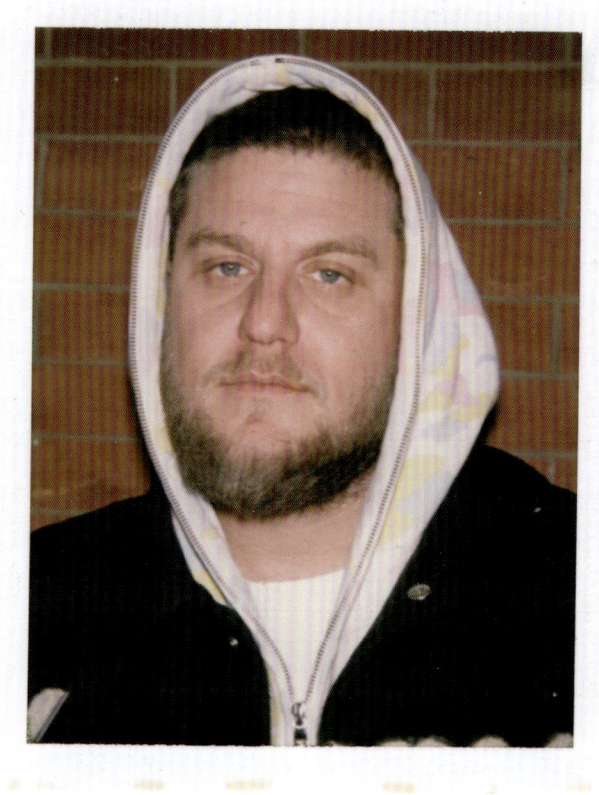

SCOTTY SELVIN - LAAMS

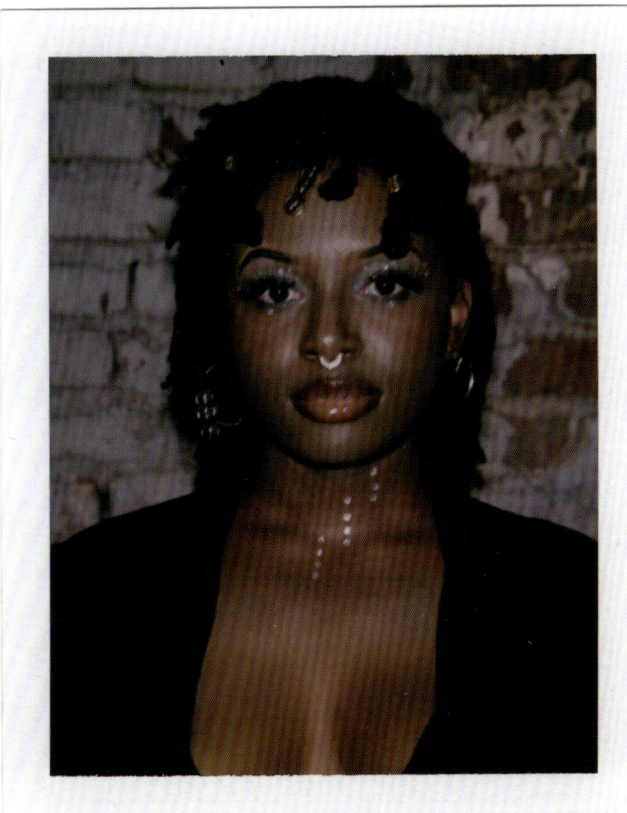

DORICA

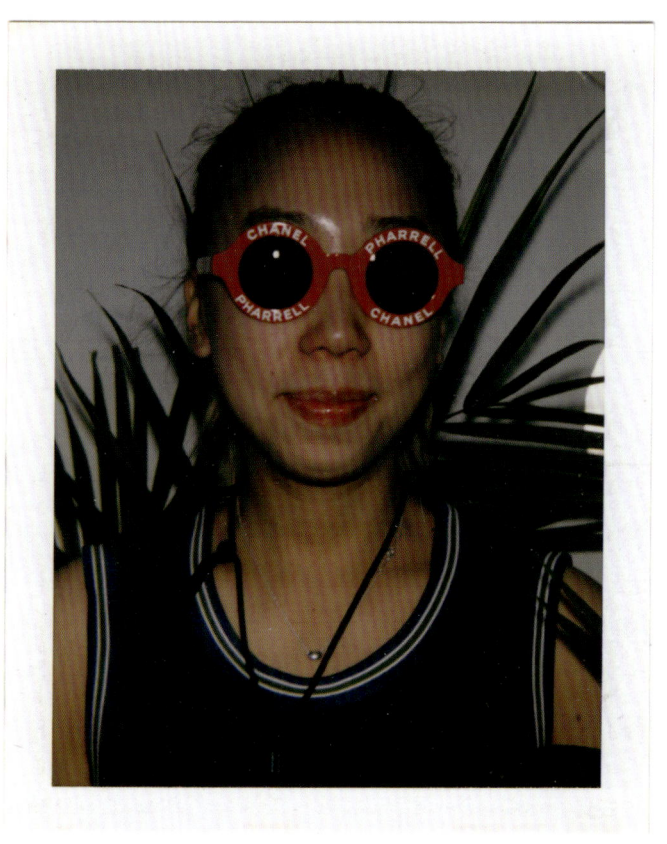

MIMI CHOI

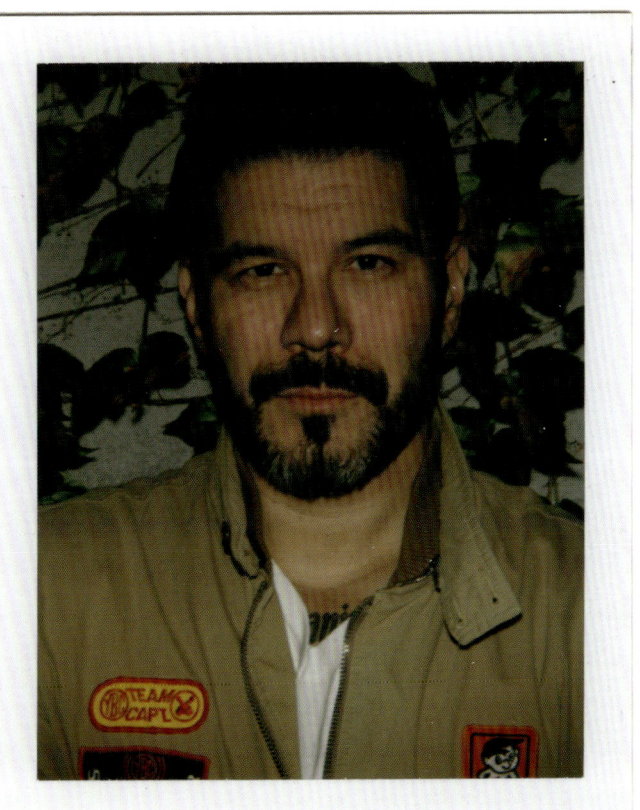

TIM OKAMURA

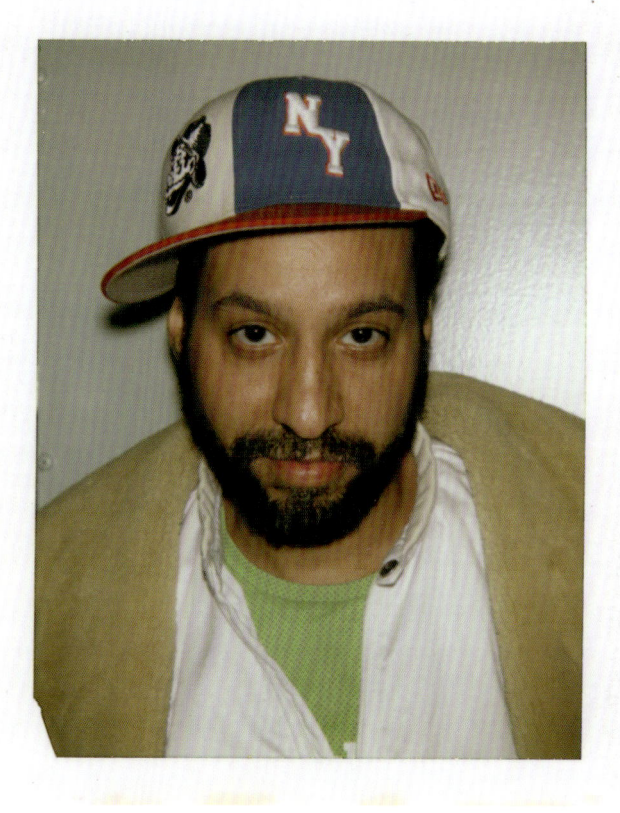

EL-SAESO

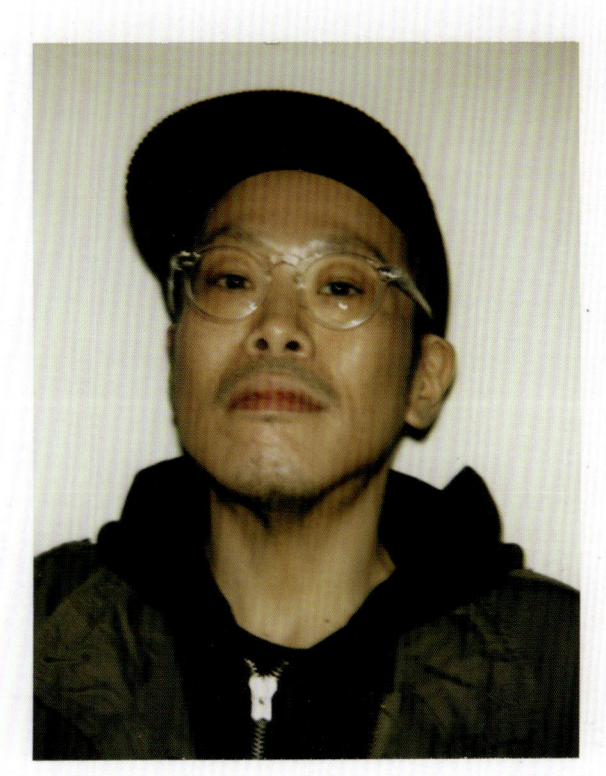

AGE - KUUMBA

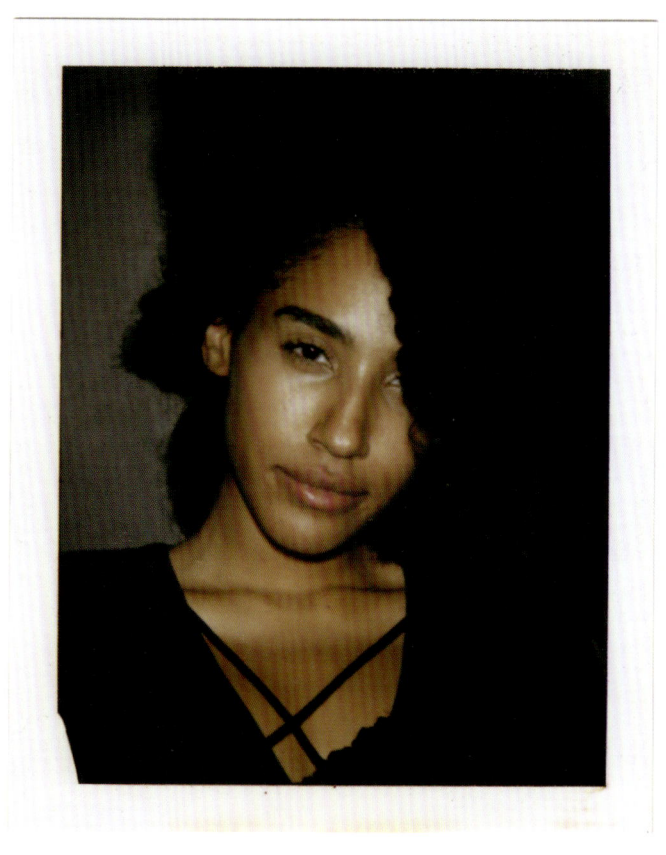

TAMAR AMABELLE HILTON SEGRE

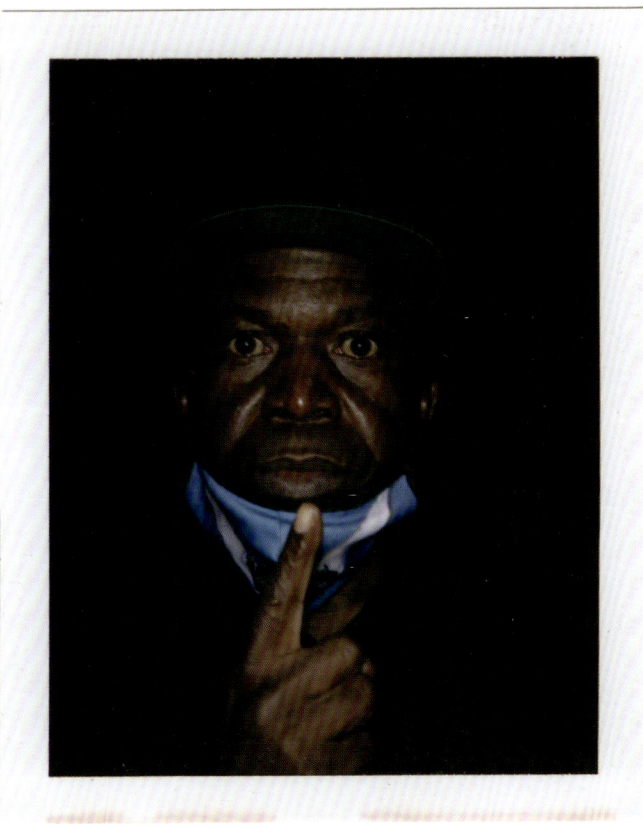

BARRINGTON LEVY

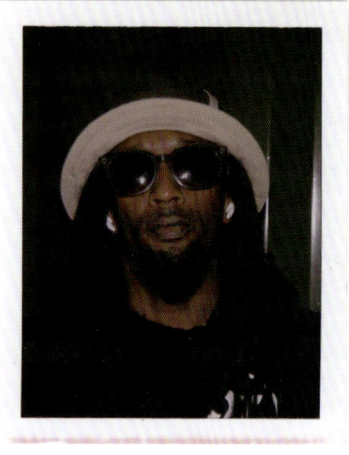

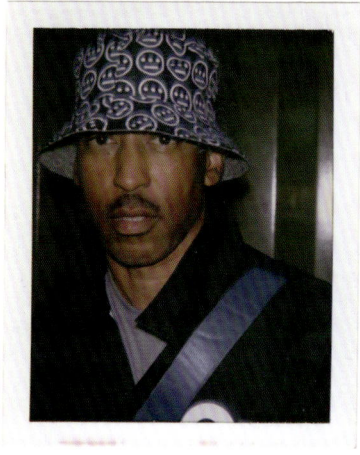

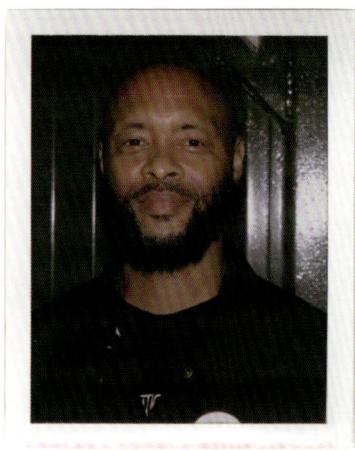

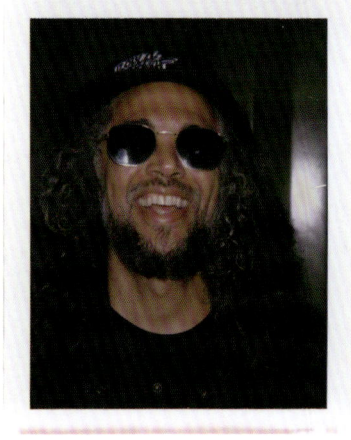

A-PLUS - SOULS OF MISCHIEF

PHESTO - SOULS OF MISCHIEF

TAJAI - SOULS OF MISCHIEF

OPIO - SOULS OF MISCHIEF

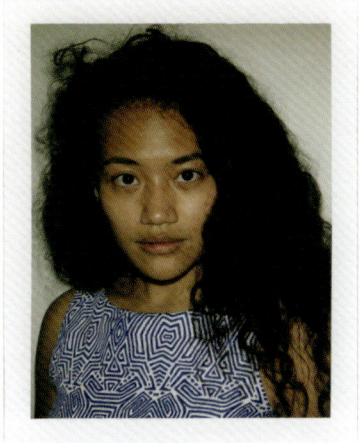

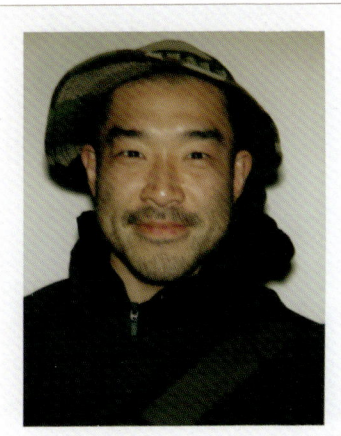

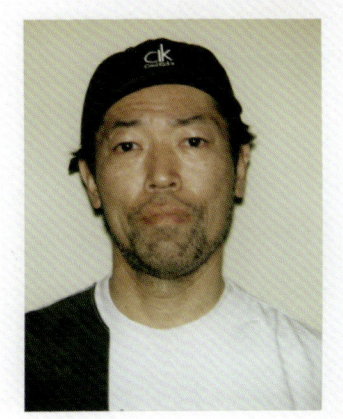

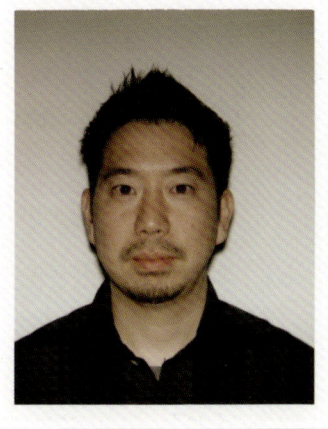

KAMALA "KAEW" THANETO

TATSUNAKA

KASE

DIAGO KASAMI

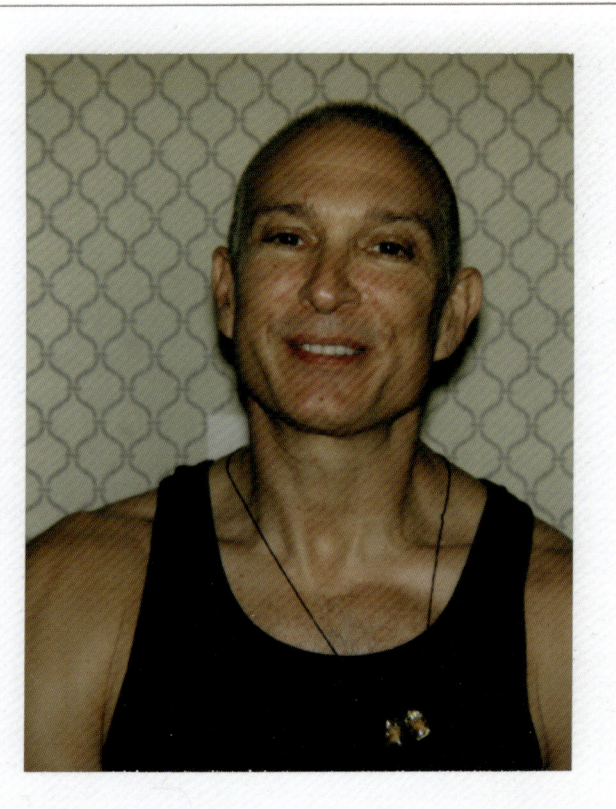

DANTE ROSS

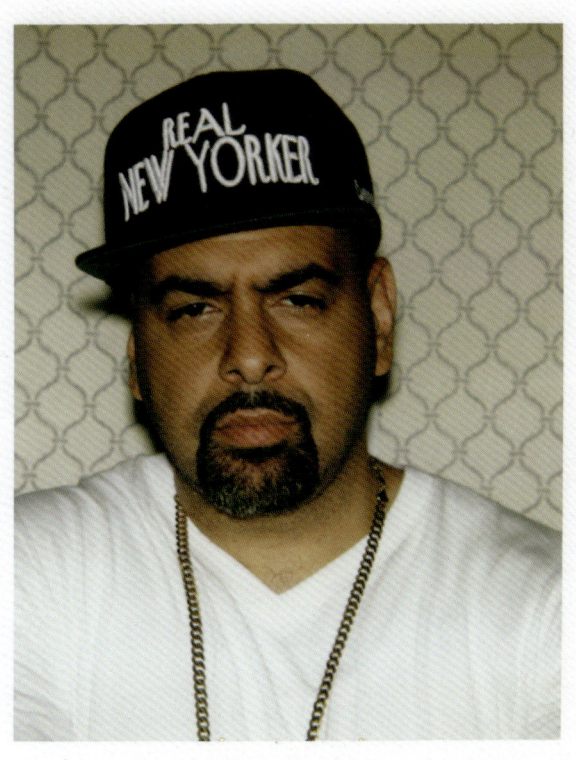

A G DA CORONER

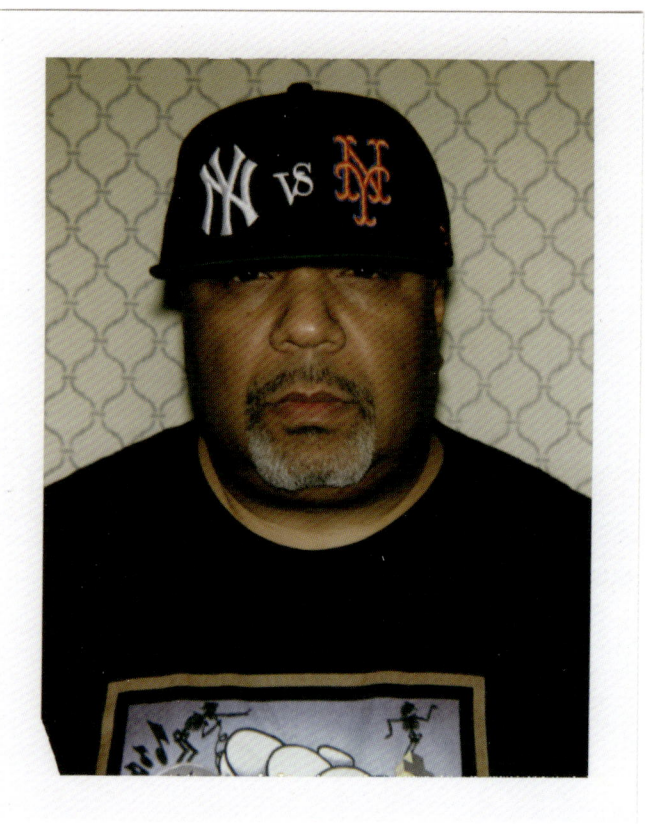

BREAKBEAT LOU

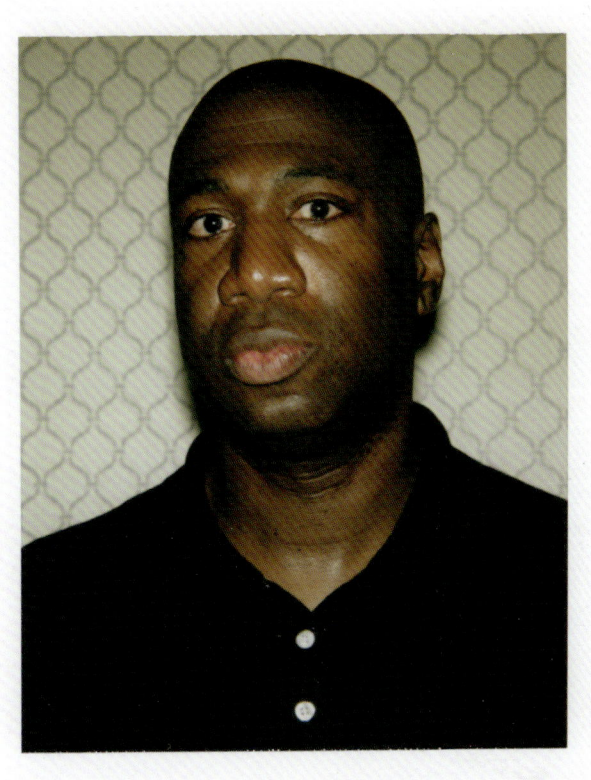

KENNY PARKER

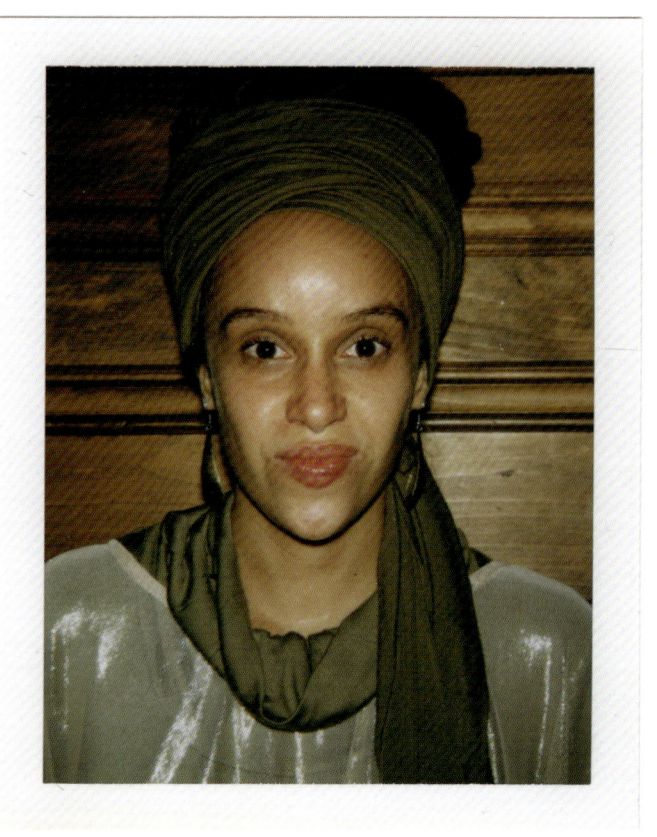

KELISSA

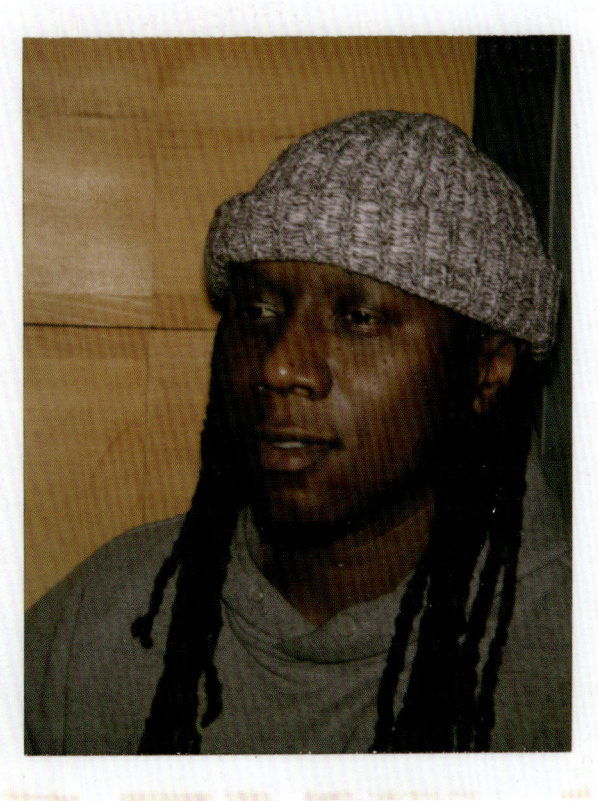

MOOSA

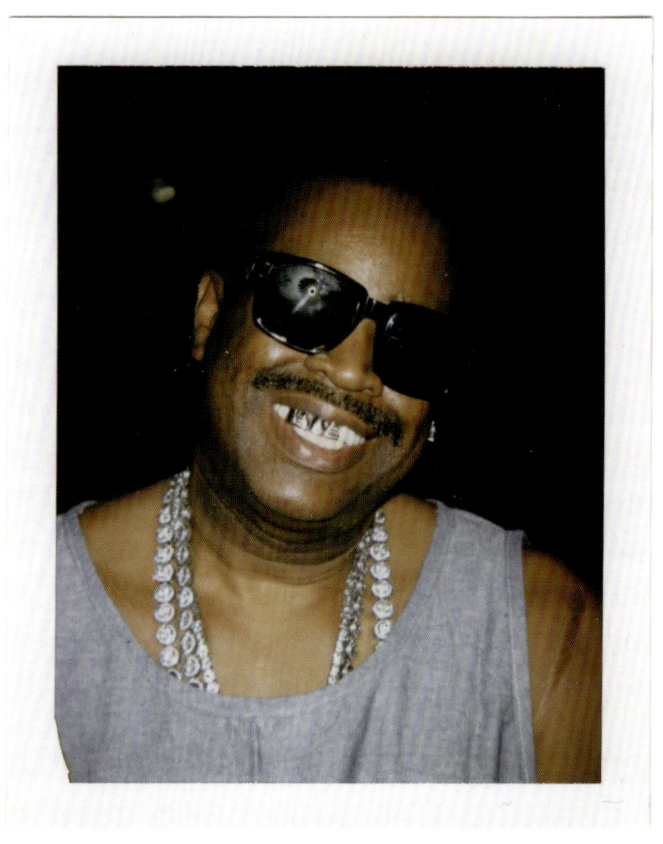

SLICK RICK THE RULER

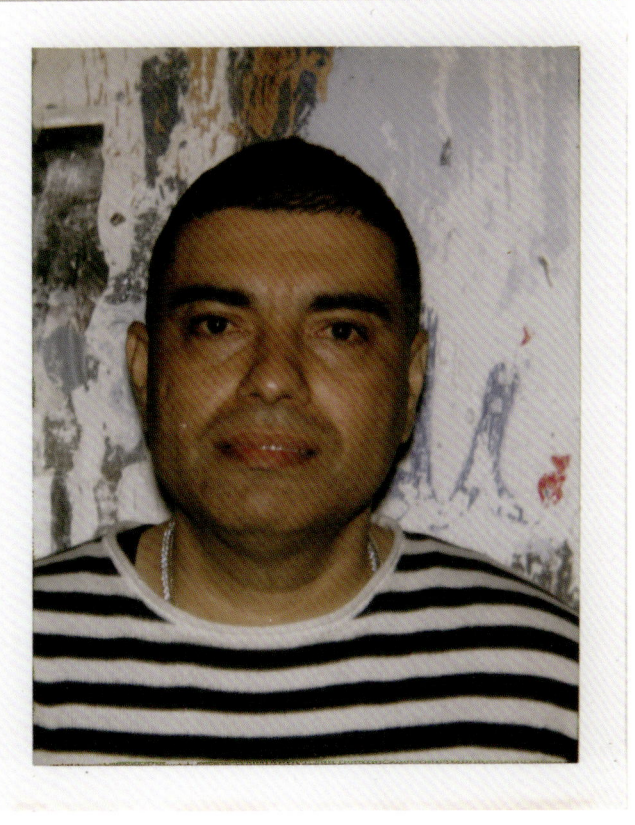

PUERTO RICO ROB

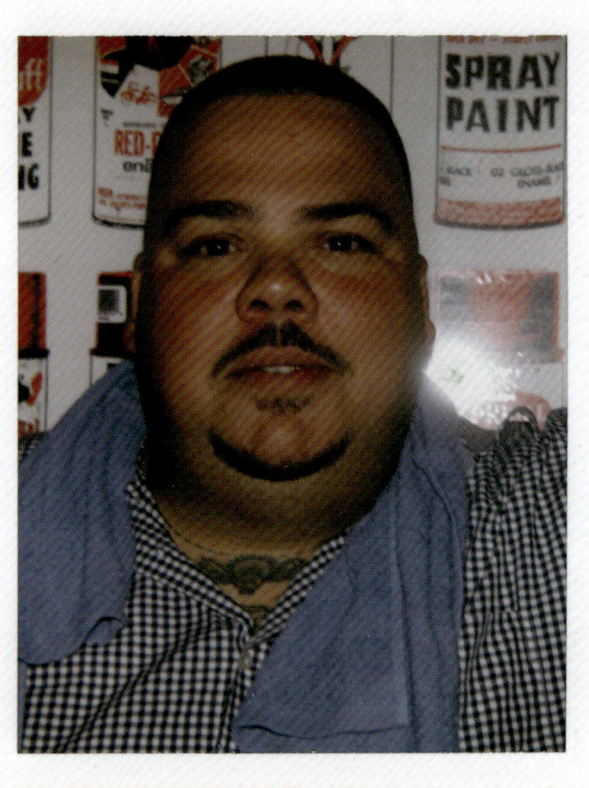

BERT KRAK

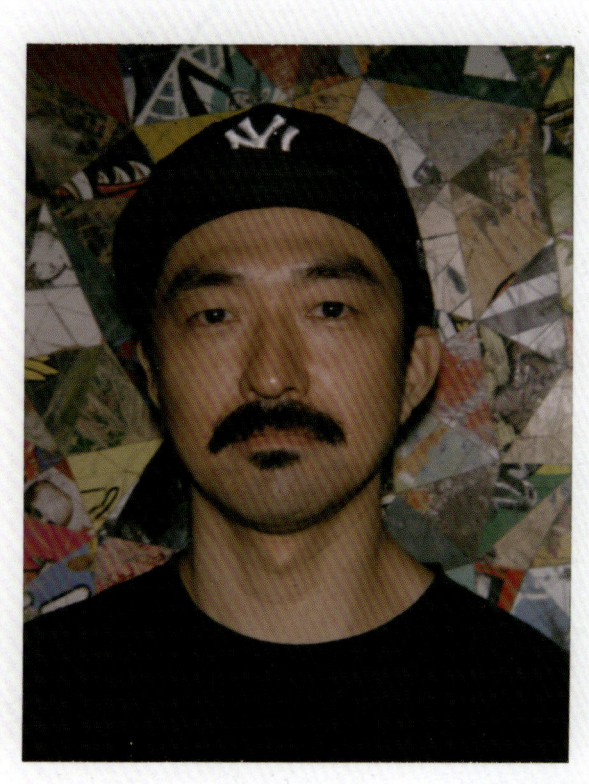

HAROSHI

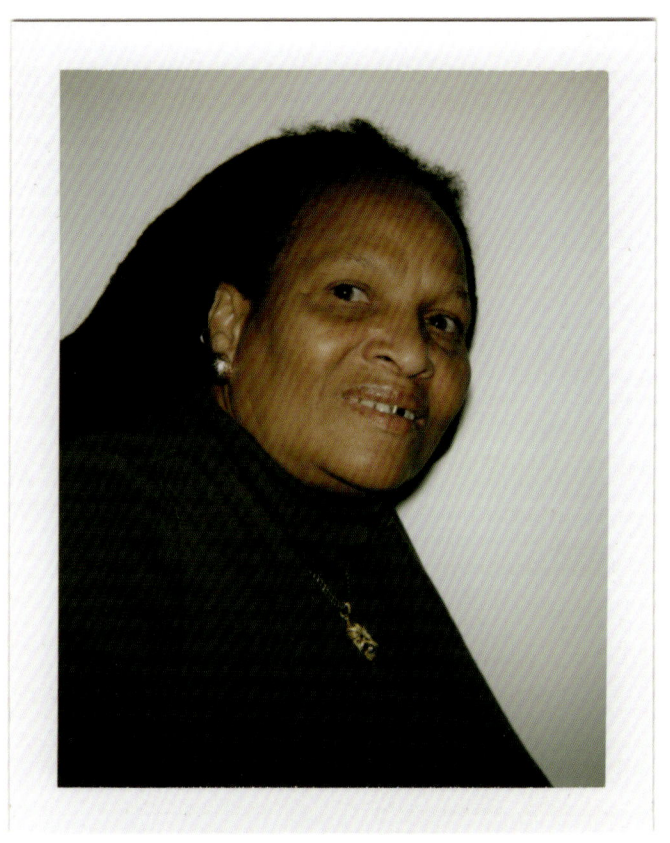

SISTER NANCY

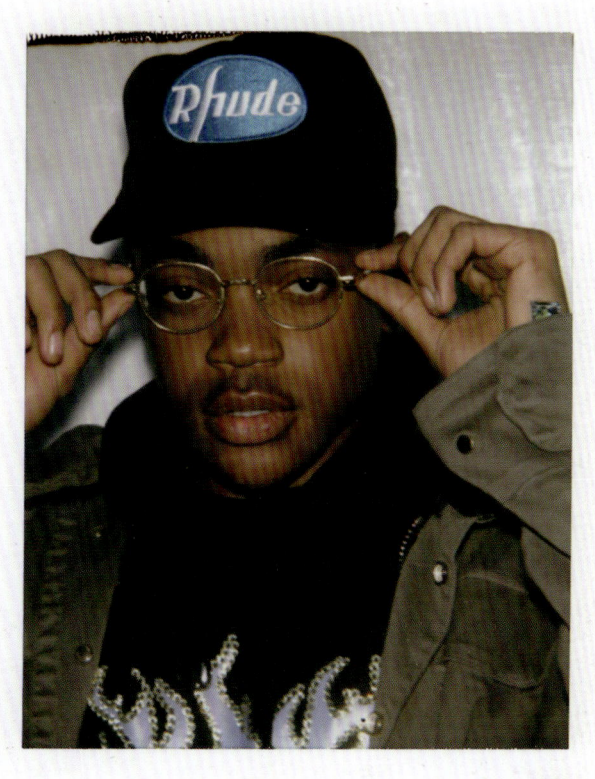

MICHAEL RAINEY JR.

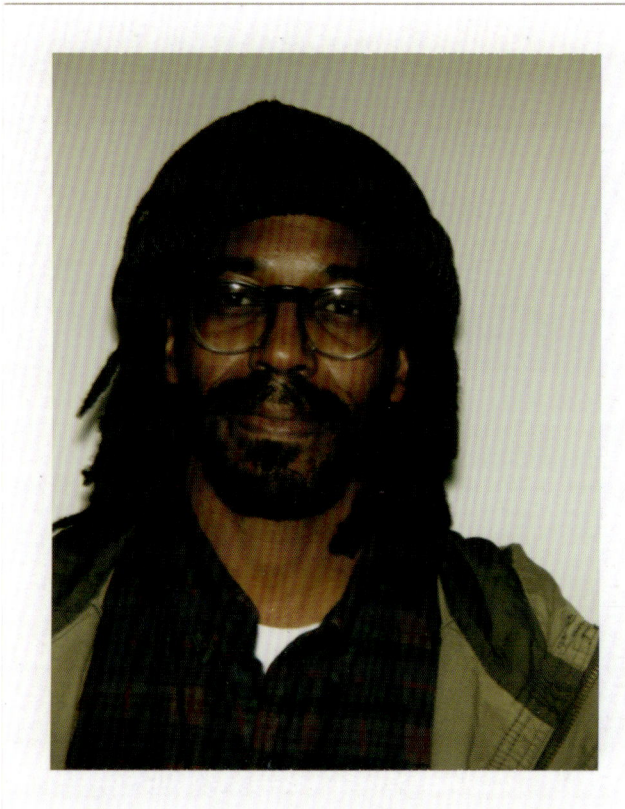

SCOTT "SWITTTCH" TURNER

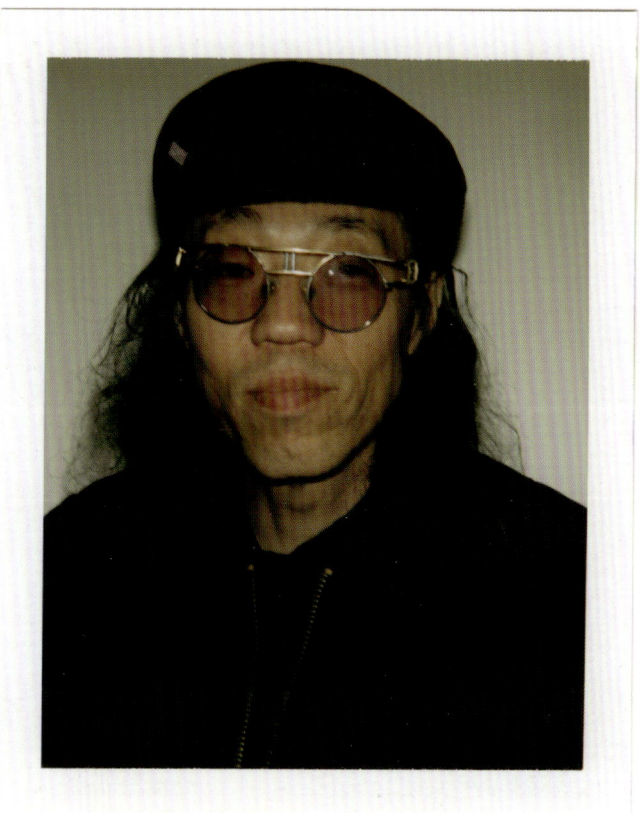

HAYAO MATSUMURA

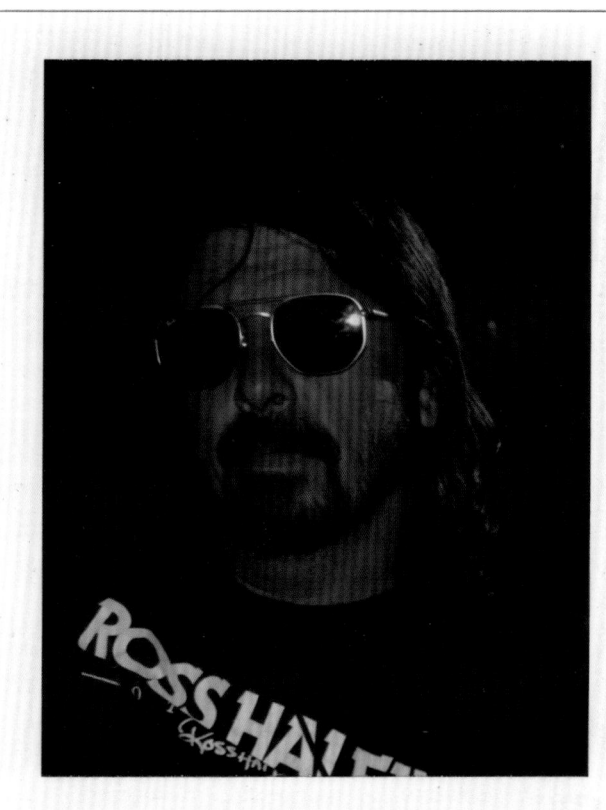

DAVE GROHL

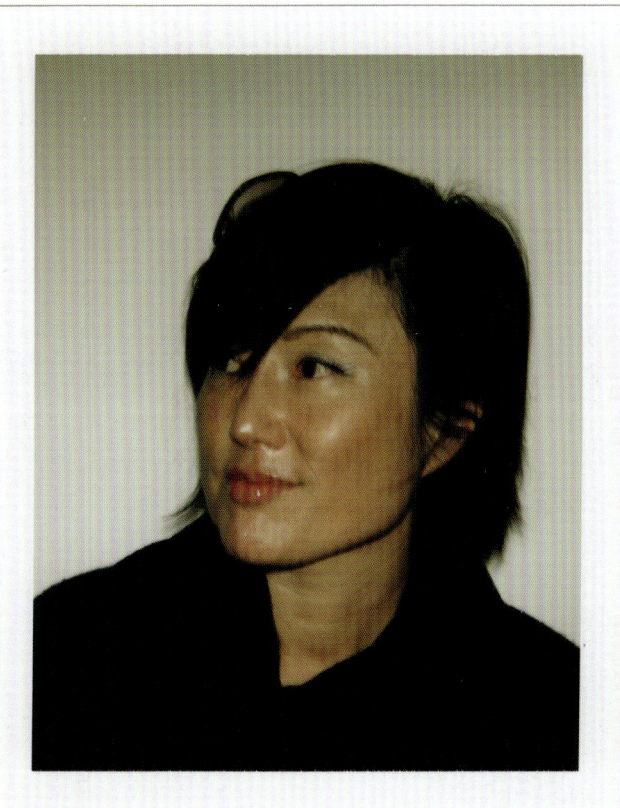

MAMI

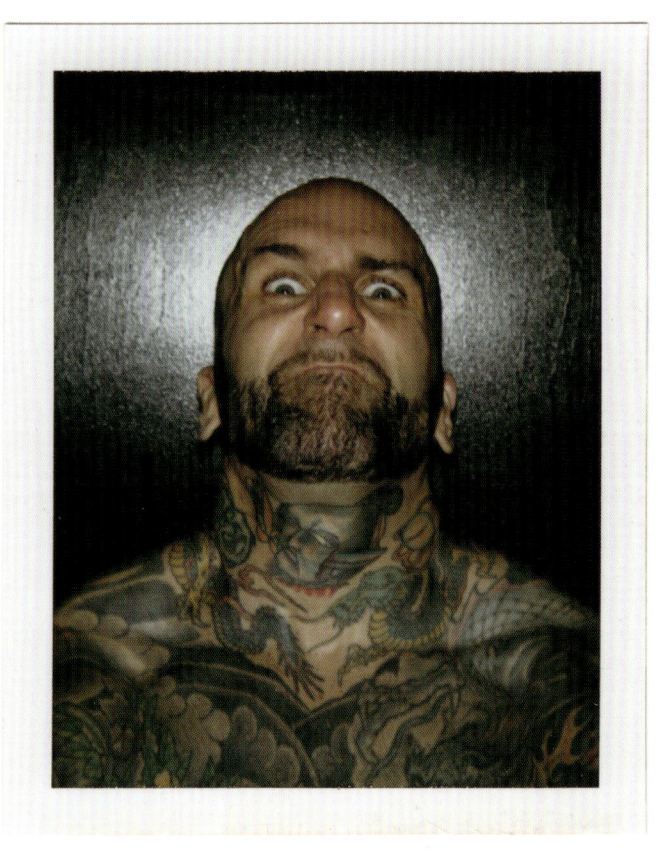

FERNANDO SCHAEFER

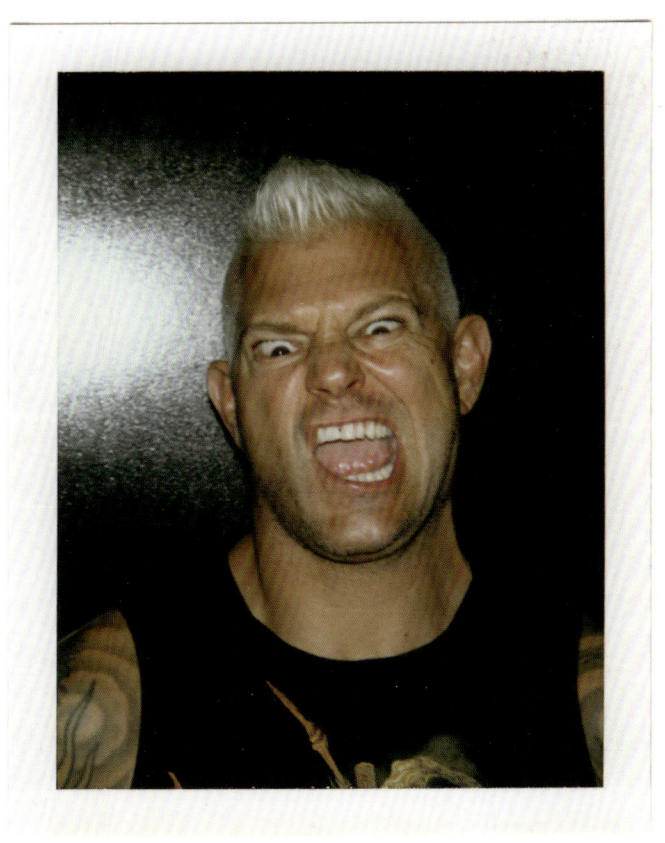

BILLY GRAZIADEI

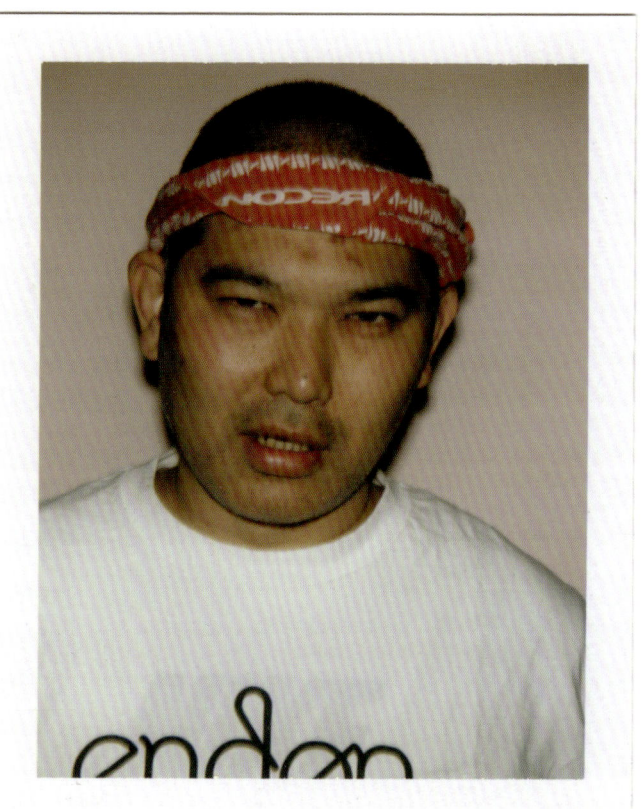

IHA

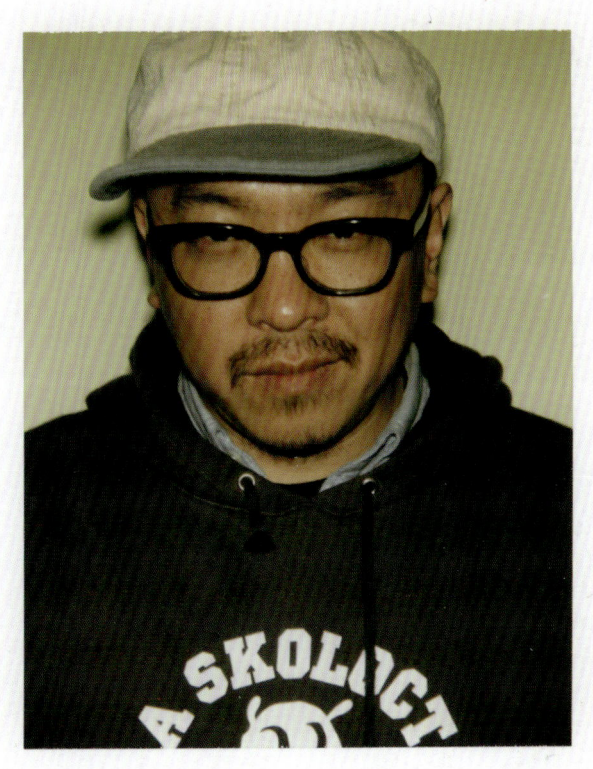

IORI

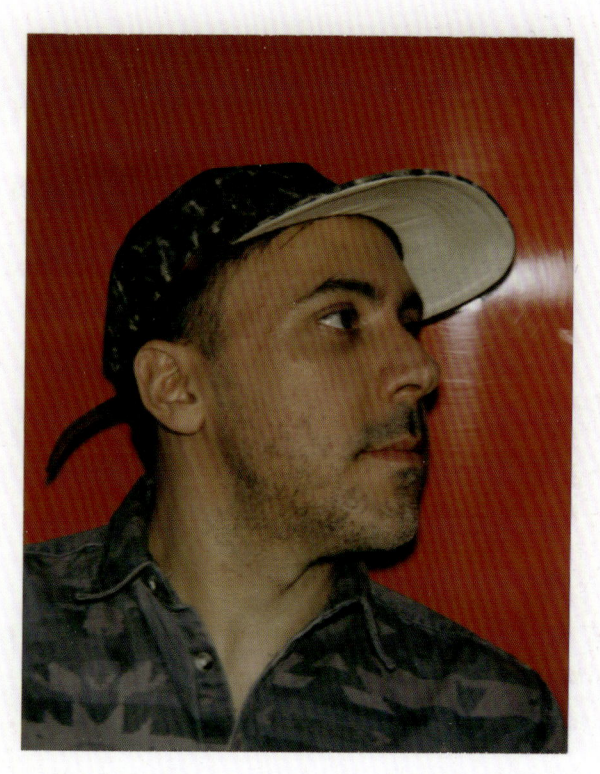

DAN PETRUZZI

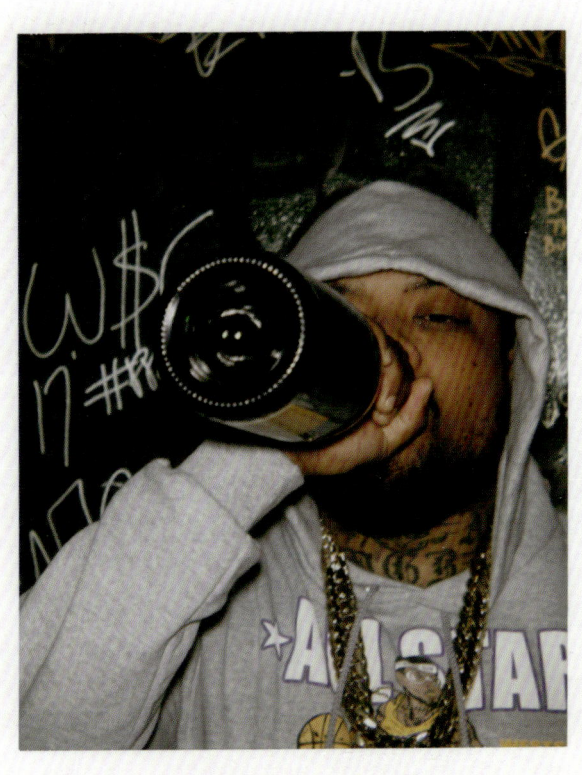

WESTSIDE GUNN

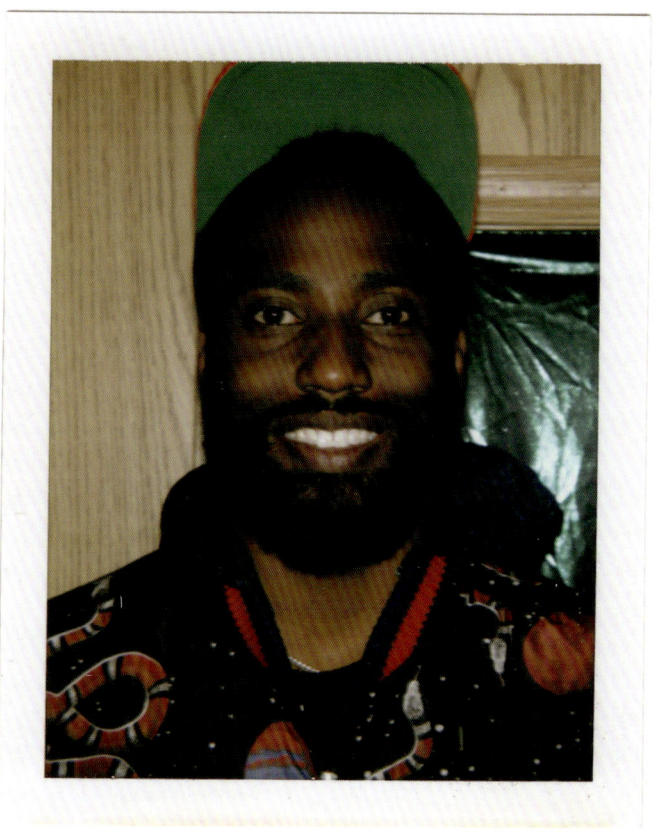

JOHN DAVID WASHINGTON

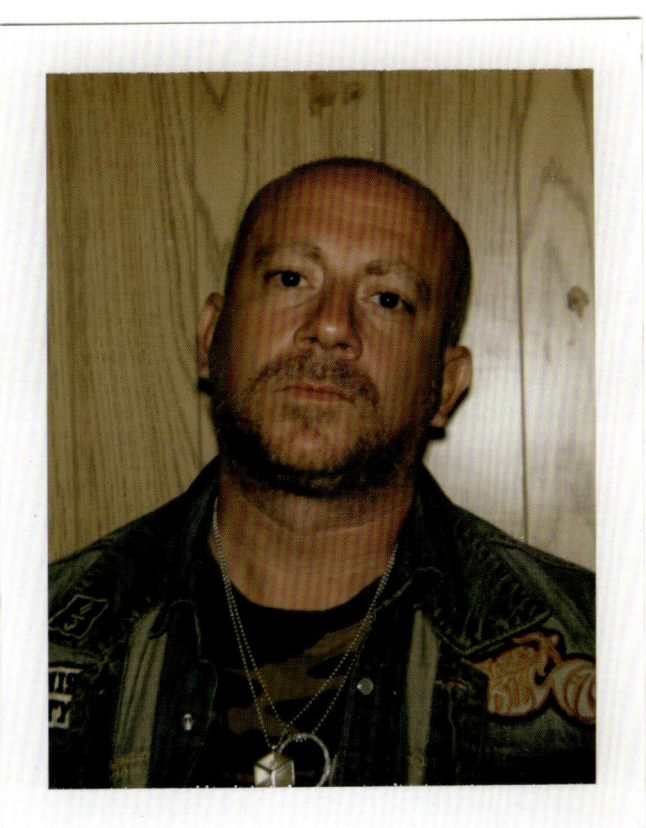

CYRIL KEBELLIAN AKA CREALKILLA

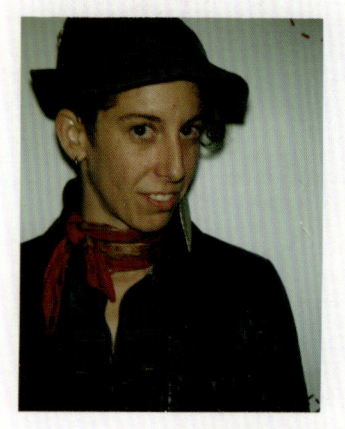
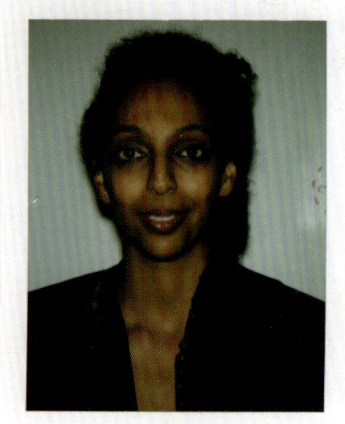
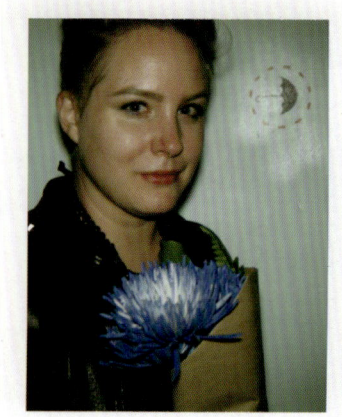
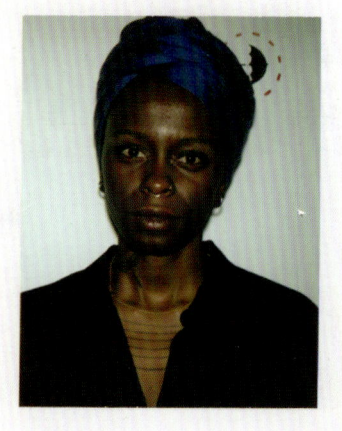

ROWAN RENEE

ALEX CHOWANIEC

ASMERET BERHE LUMAX

TOYIN OJIH ODUTOLA

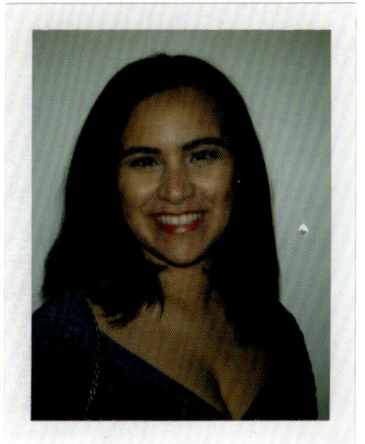

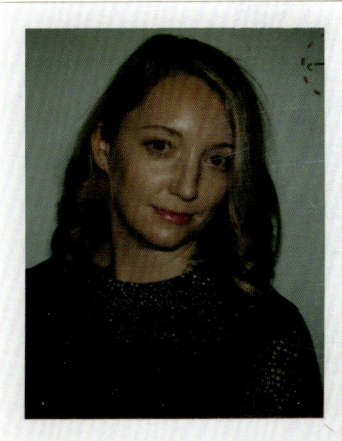

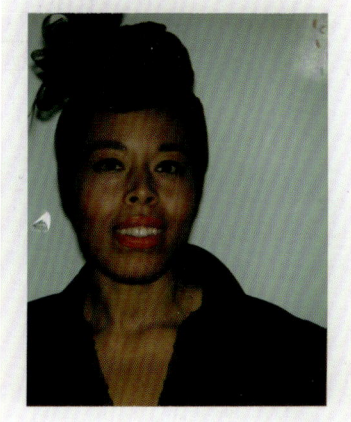

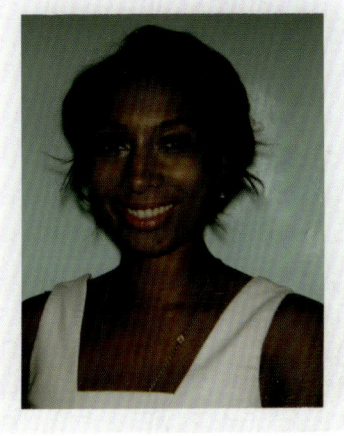

SIHAN JAOUI

ANDREA YELESIAS

DANIELLE BROWN

SIMONE HOYTE

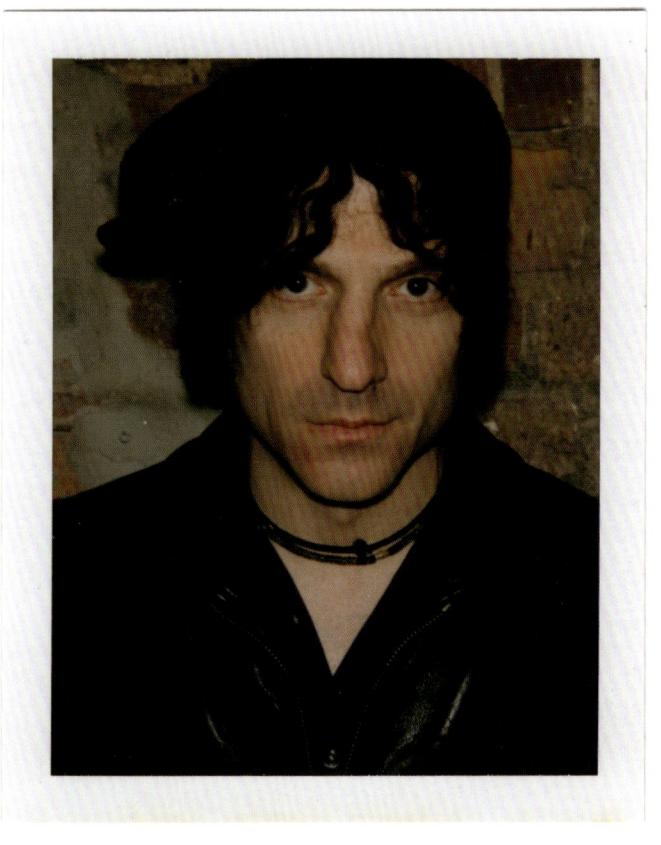

JESSE MALIN

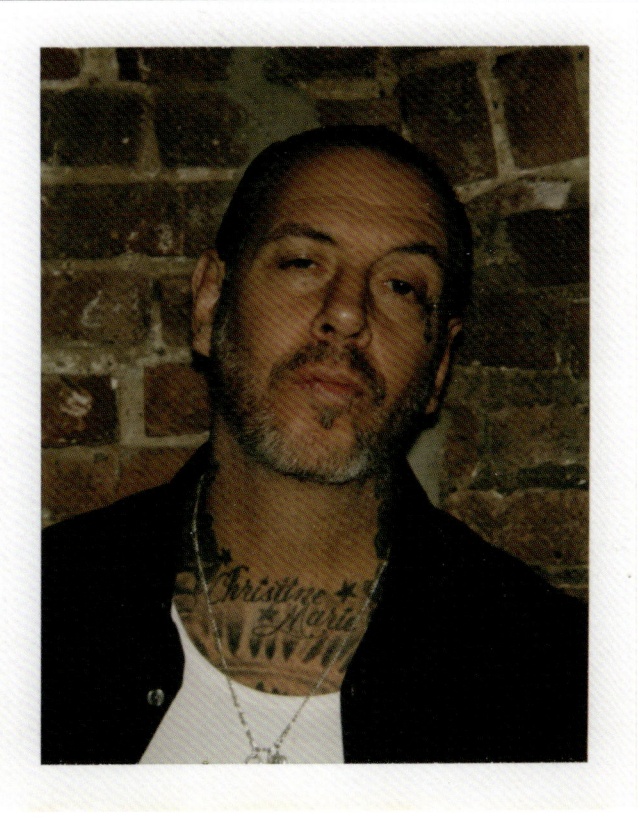

MIKE NESS

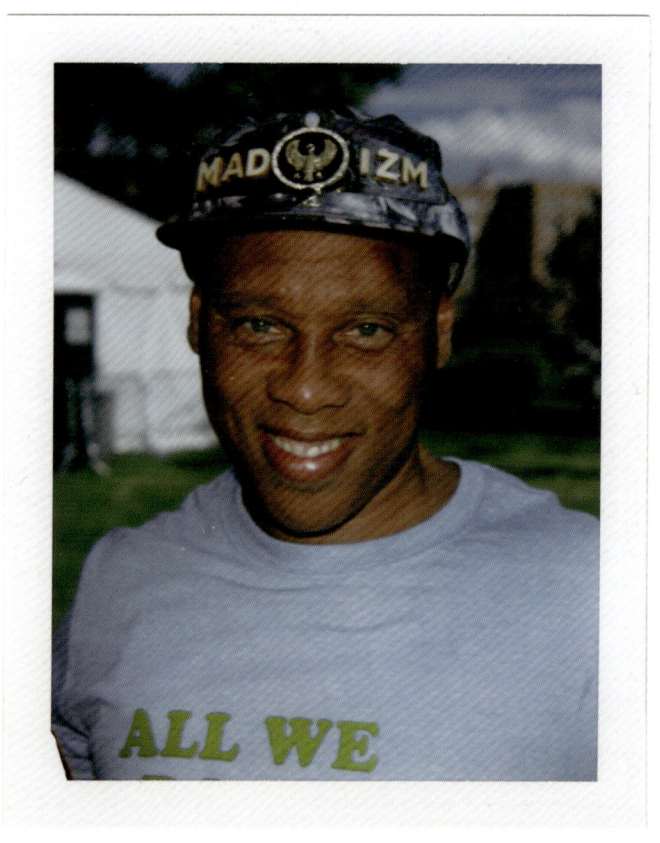

HAKIM GREEN

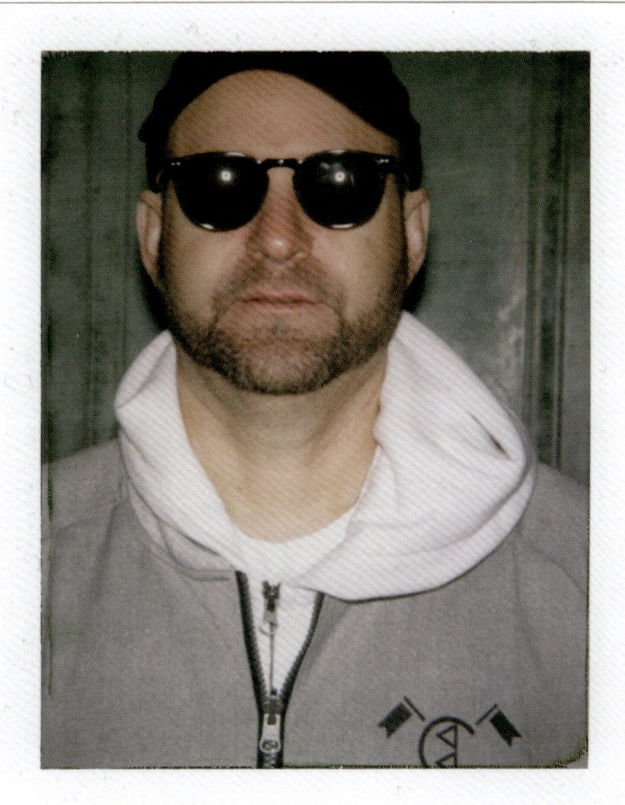

CHAMPELLI

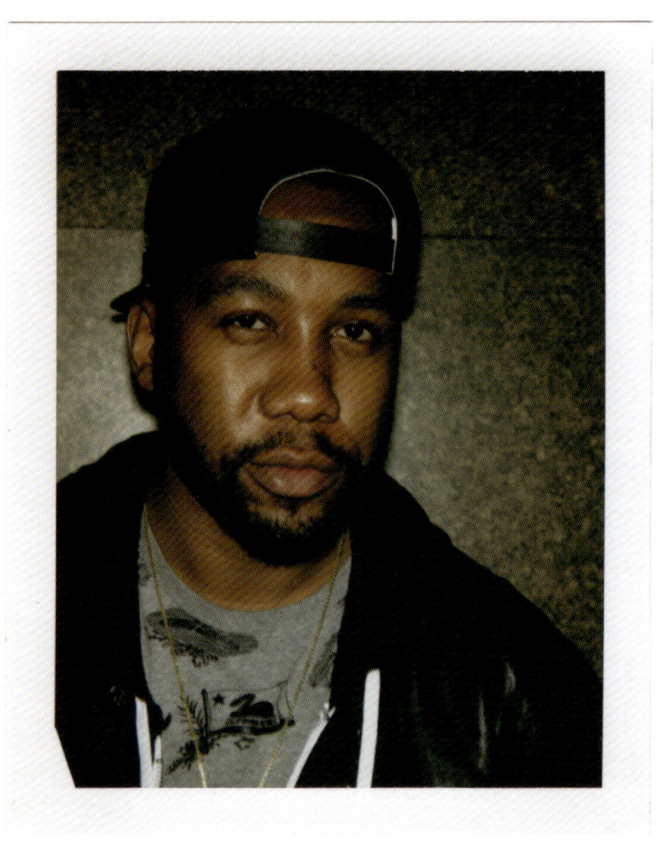

NDABA MANDELA

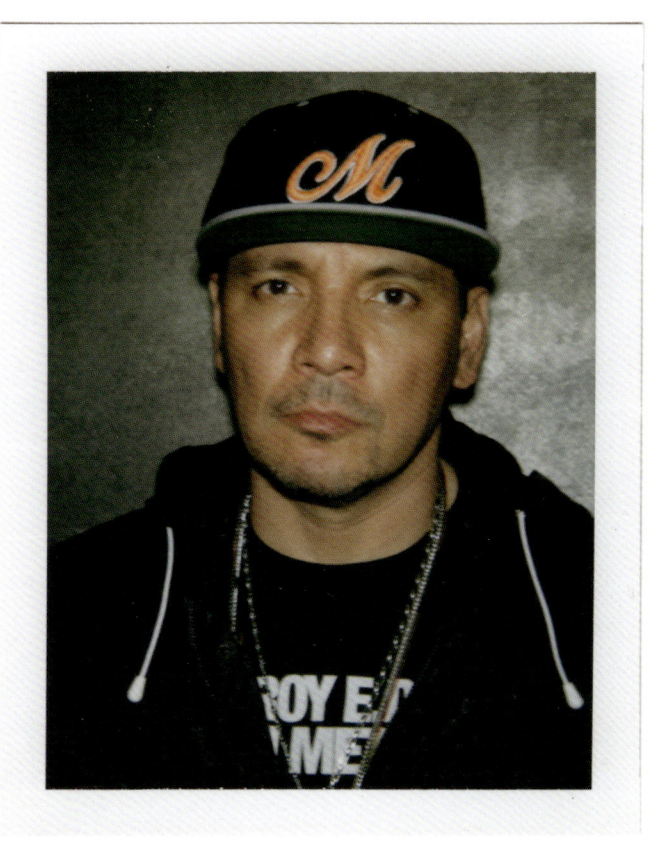

MIX MASTER MIKE

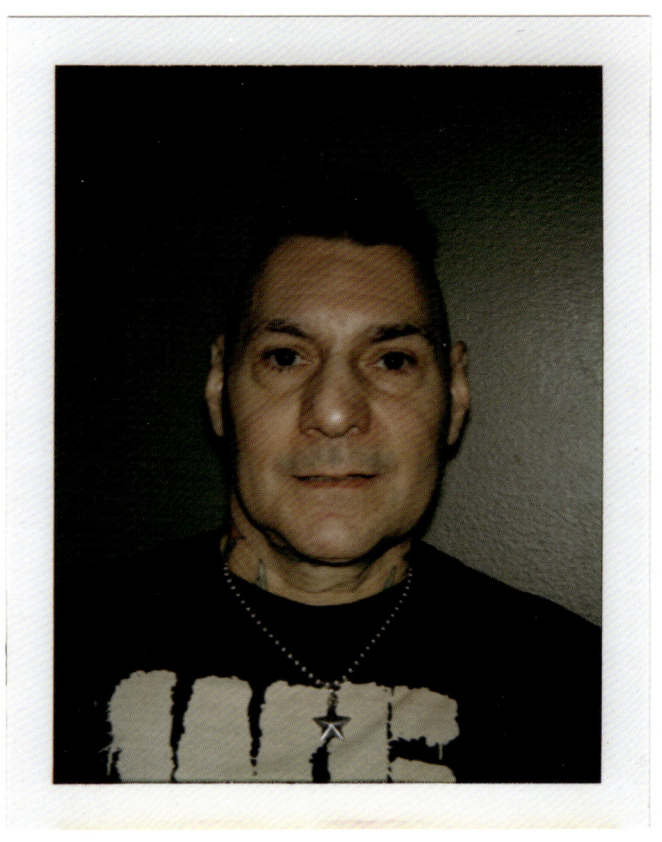

VINNIE STIGMA

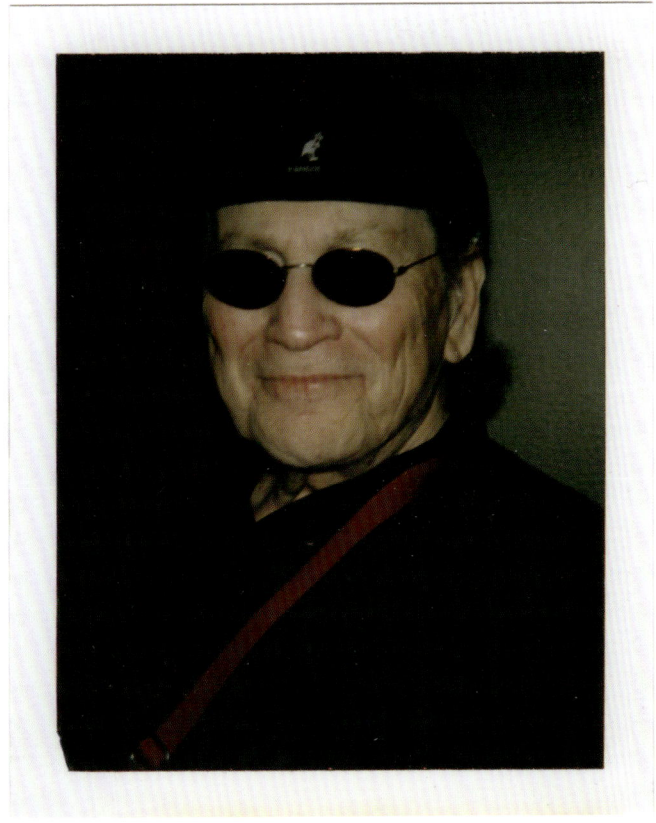

ARNY STONE

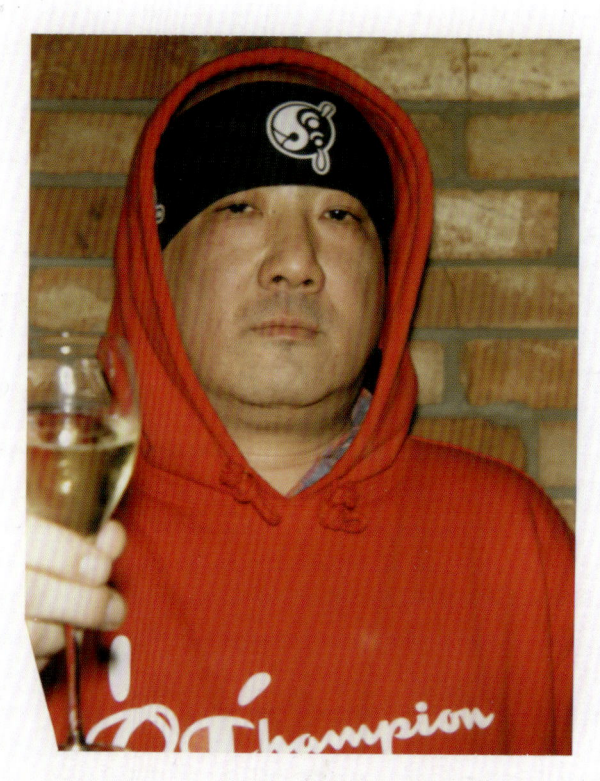

SKOLOCT

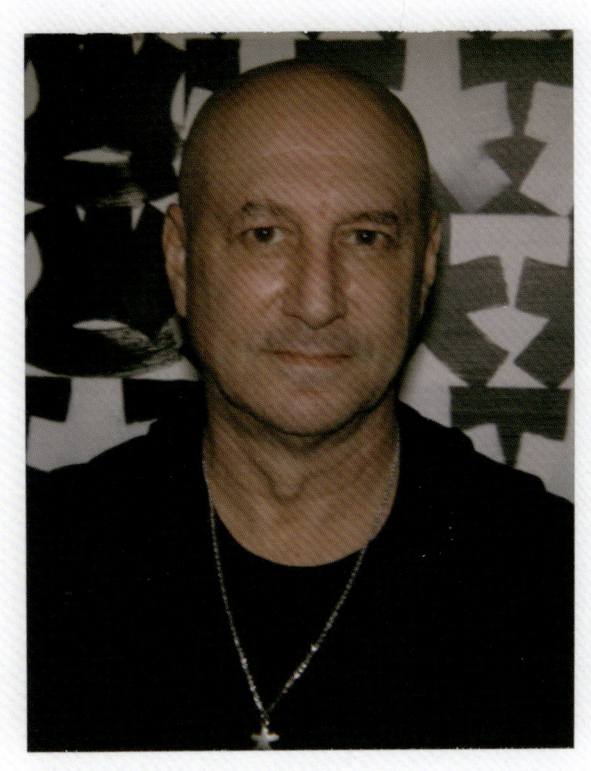

ERIC HAZE

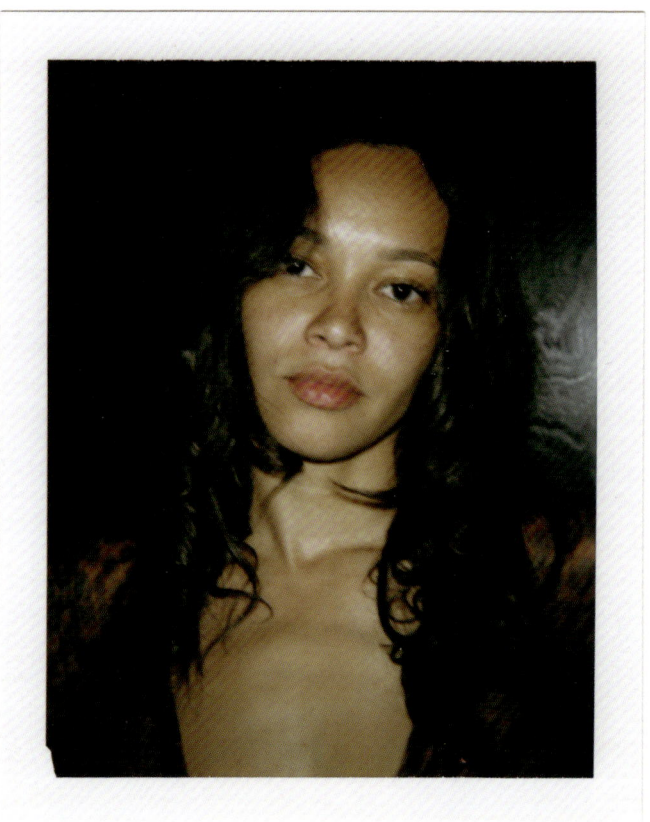

MARZ LOVEJOY

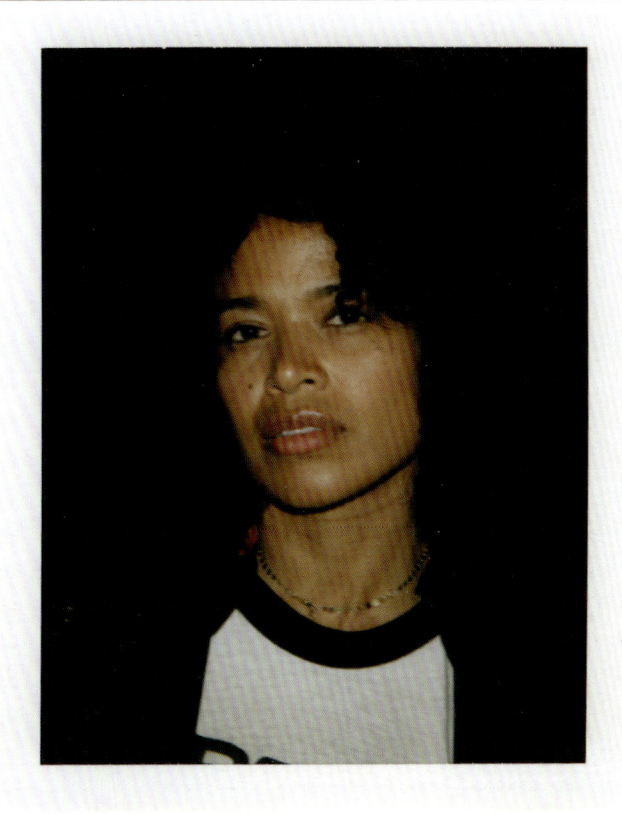

MONICA REYES

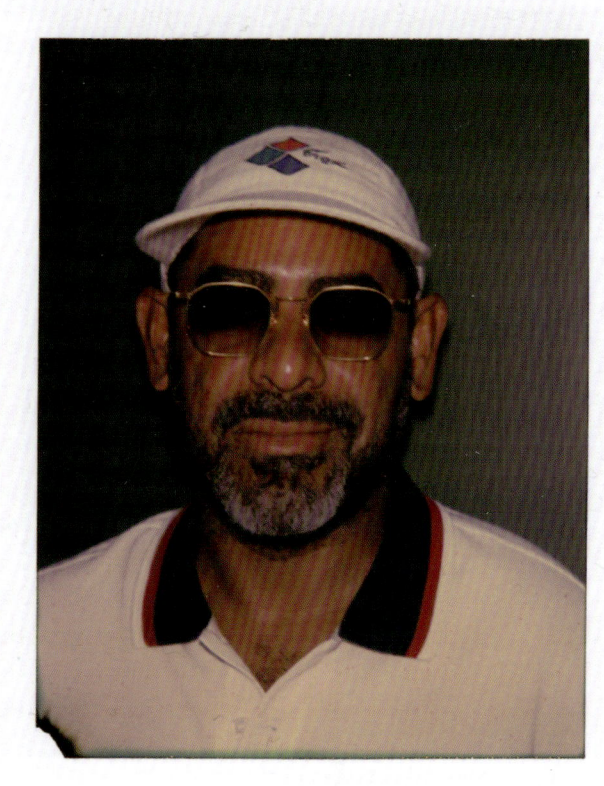

HIRMANE aka THE DWICHTORIALIST

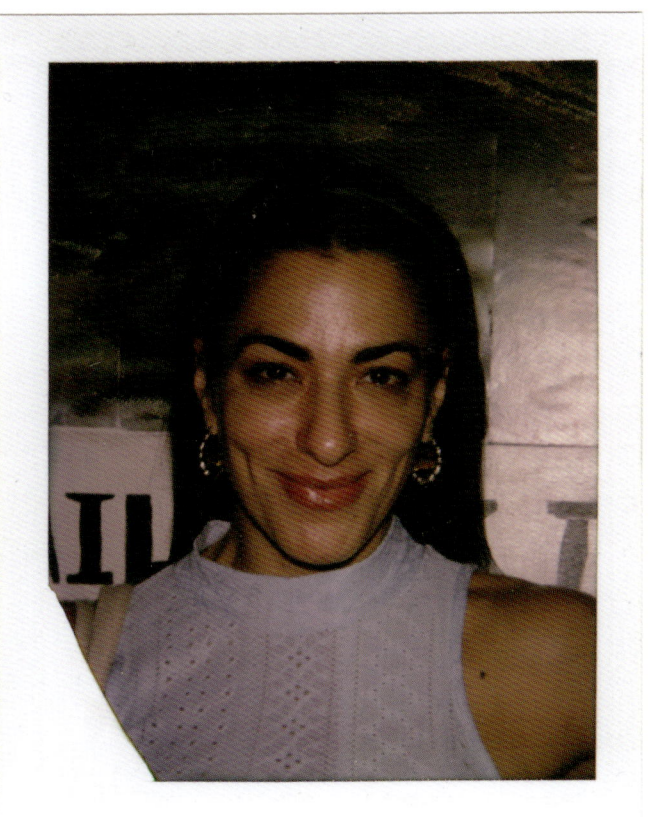

KATE NYC

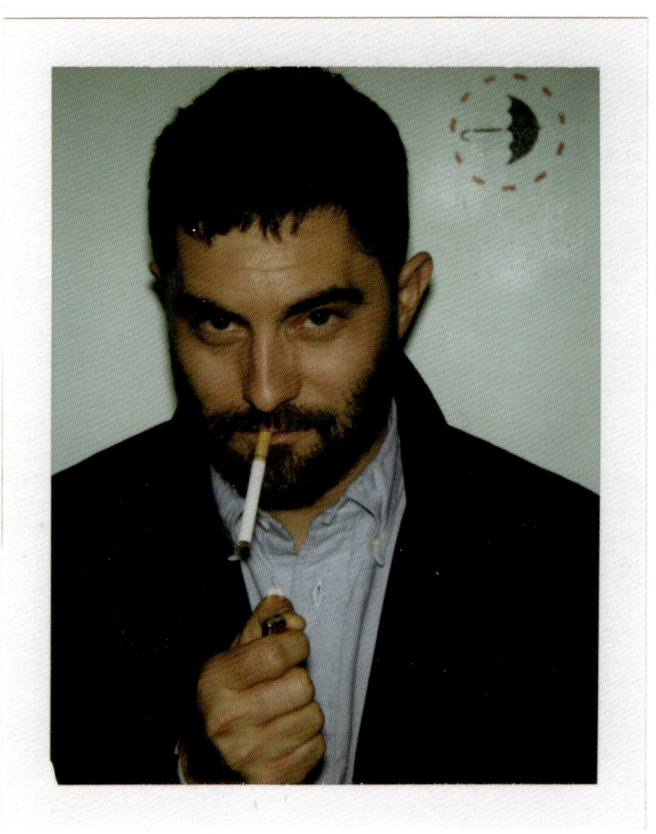

EVAN PRICCO

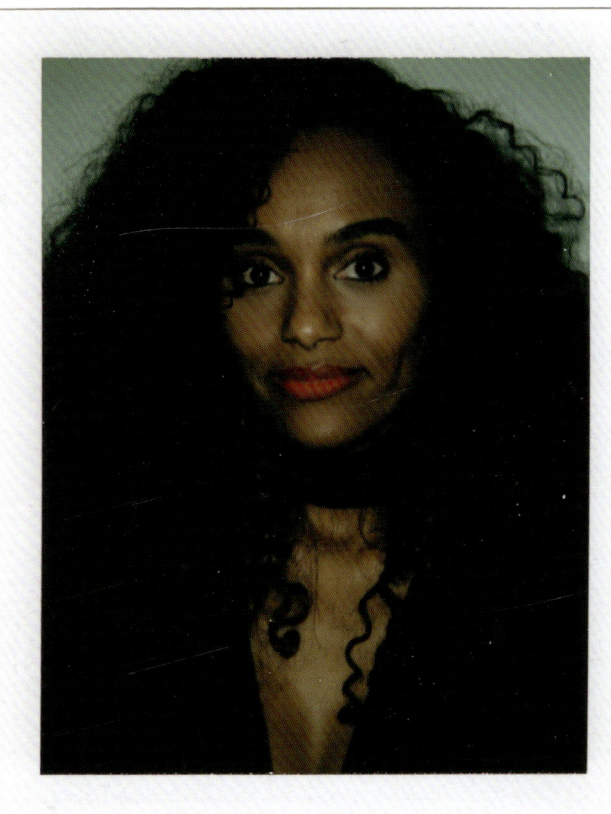

GELILA BEKELE

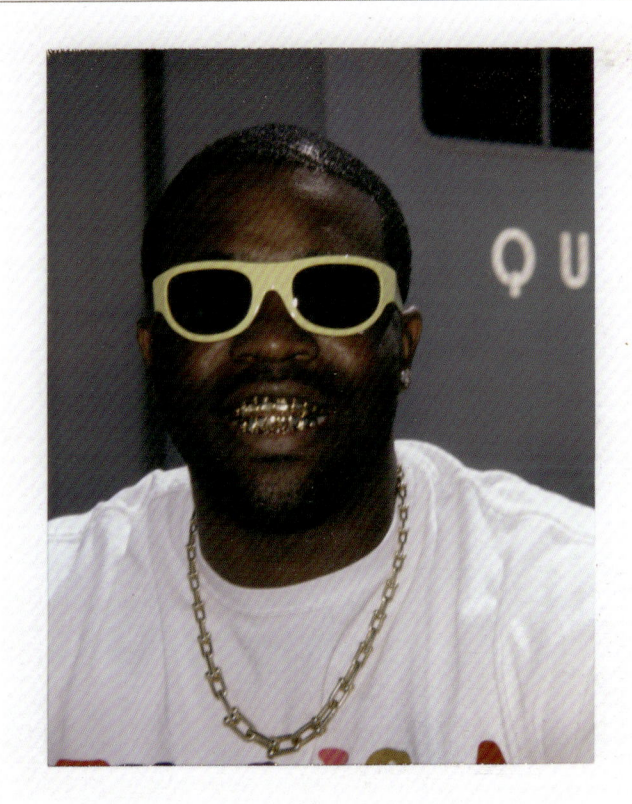

A$AP FERG

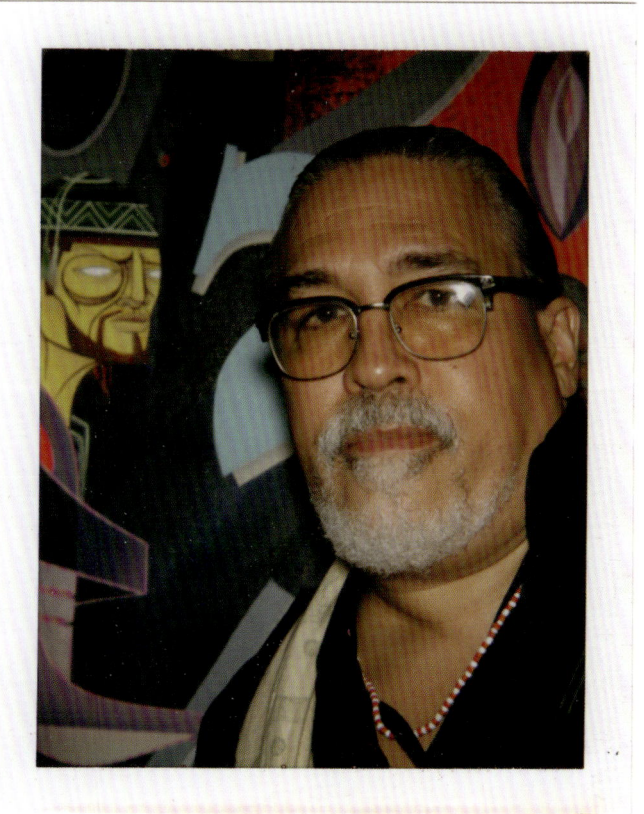

DOZE GREEN

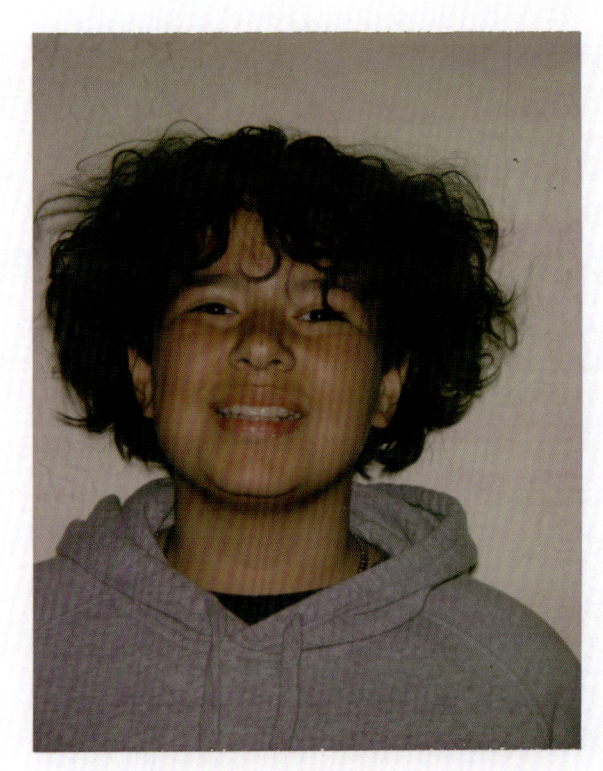

TEDDY LEEDS

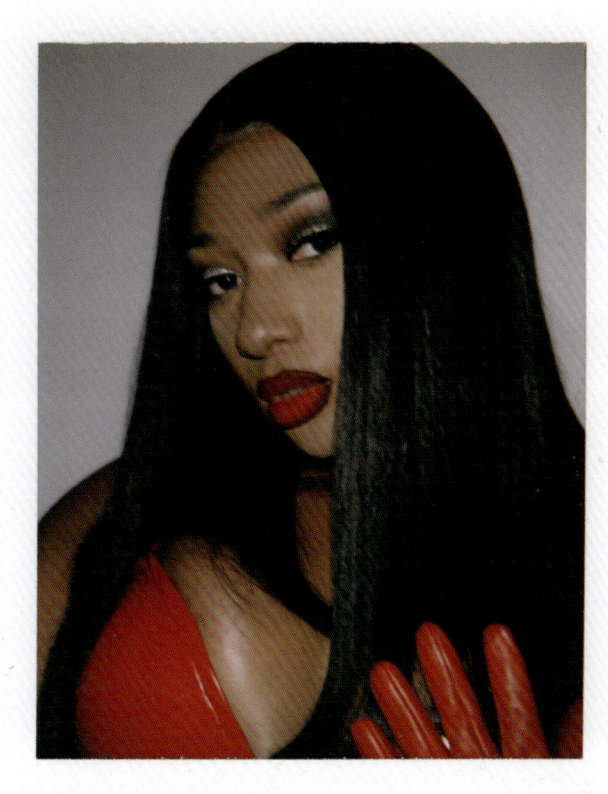

MEGAN THEE STALLION

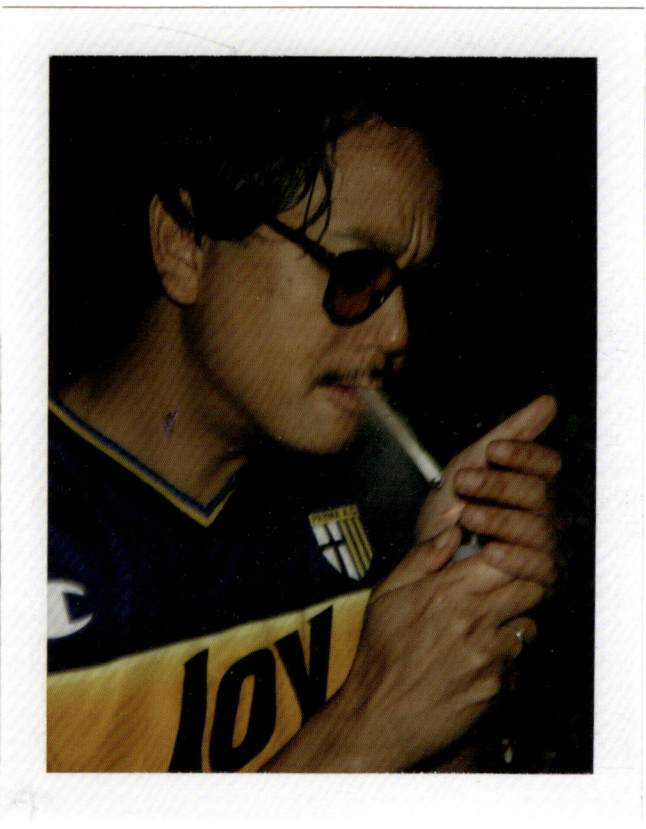

NAT SARASAS

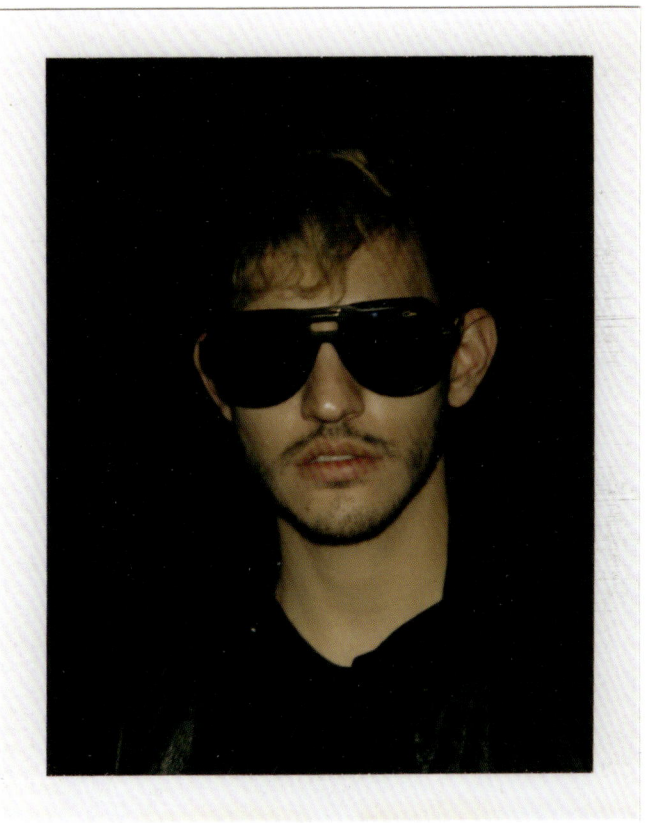

NICK HISSOM

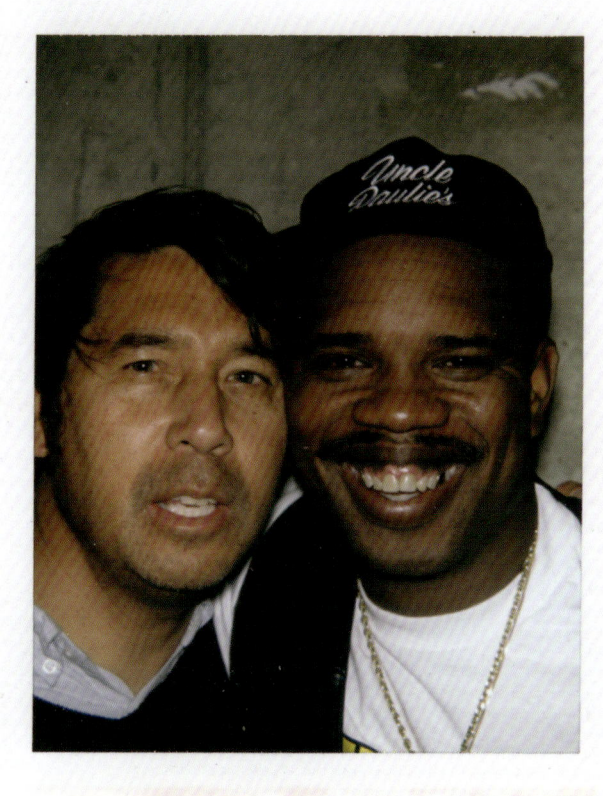

BARRY McGEE & KUNLE F. MARTINS JR.

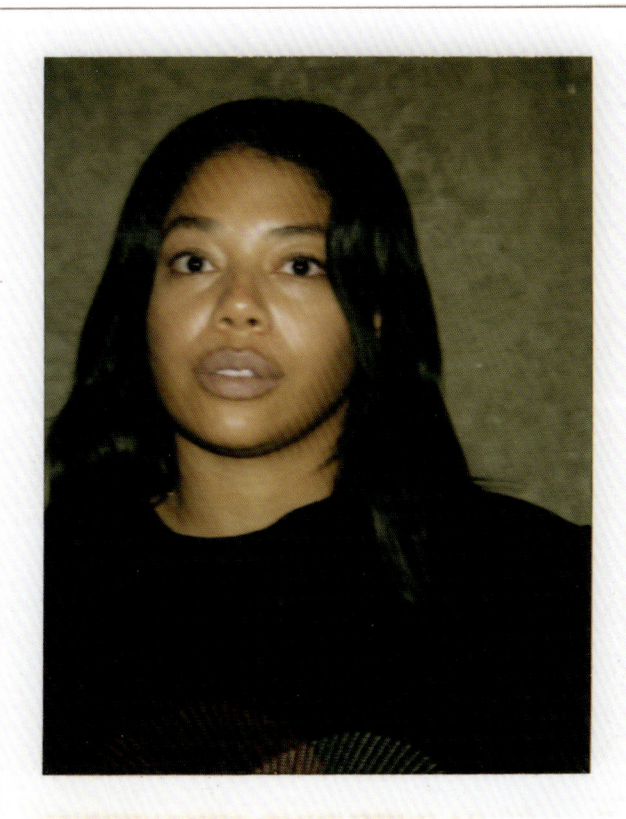

TIESHA LESHORE

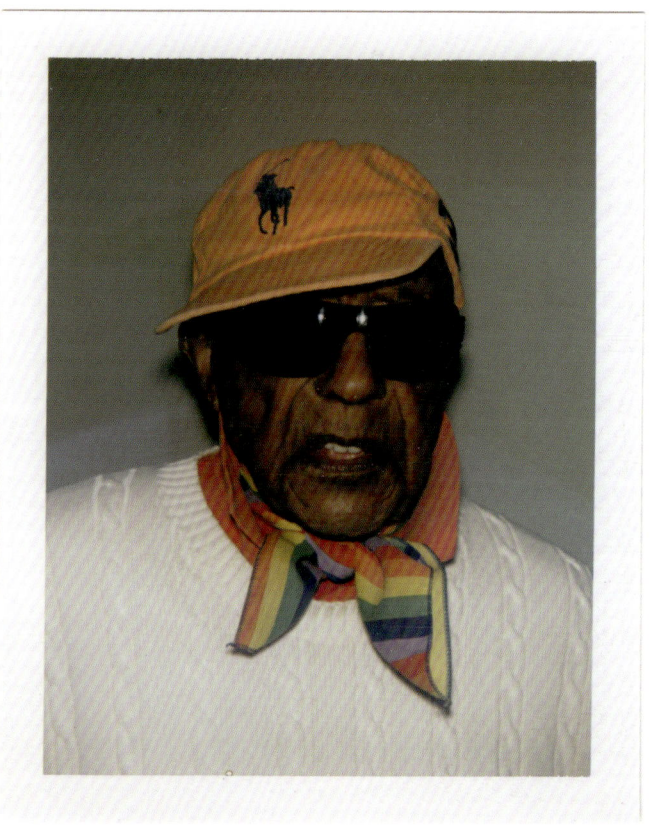

THEO DIXON

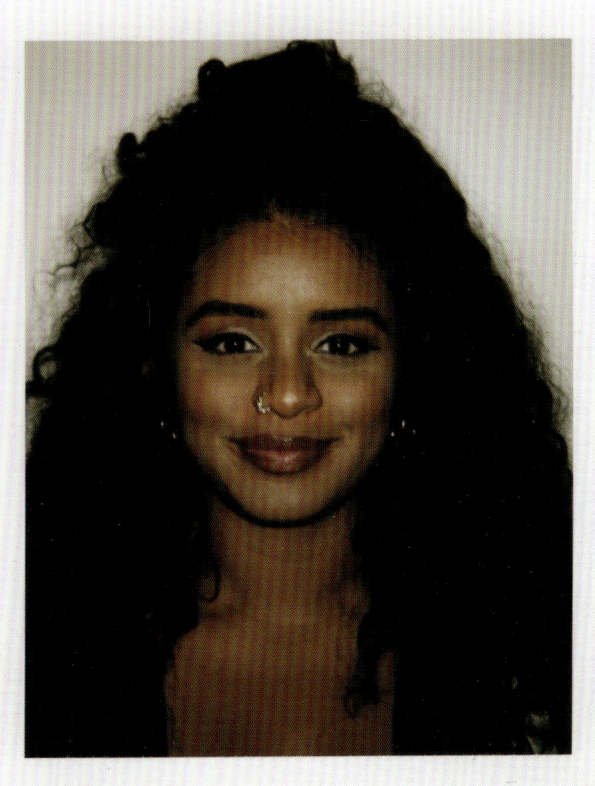

STELLA BLU

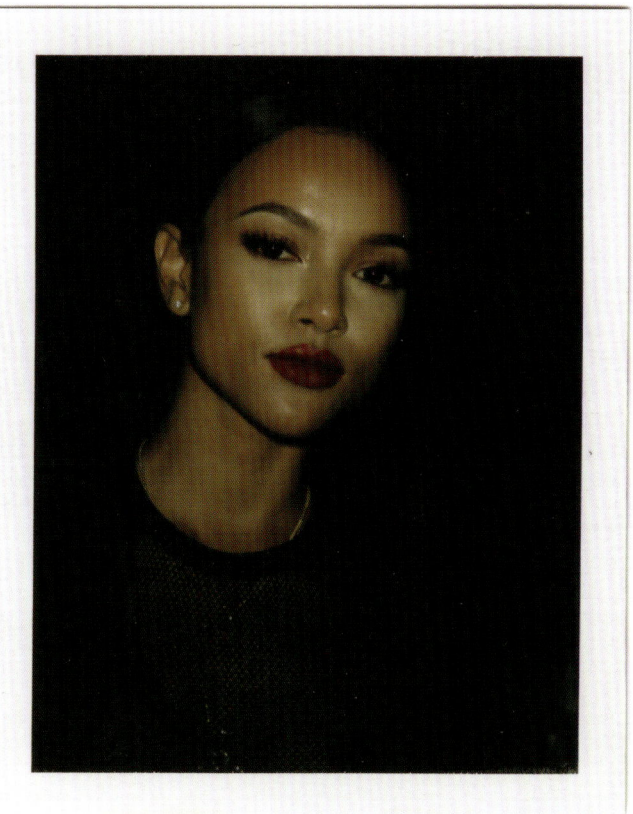

KARRUECHE TRAN

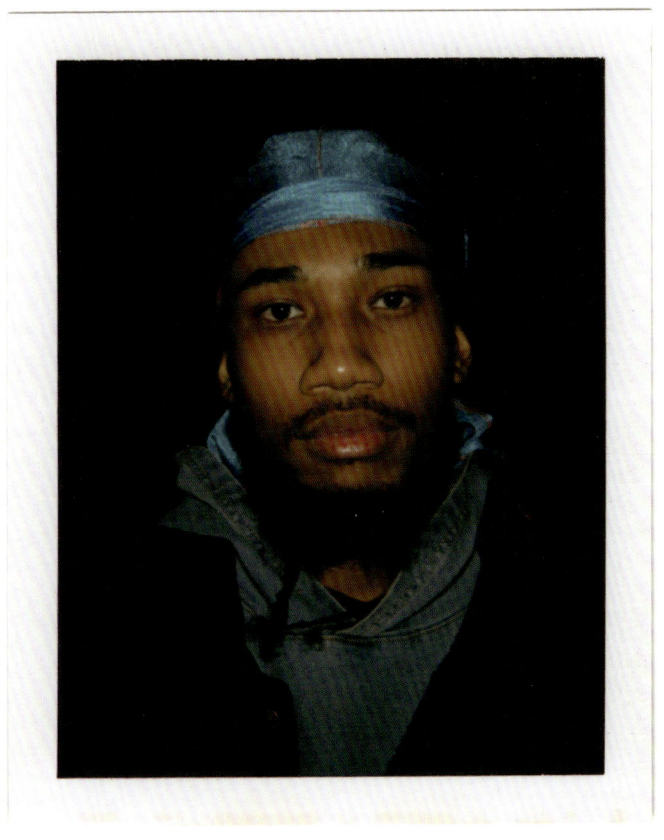

STONED SOUL STEEZ FLOSSIN

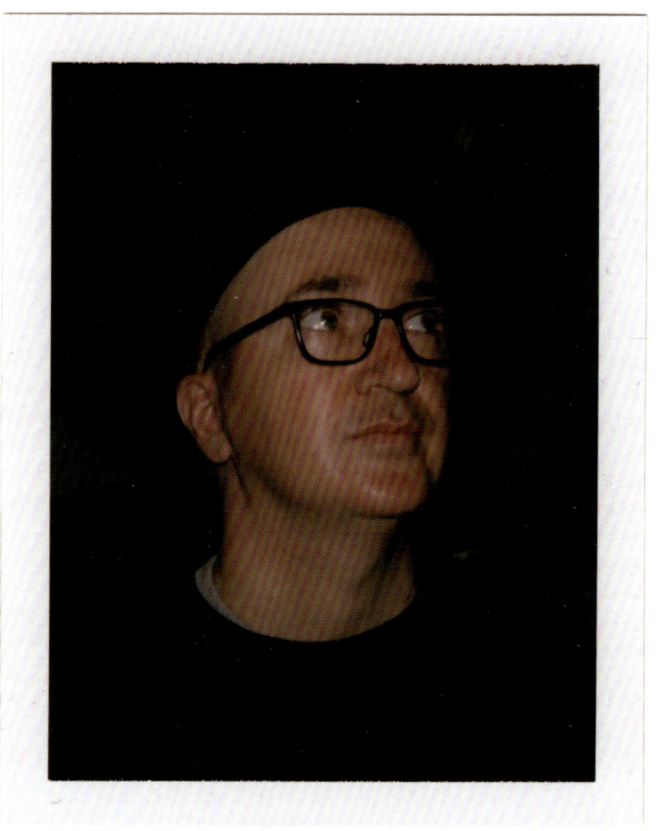

KAWS

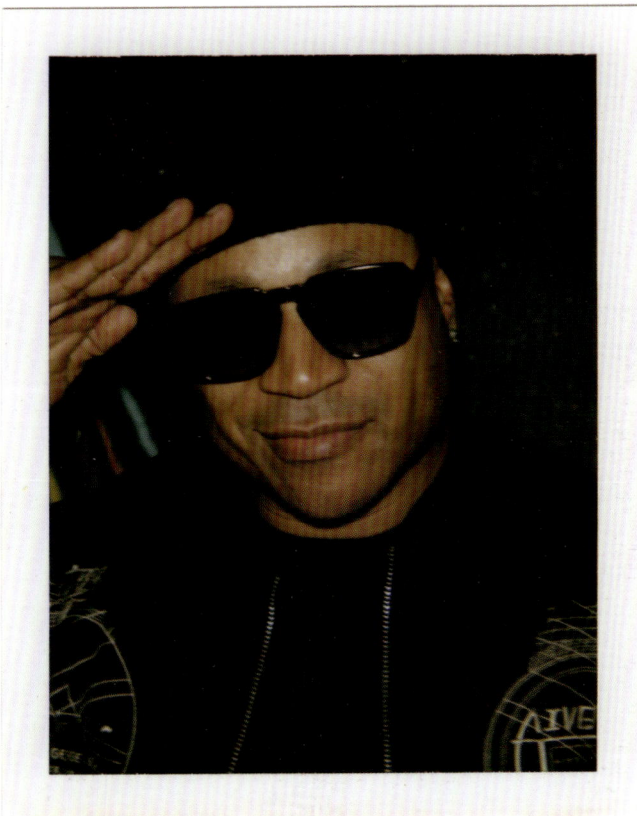

LL COOL J

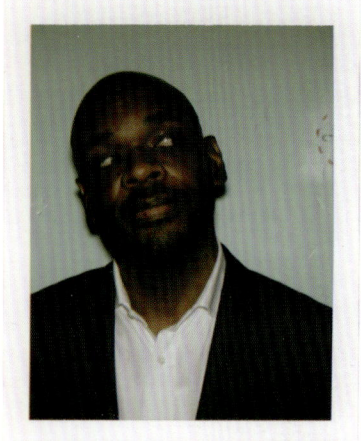

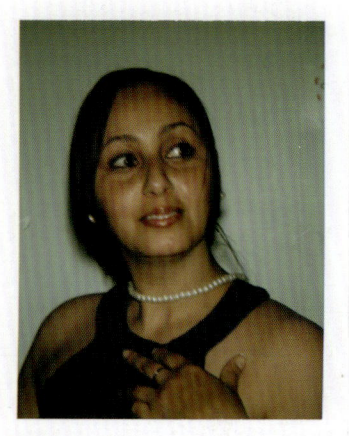

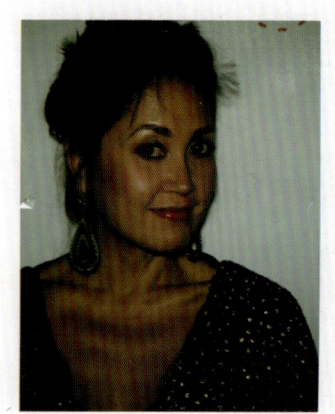

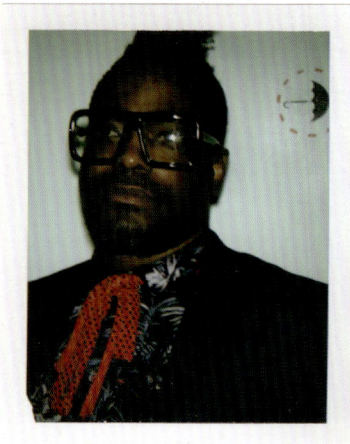

JERMAINE HALL

FOZIA ALMONTASER

JENIFER WELK

AYO OKUNSEINDE

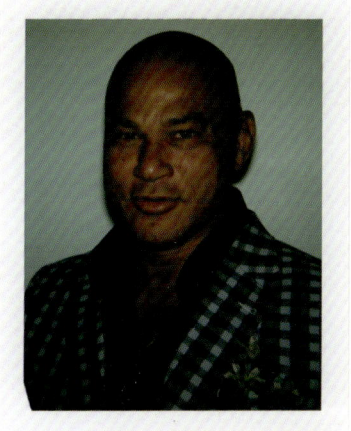

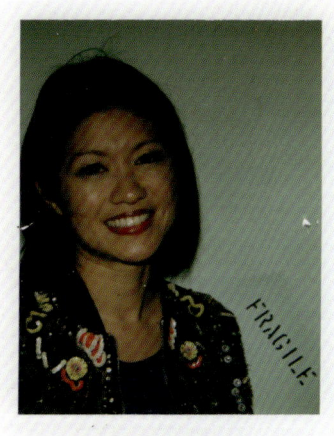

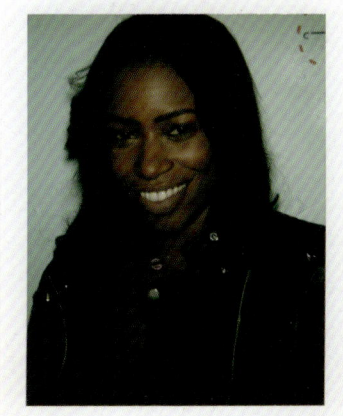

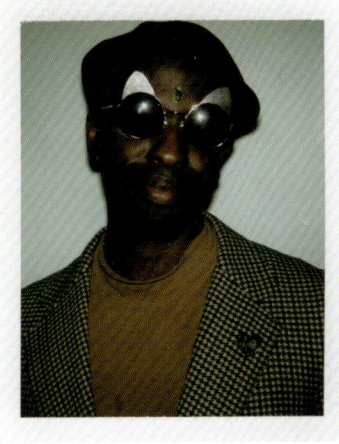

FERNANDO MATEO

FRANCOISE BLANCHETTE

JENNIFER PURITZ

ISSAC OWENS

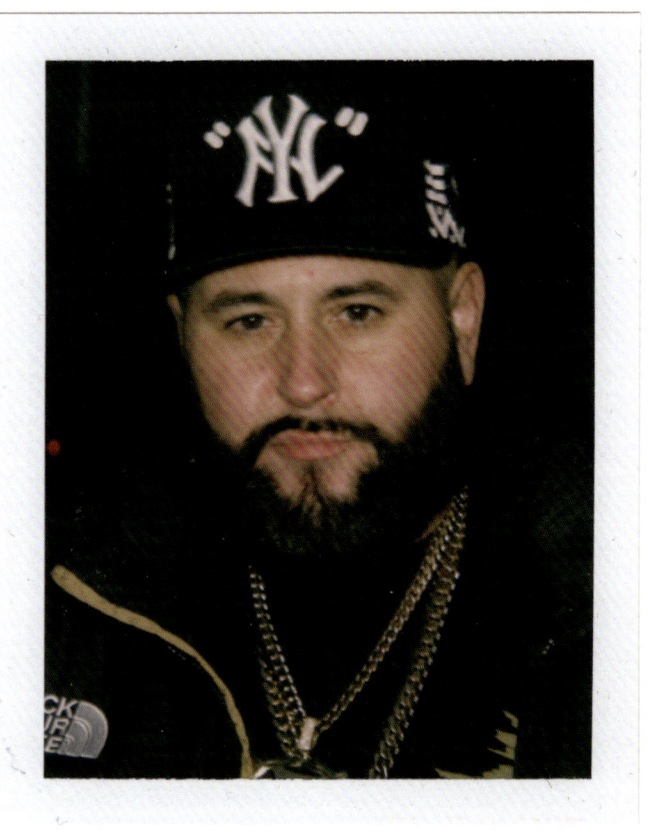

NEMS - FYL

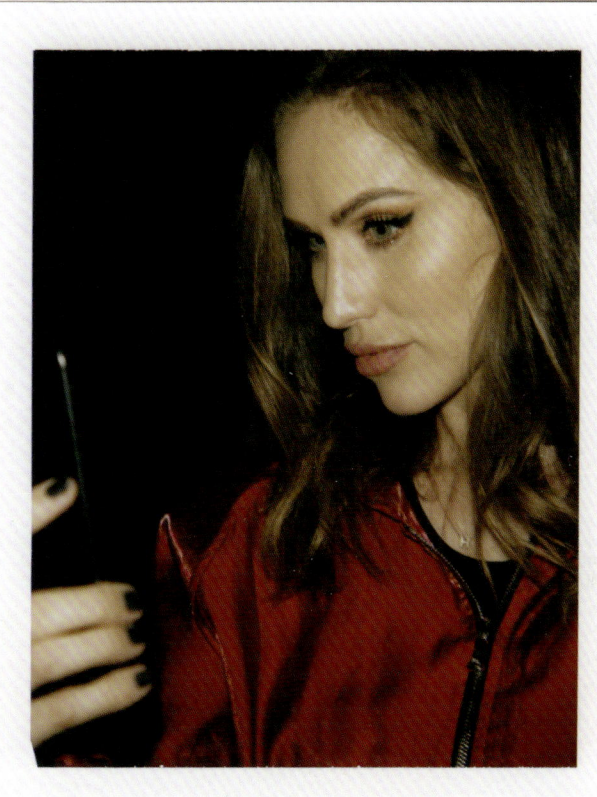

RACHEL ANGELINI

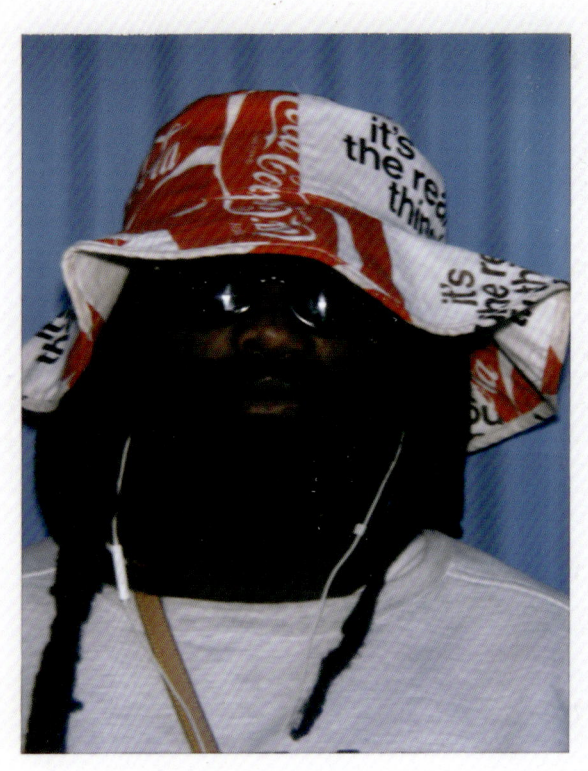

TREMAINE EMORY

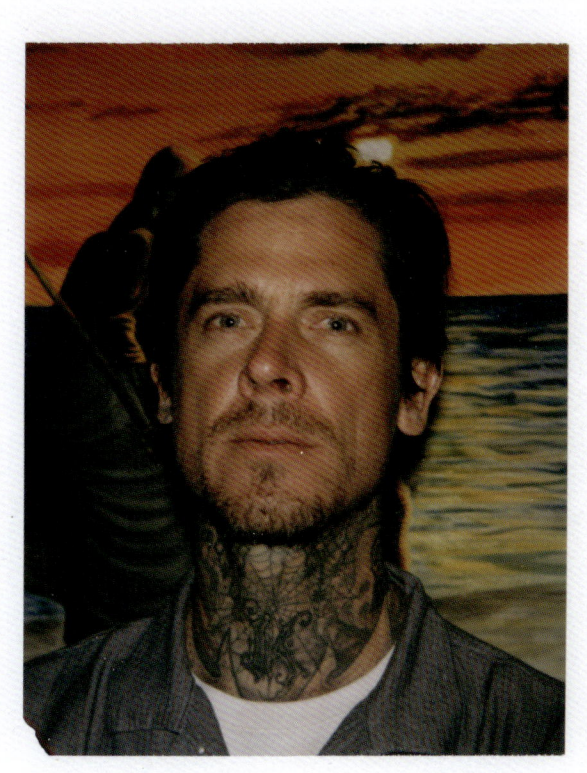

NATHAN KOSTECHKO

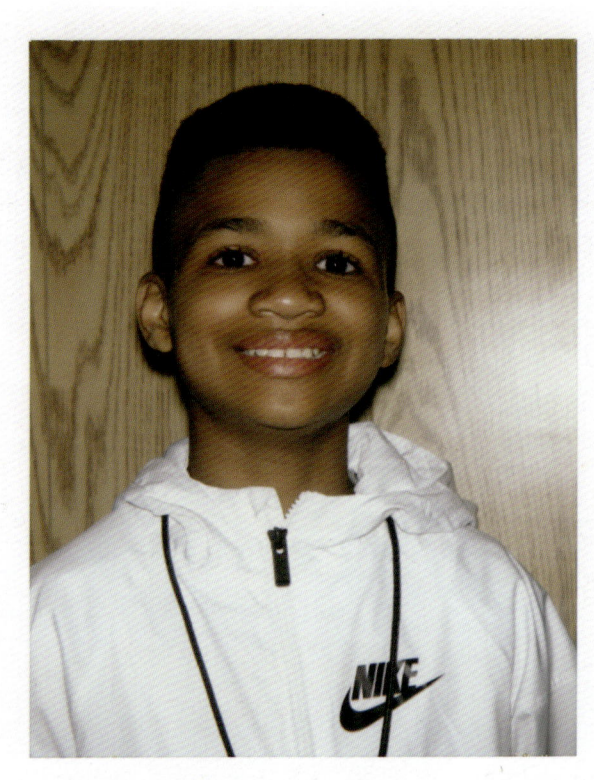

DEMARJAY SMITH

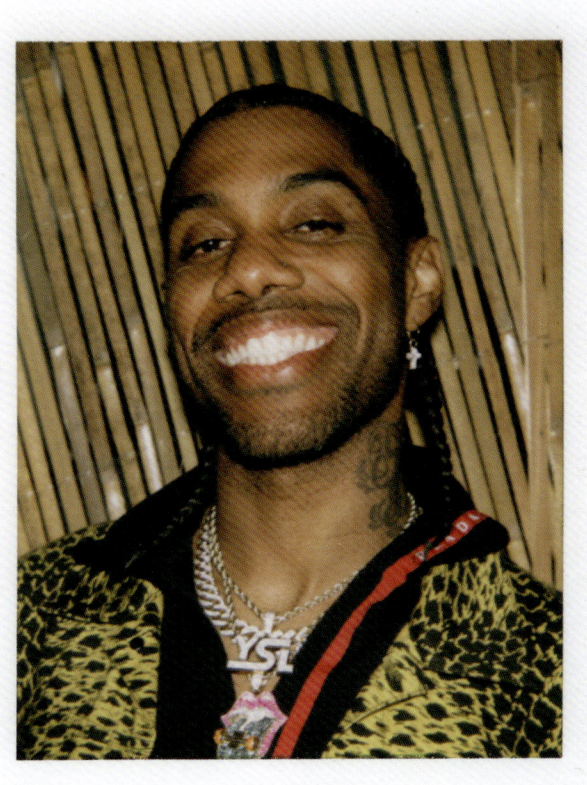

REESE LAFLARE

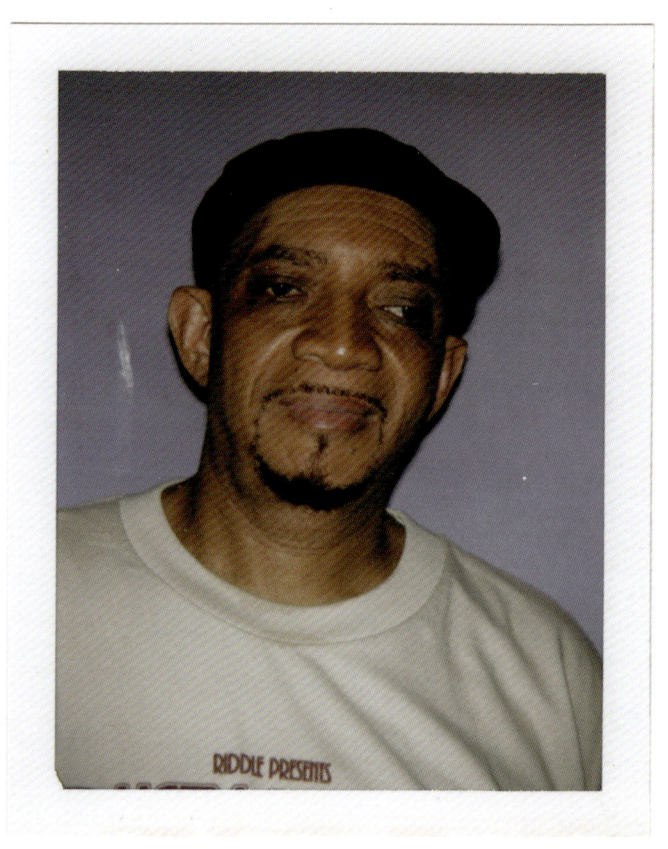

KOOL DJ RED ALERT

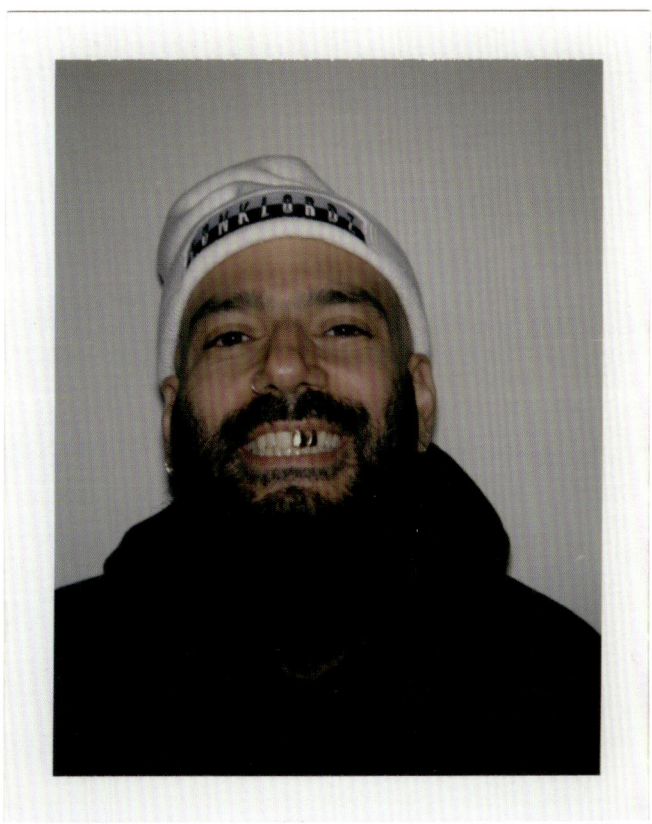

P-THUGG

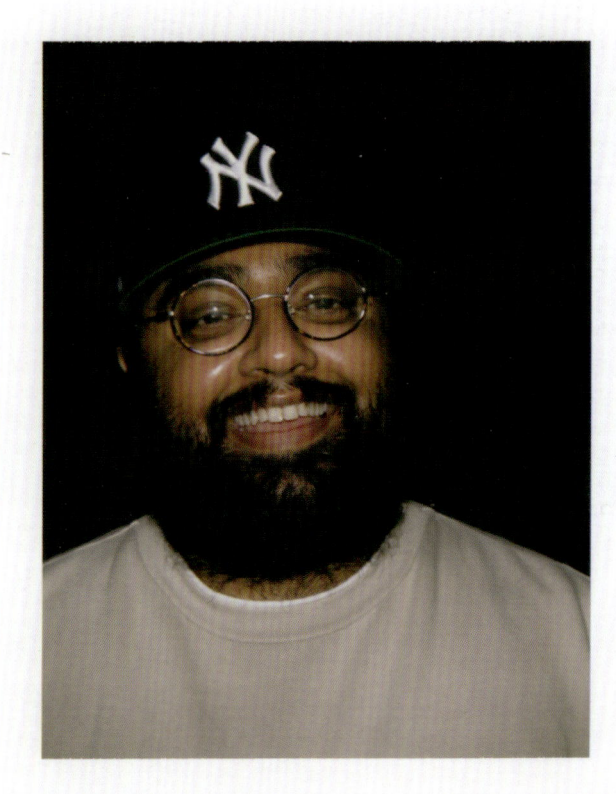

SHIVAM PANDYA

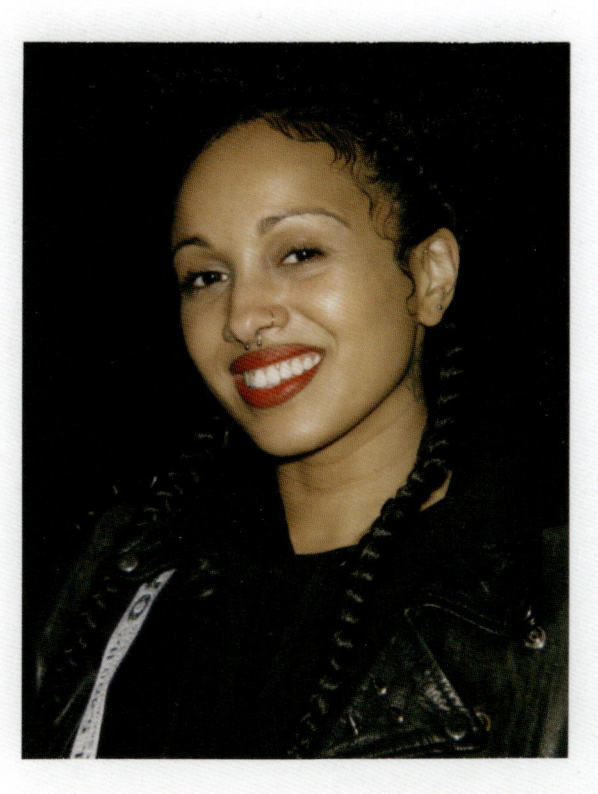

VENUS X

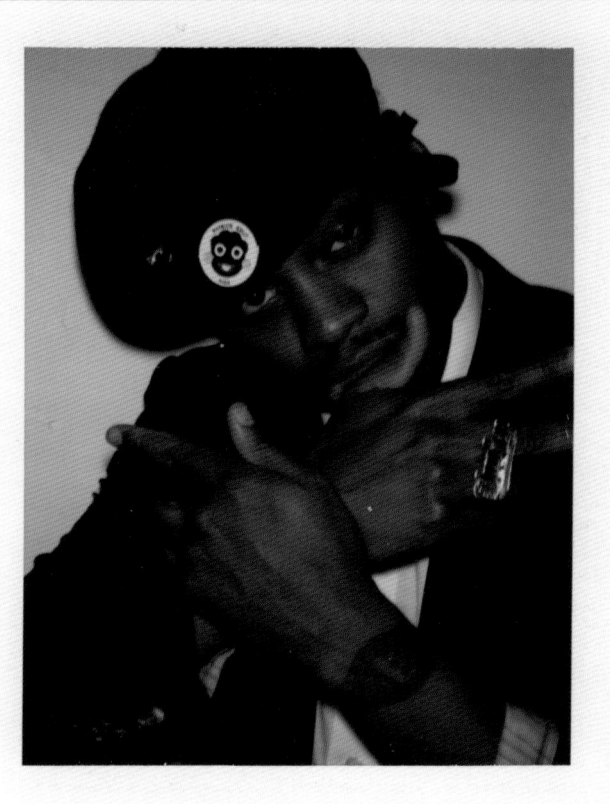

RICARDO JACKSON

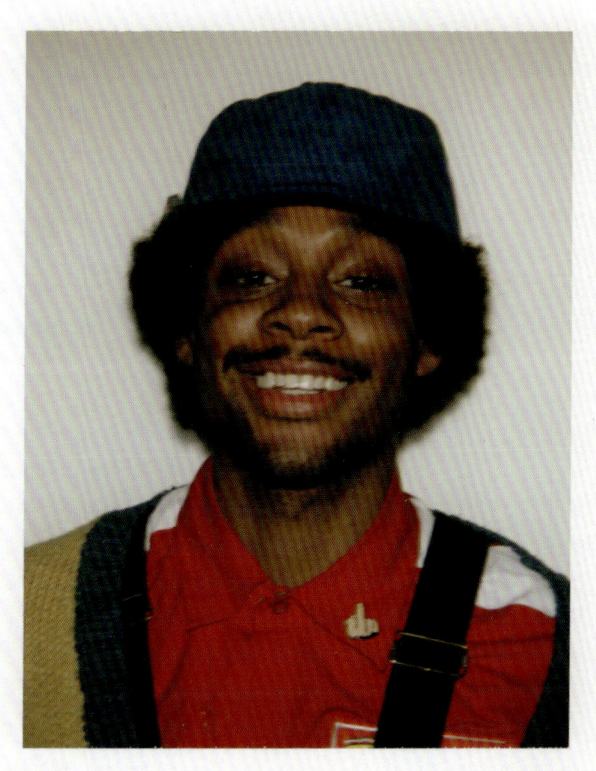

DIMIETRUS JACKSON

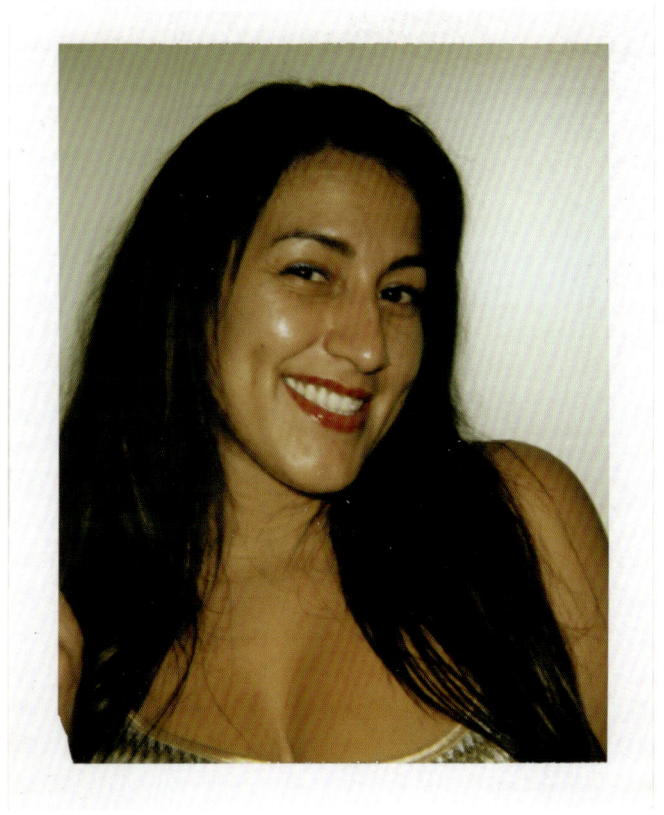

MONICA QUINTANILLA

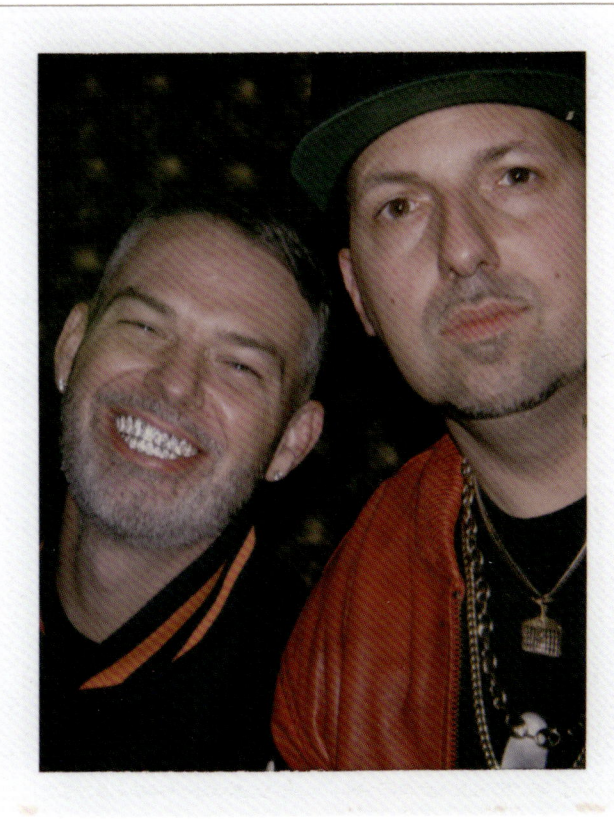

PAUL WALL & TERMANOLOGY

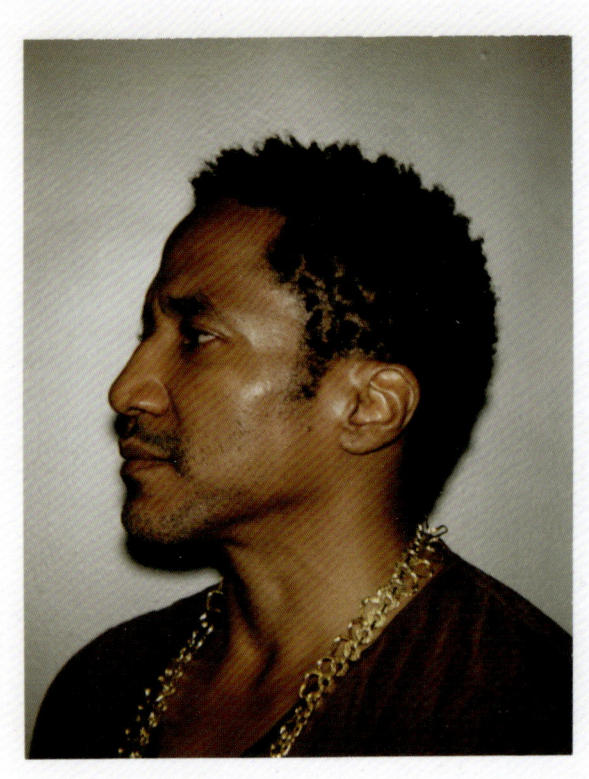

Q-TIP

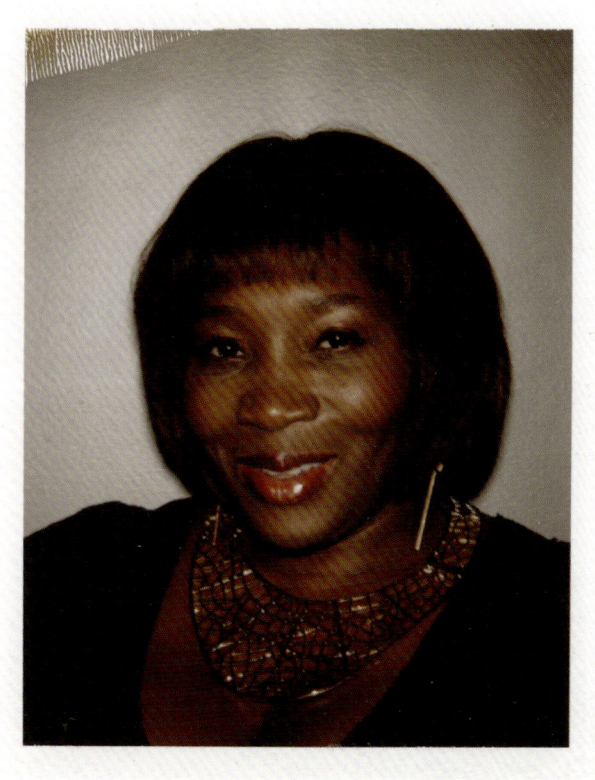

BEVY SMITH

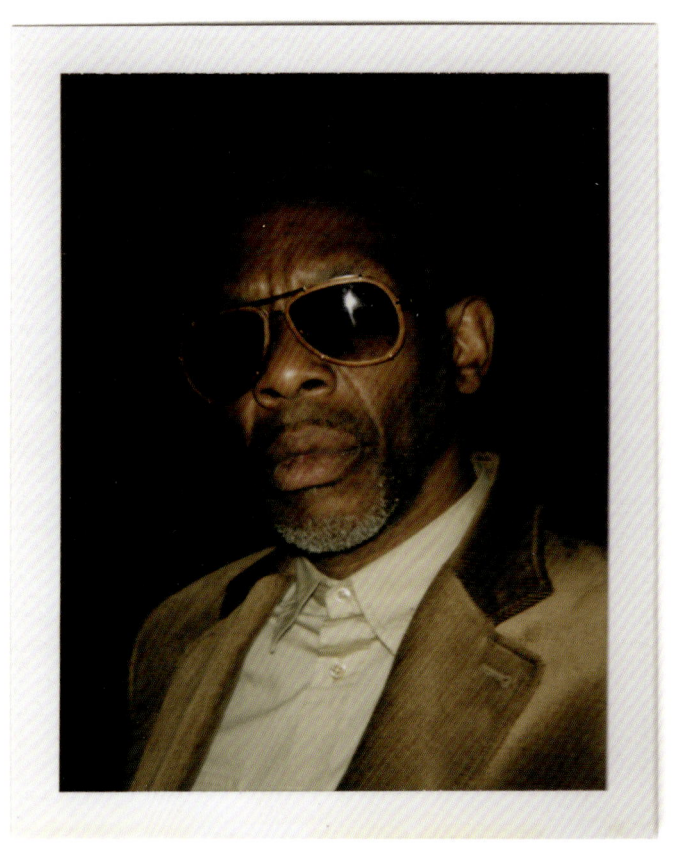

O.G. BAR

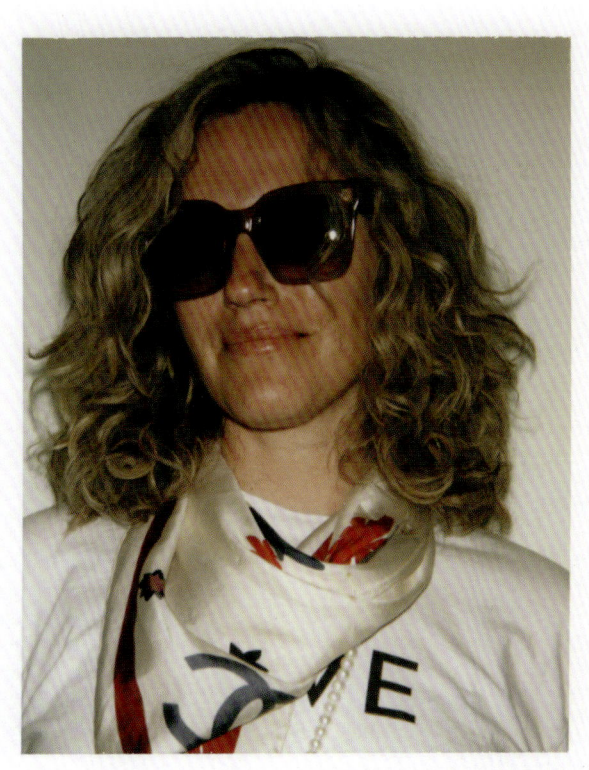

MELISSA DISHELL

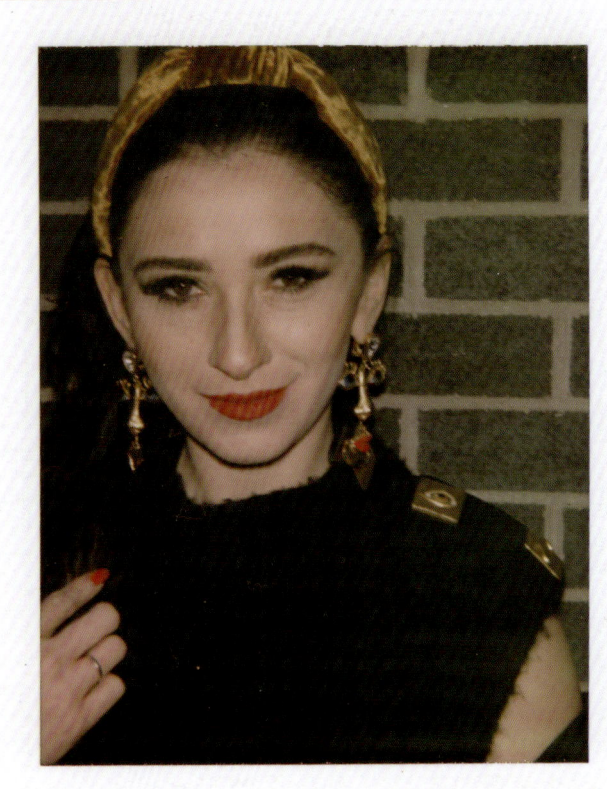

ANYA FIRESTONE

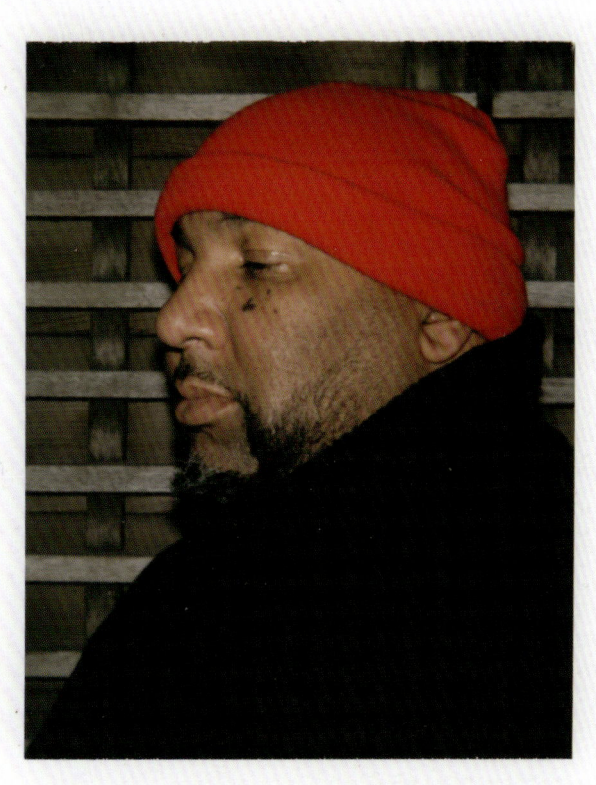

BERNARD ALEXANDER

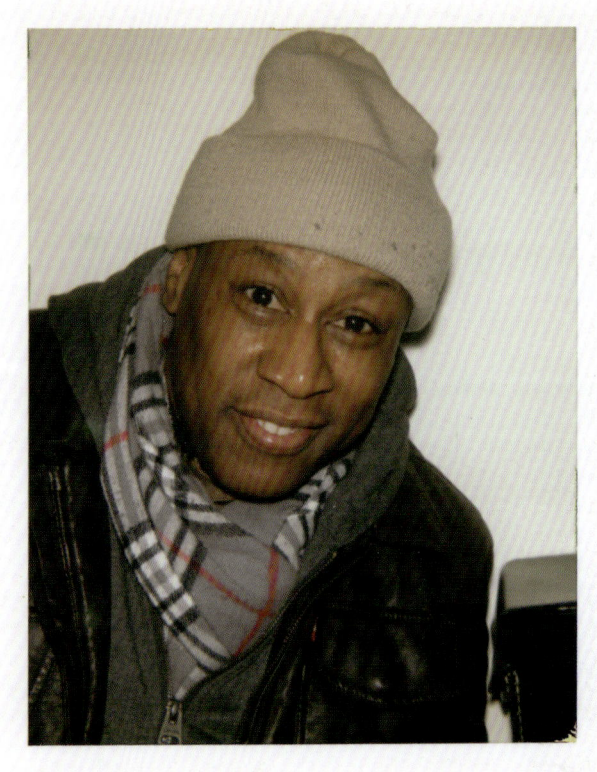

A B BUTLER

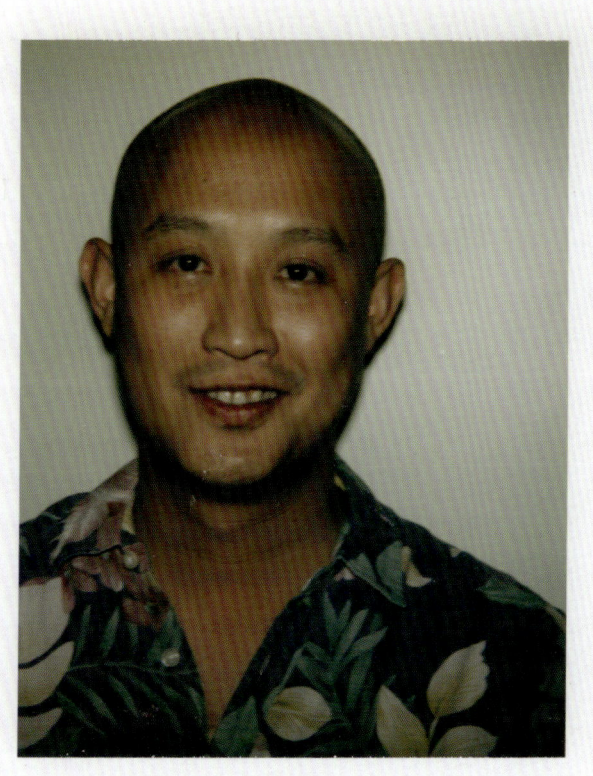

VUDI

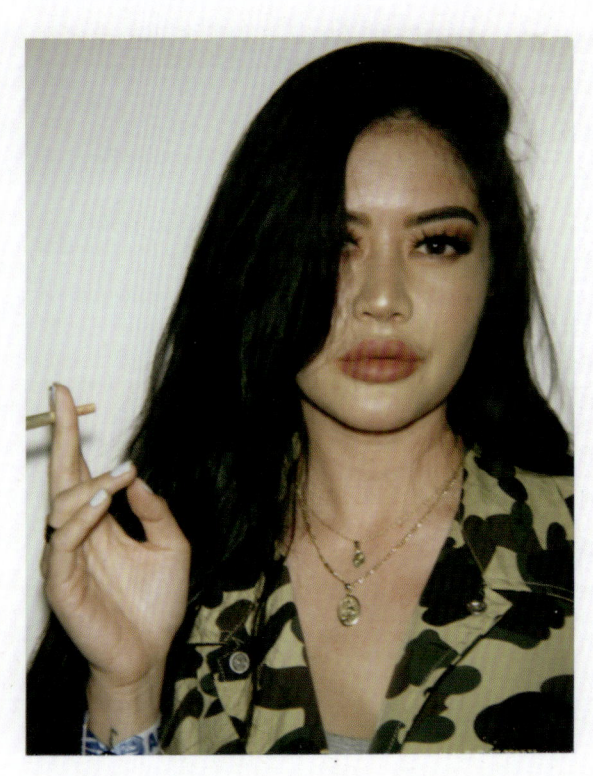

KIM LEE

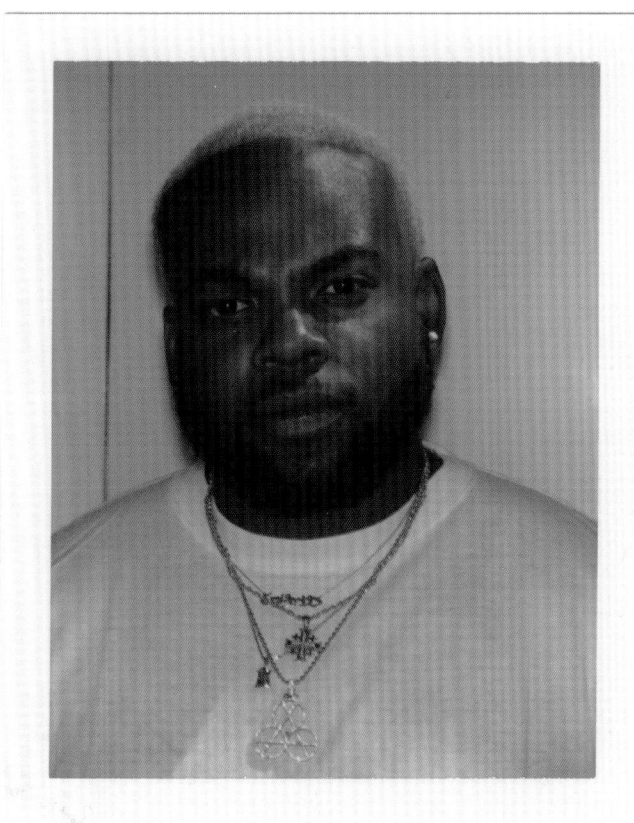

T J MIZELL

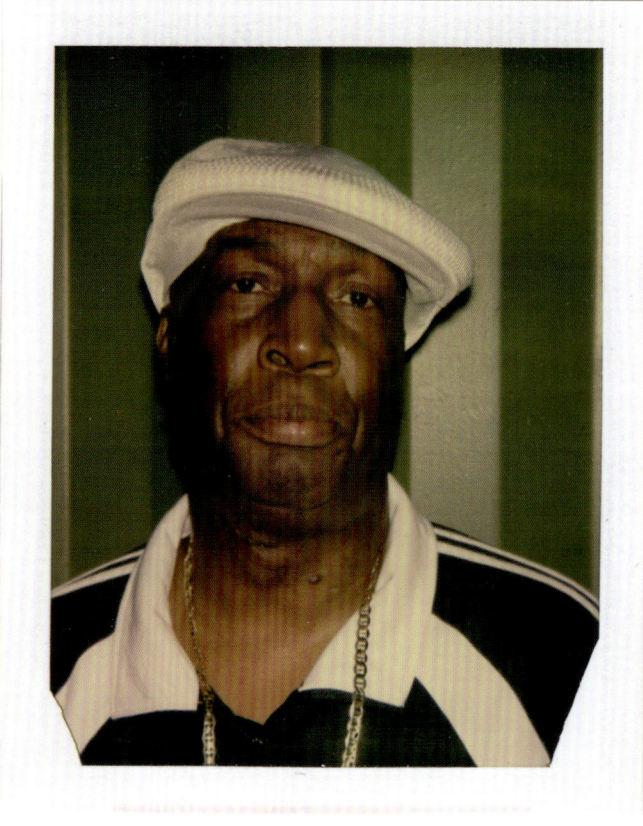

GRANDMASTER FLASH

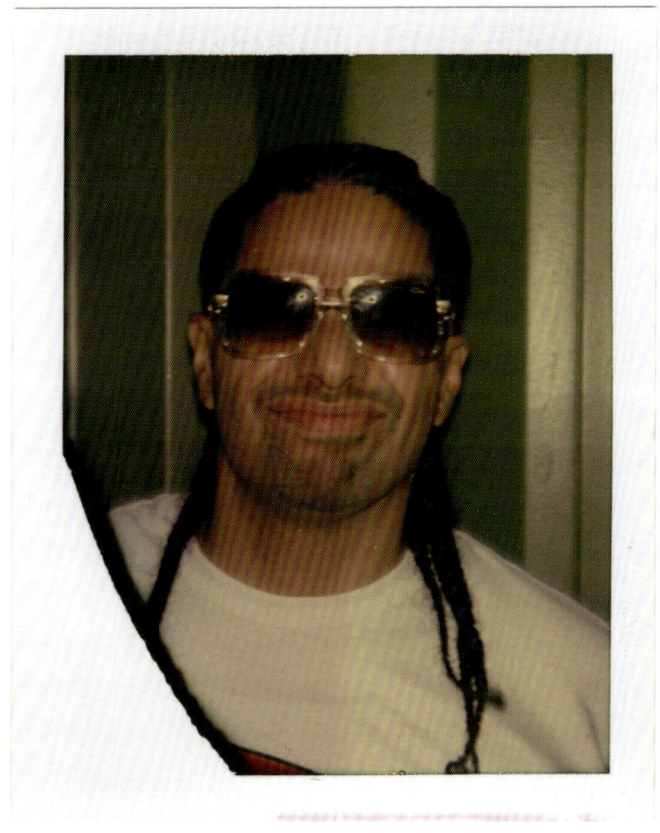

D-STROY

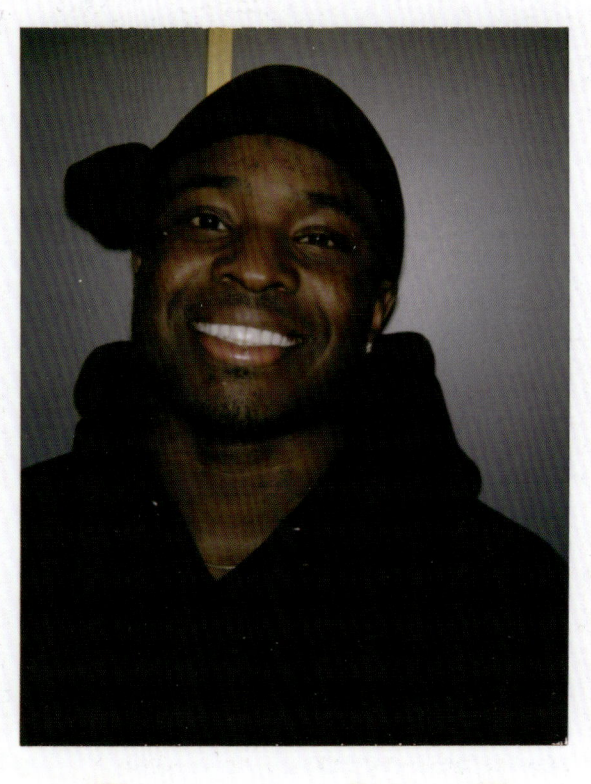

IDK

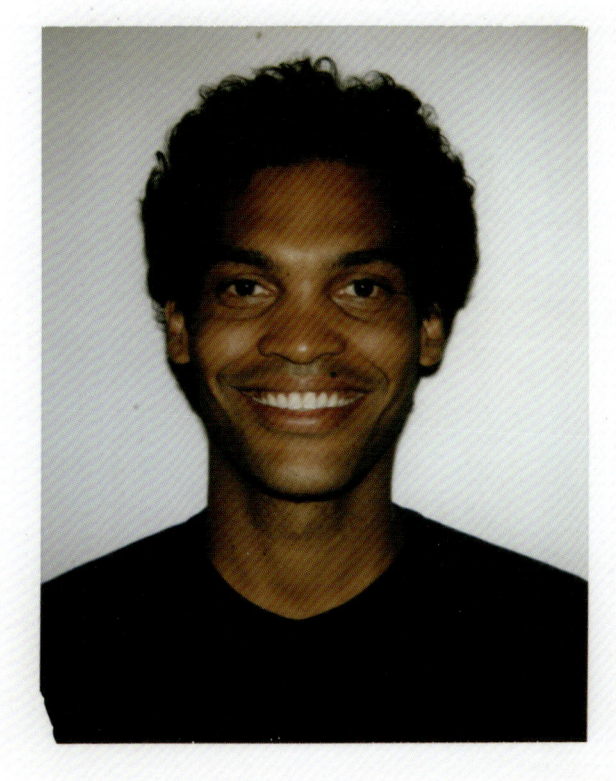

SCOTT ROBERT WILLIAMS

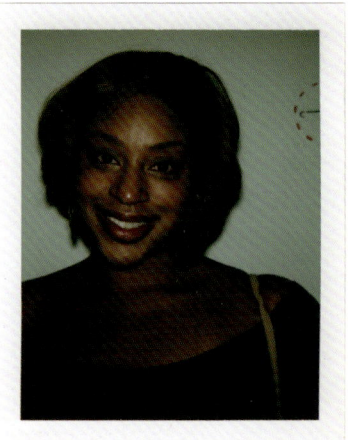

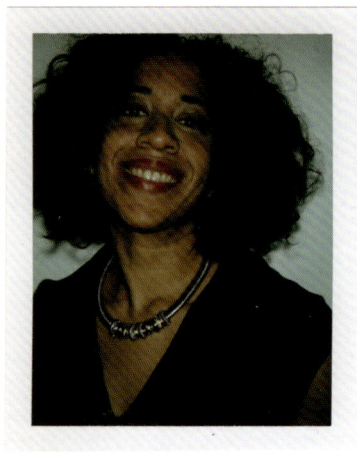

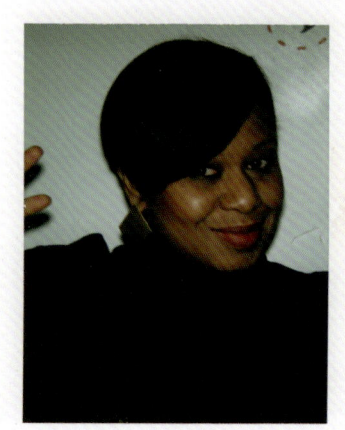

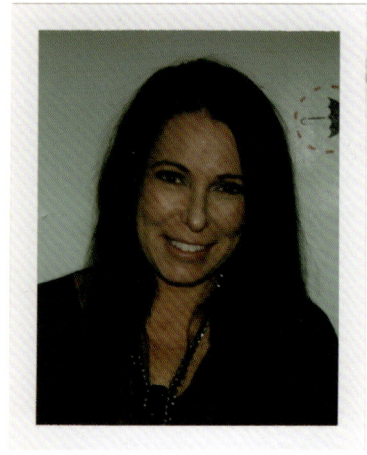

VANESSA JOSEPH   STEPHANIE TREVINO

YASMINE DEETJEN   SUSAN GROGAN

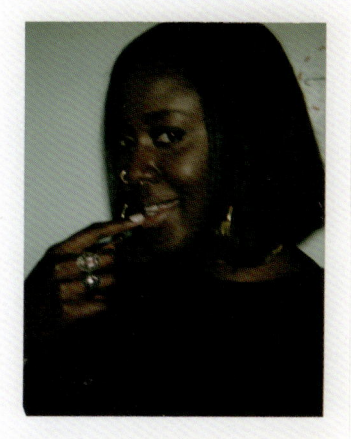

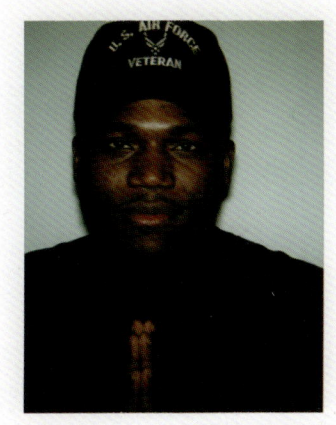

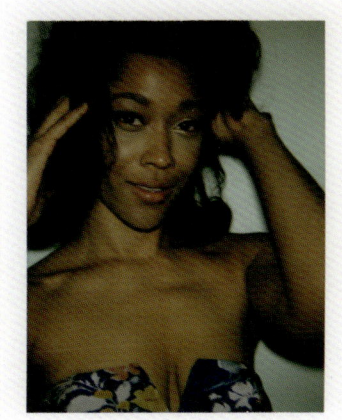

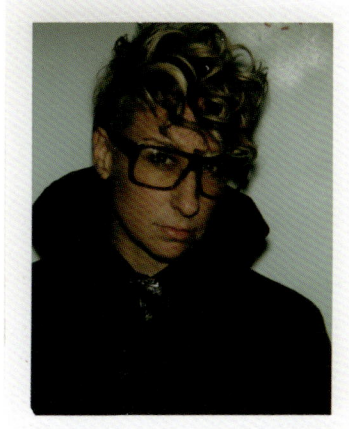

JET TOOMER

TIMO BLAKE

TABITHA HOLBERT

L K NAPS

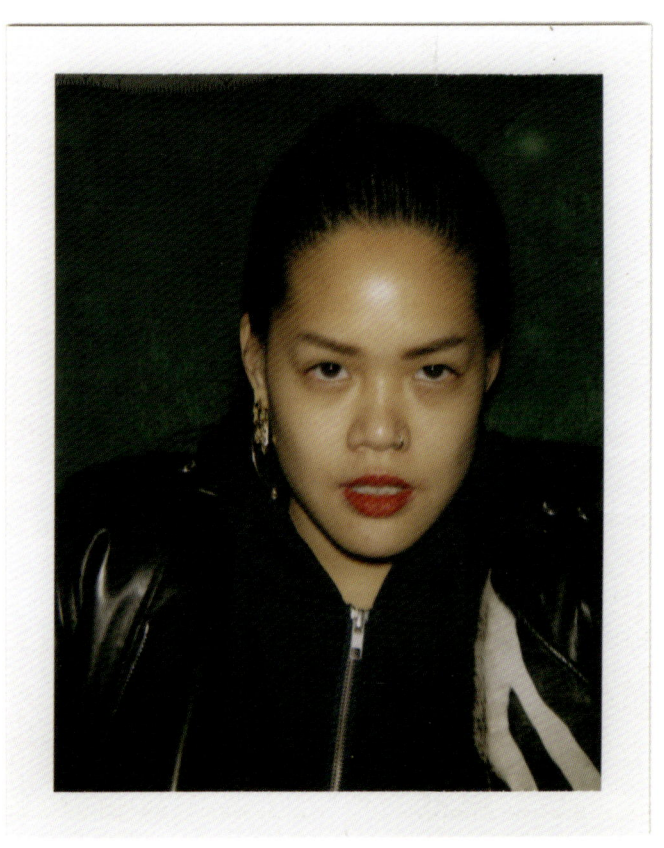

O THONGTHAI

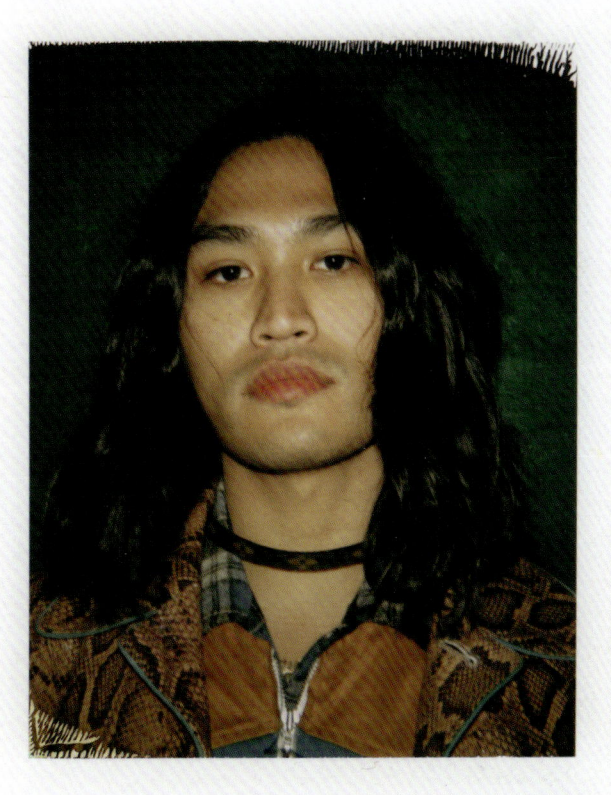

PUN SARASAS

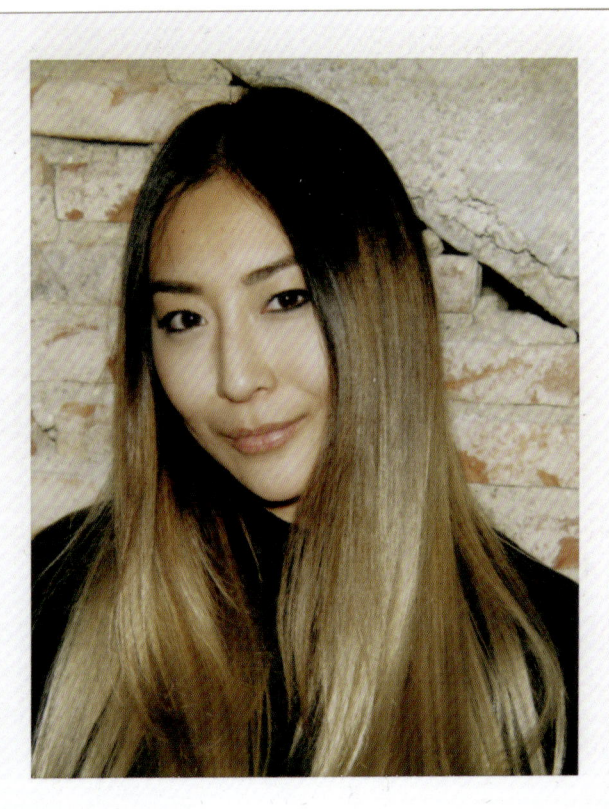

JESSIE CHLOE

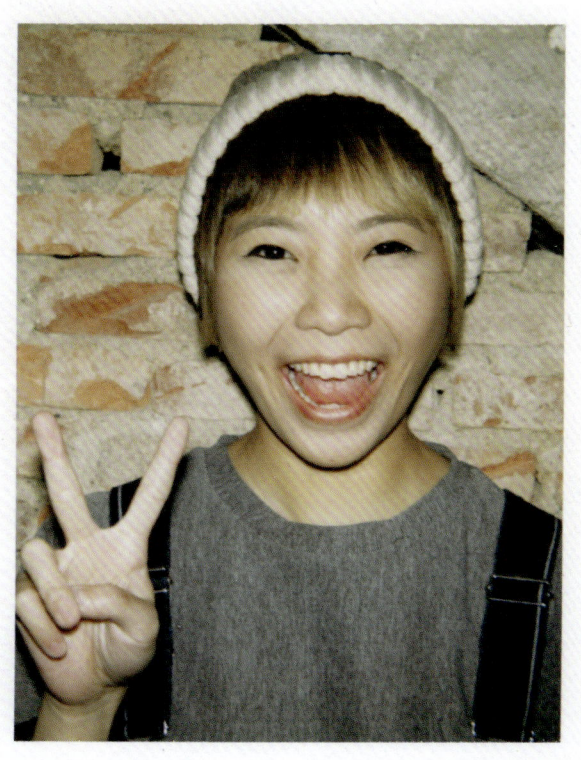

PHOEBE CHAN

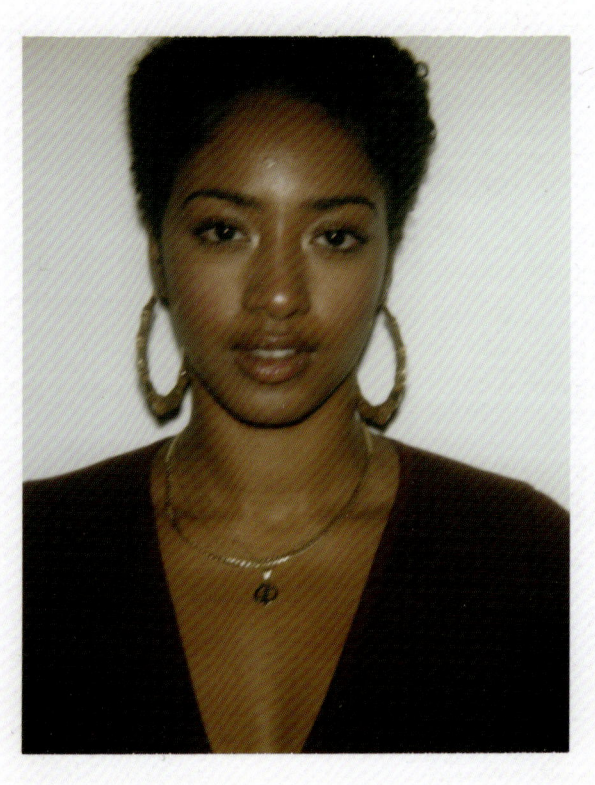

MAHANEELA

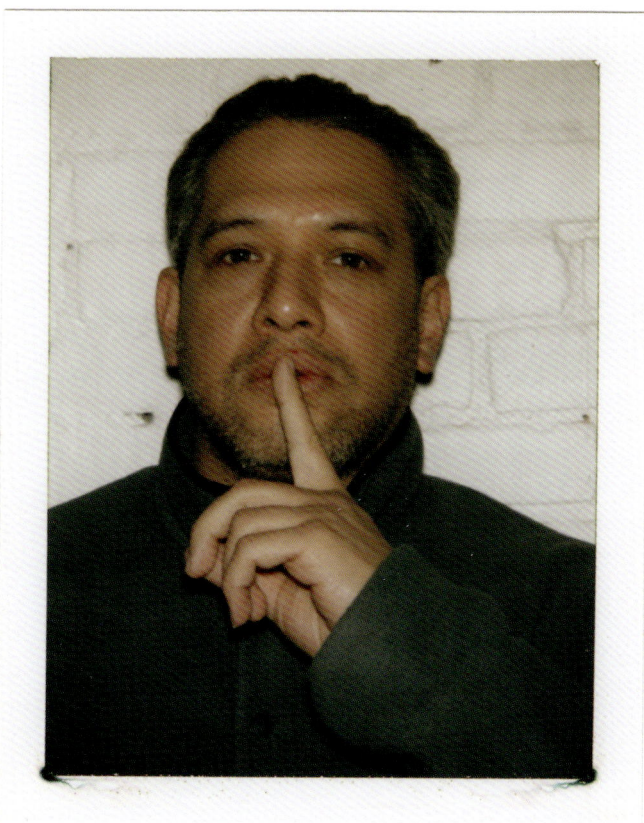

SIMONEZ

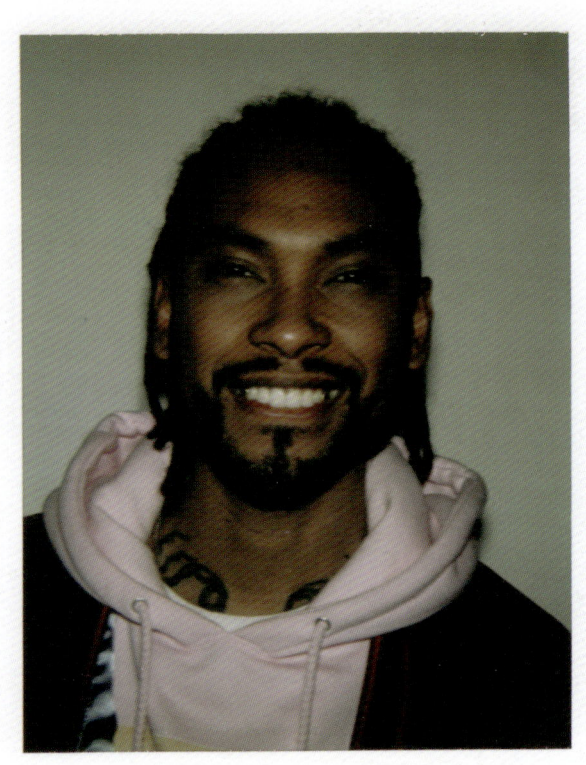

MIGUEL

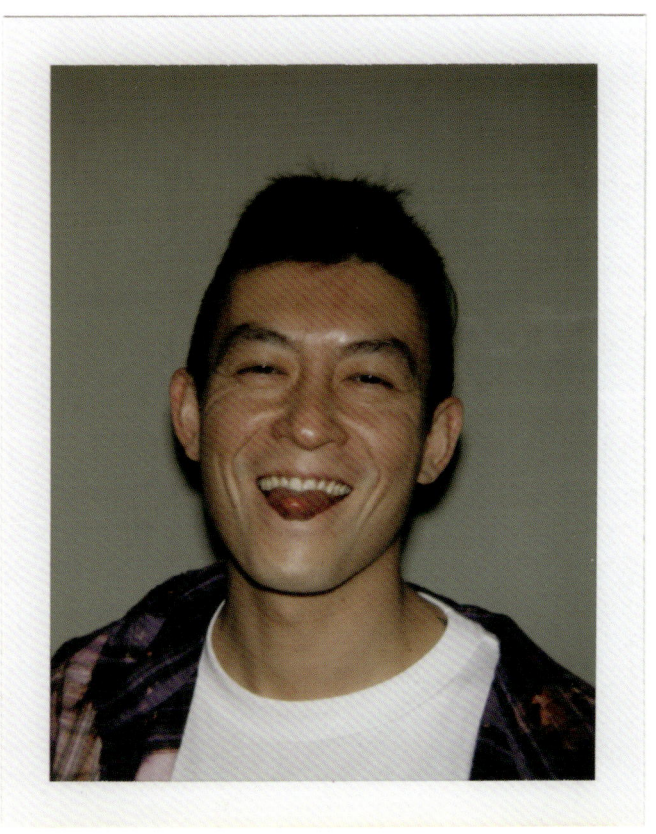

EDISON CHEN

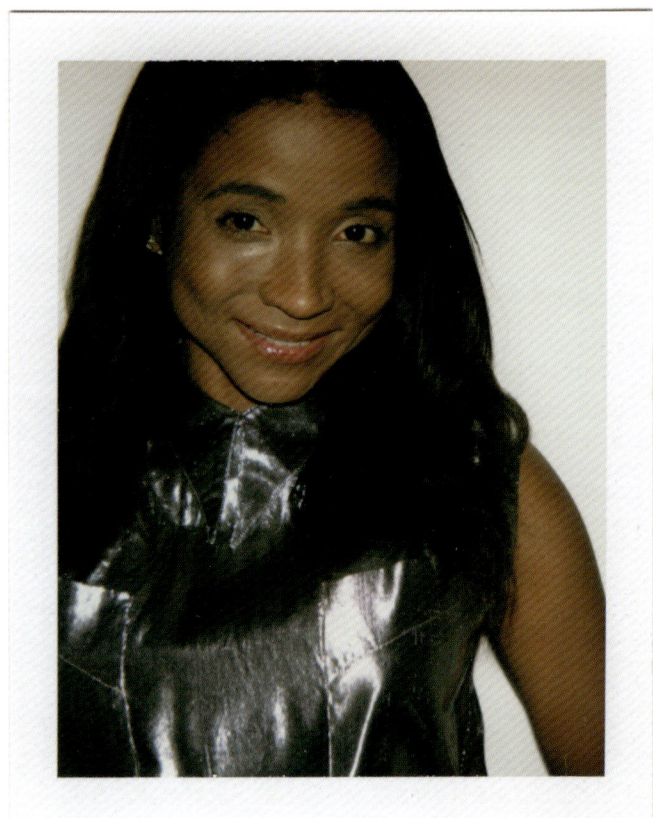

GENEVIEVE JONES

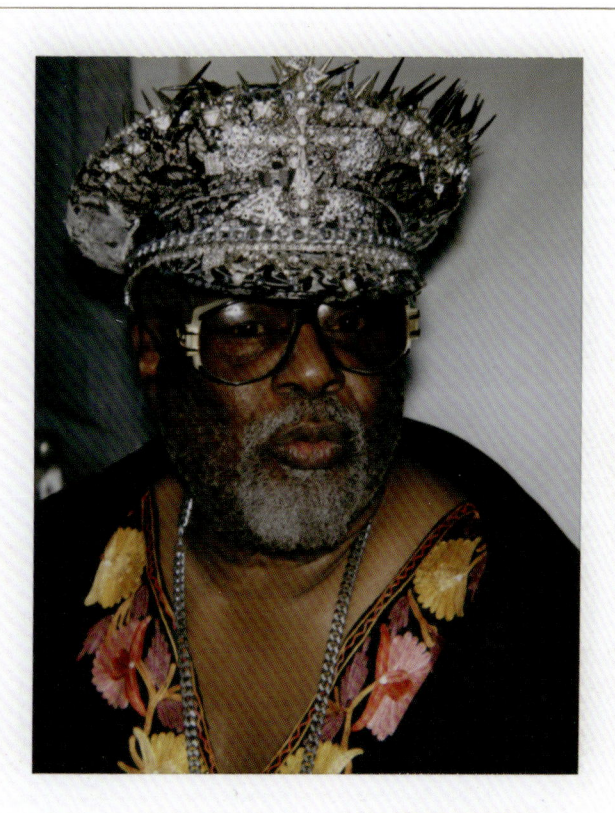

GEORGE CLINTON

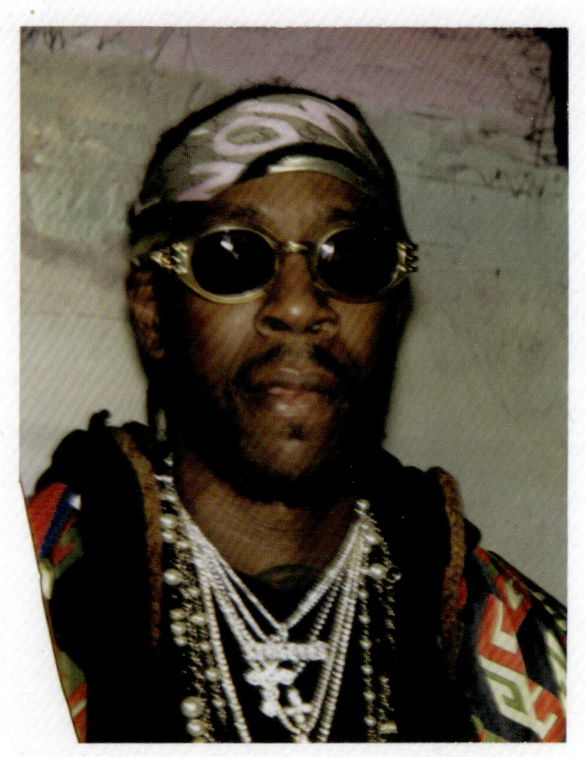

2 CHAINZ

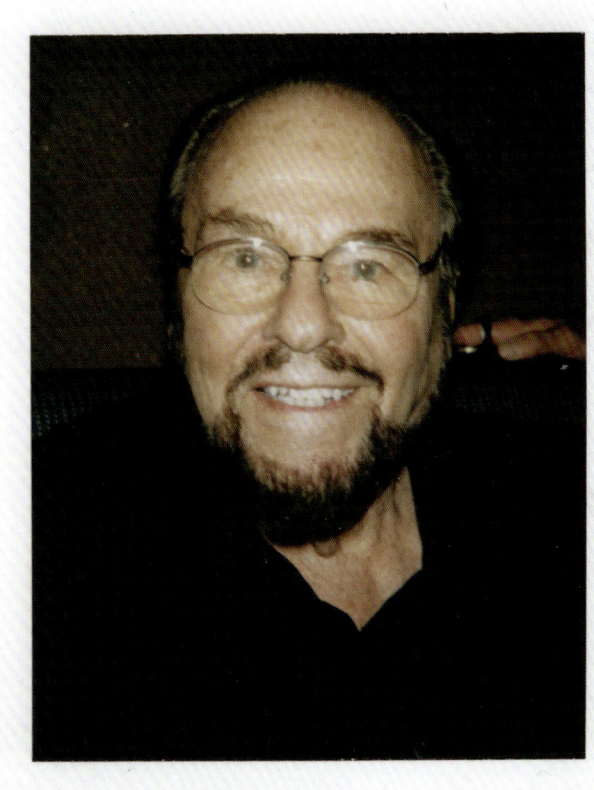

JAMES LIPTON

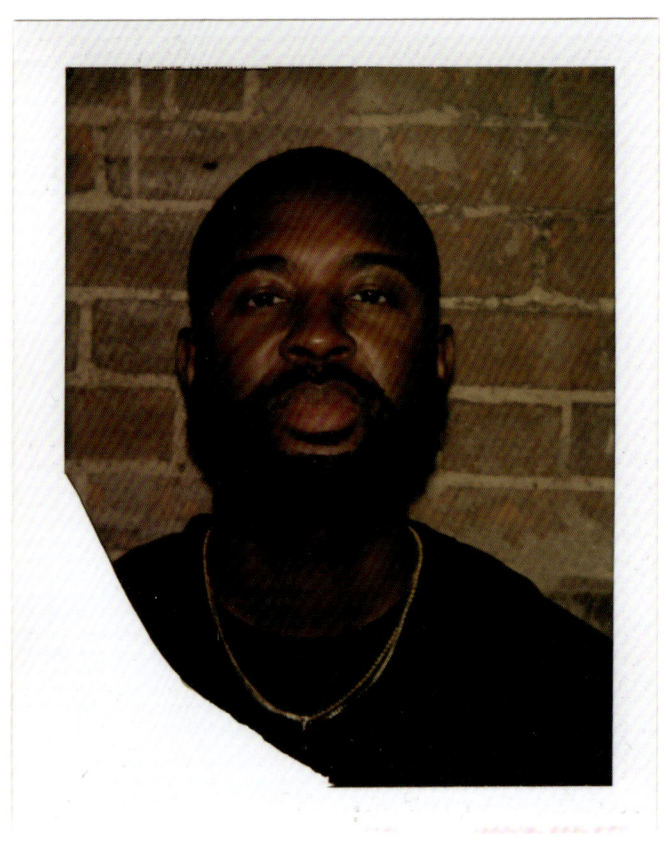

MIKE NASTY

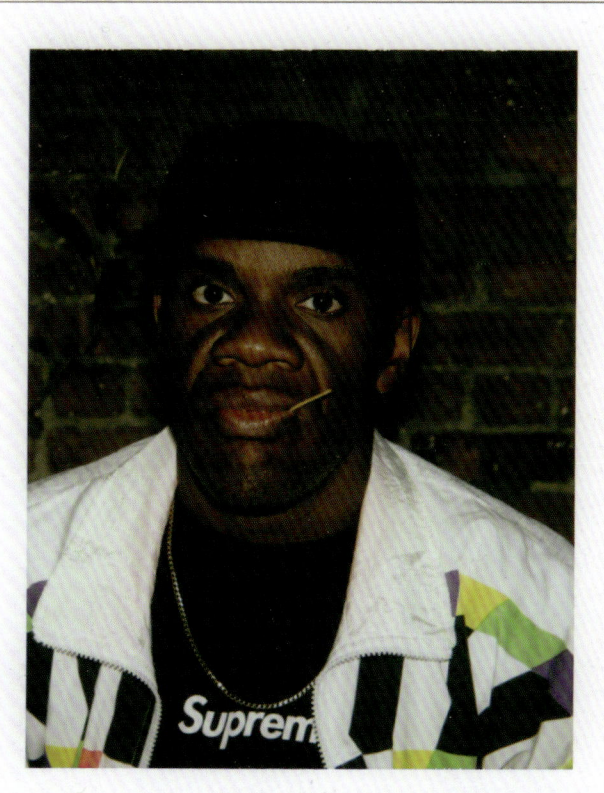

BAHR BROWN

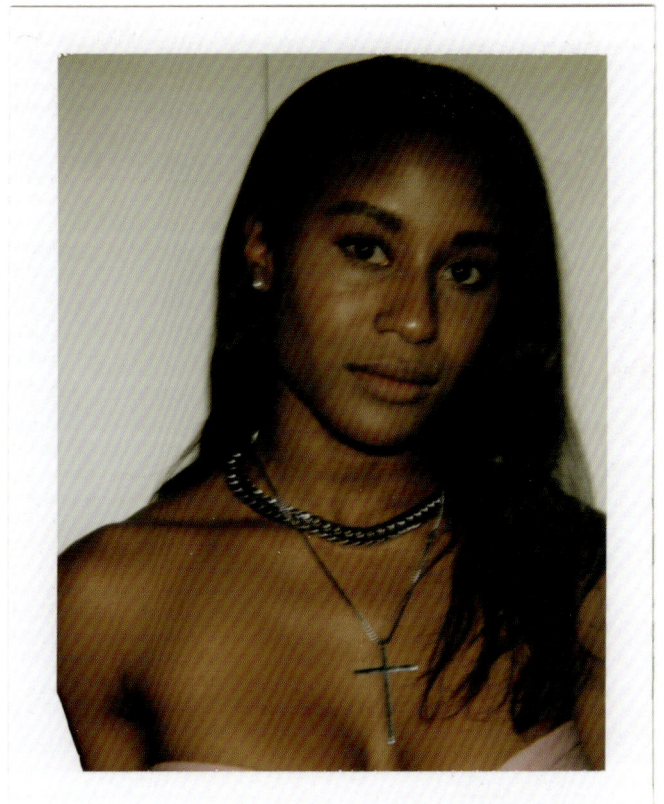

ANGEL

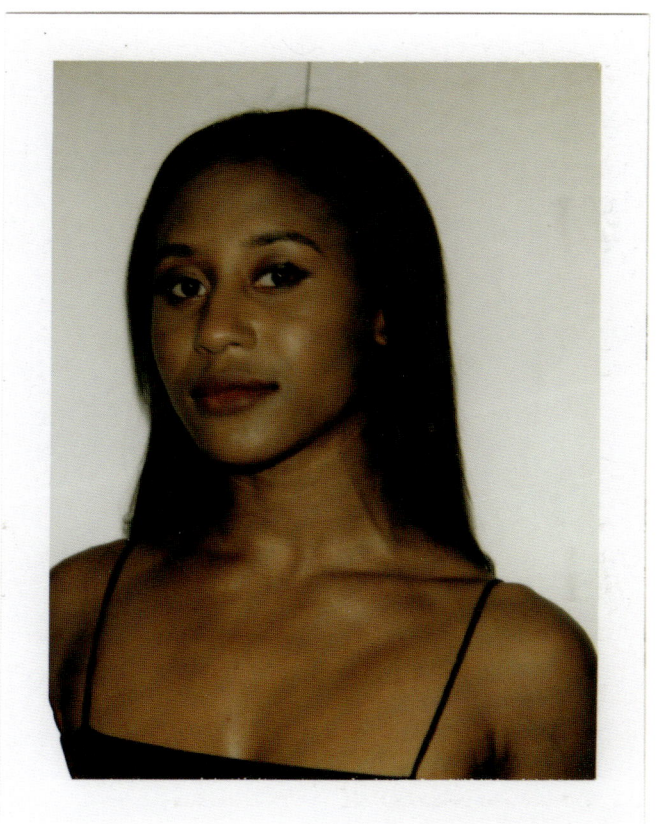

DREN

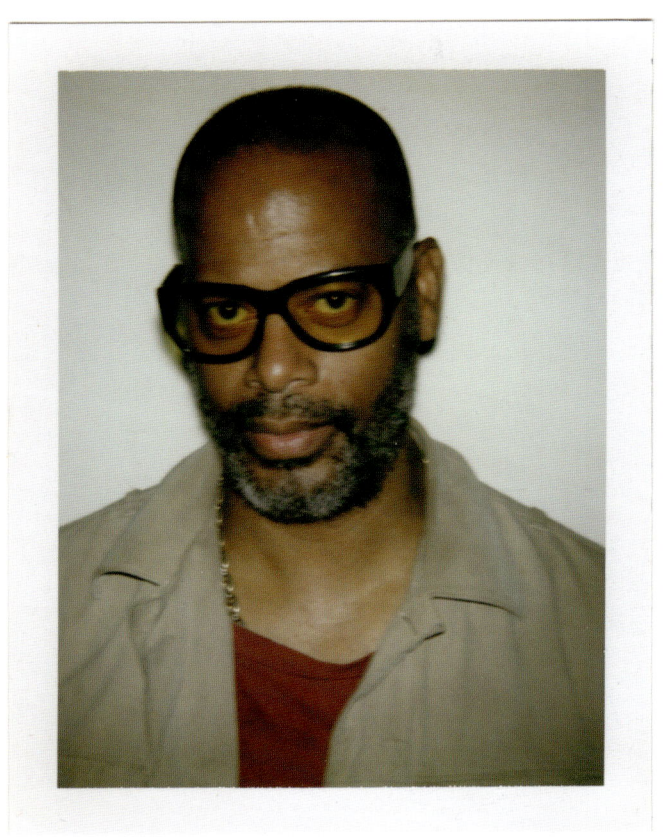

ALI RICHMOND

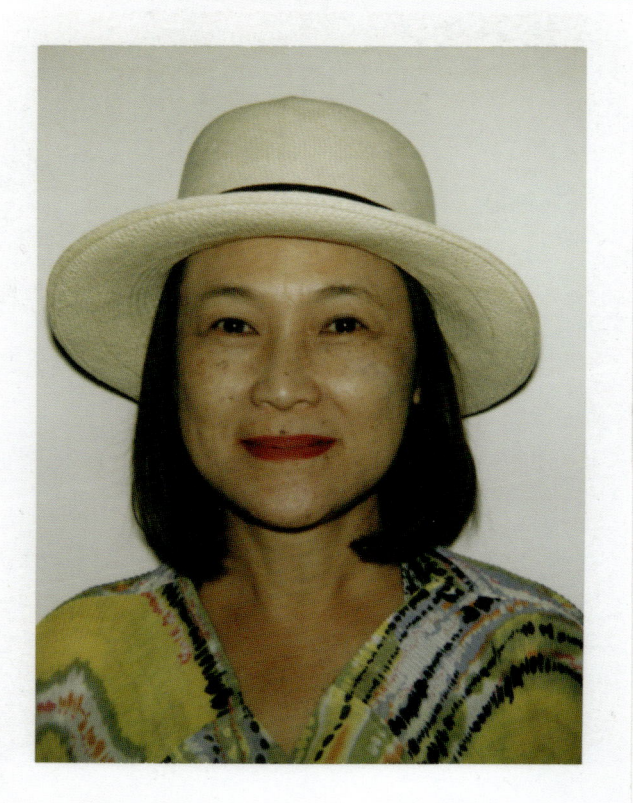

ALISARA SIRICHOOMSANG

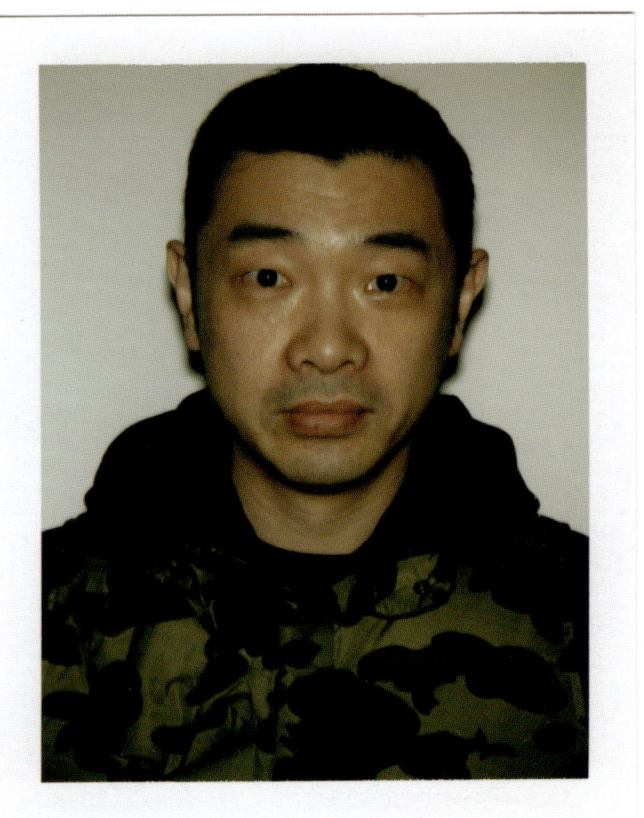

KANZUNORI

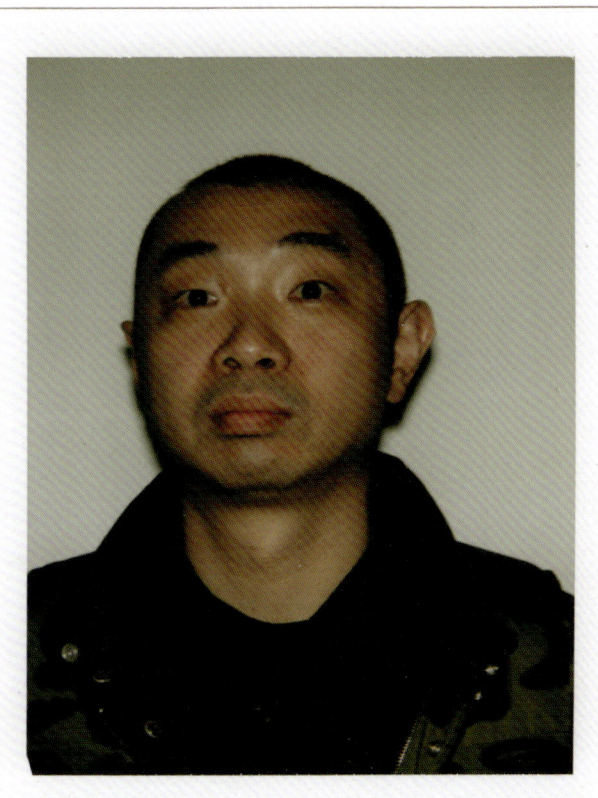

KANJI

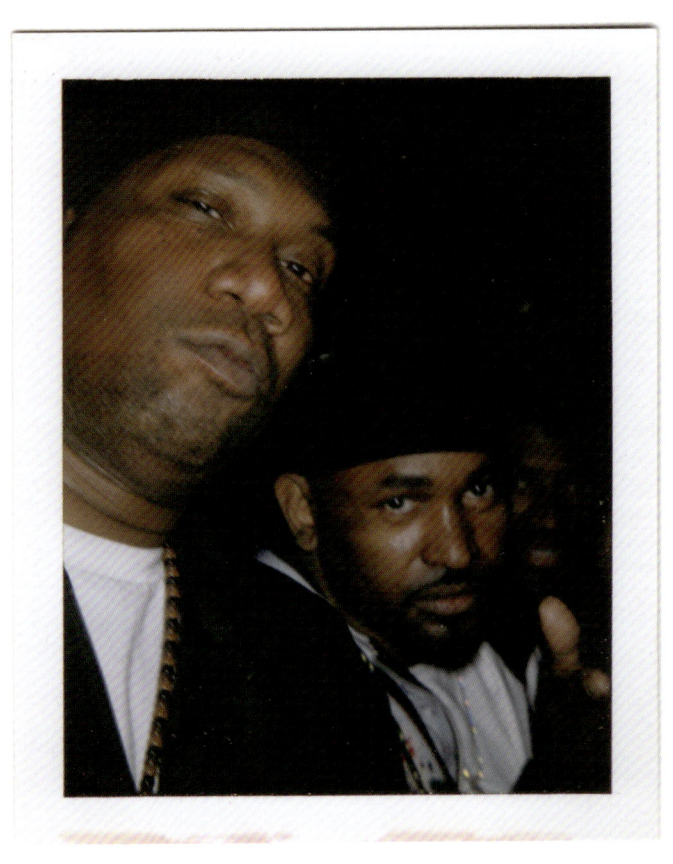

KRS ONE & MAD LION

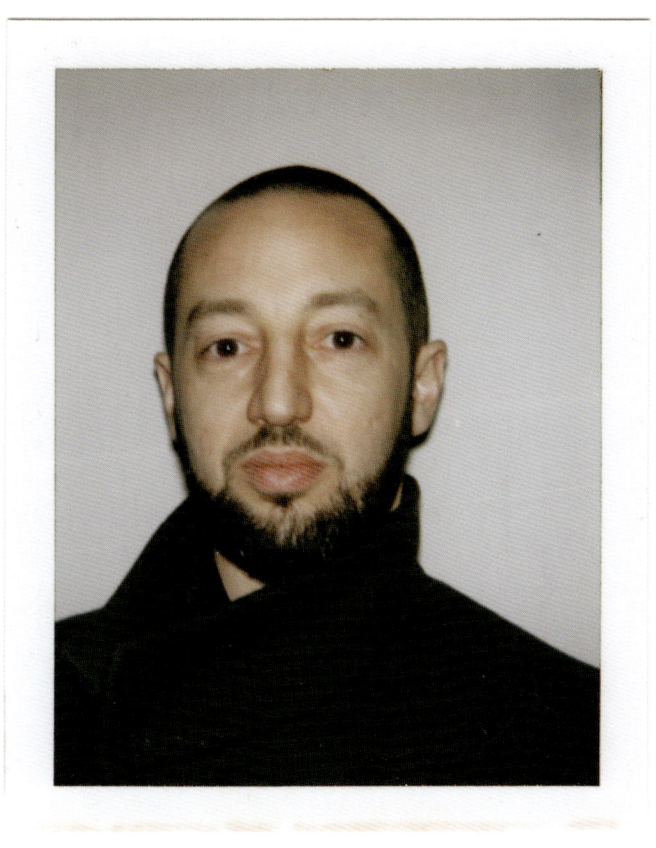

J.PERIOD

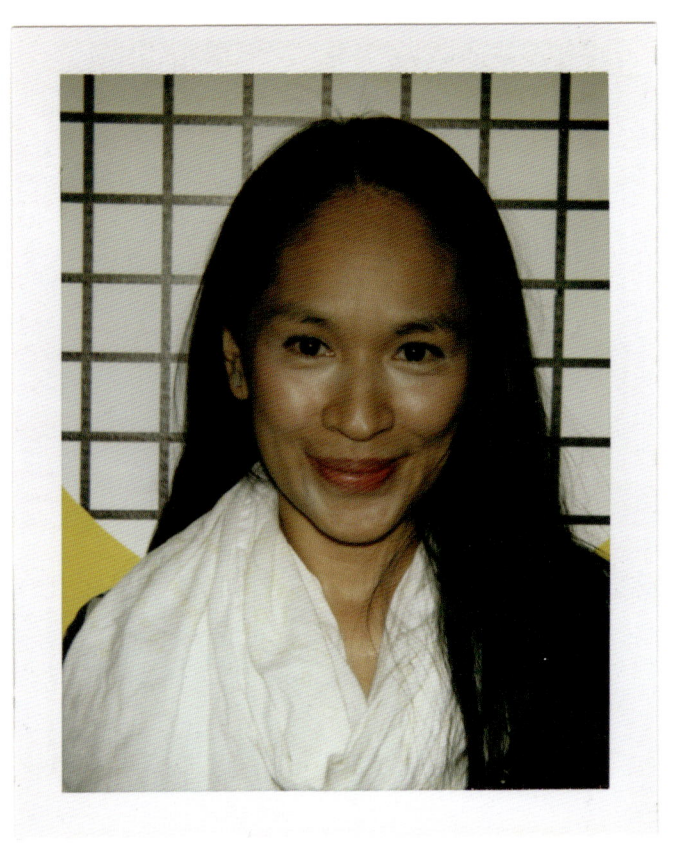

KARMELA ORETA

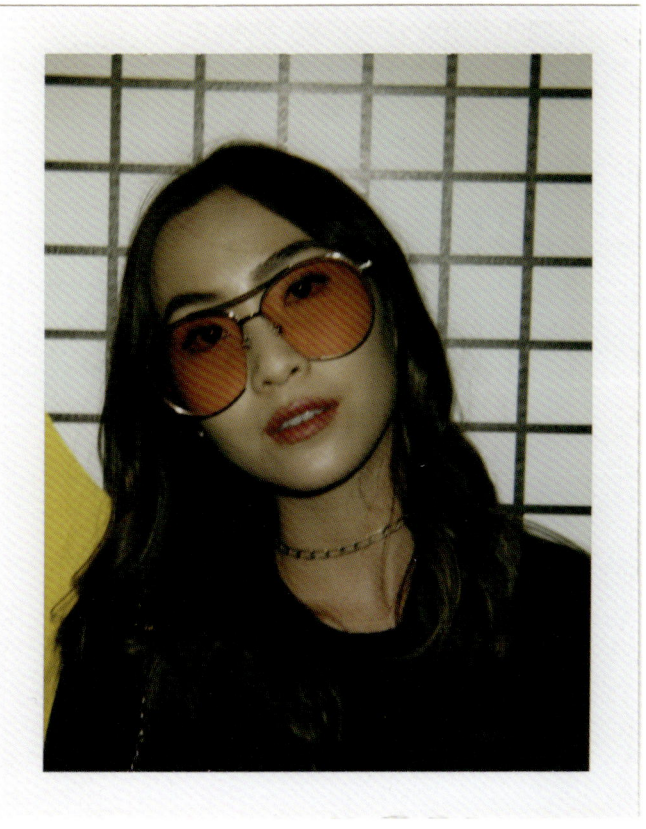

SONIA CHEW

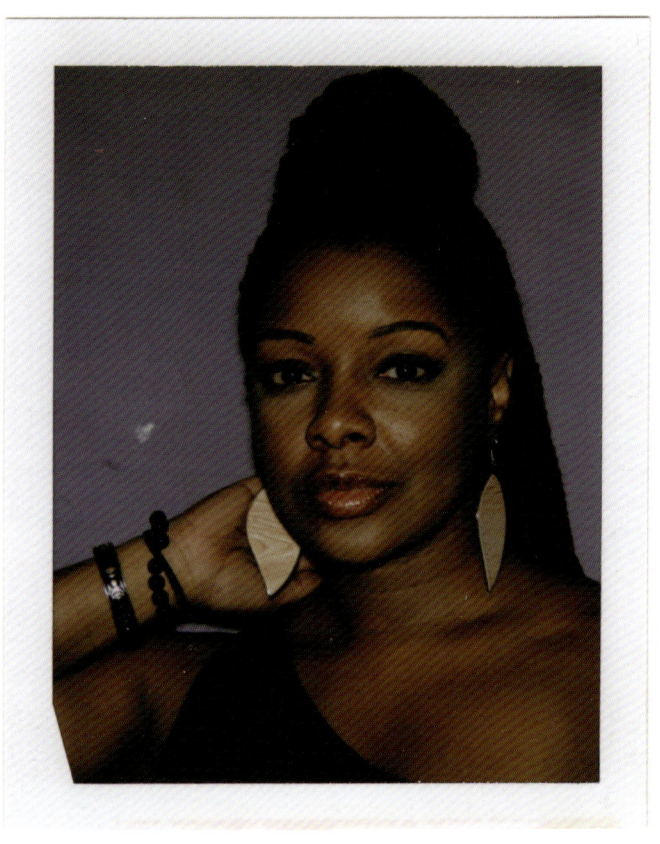

CORI ROBINSON

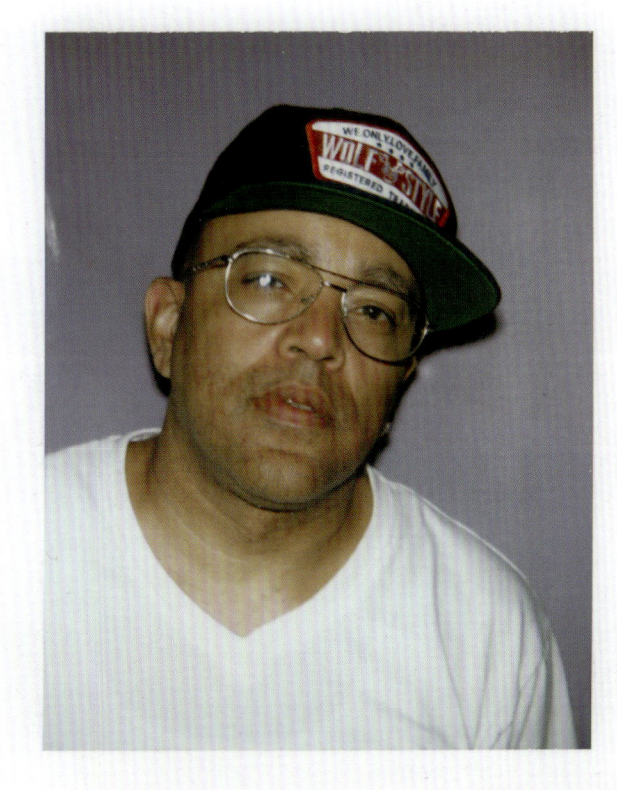

DERIC "D-DOT" ANGELETTIE

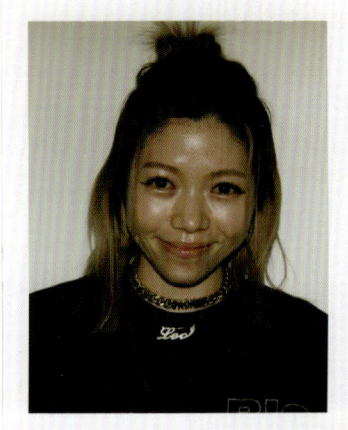

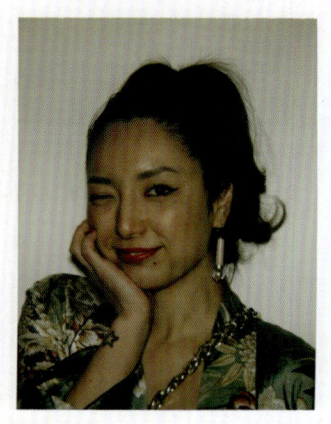

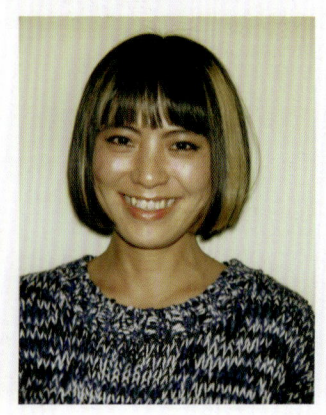

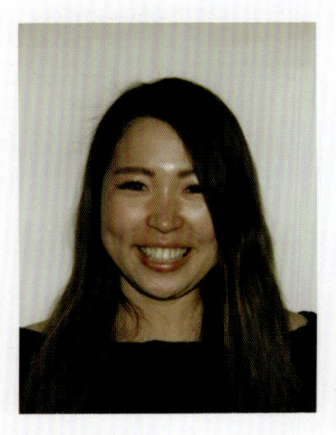

MICHIKO

IKUMI

MIYU

AYUMI

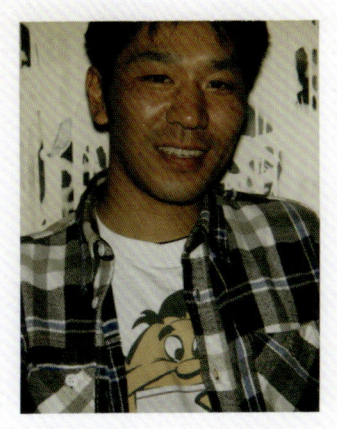

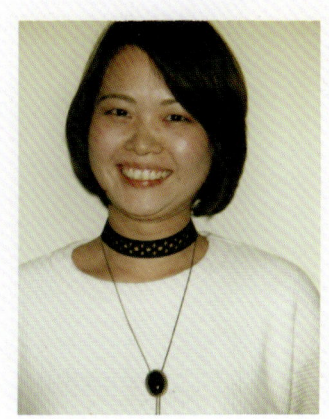

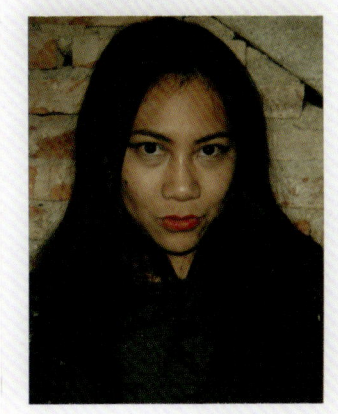

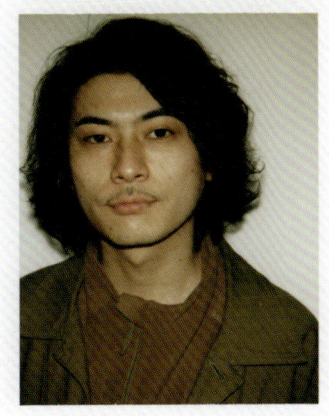

KASUGA

CHIE

KHANH-LINH

RUEED

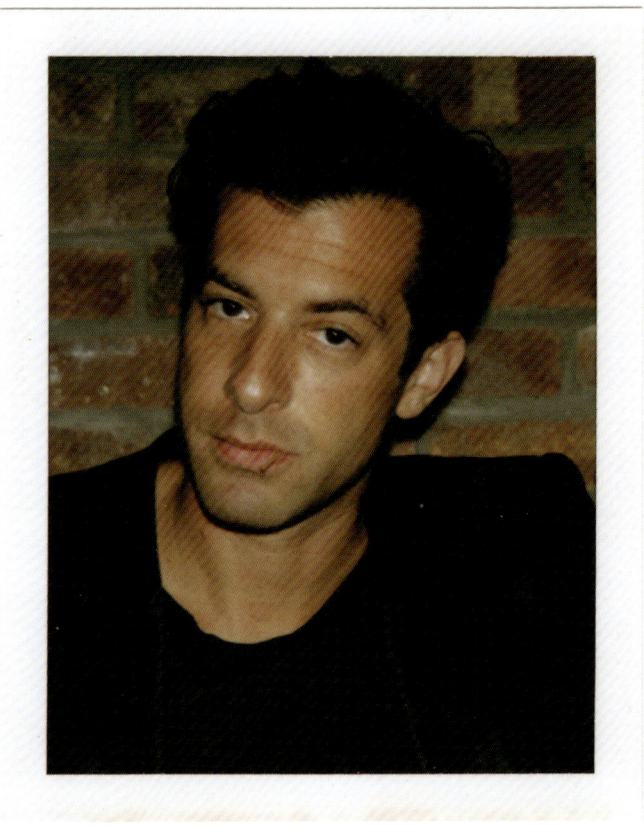

MARK RONSON

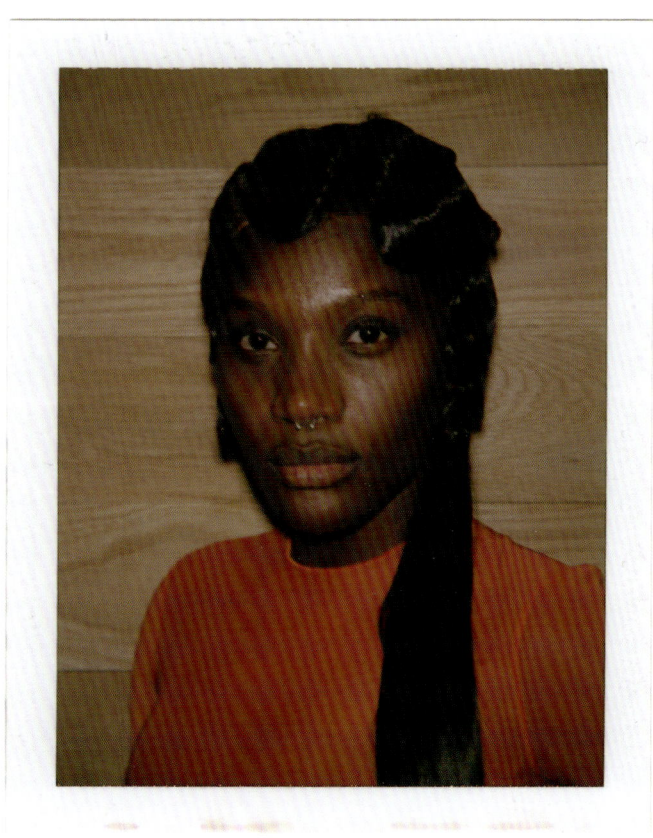

DOECHII

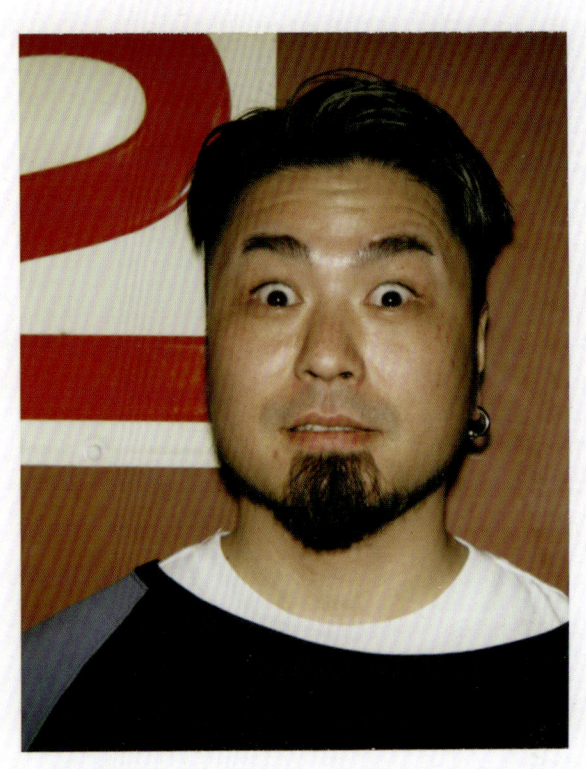

HISHI

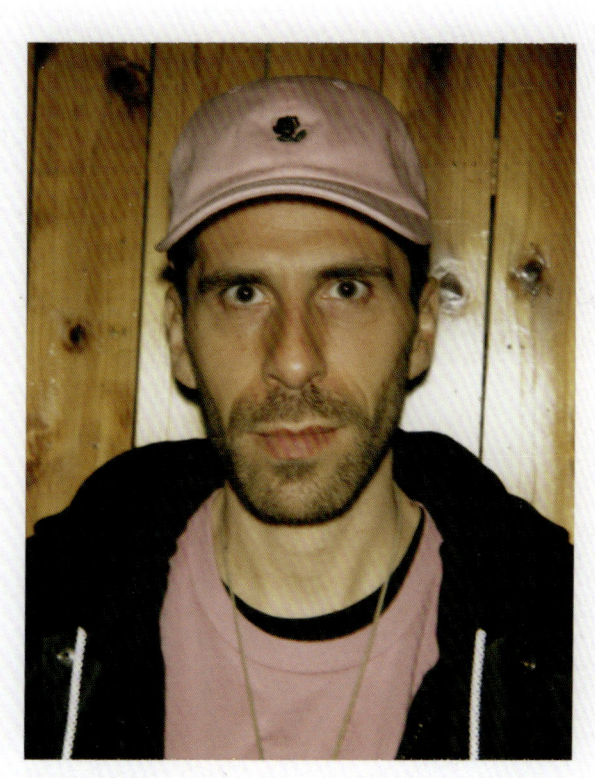

MICHAEL DUPOUY

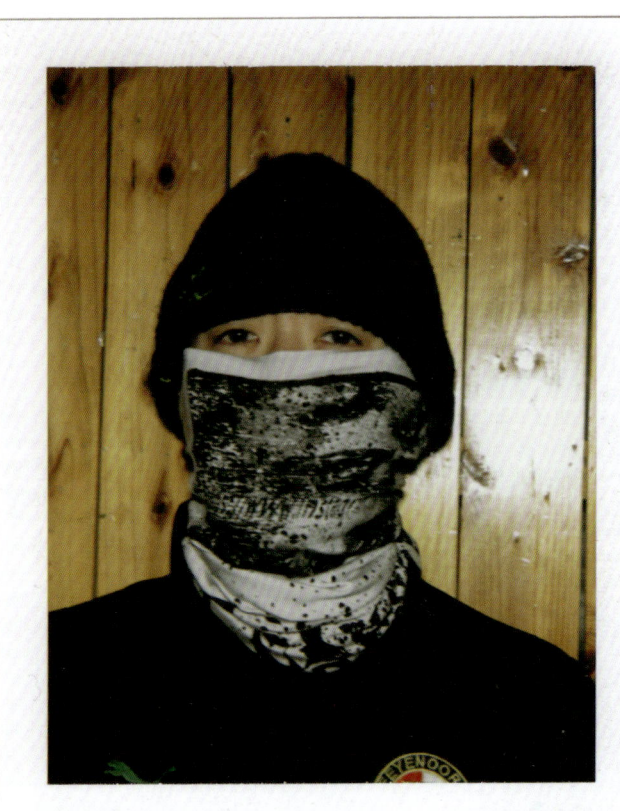

SK8 THG

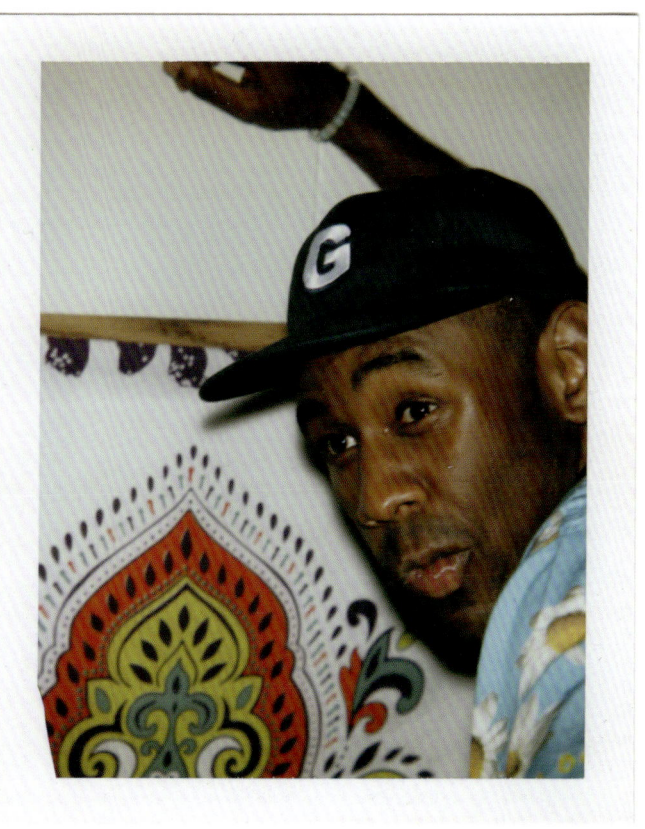

TYLER, THE CREATOR

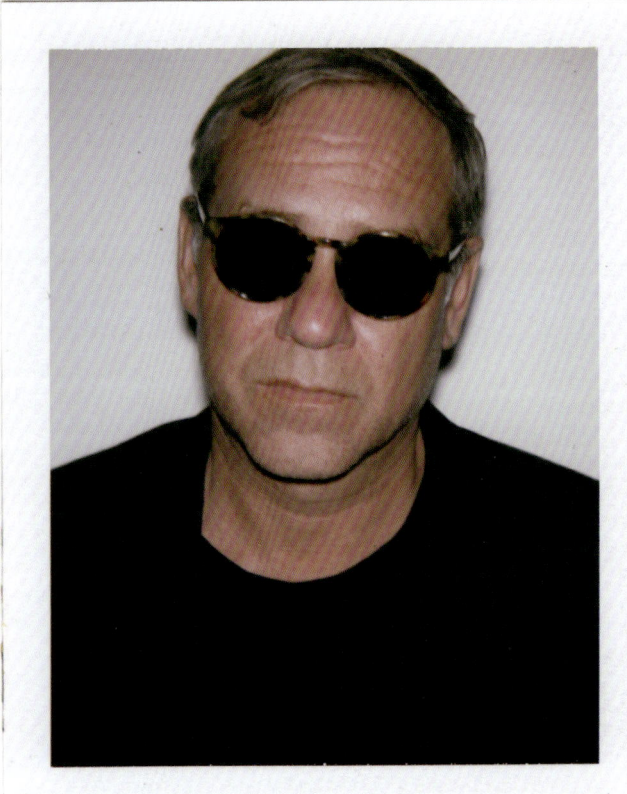

PAUL SEVIGNY

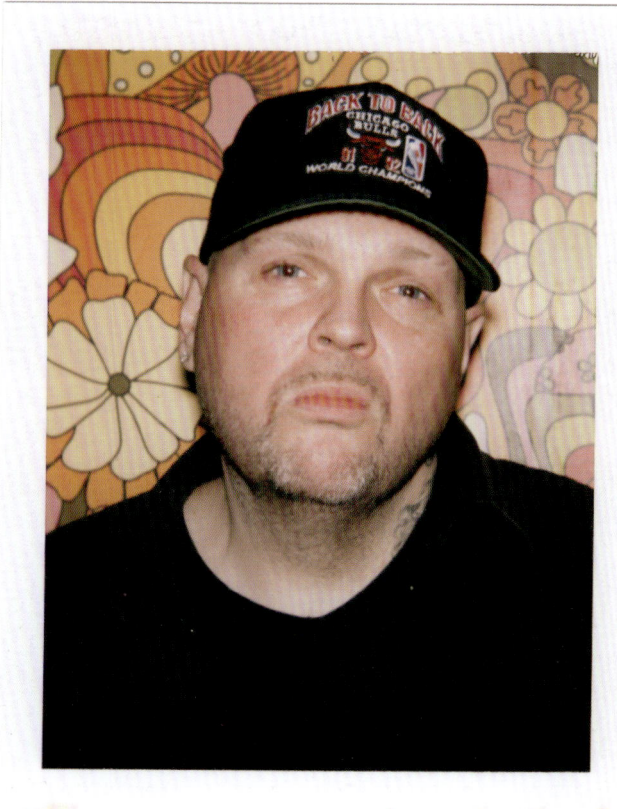

SEAN SULLIVAN - LAYERCAKE

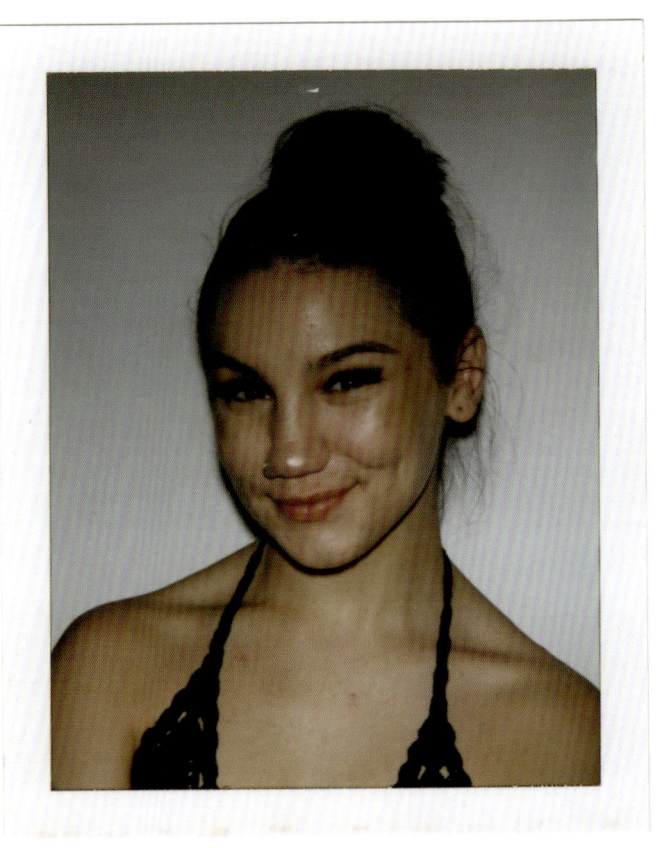

ALEXIE BLUE

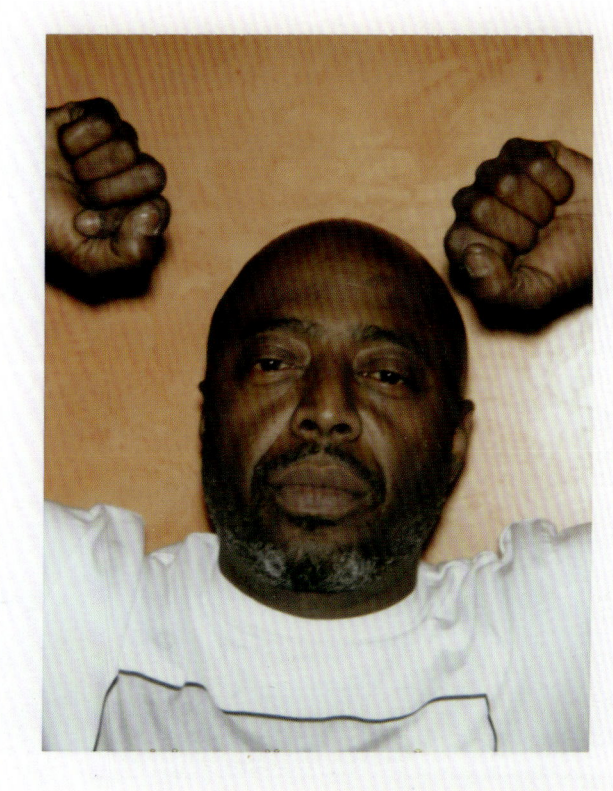

DONNELL RAWLINGS

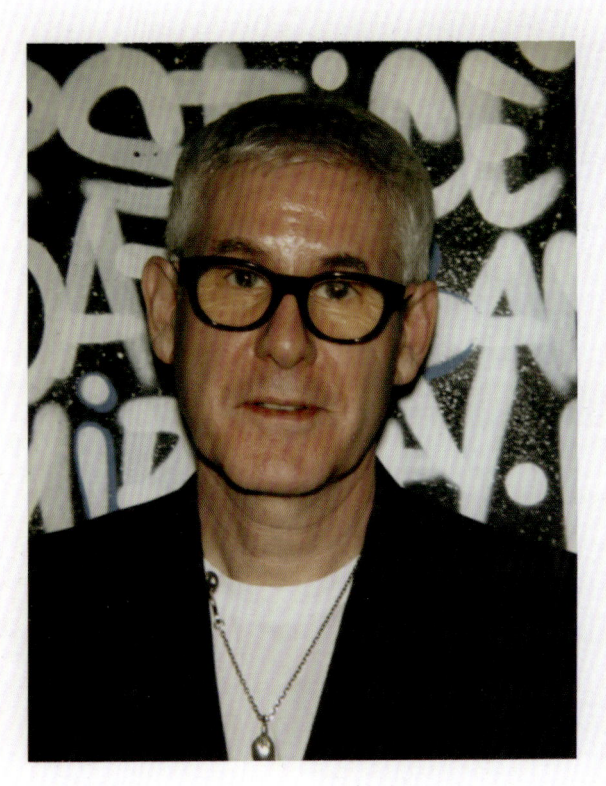

MARC FRASER COOKE

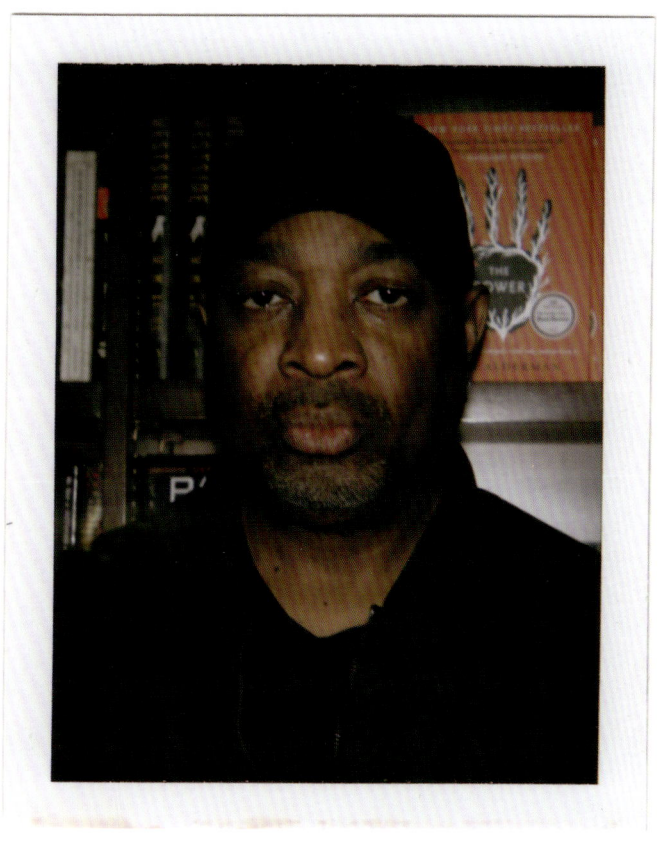

CHUCK D

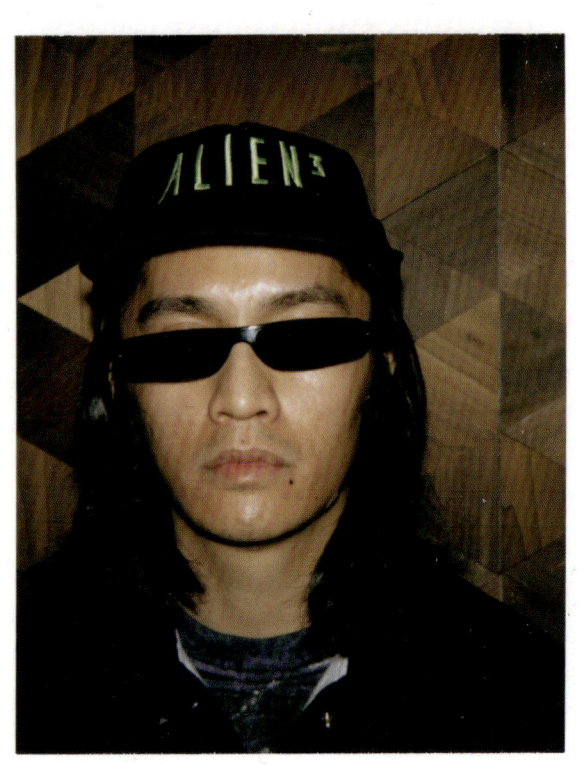

EYEDRESS

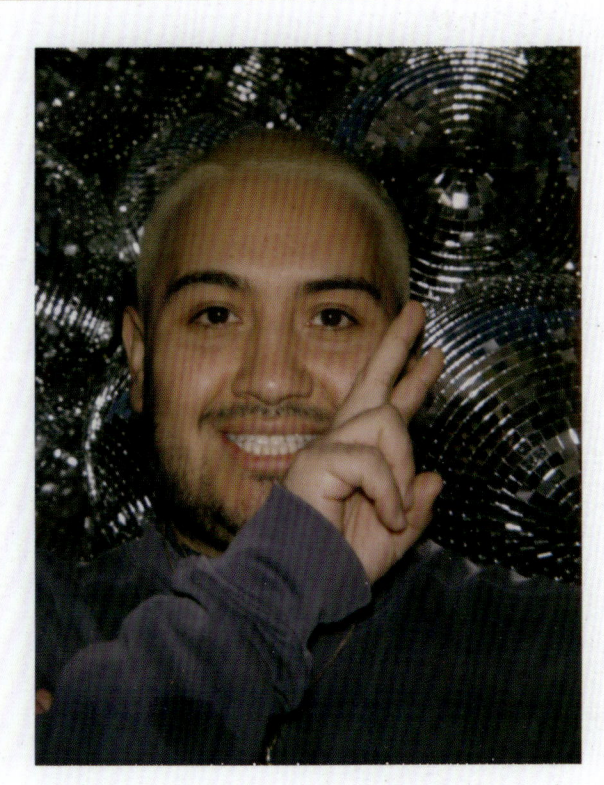

PAULO CALLE

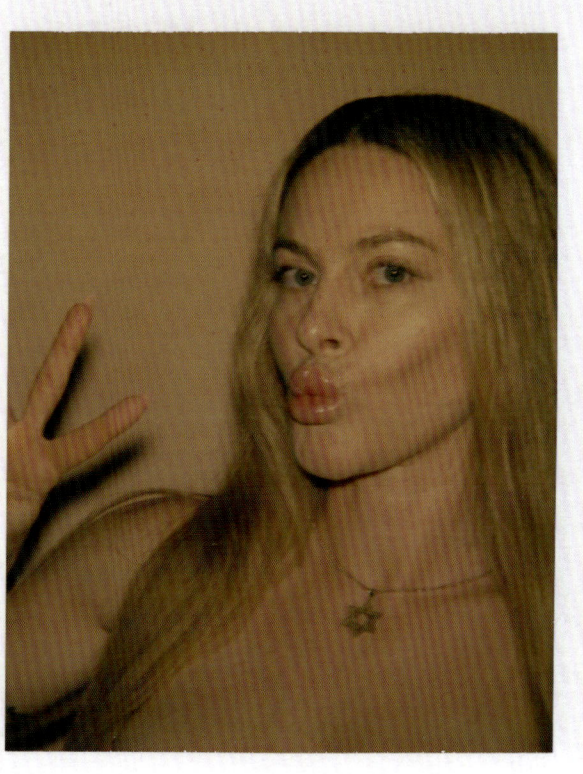

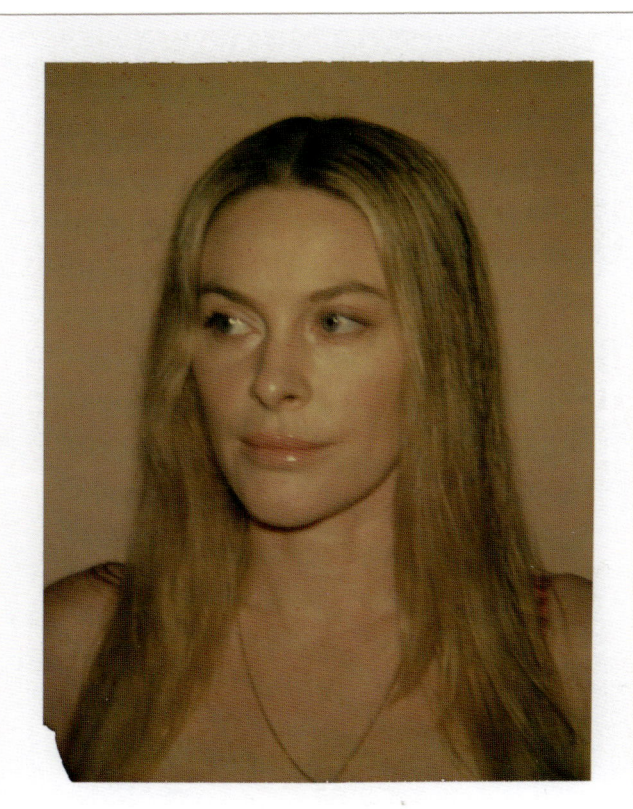

LEAH McSWEENEY

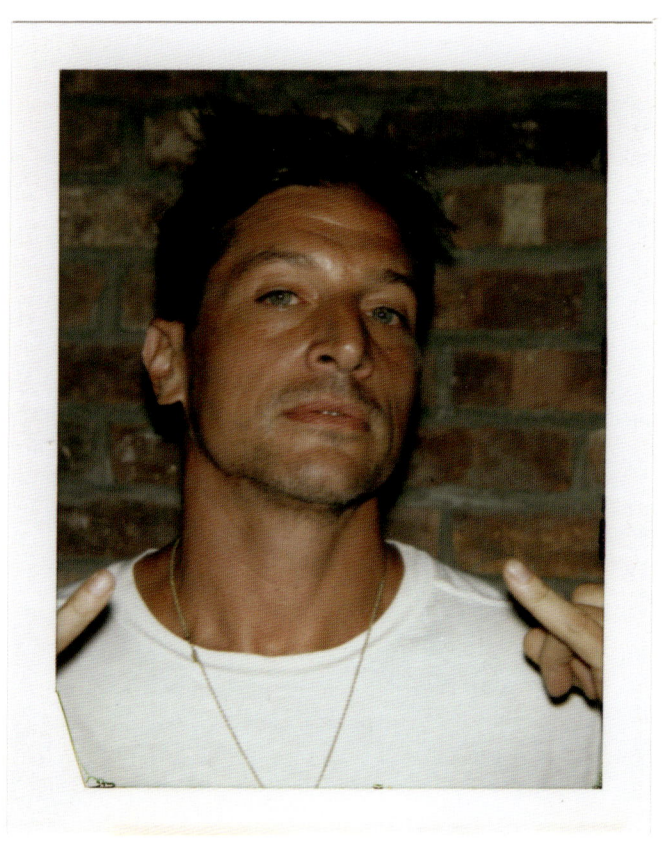

SIMON REX

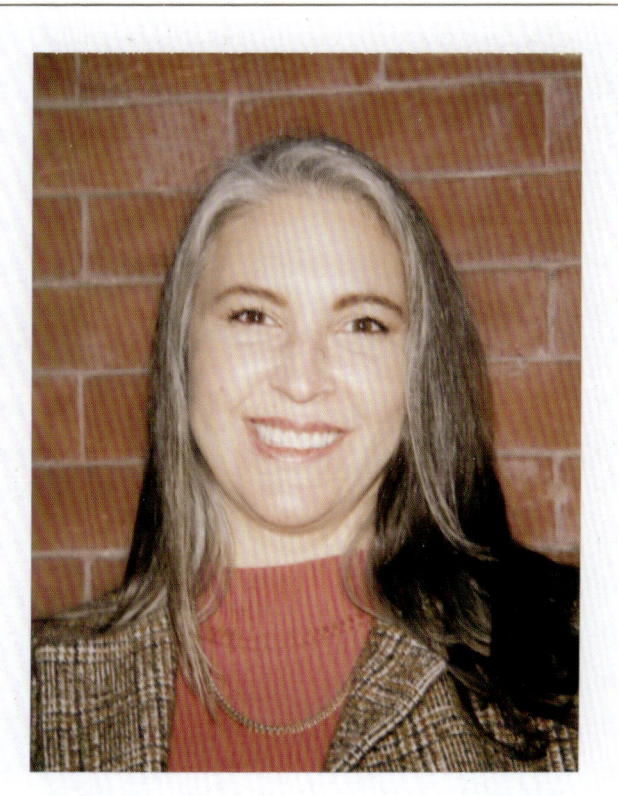

TIFFANY LOVE MEA

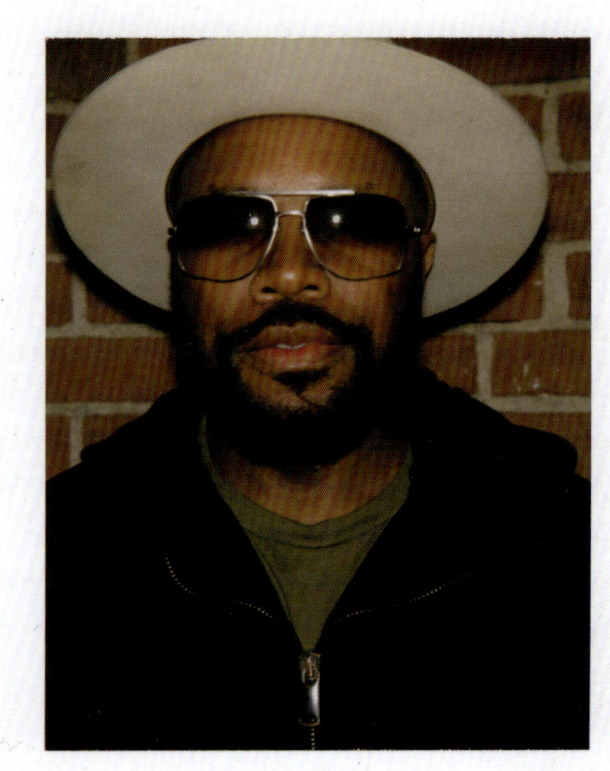

D-NICE

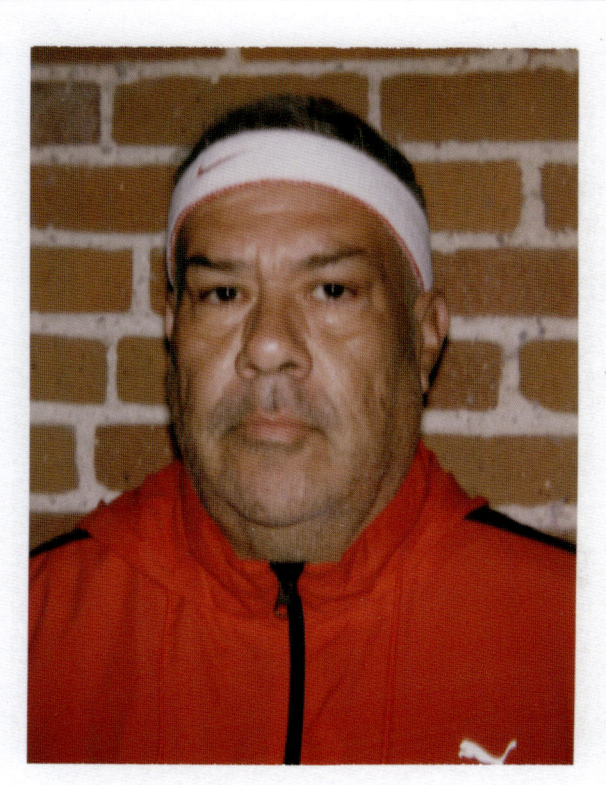

RAY OROPEZA

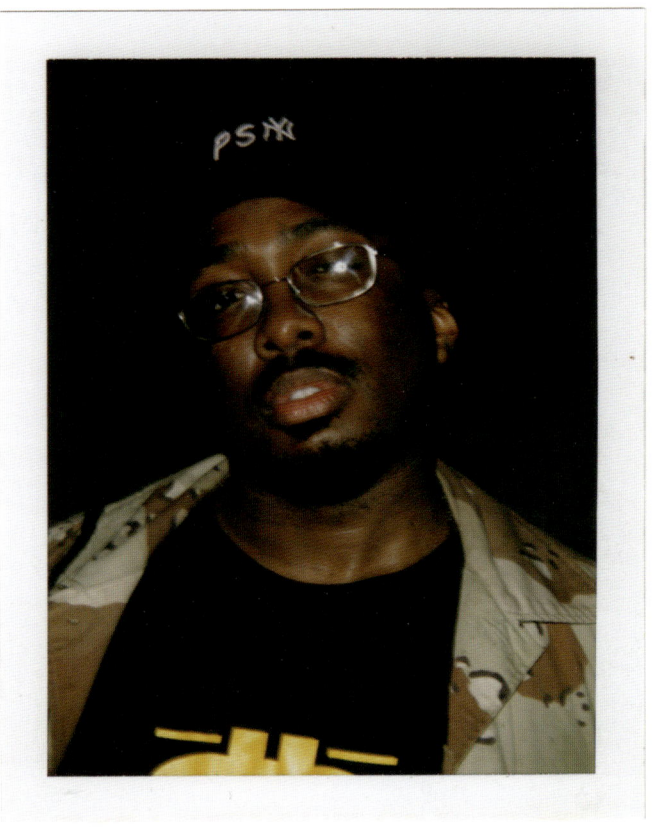

TUBBS KRUEGER

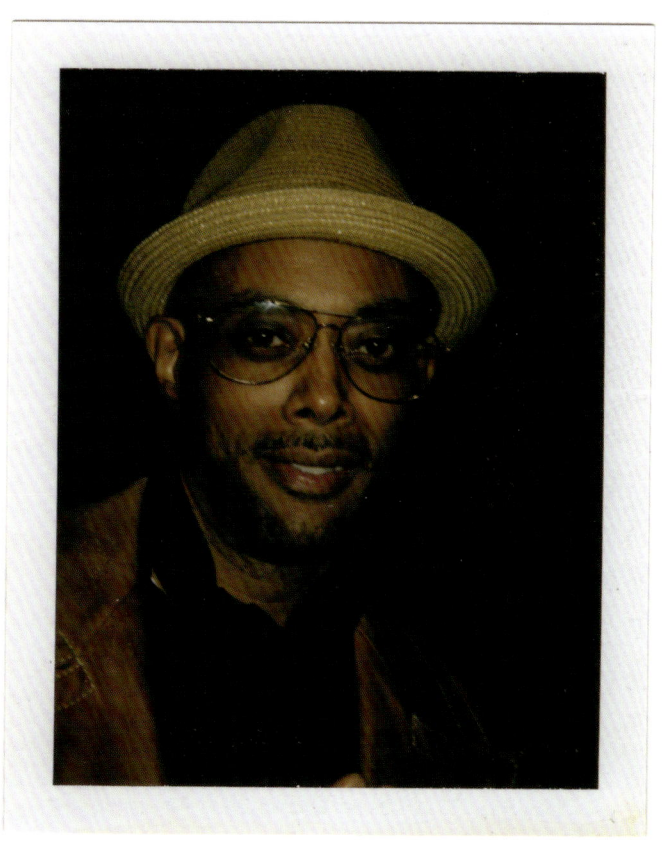

BROTHER RICH MASON

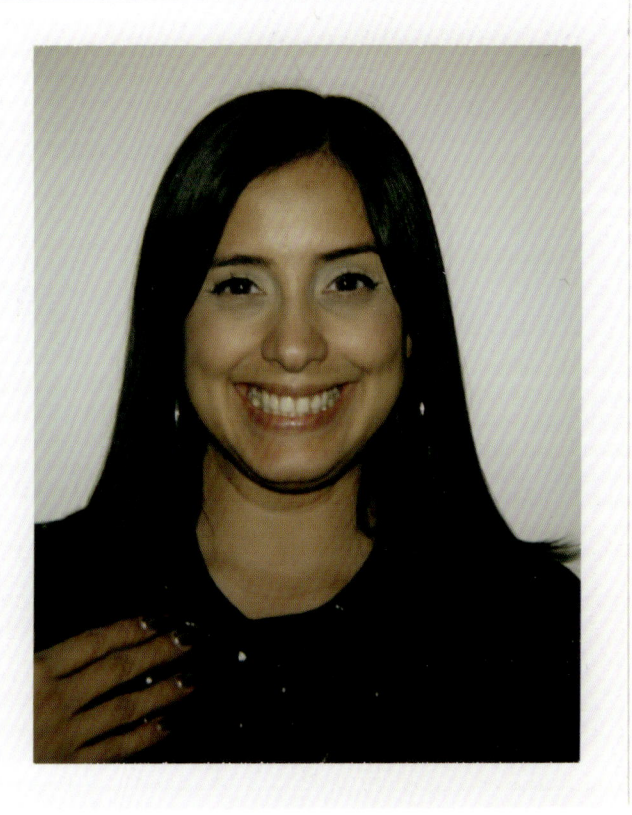

LAURA STYLEZ

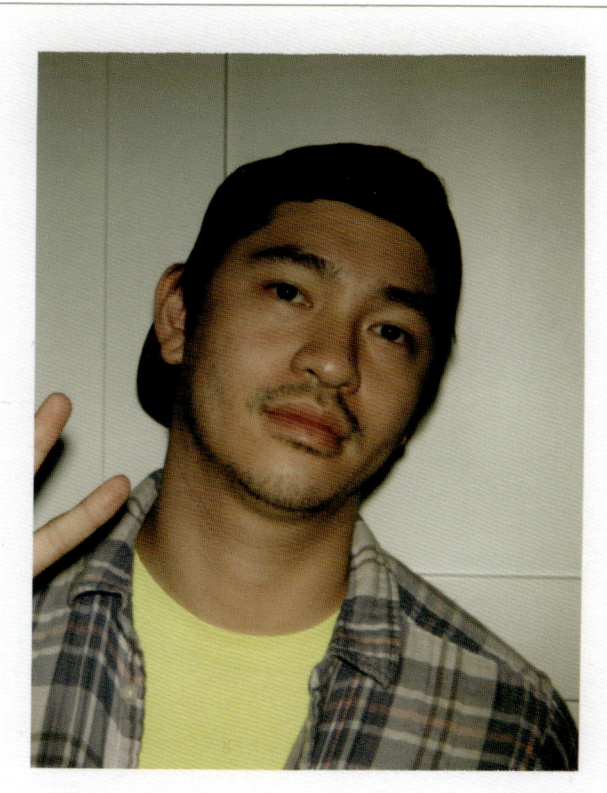

MOTLEY NICK

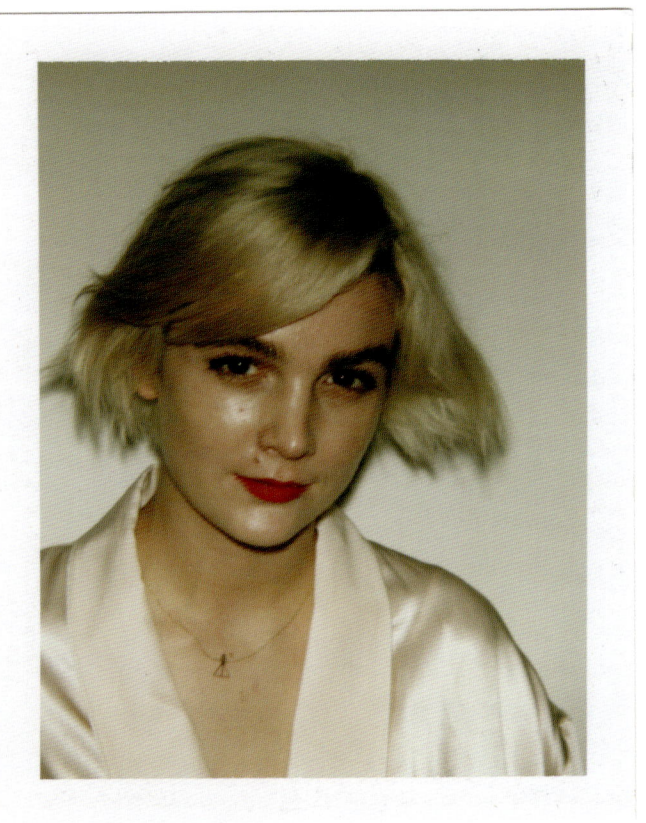

ALLIE TEILZ

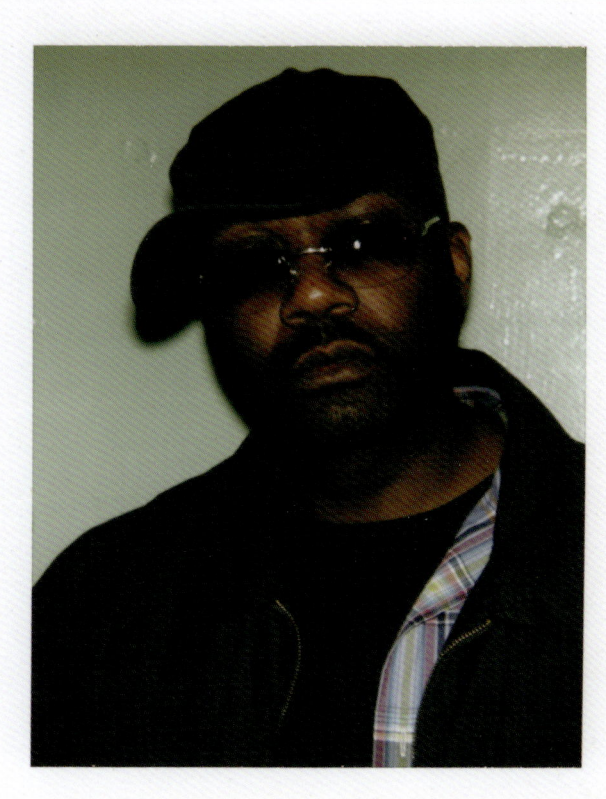

MASTA KILLA

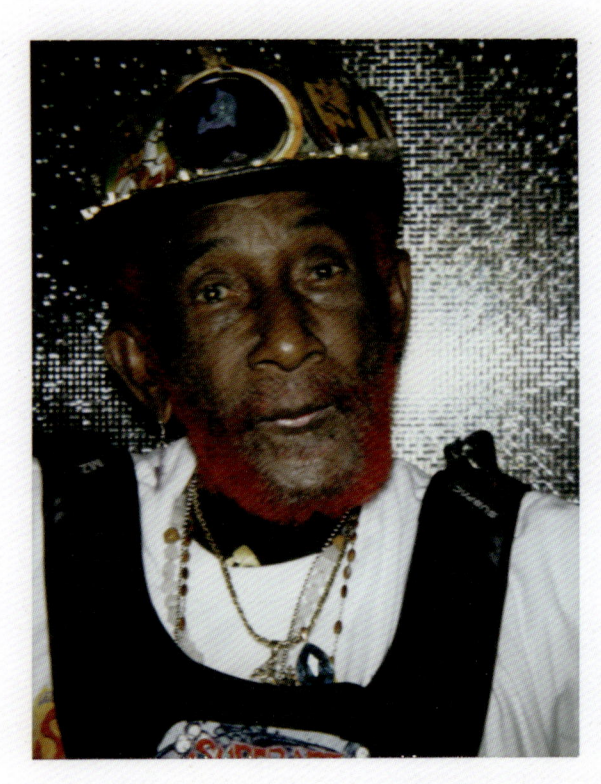

LEE "SCRATCH" PERRY

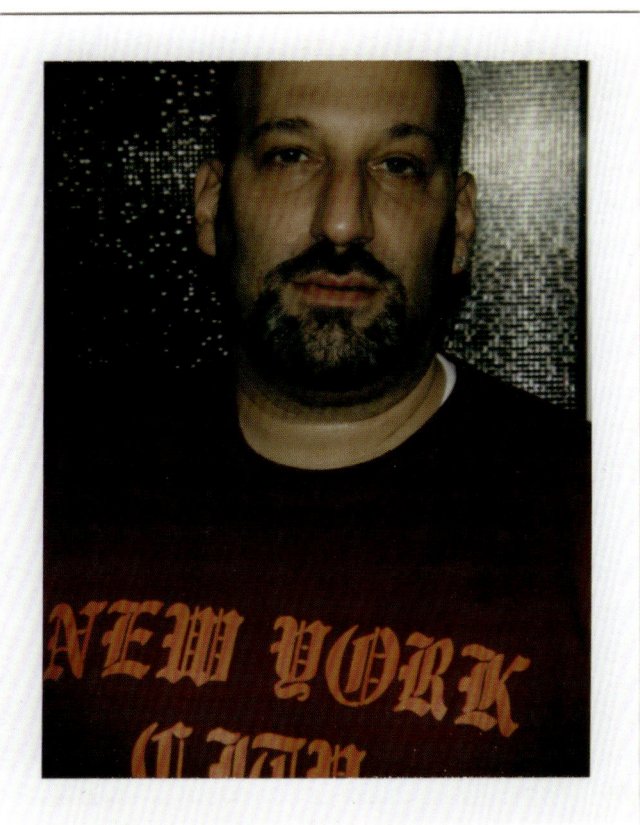

ROB "REEF" TEWLOW

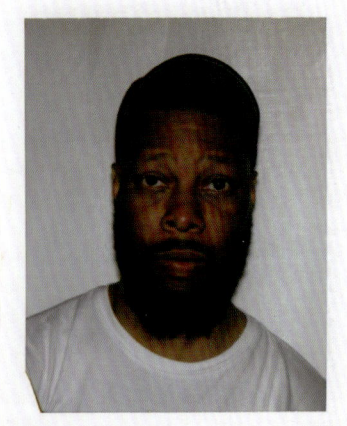

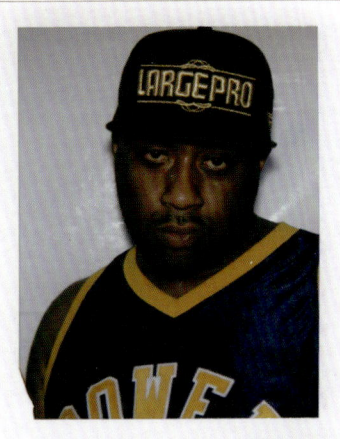

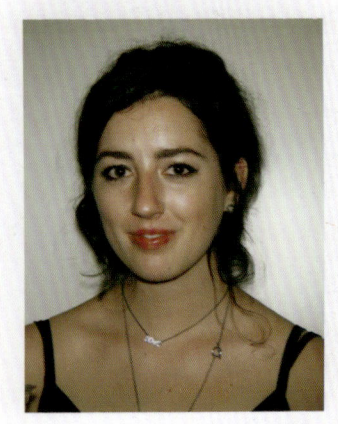

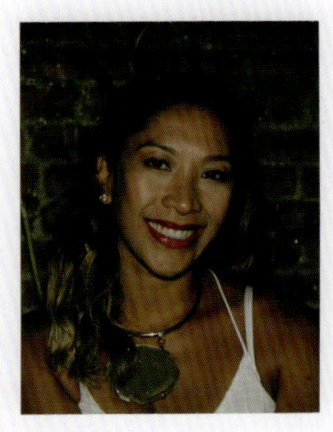

K-CUT

ROYAL FLUSH

ALLY WARSON

DIANE GAMINO

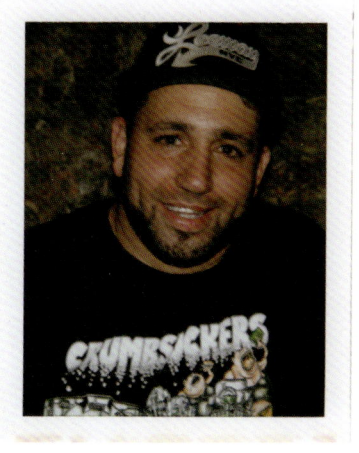
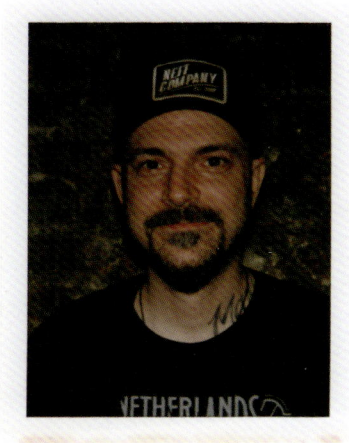
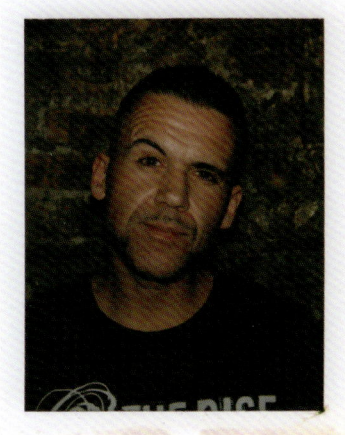
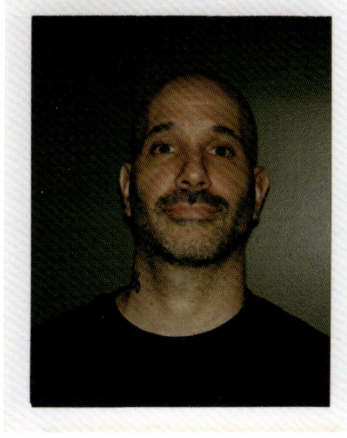

COUSIN JOE

JIMMY FERRARI

JOHN LAMACHIA

DON CAPRIA

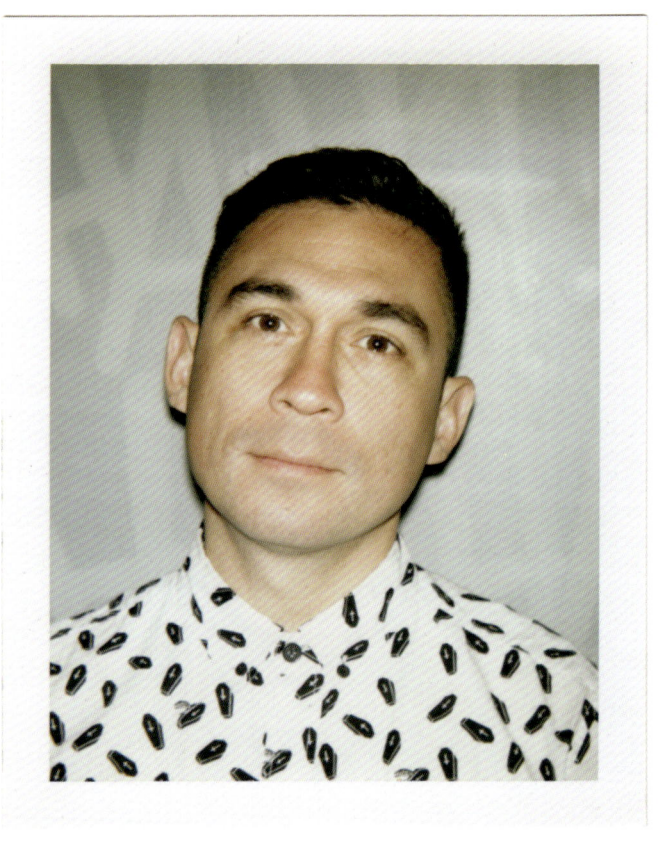

RONNIE BUDERS

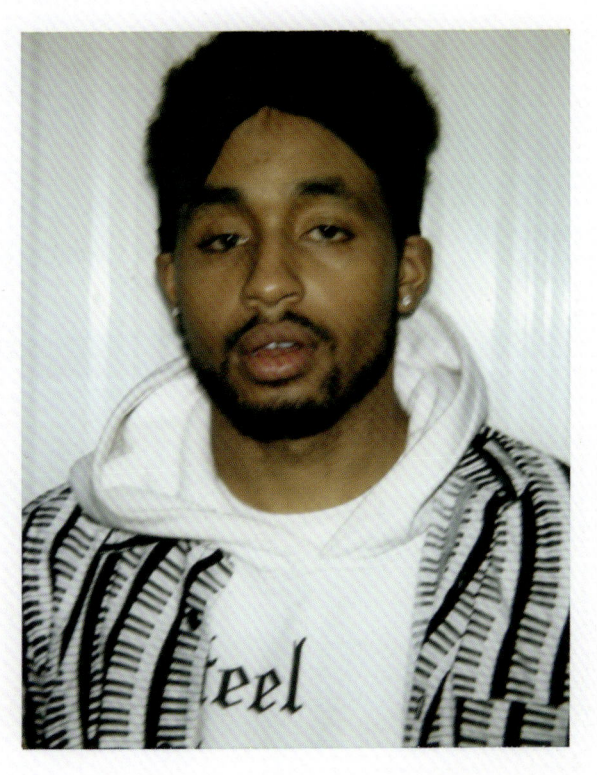

QUENTIN CHANDLER CUFF

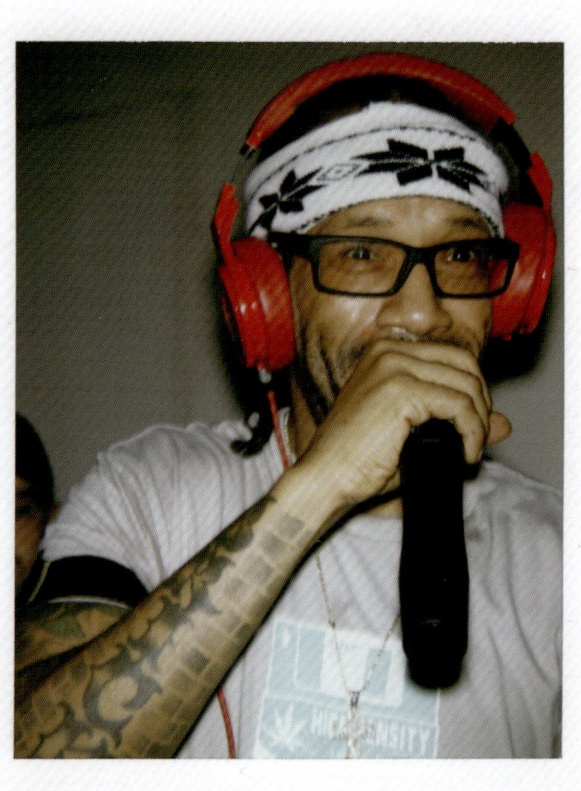

REDMAN

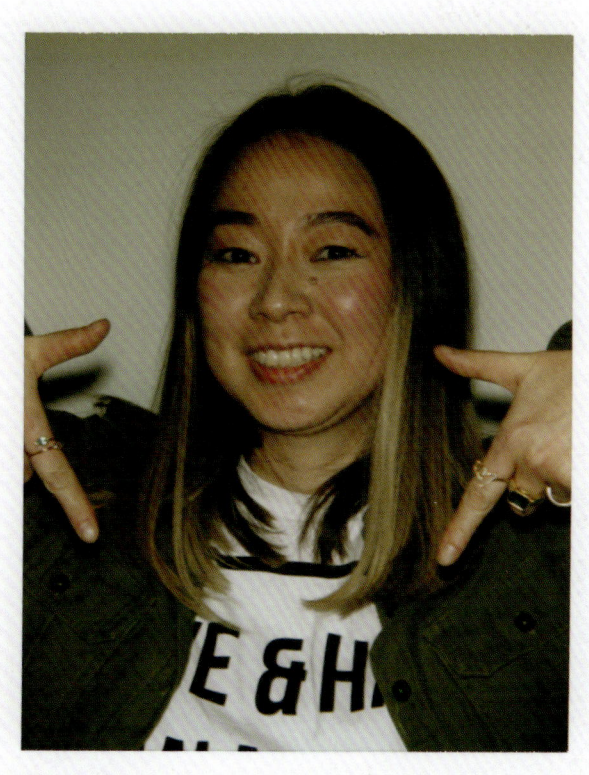

MOE NARUSE

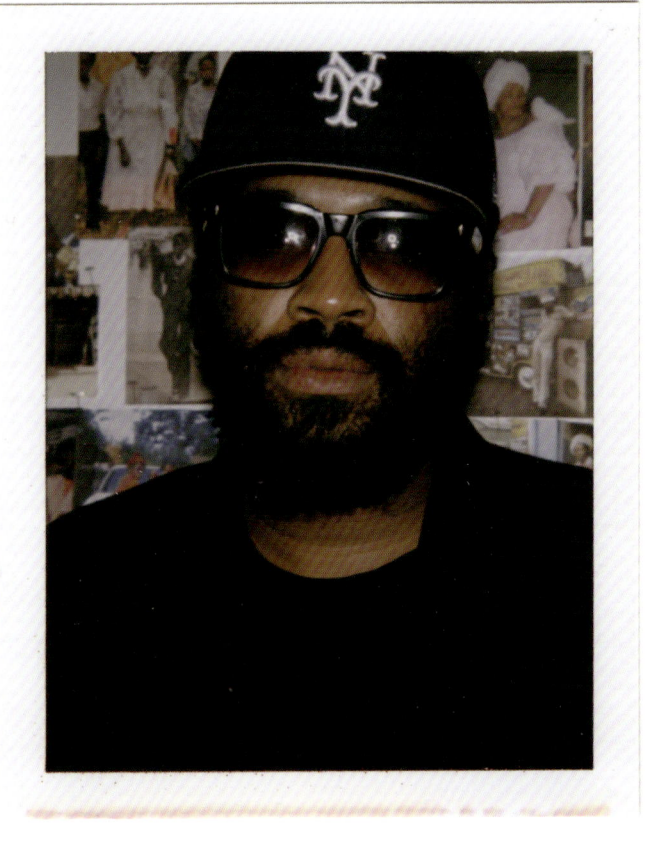

MAXWELL OSBORNE

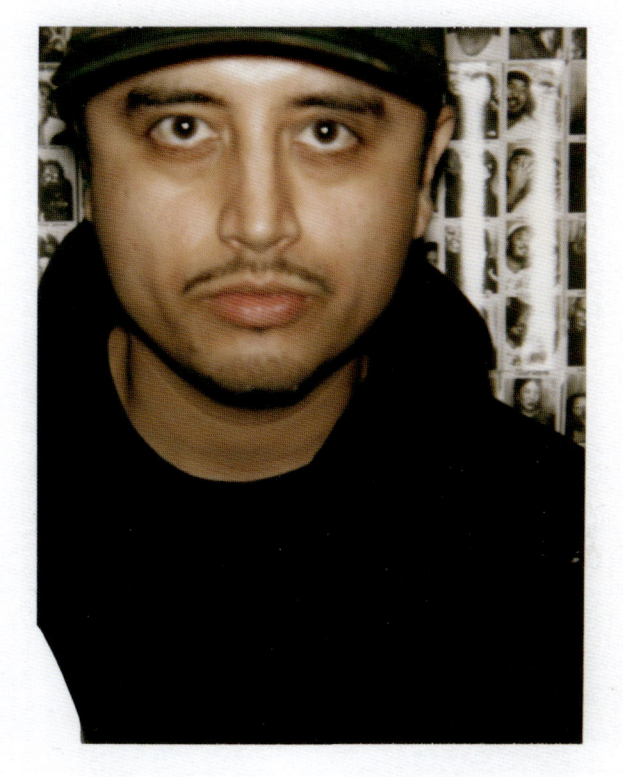

BRAINFREEZE

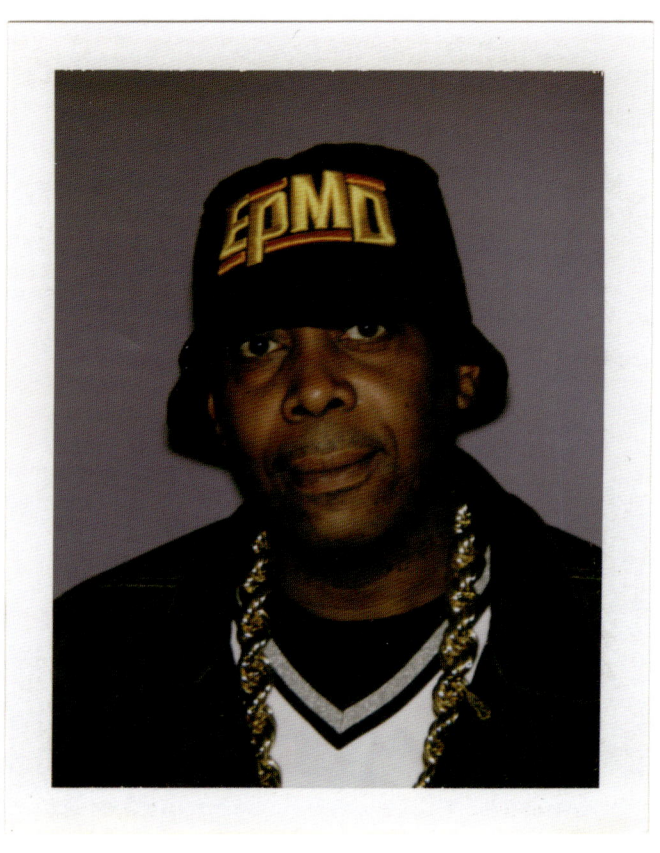

PARISH SMITH AKA PMD

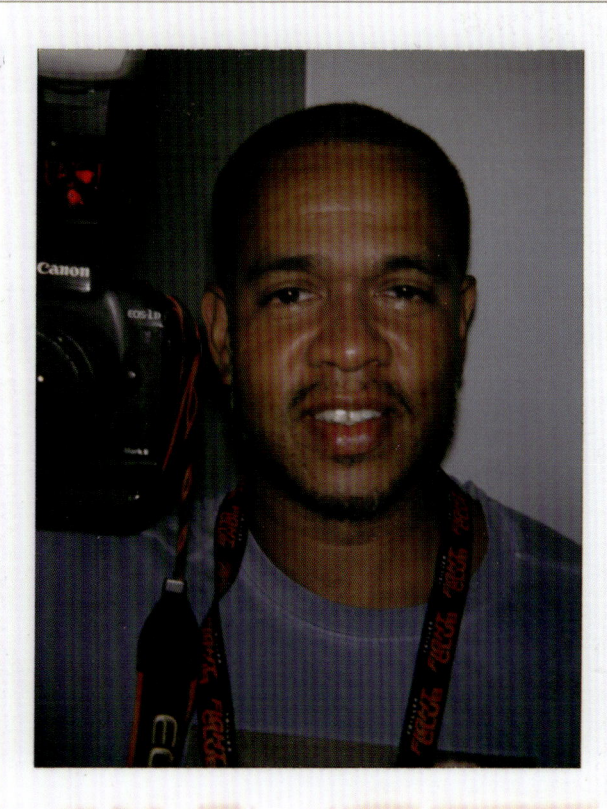

JOHNNY NUNEZ

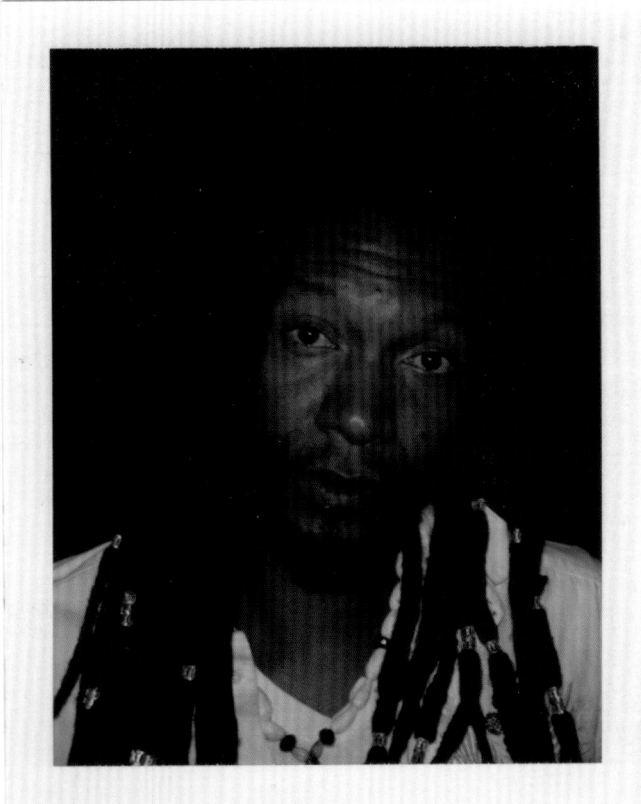

SELAHDON BENGBENG

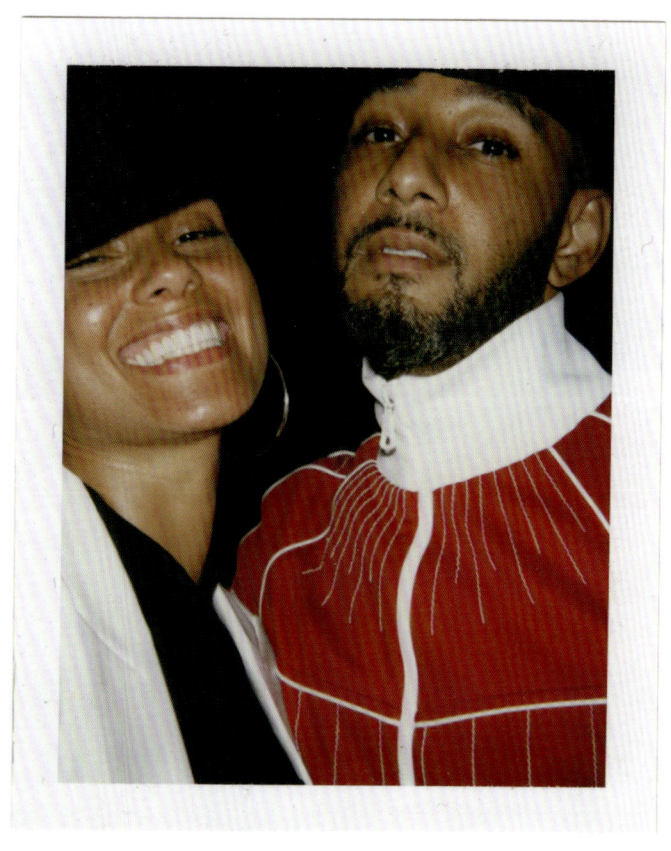

ALICIA KEYS & SWIZZ BEATZ

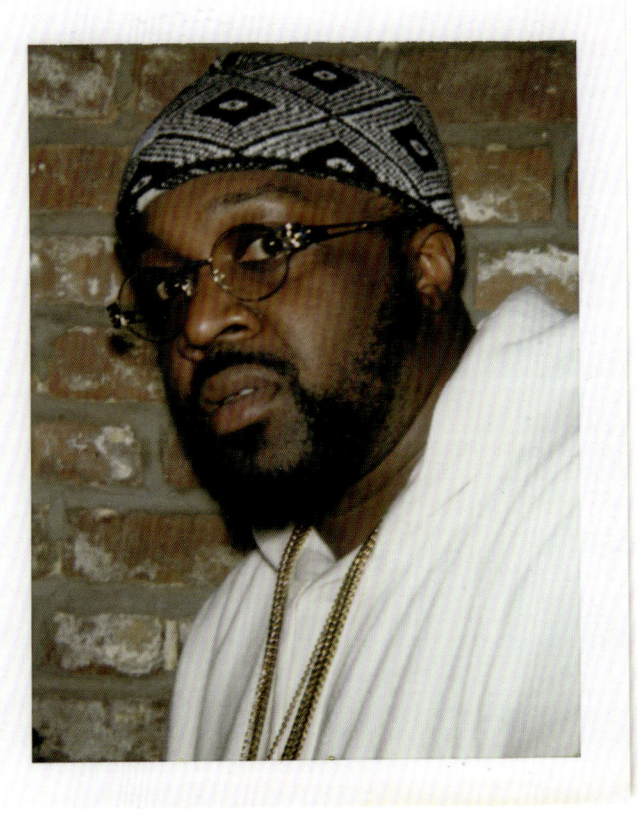

SMOKE DZA

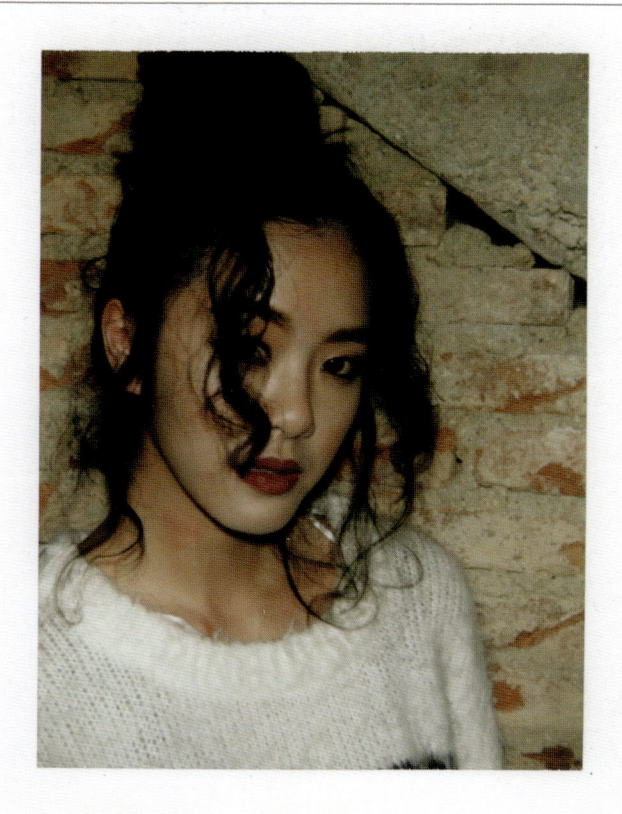

SIUWAN

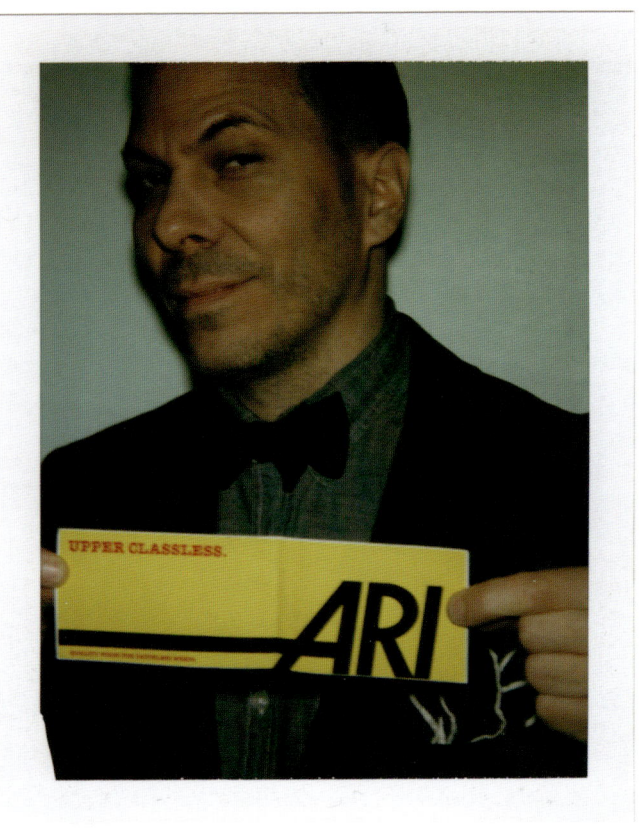

ARI SAAL FORMAN

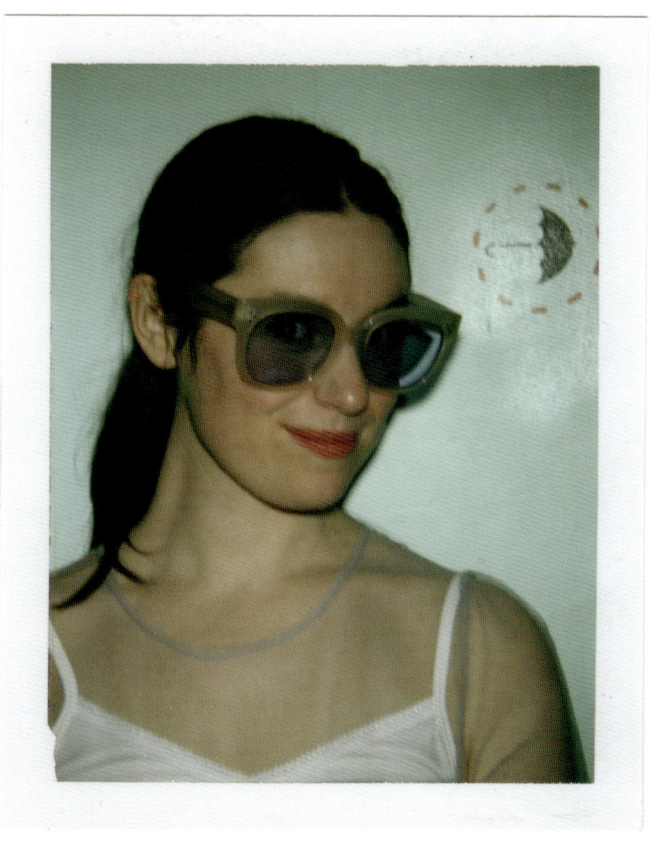

DANA GLUCK

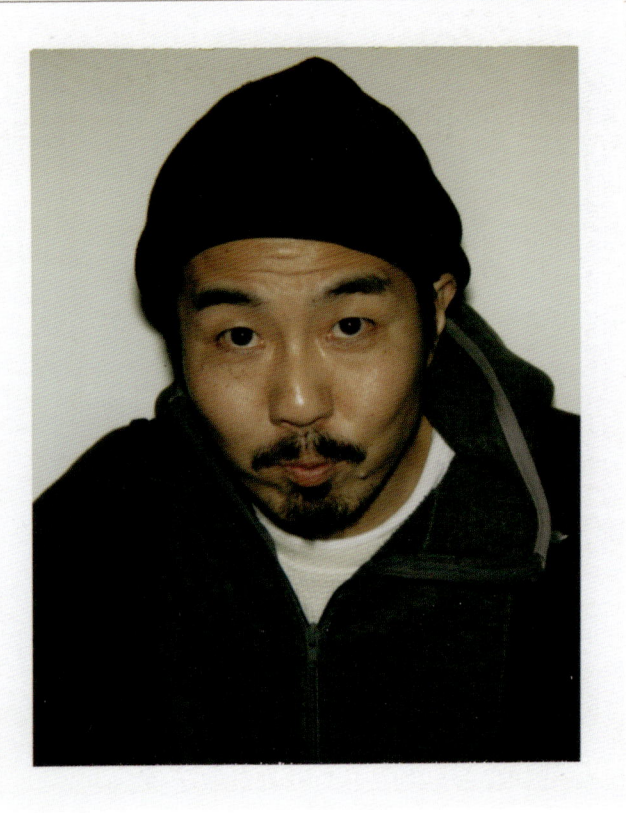

SHITARA DAISUKE

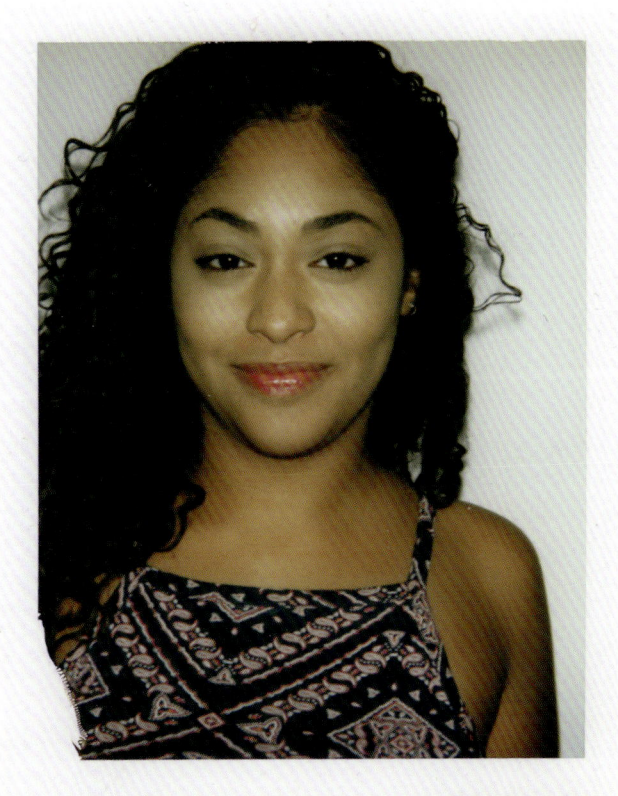

SHANEEL LOVERA

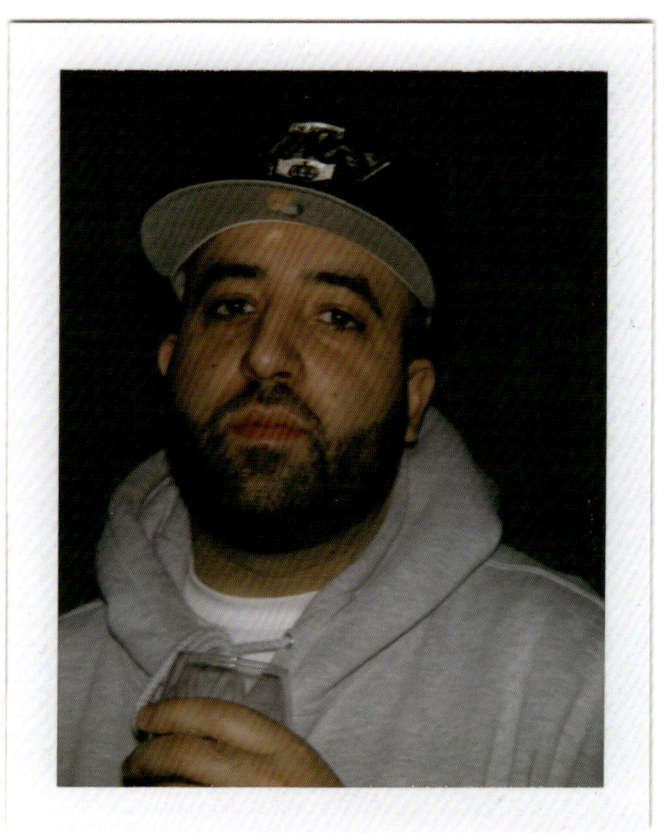

JAY WORTHY

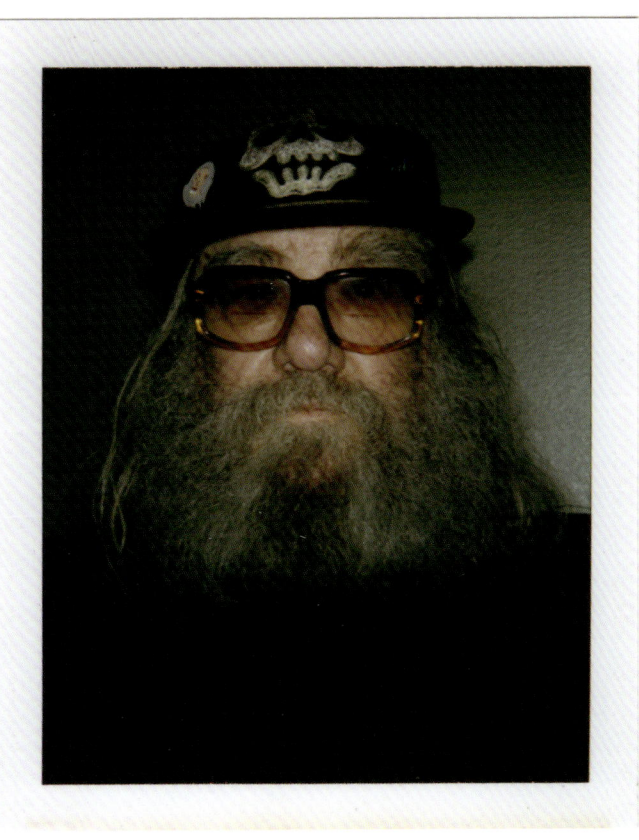

CLAYTON PATTERSON

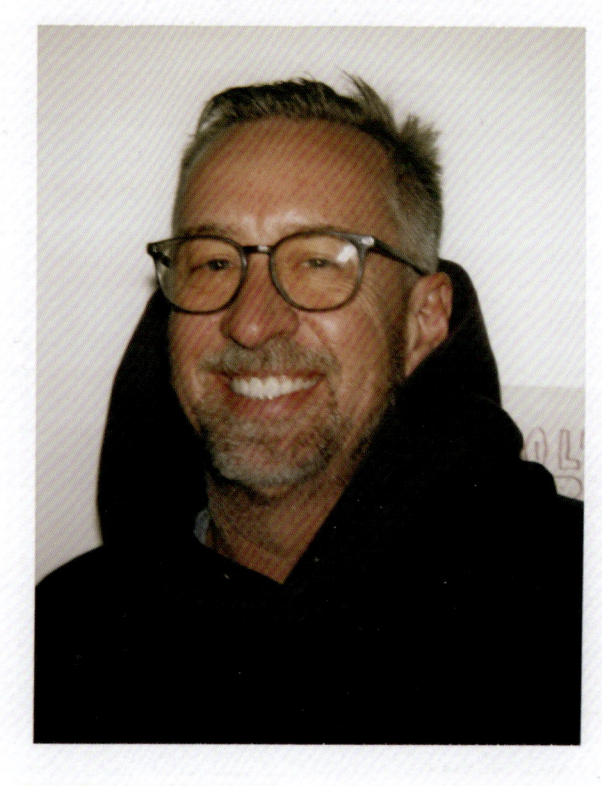

TYLER GIBNEY

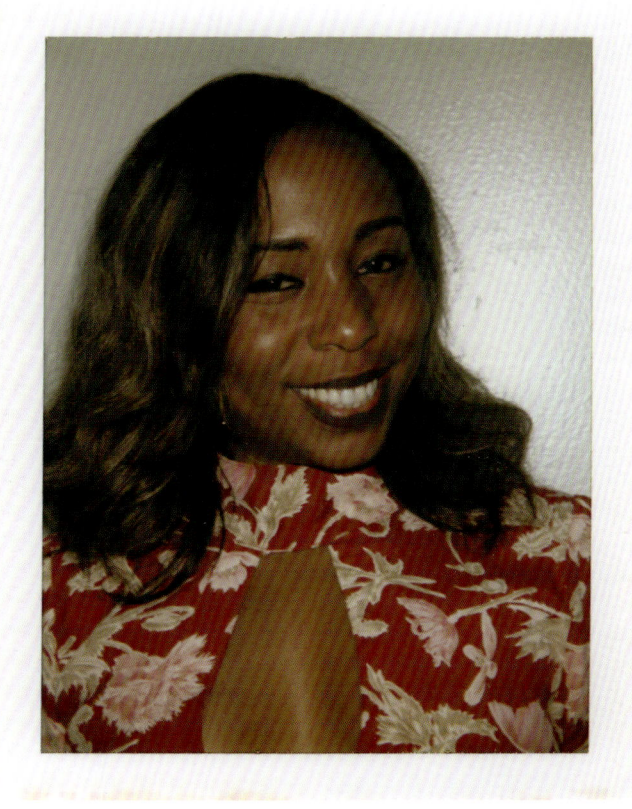

NICOLE PLANTIN

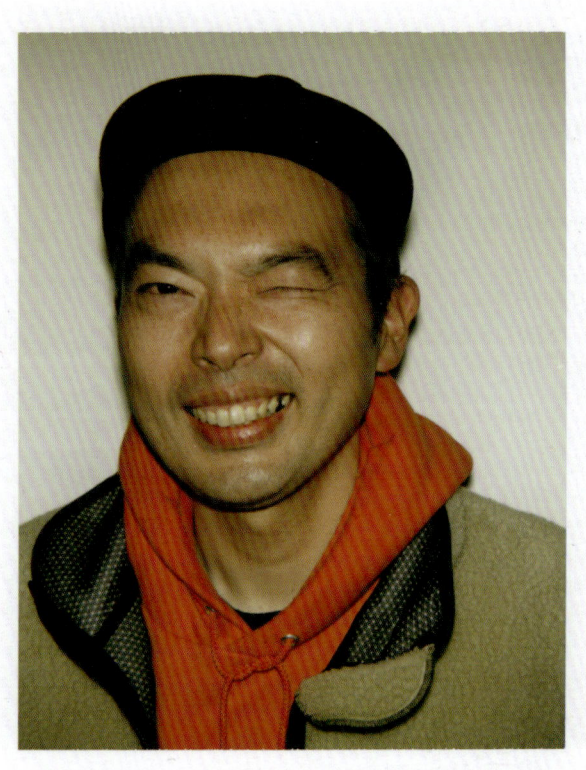

MISTER ZONE

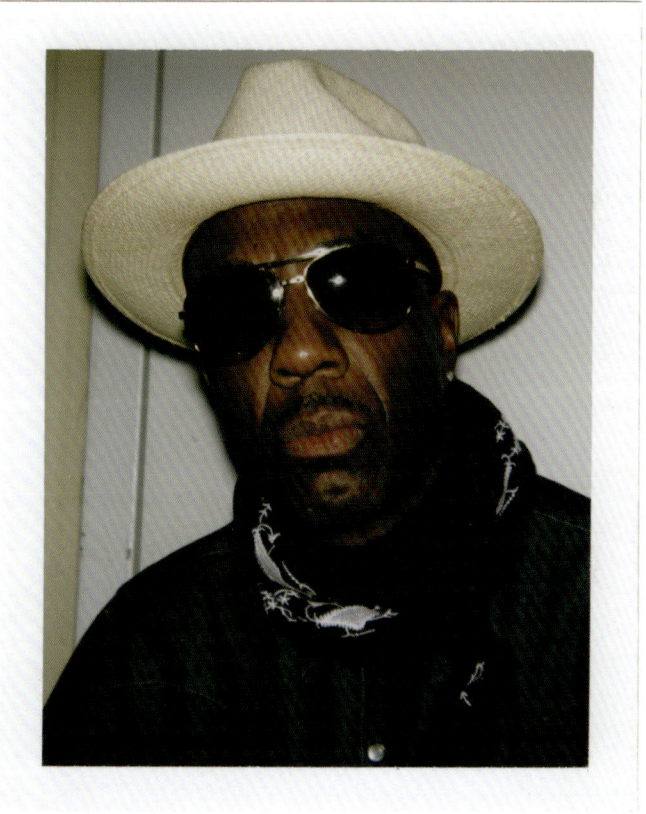

J B SMOOVE

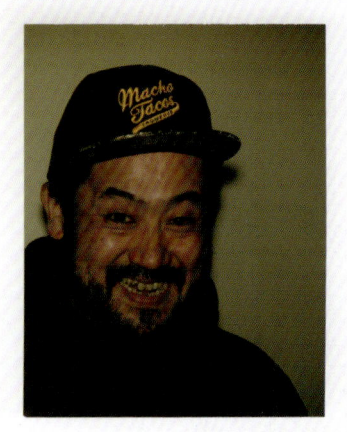

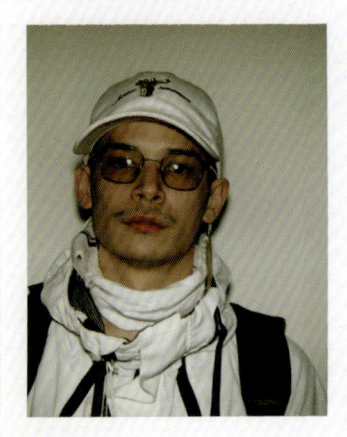

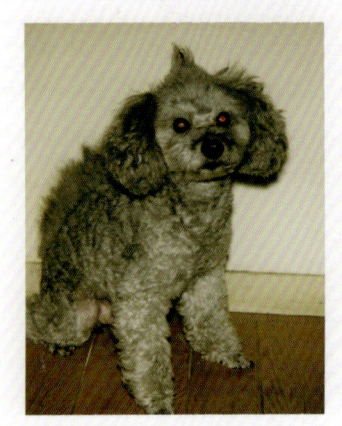

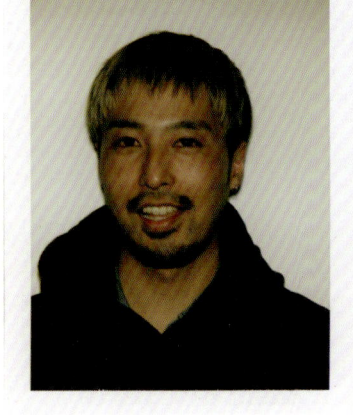

KAZU

KINZO

ALEK

KOMA

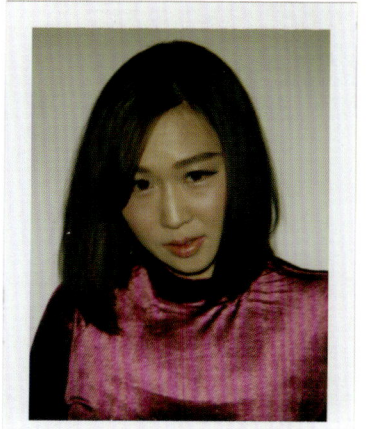

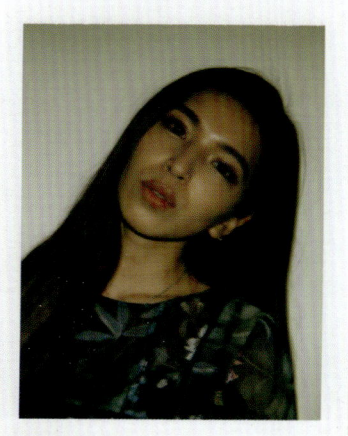

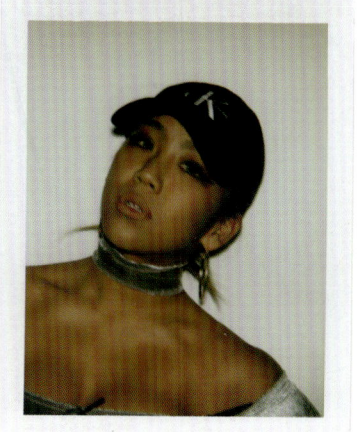

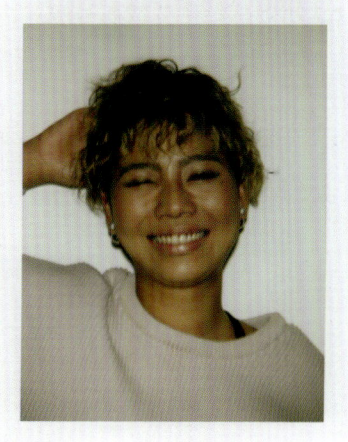

CYBERJAPAN DANCER 1

CYBERJAPAN DANCER 2

CYBERJAPAN DANCER 3

CYBERJAPAN DANCER 4

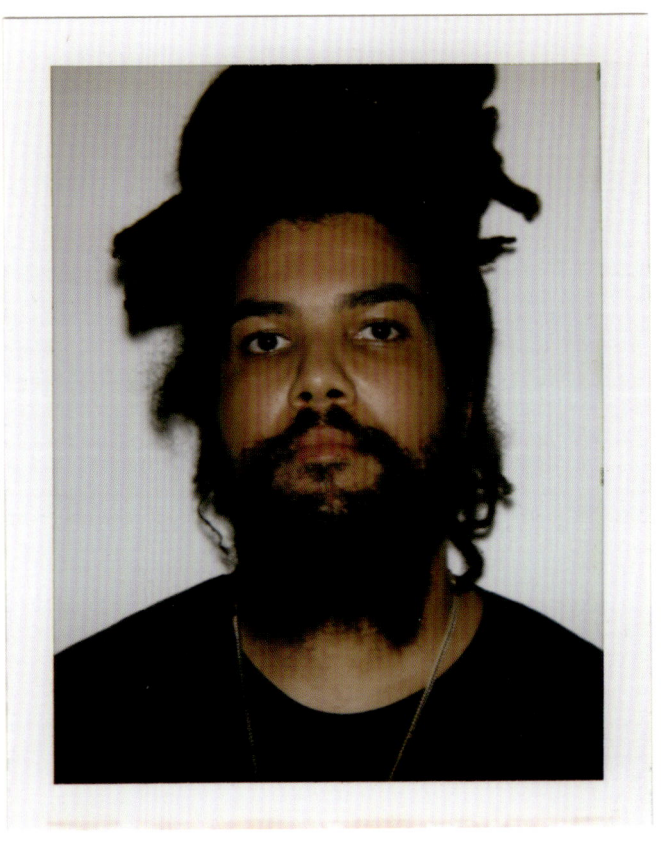

CHRIS GRIGGS

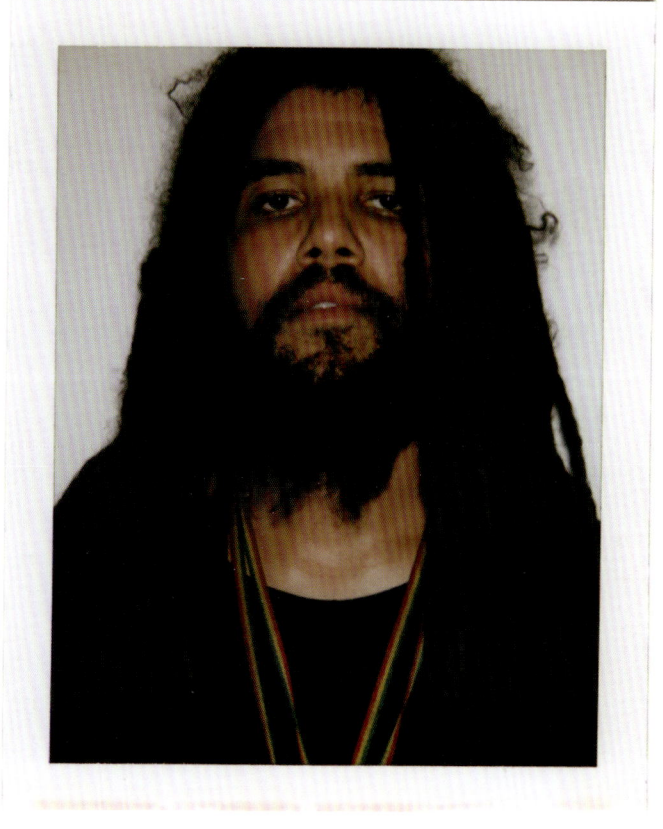

CLAYTON GRIGGS

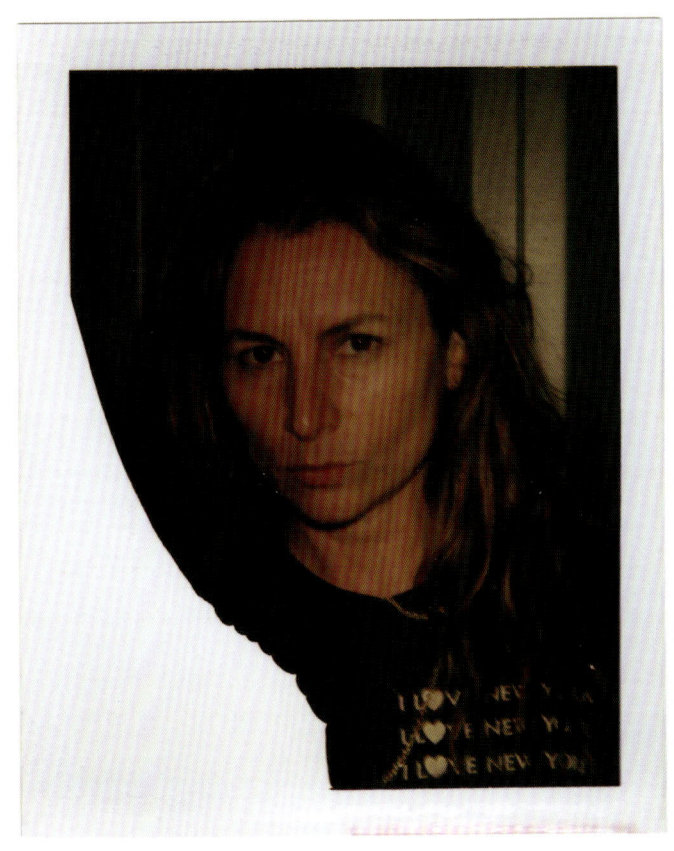

HEIDI HARTWIG

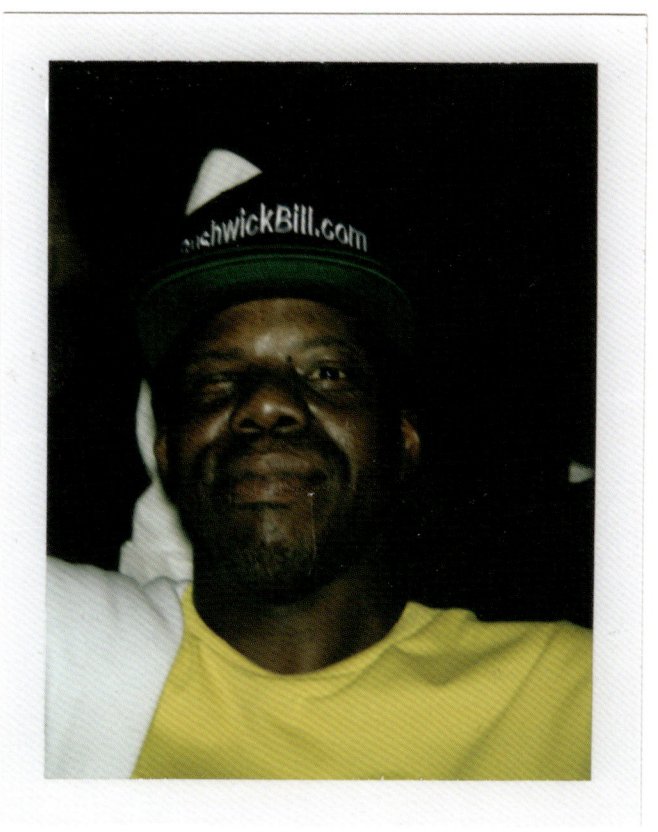

BUSHWICK BILL

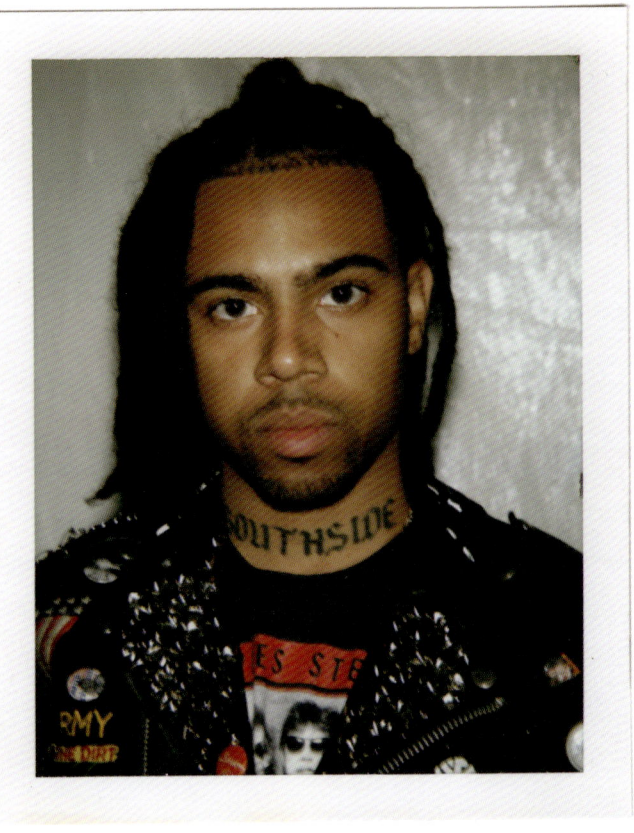

VIC MENSA

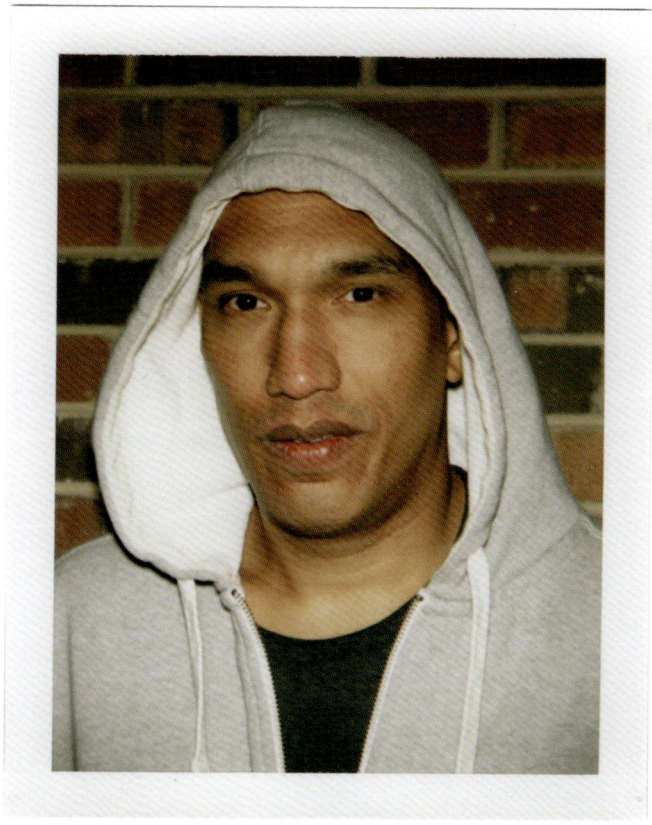

DAVID "CHINO" VILLORENTE

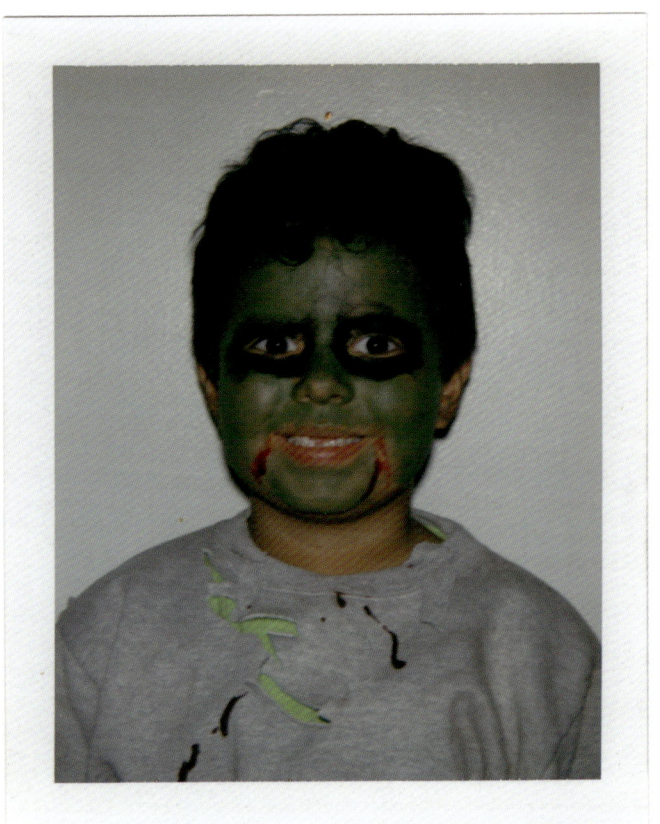

ZOMBIE THEODORE

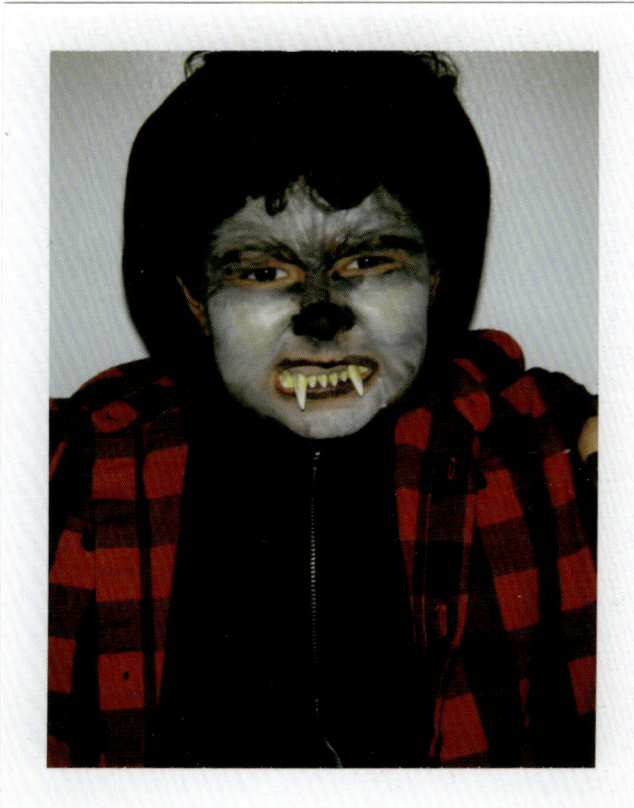

WEREWOLF THEODORE

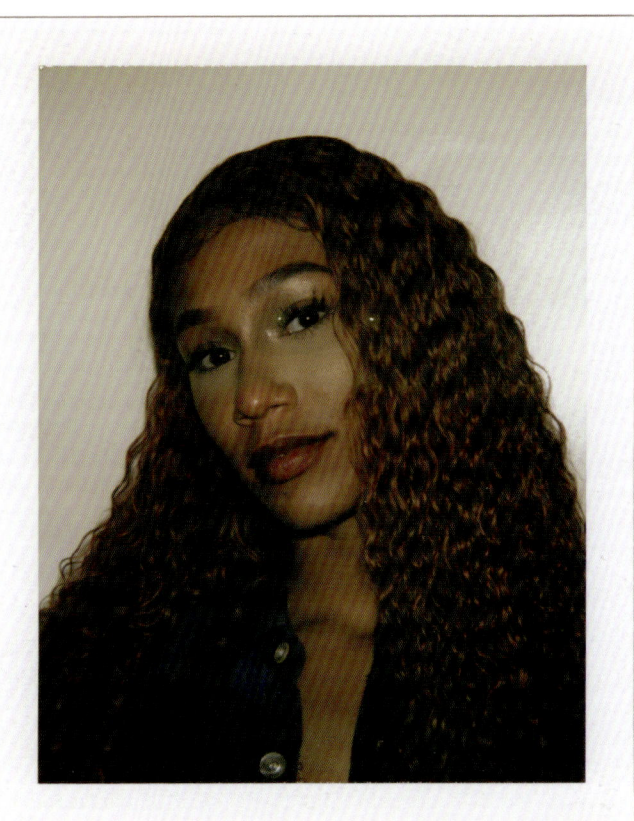

BIA

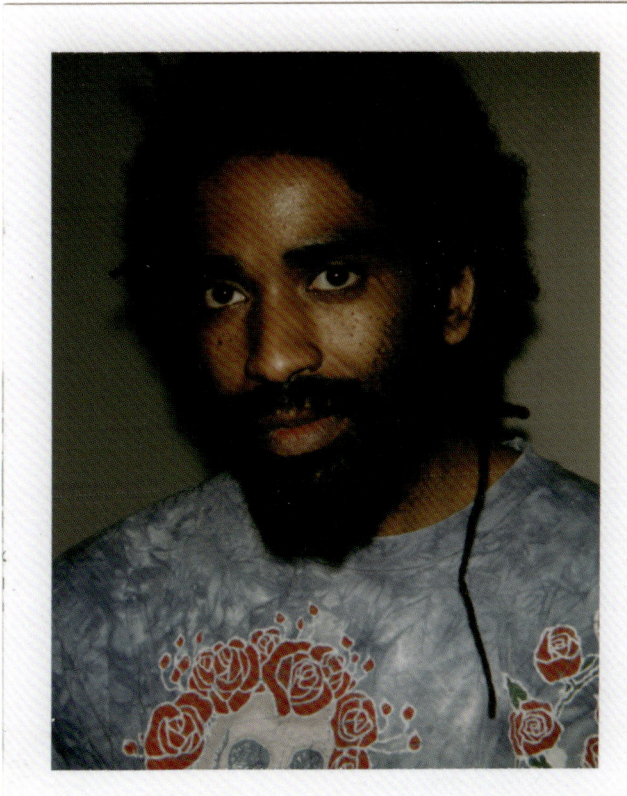

MARCUS BURROWES

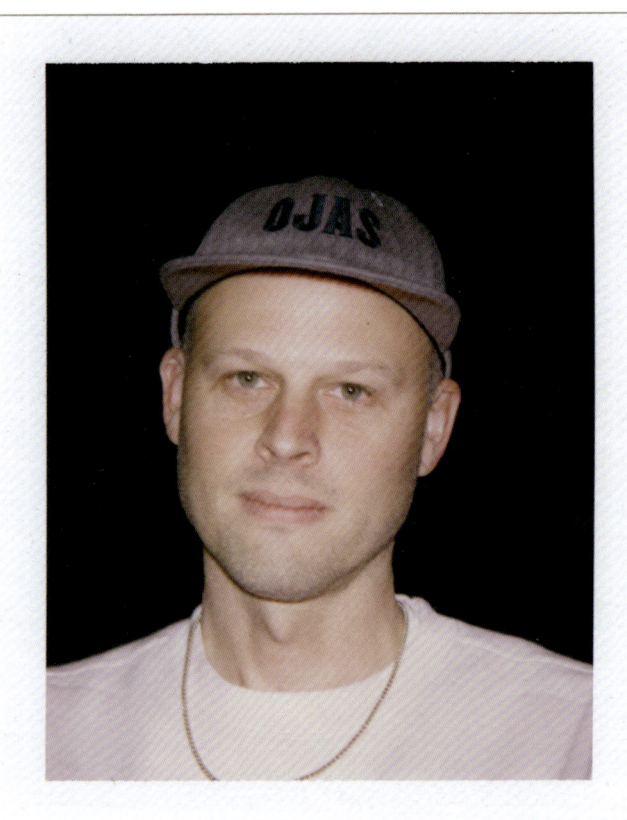

DEVON OJAS

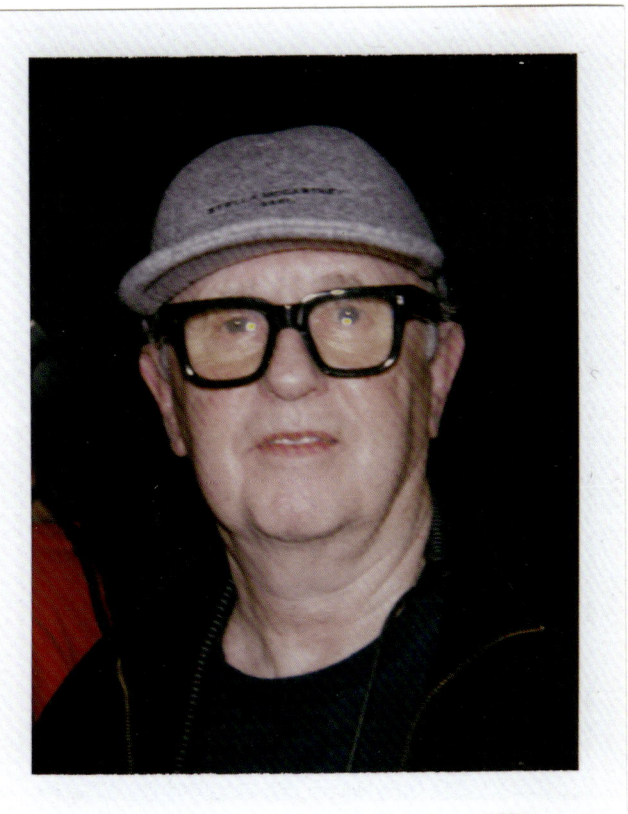

DAVID RODIGAN

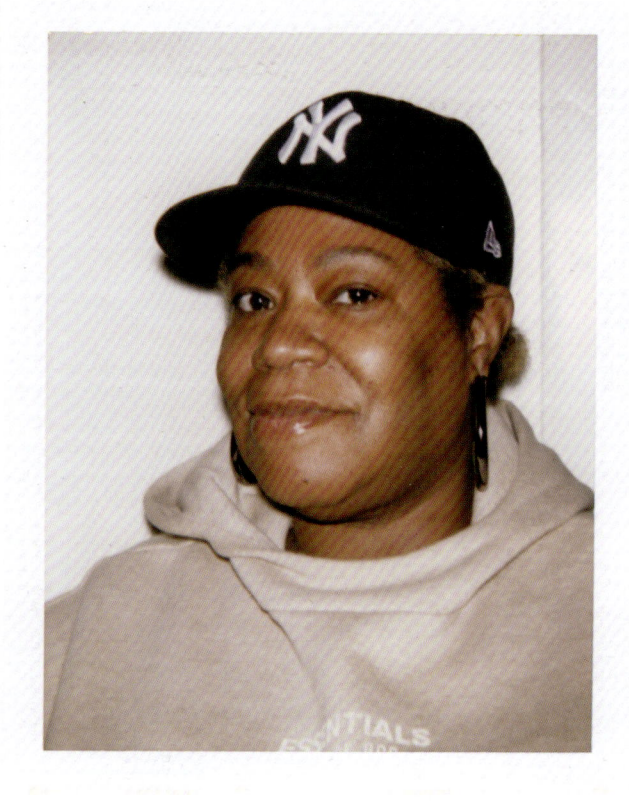

VICKEY FORD - SNEAKSHOT

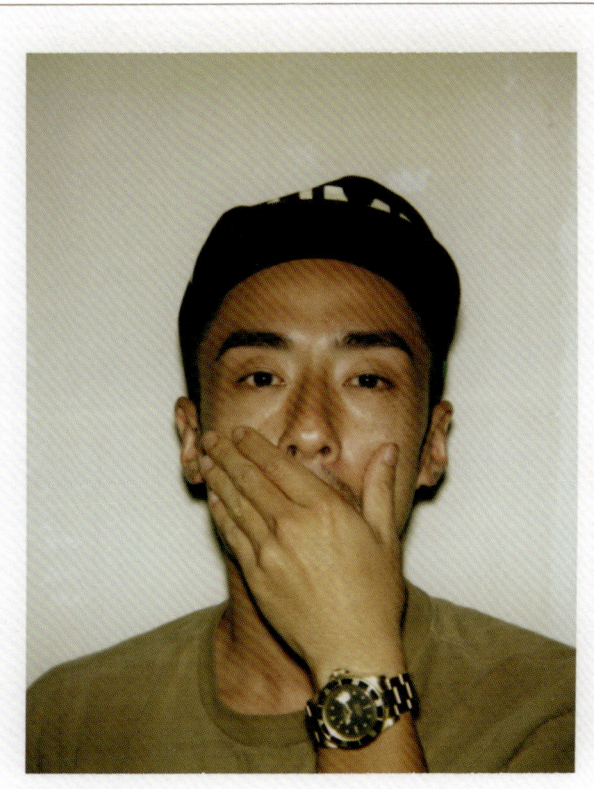

KEVIN POON

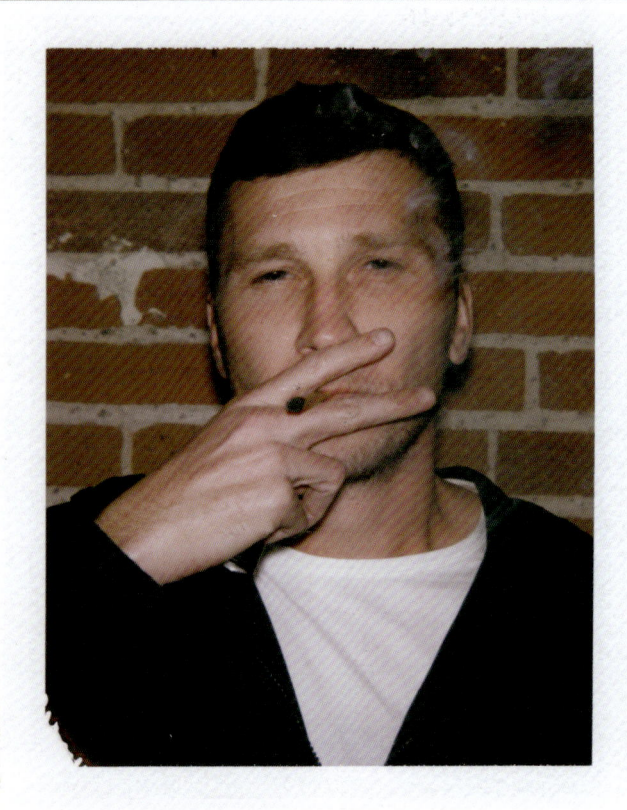

EMMETT DUFFY

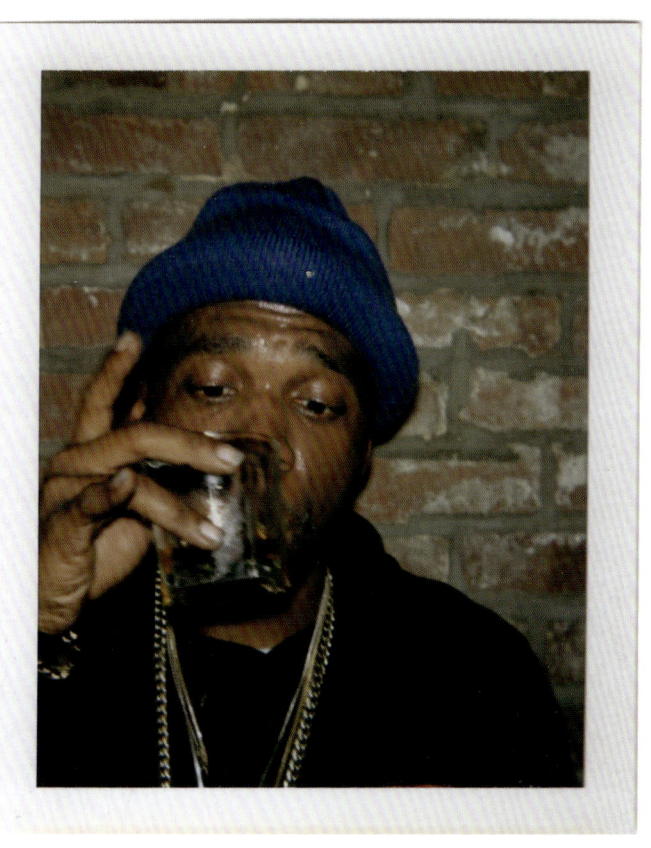

CURREN$Y

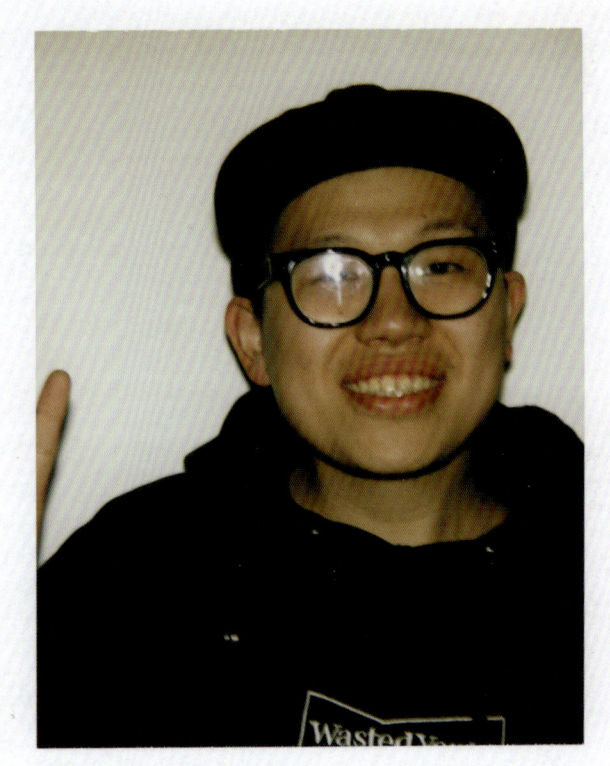

VERDY

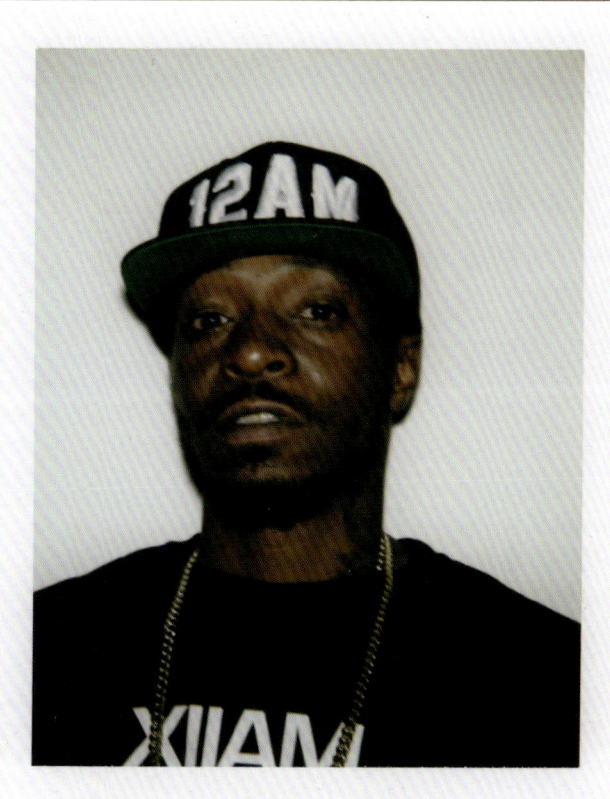

JUNGLE

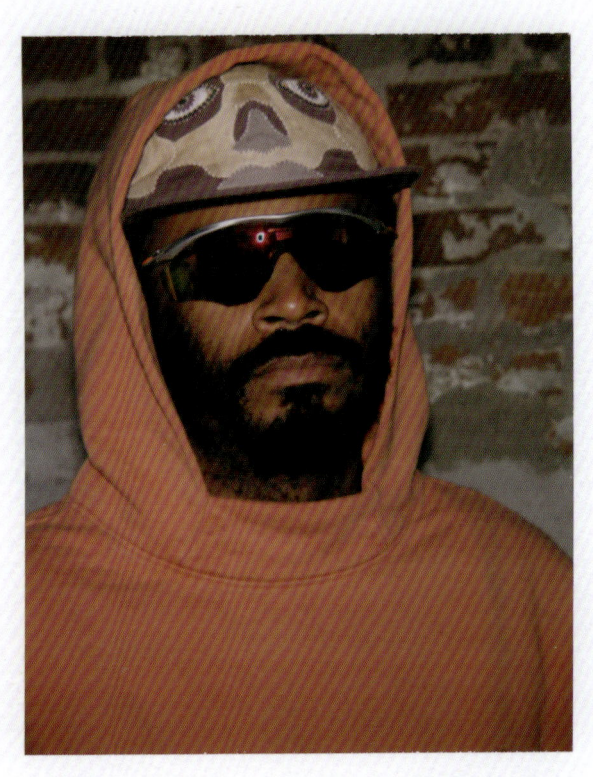

SALEHE BEMBURY

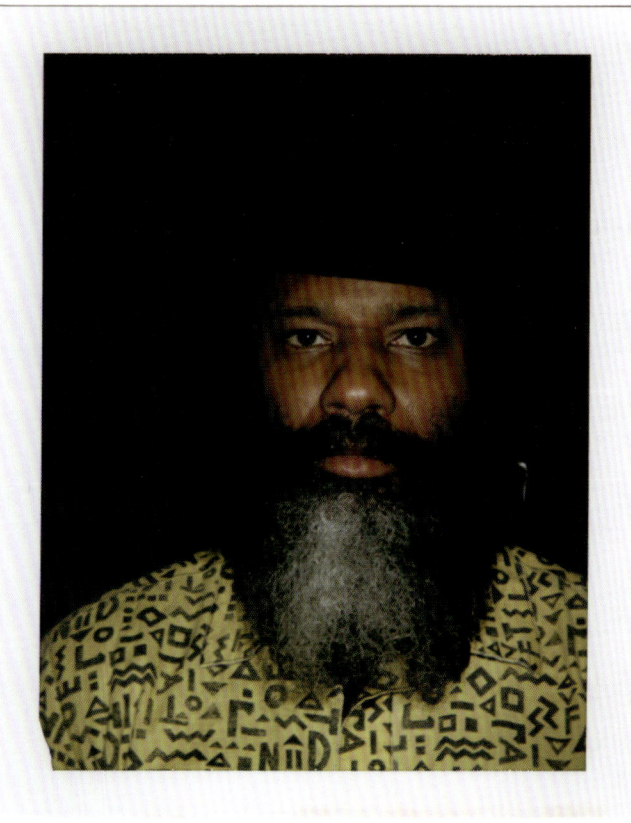

D PROSPER

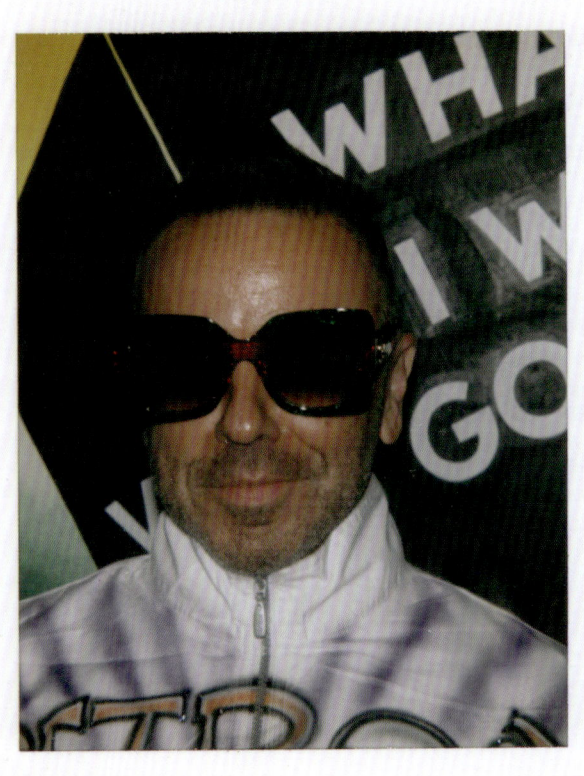

LEGENDARY DAMON

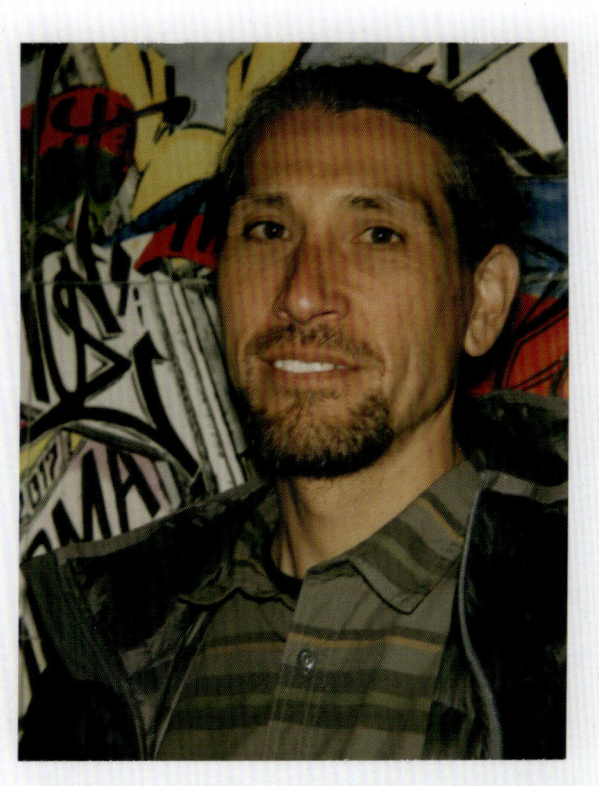

ERIC SPIE

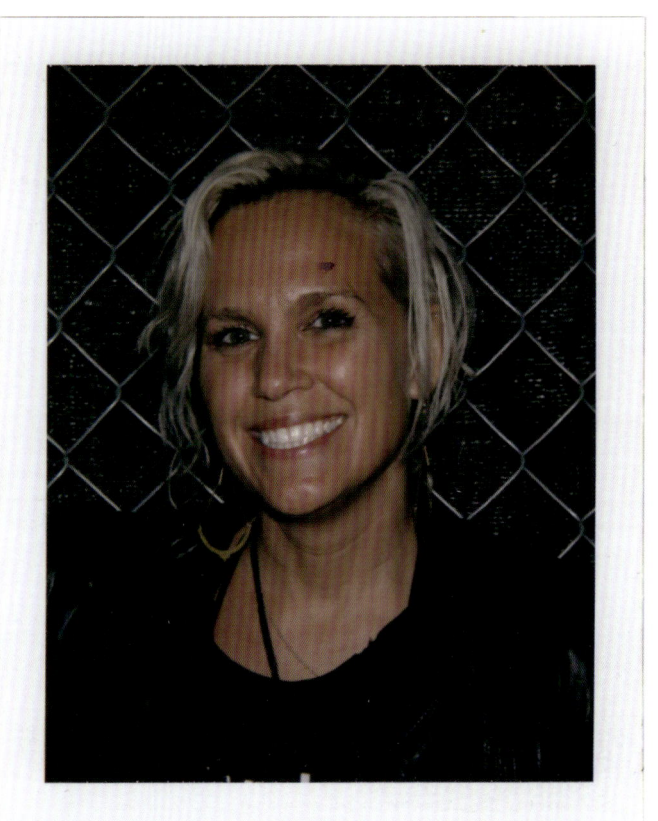

GINNY SUSS

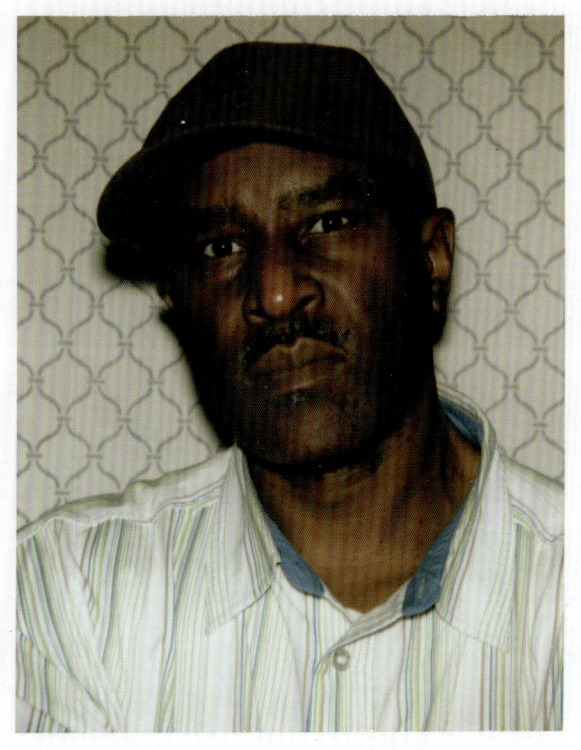

EASY MO BEE

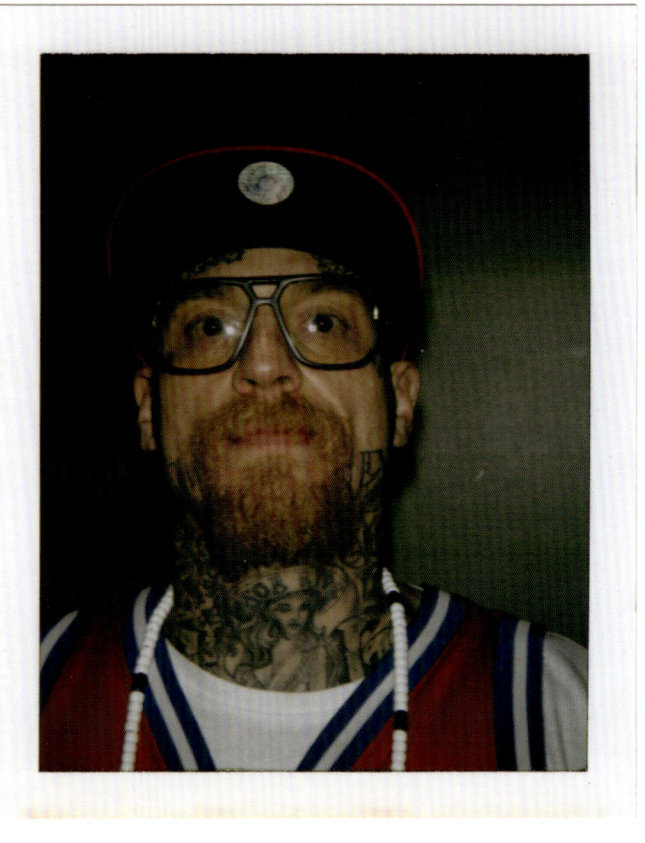

LORD EZAC AKA DANNY DIABLO

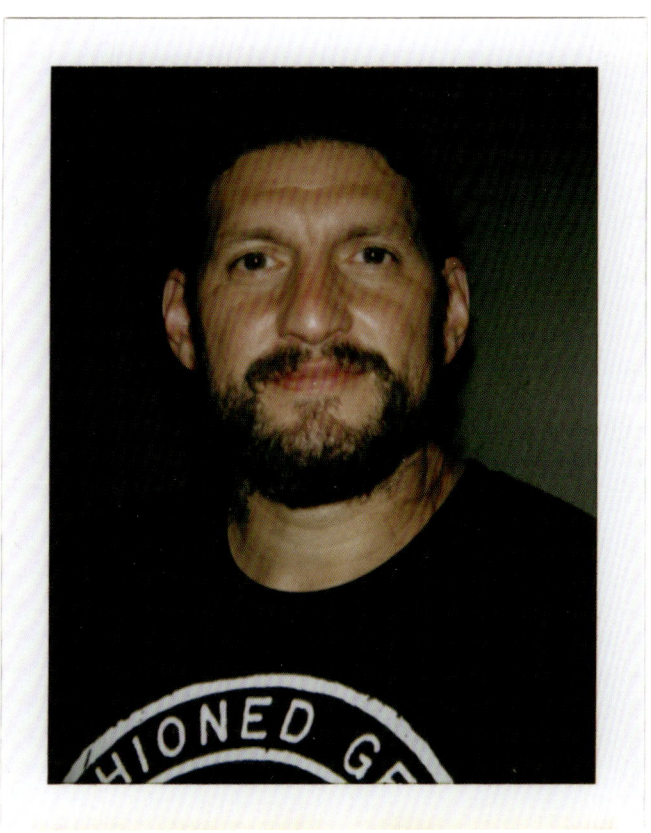

FREDDY CRICIEN

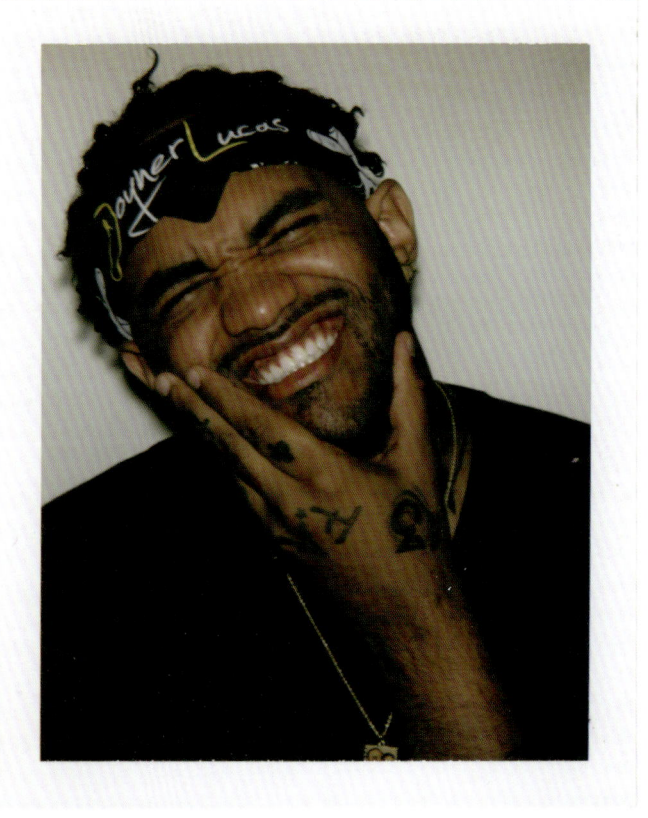

JOYNER LUCAS

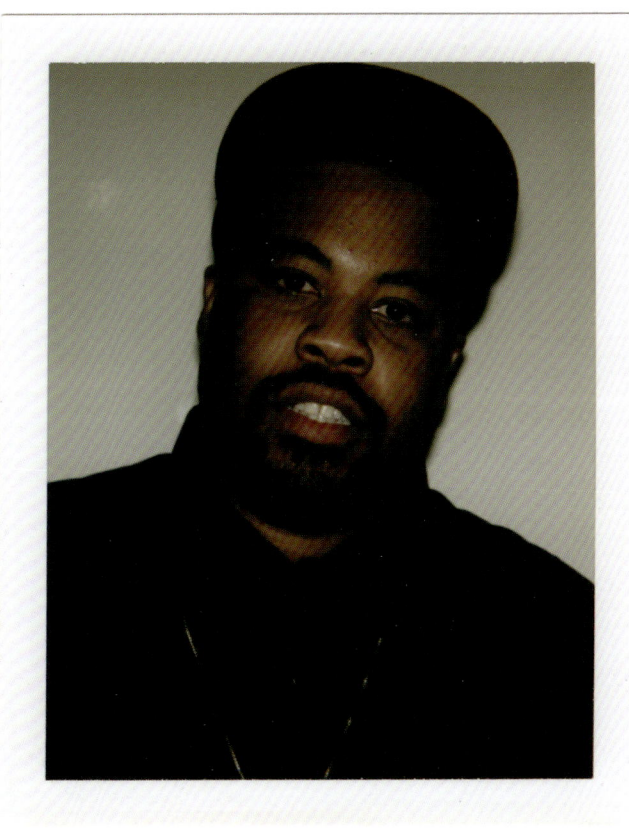

DARRELL ROBINSON JR.

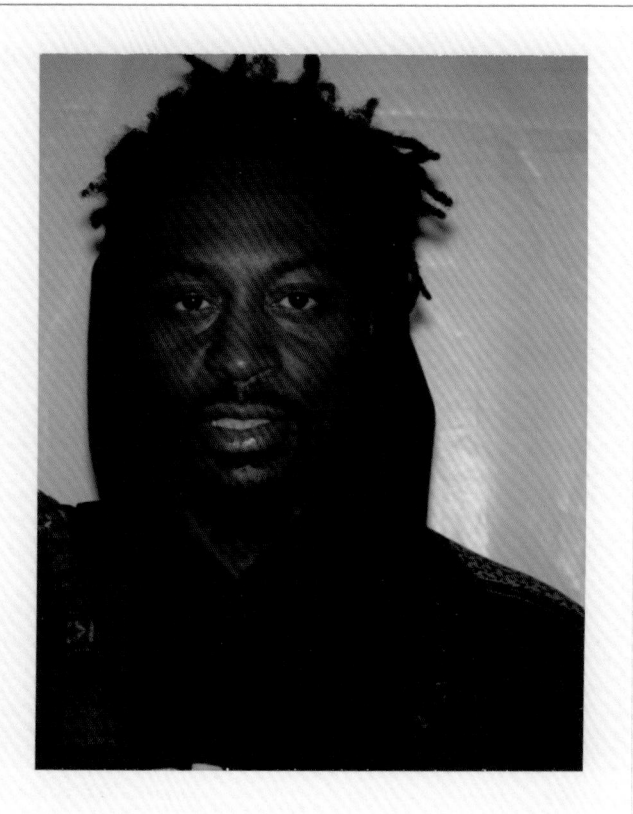

MEL D. COLE

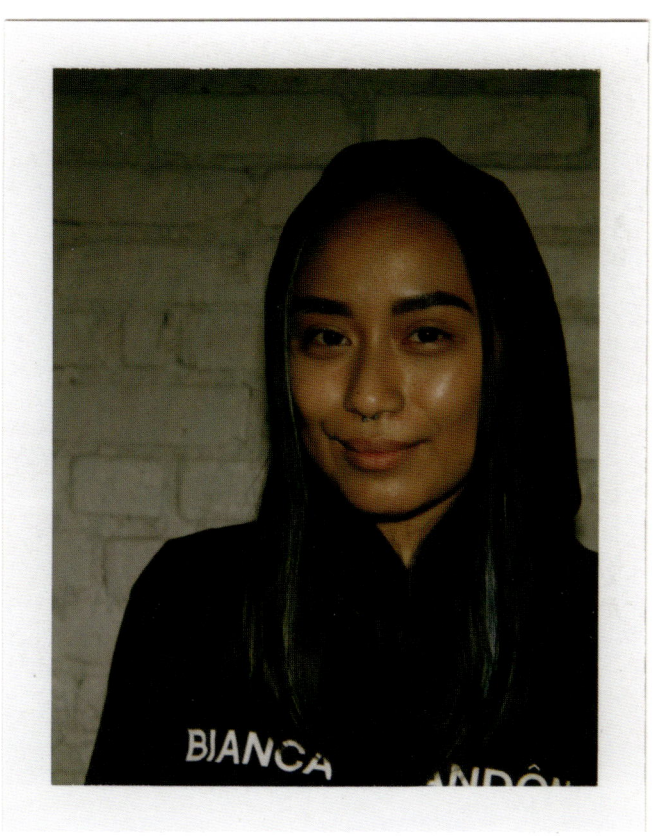

NIKKI MARTINEZ - HIGHKEYZ

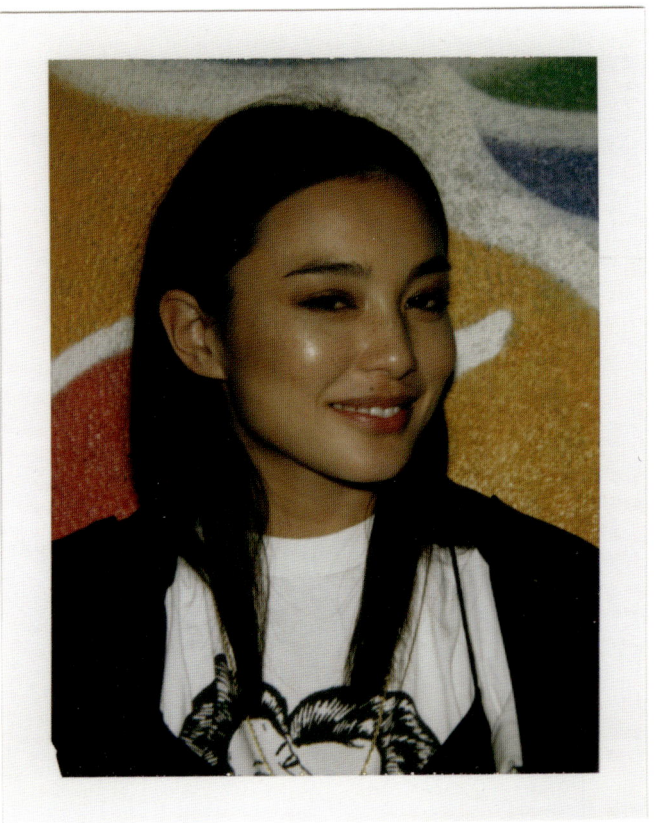

SOSUPERSAM

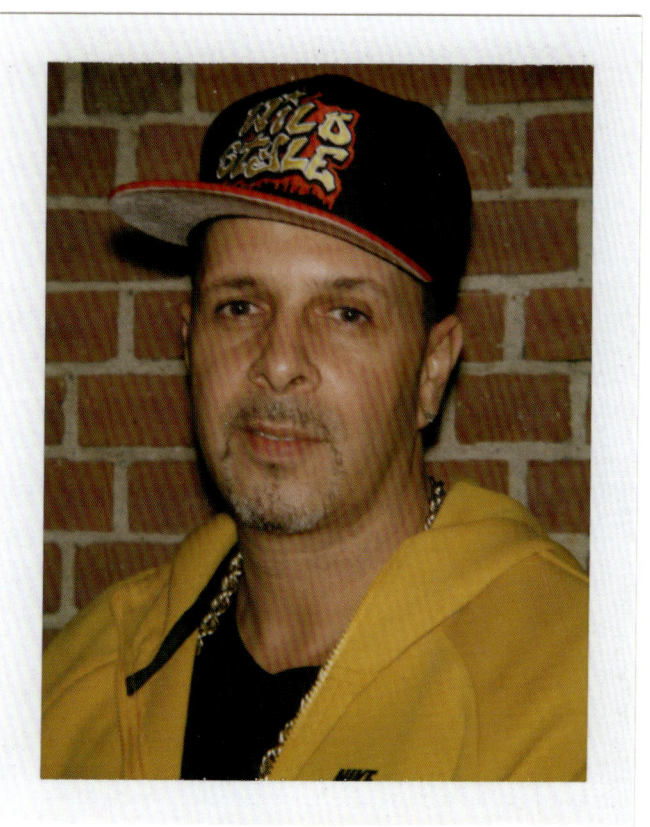

TONY TOUCH

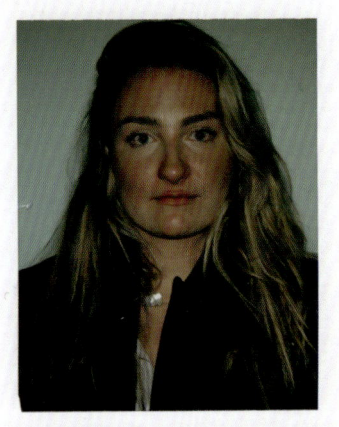
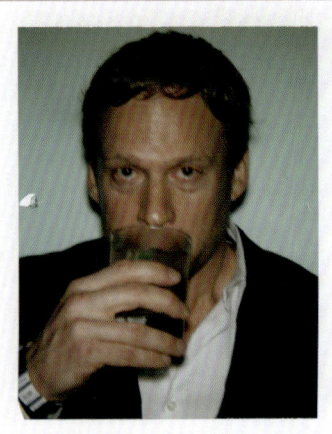
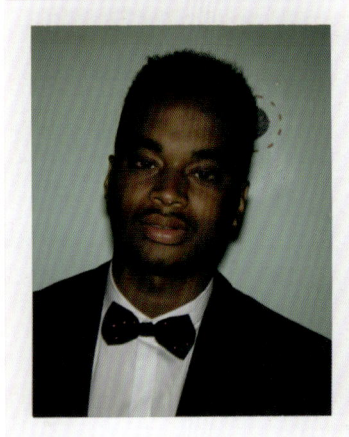
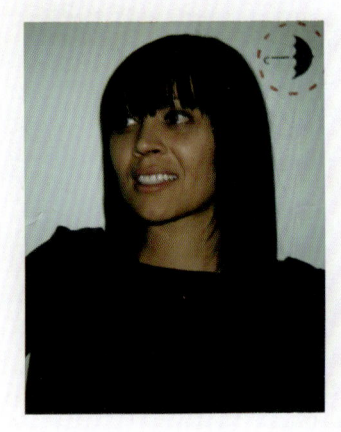

MACKENZIE JOHNSON

SCOTT SCHROEDER

PATRICK TOUSSANT

LATOYA JACKSON

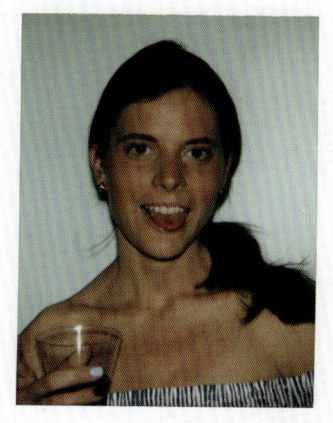

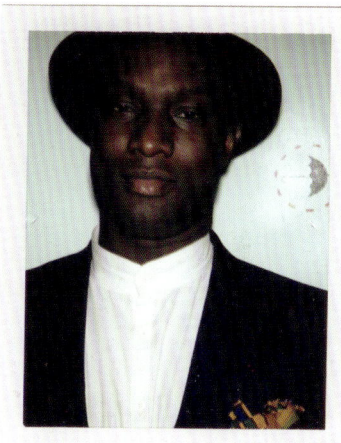

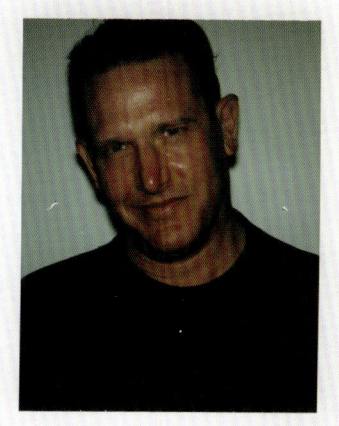

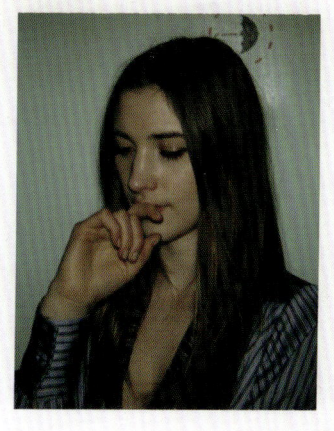

LAUREN JOYCE

JETT KAIN

STANLEY LUMAX

LILI VALCARENGHI

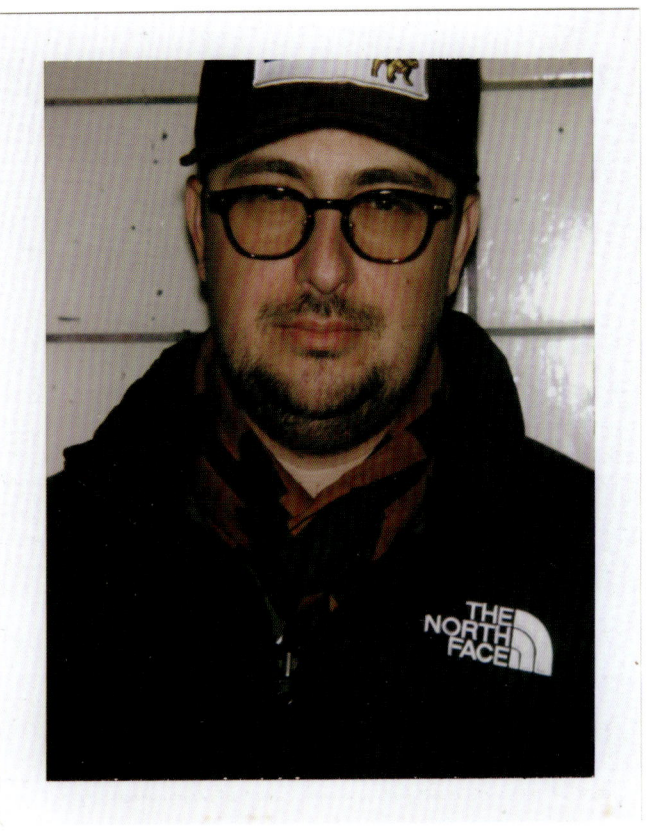

VLAD ELKIN

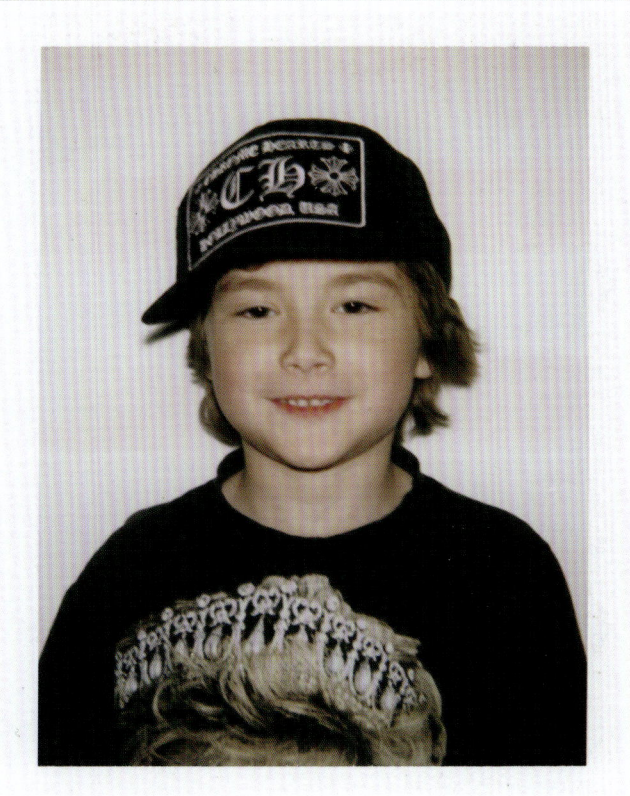

MAXWELL ELKIN

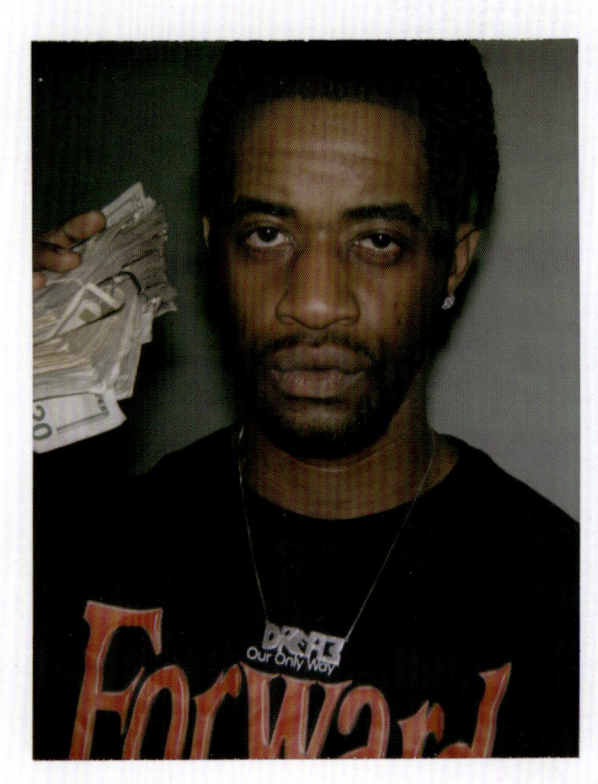

SLIM DOLLARS

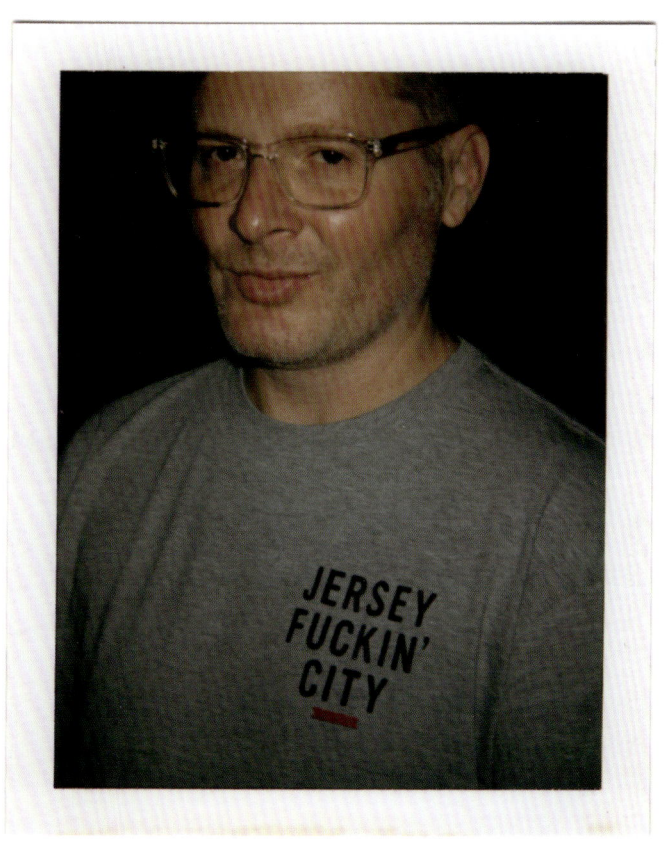

JON DEUS AKA DON JEUS

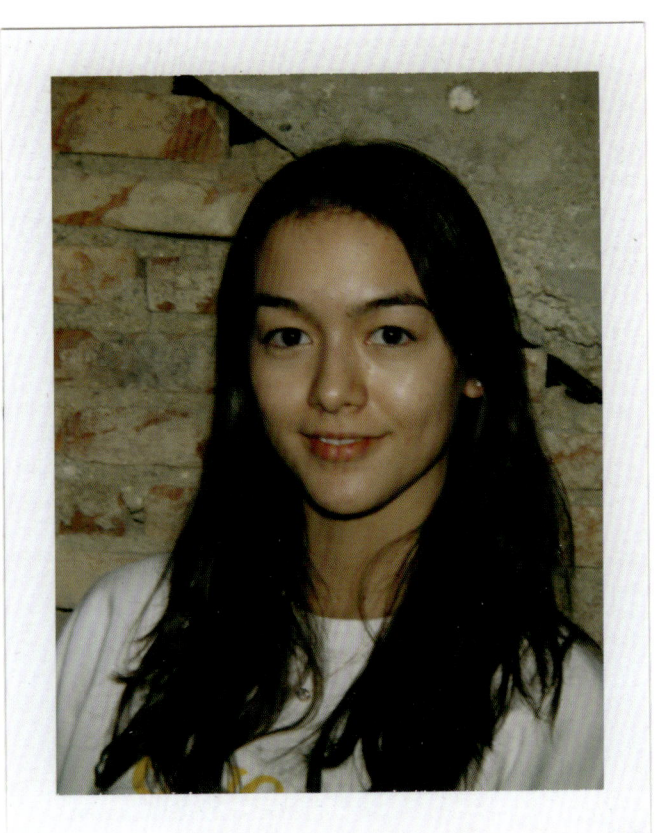

FIONA McLEISH

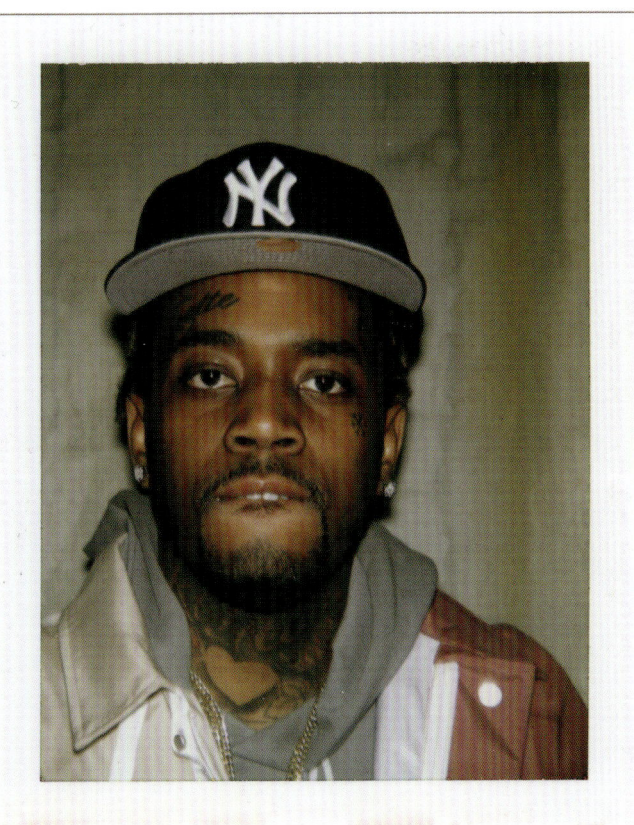

FIVIO FOREIGN

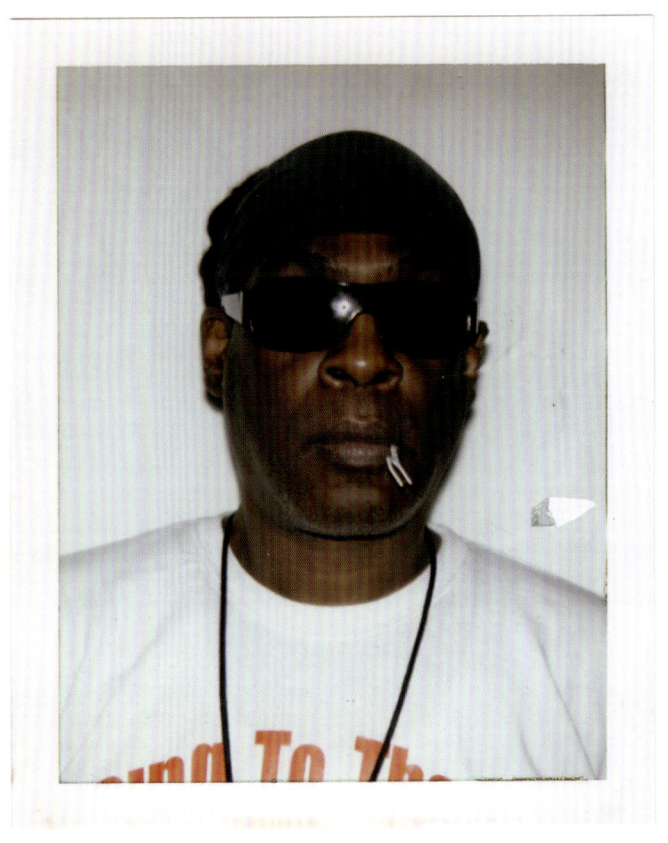

GRANDMASTER VIC

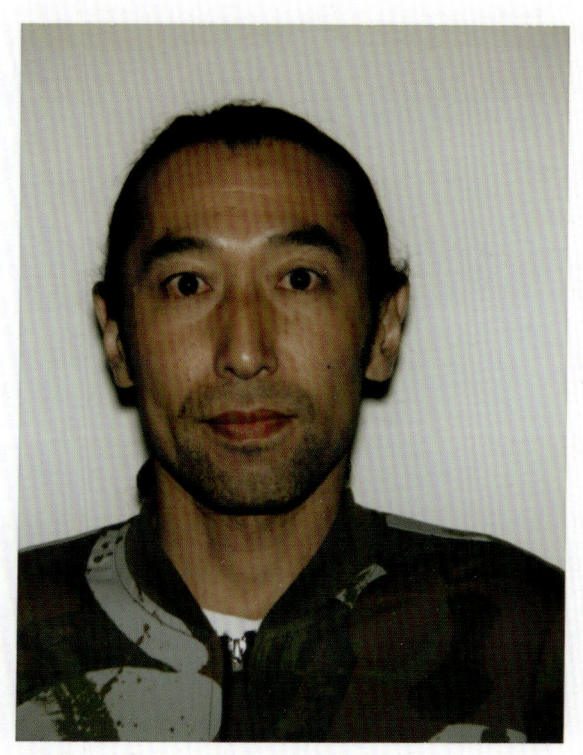

FUMI

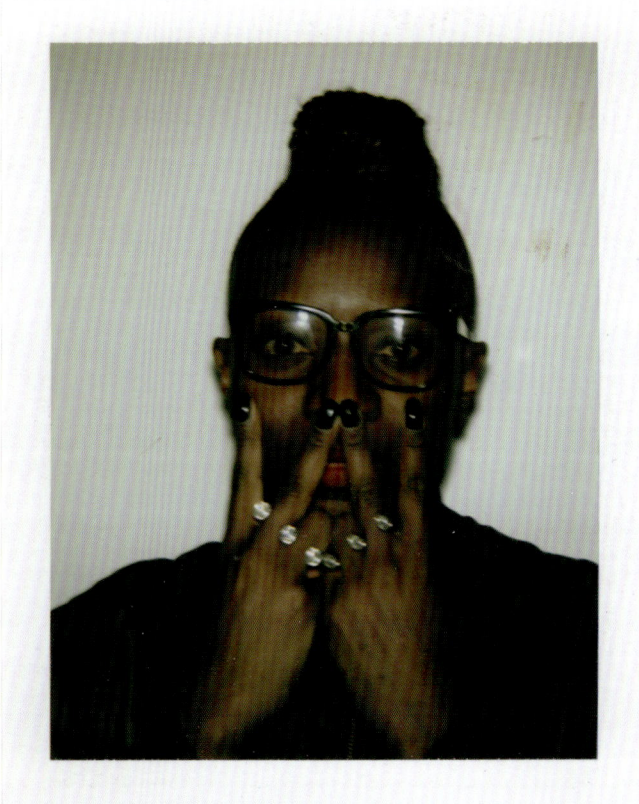

BABY SAM

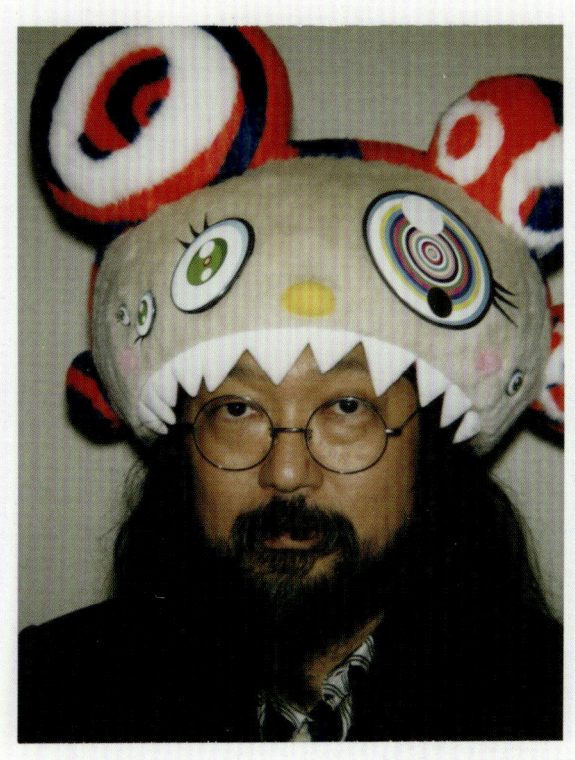

TAKASHI MURAKAMI

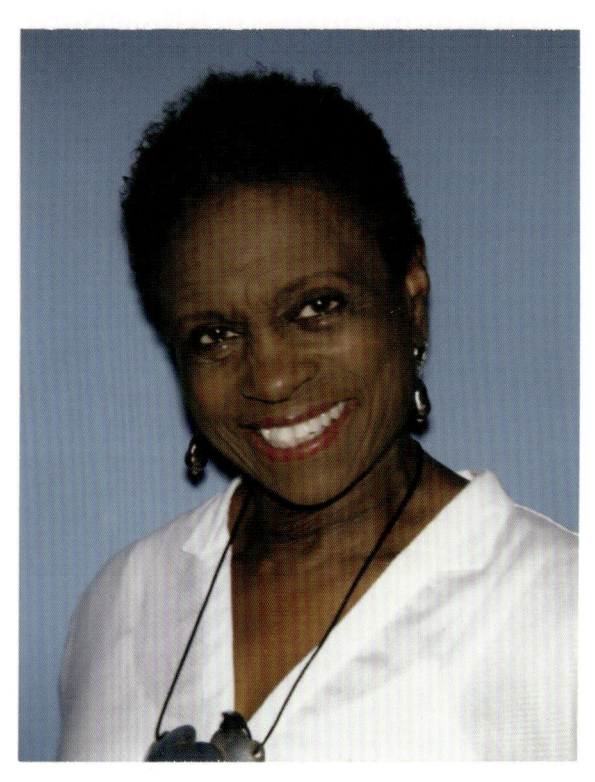

AUDREY ROWE

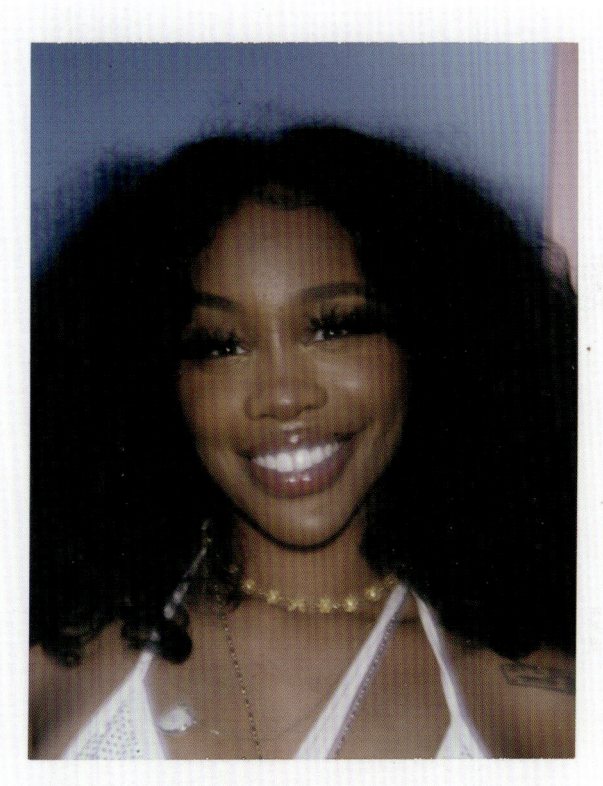

SZA

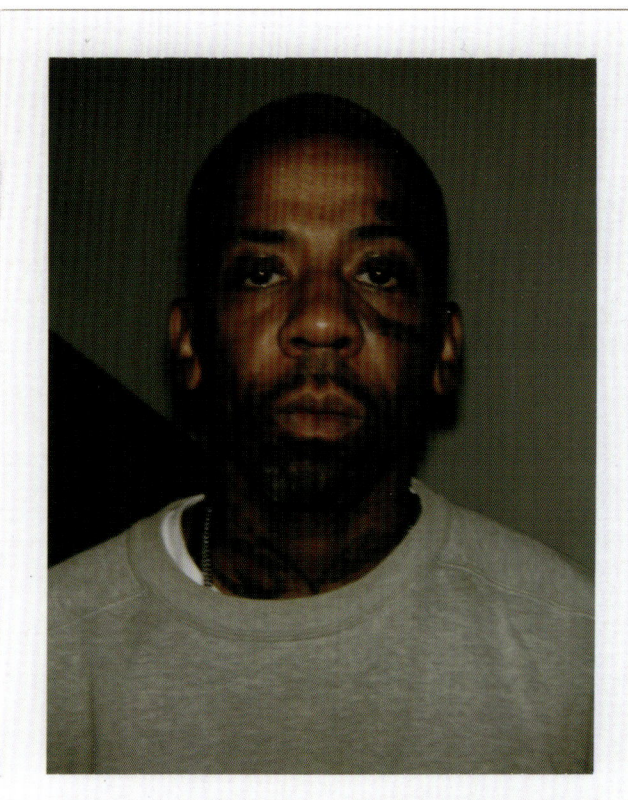

CHRISTIAN ALEXANDER

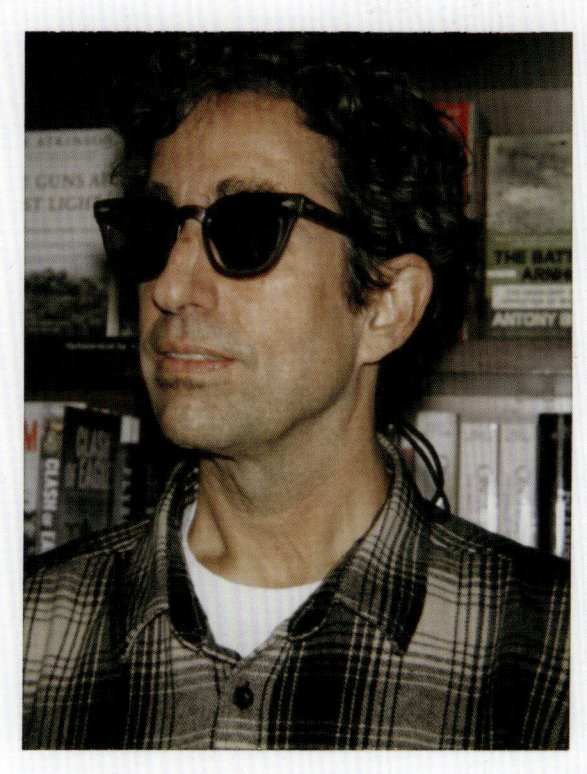

GLEN E. FRIEDMAN

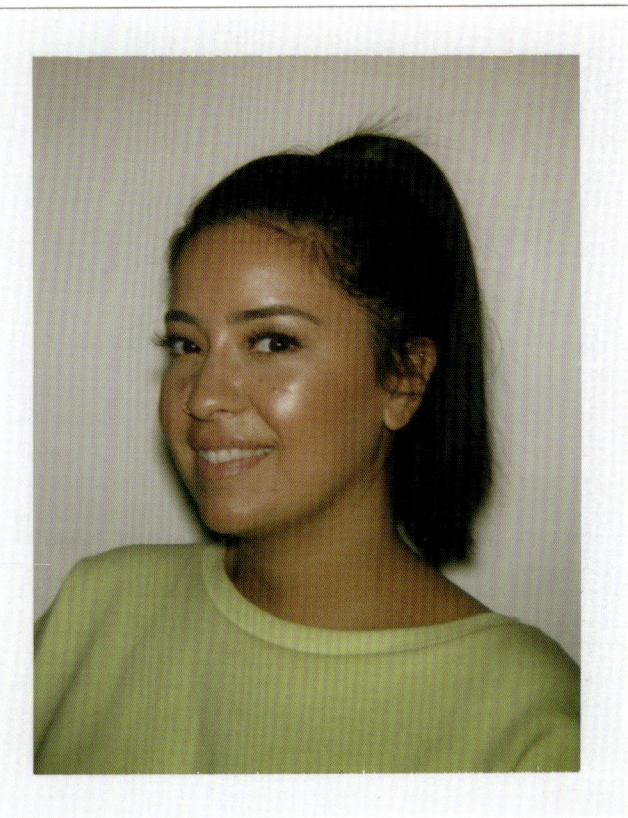

BAHAR BAMBI

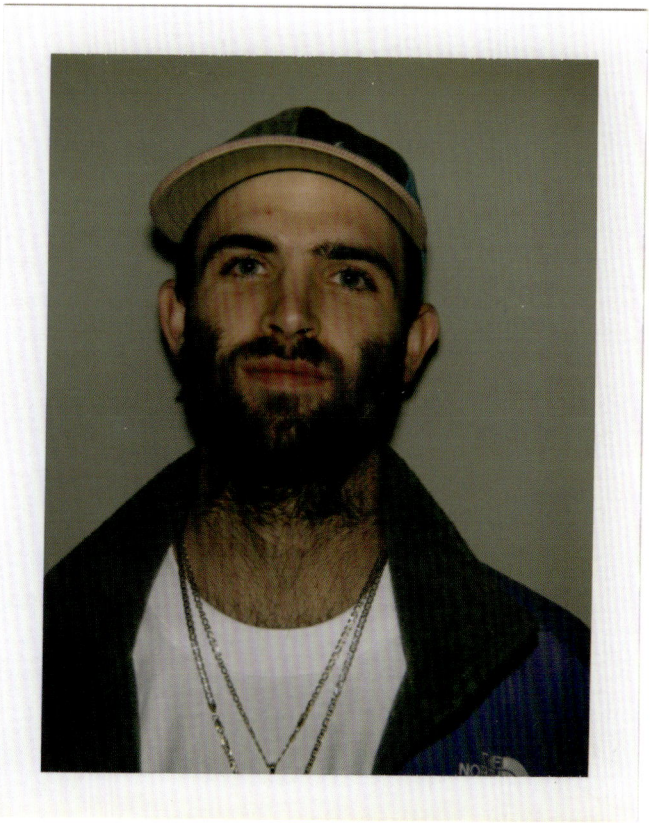

SEAN WOTHERSPOON

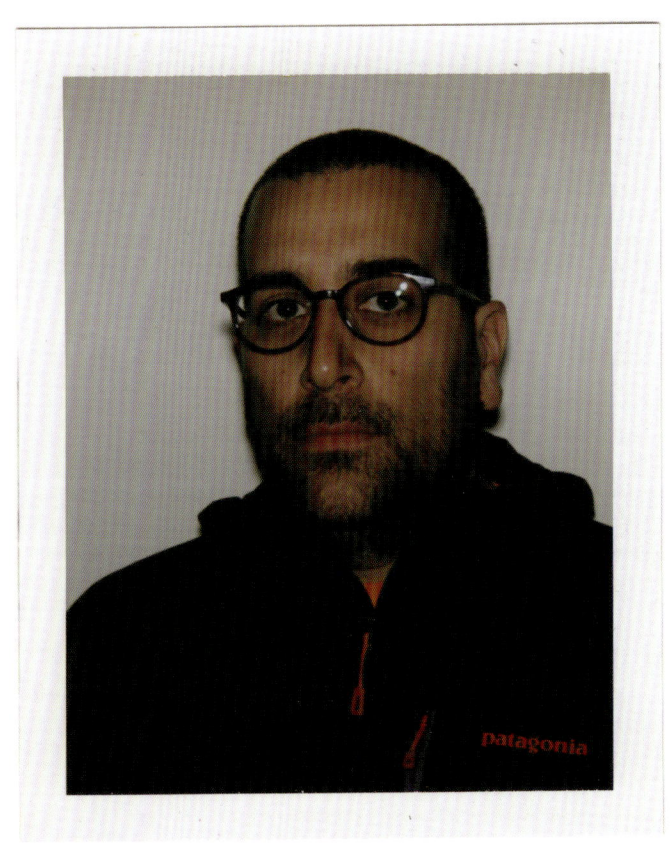

ARTHUR SOLEIMANPOUR - PARKS DEPARTMENT

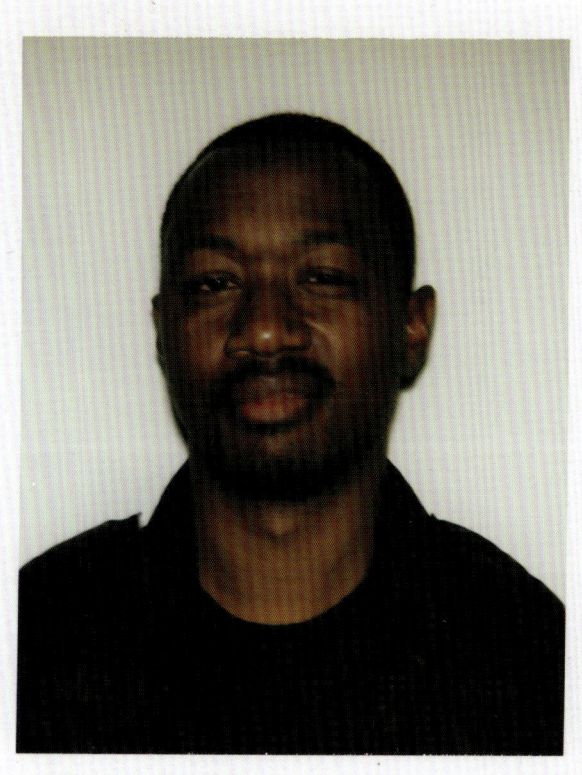

CURTAINS

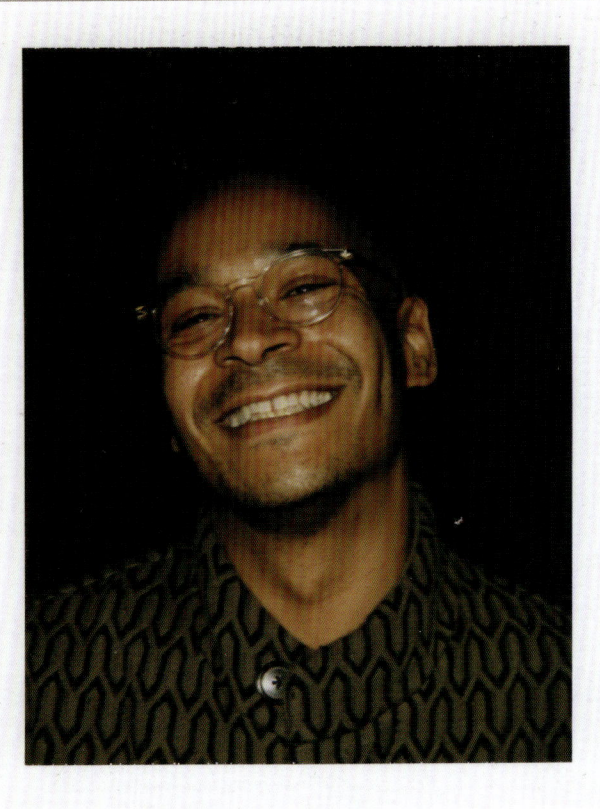

LAURENT SEGRETIER

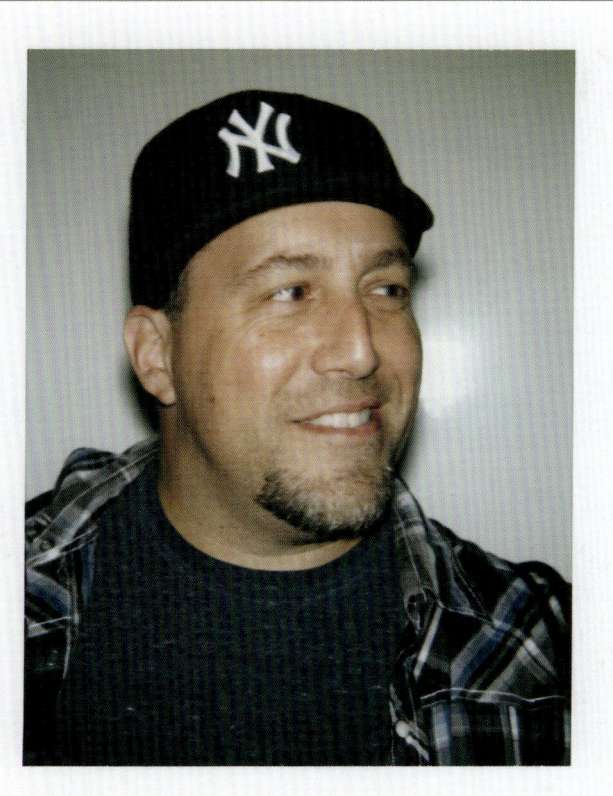

DANNY SCHULER

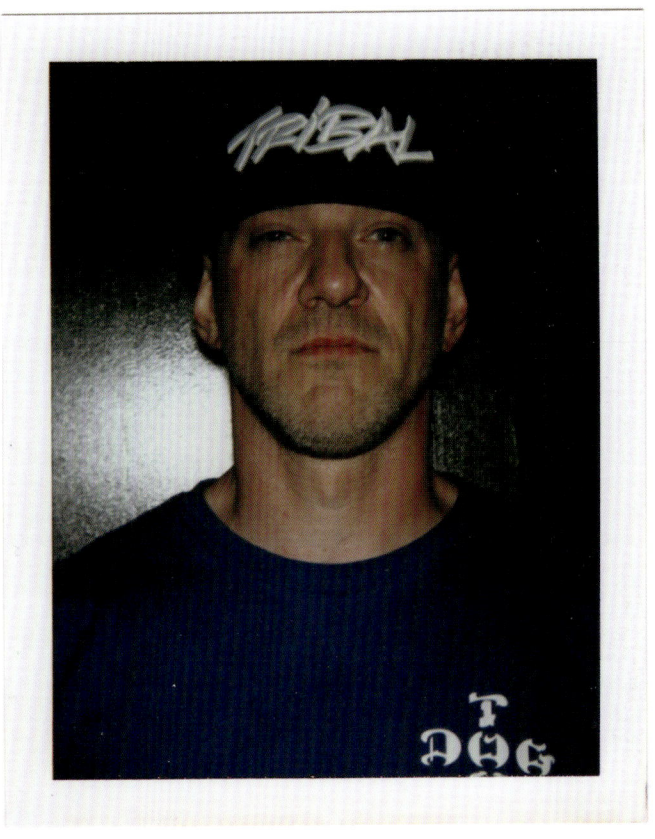

CHRISTIAN OLDE WOLBERS

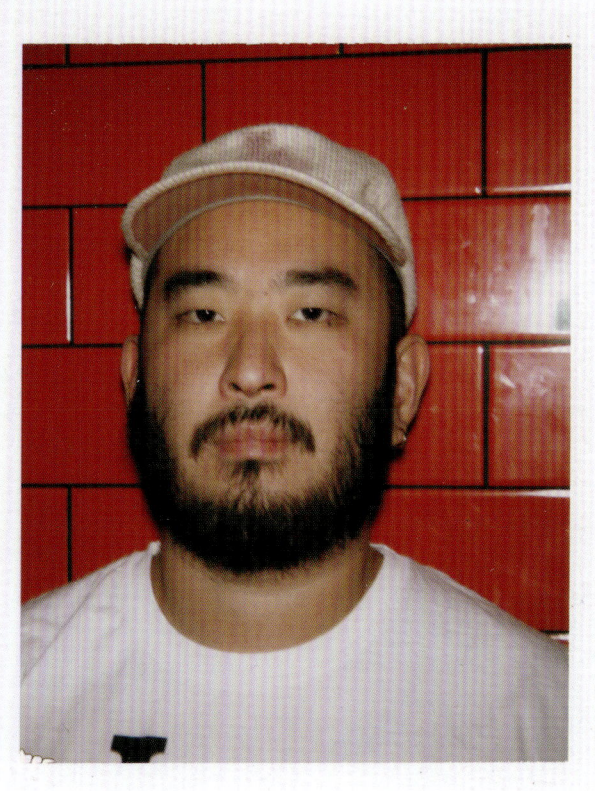

MICHAEL PAK

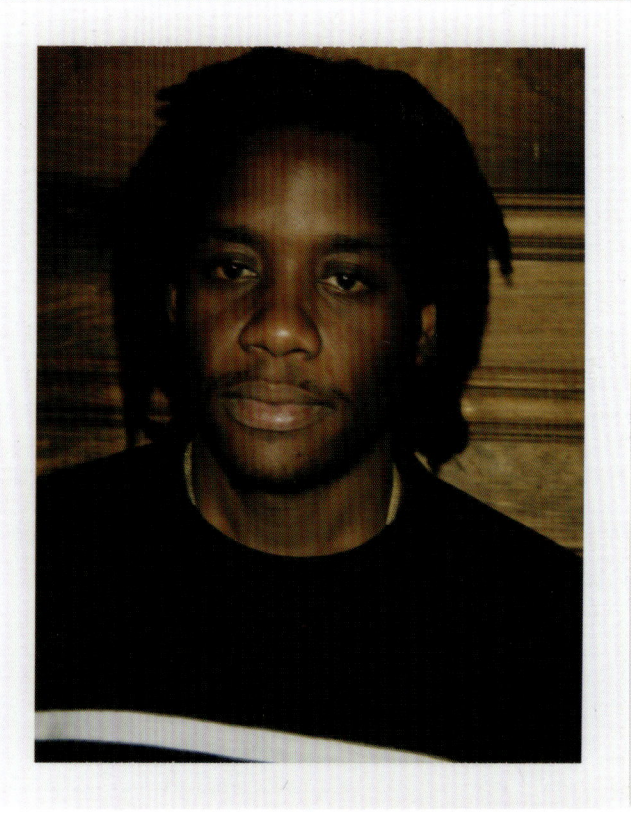

BRENDON SHARPE AKA DADDI BARNZ

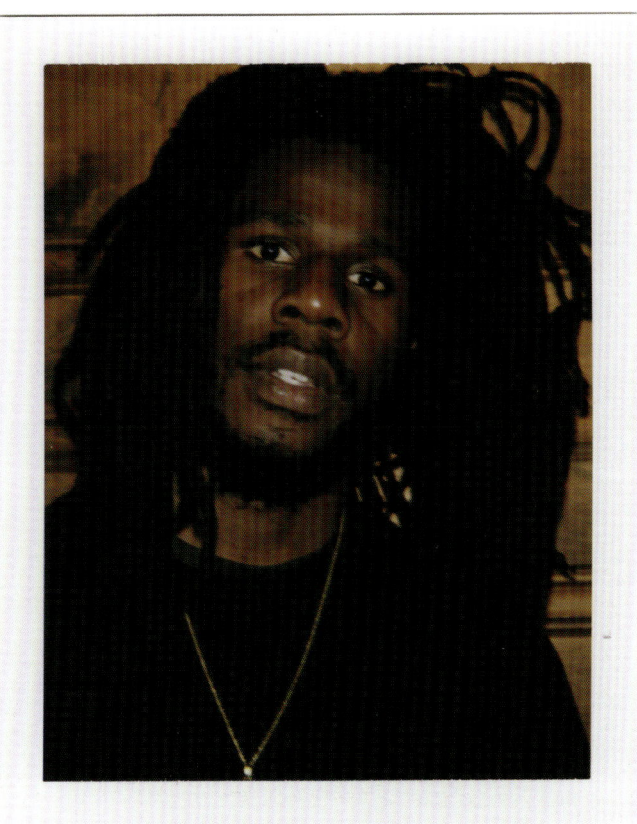

CHRONIXX

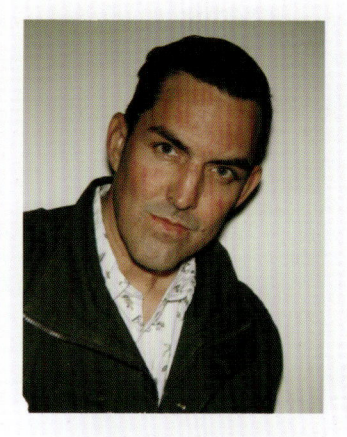

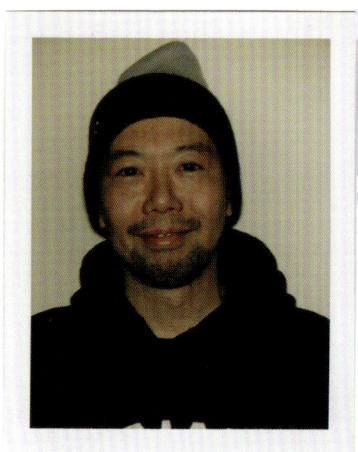

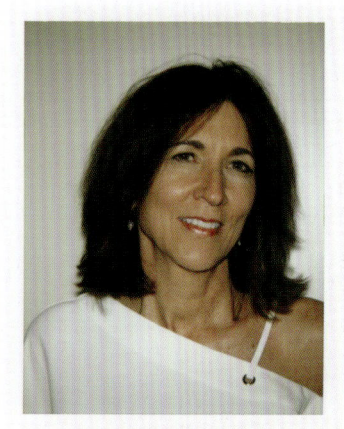

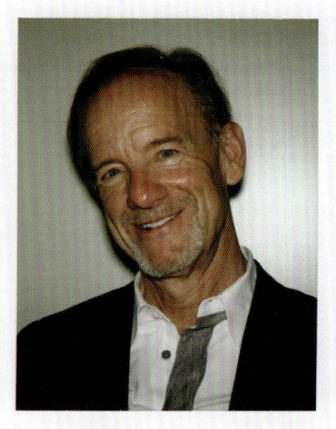

SAM FLORES

YOSUKE ITO

DONNA POHLAD

JIM POHLAD

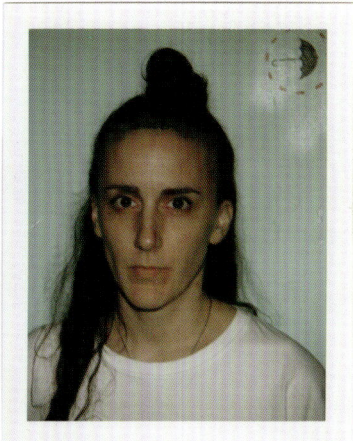

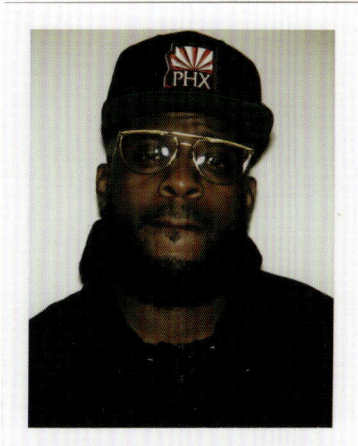

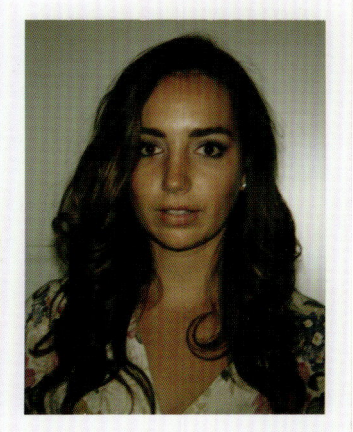

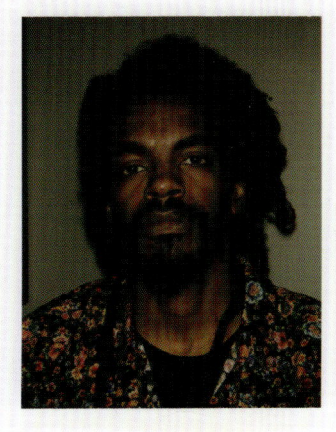

LAUREN FLAX

DJ SMYPHONY

KENDALL WARSON

I'KYORI SWABY

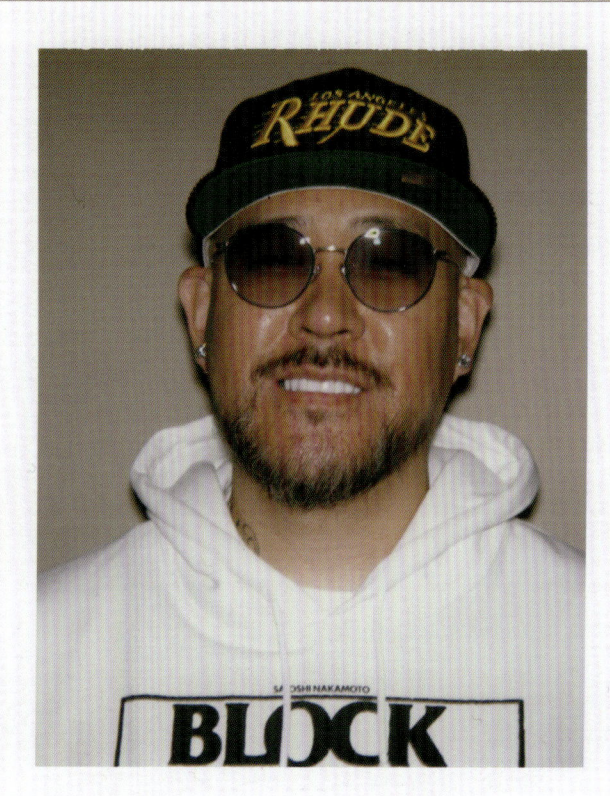

BEN BALLER

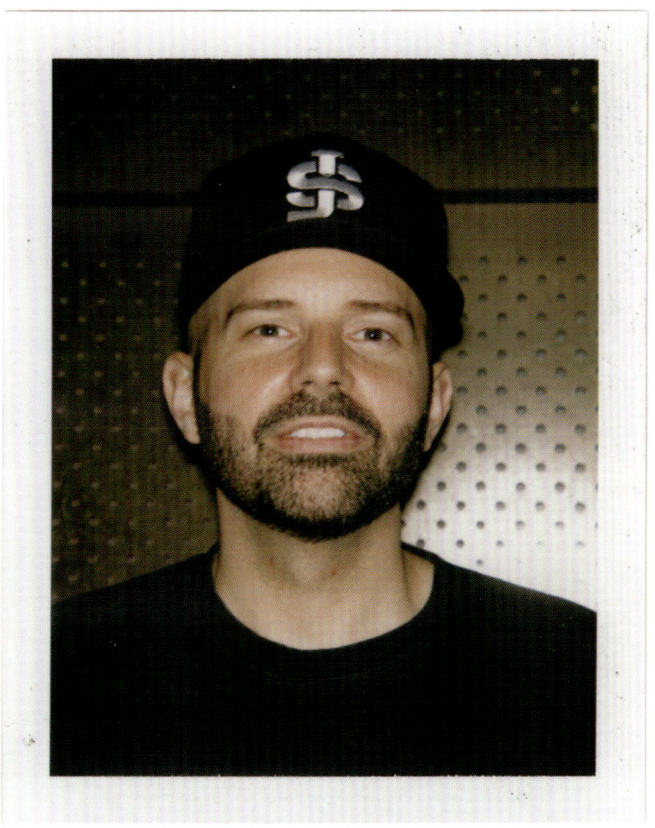

DJ WONDER

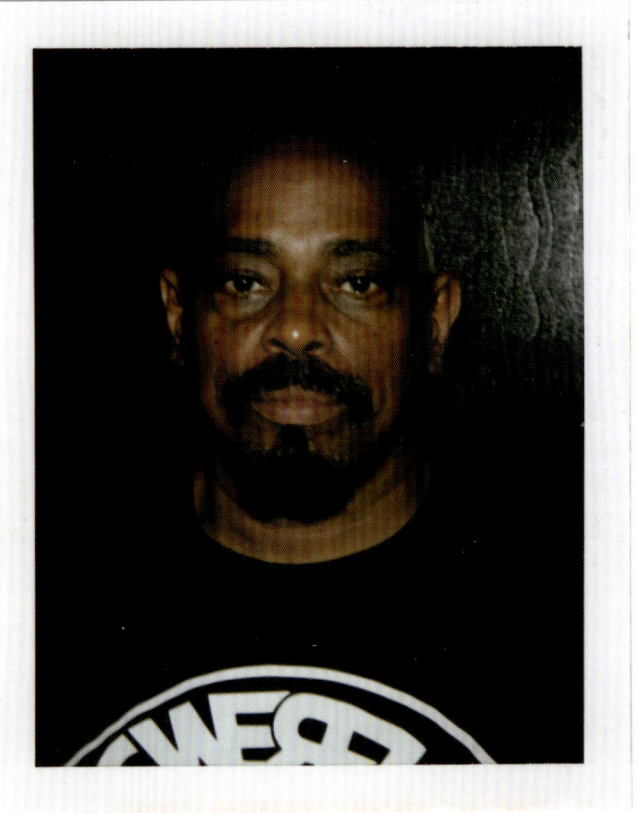

SEN DOG

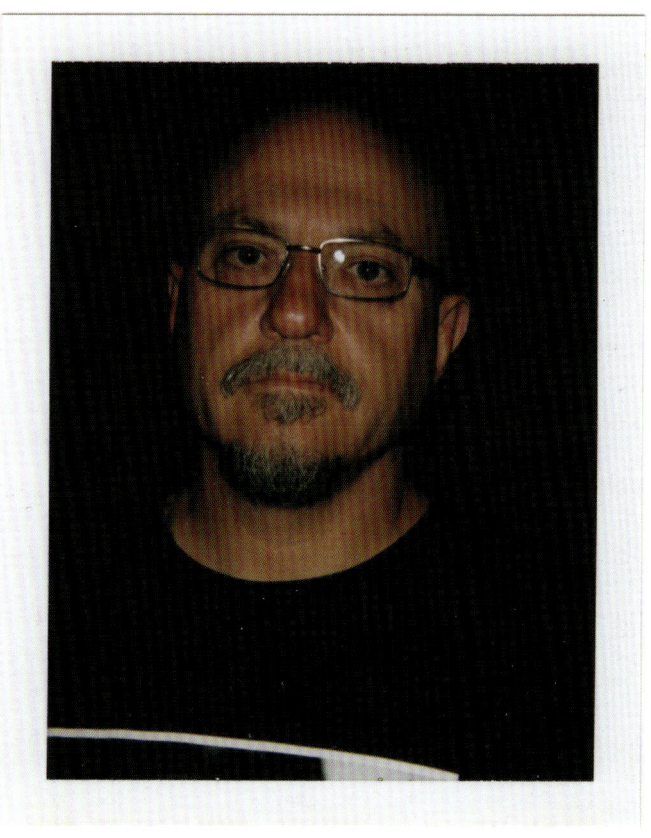

ESTEVAN ORIOL

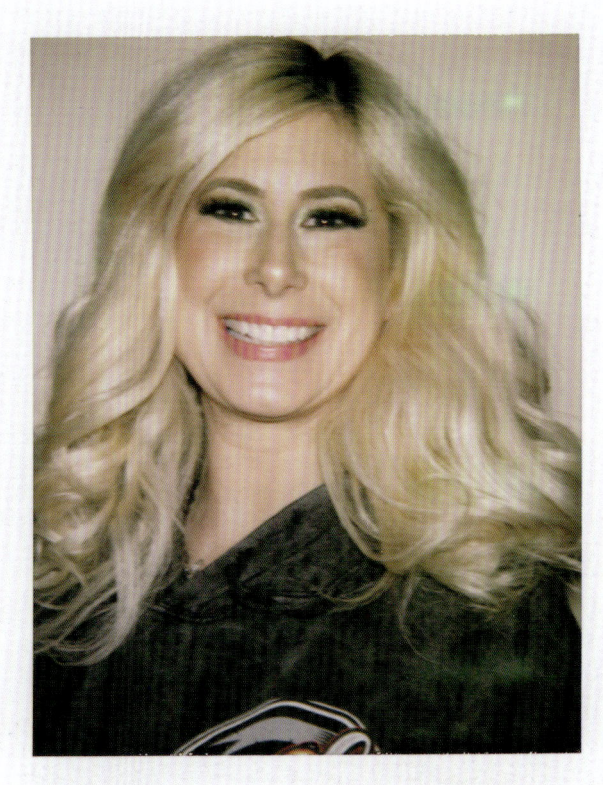

ELANNA BURKE

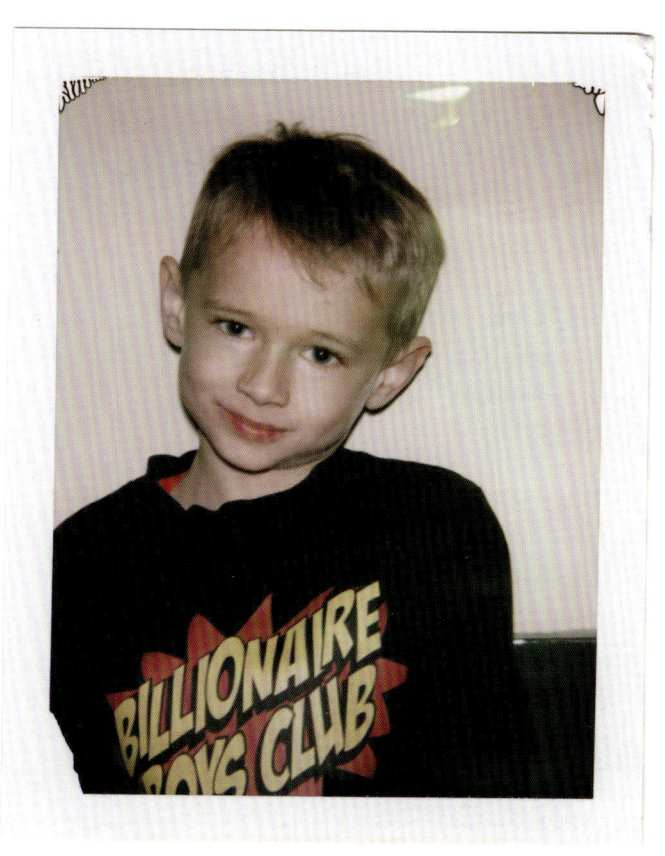

BRYSON BLAZE BURKE

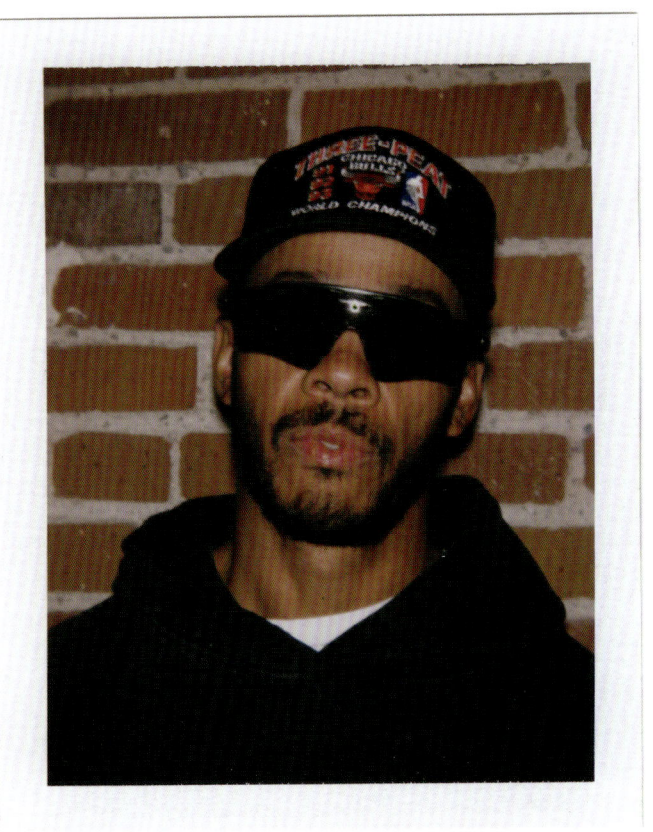

GEORGE ROBERTSON

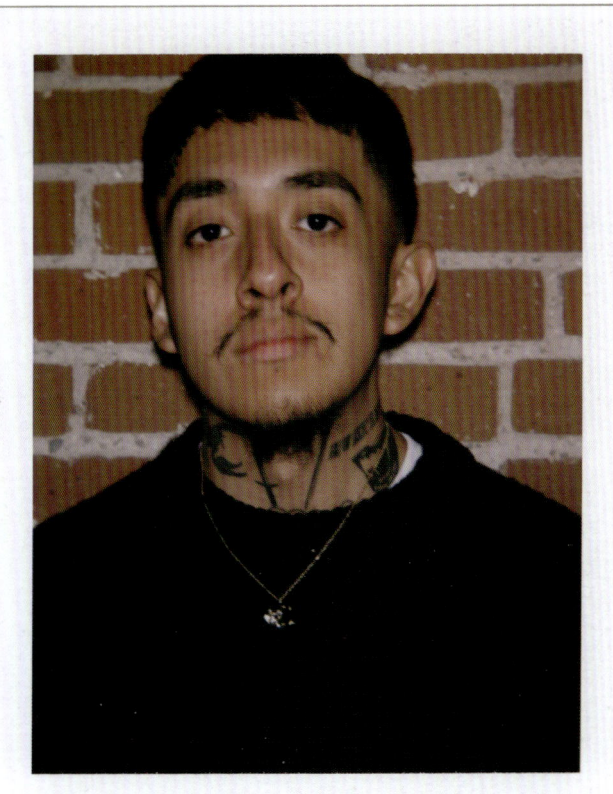

CUCO

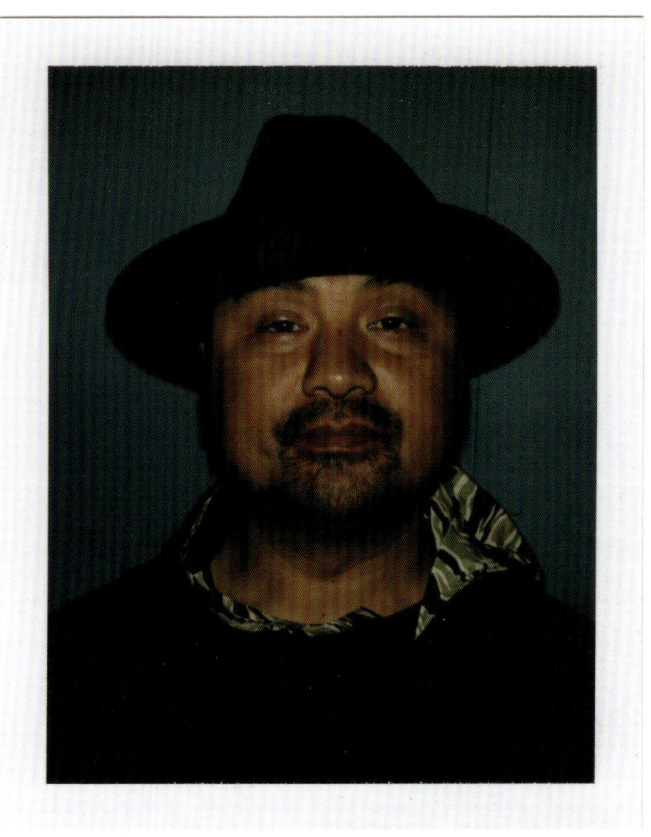

ALEX AQUINO

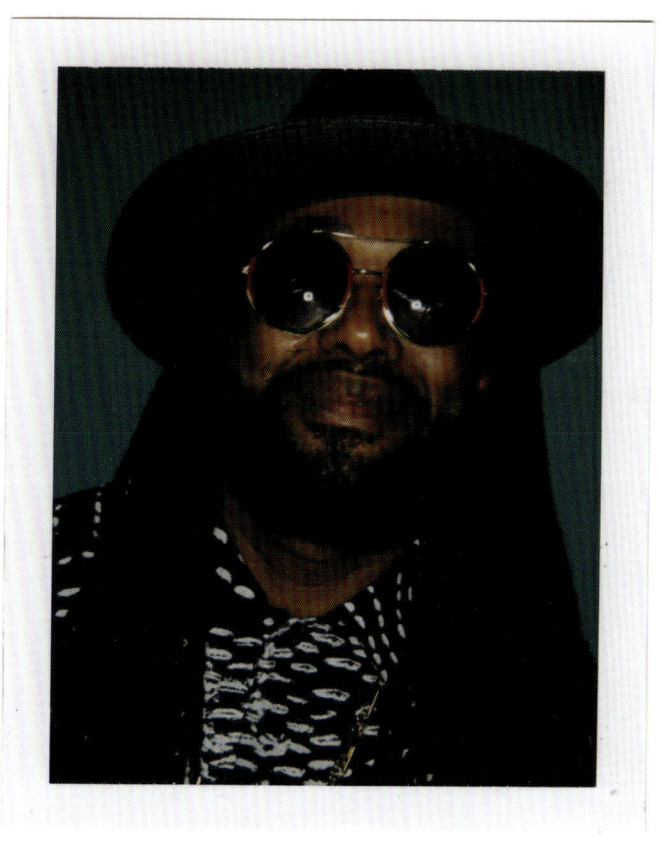

SUPERNATURAL

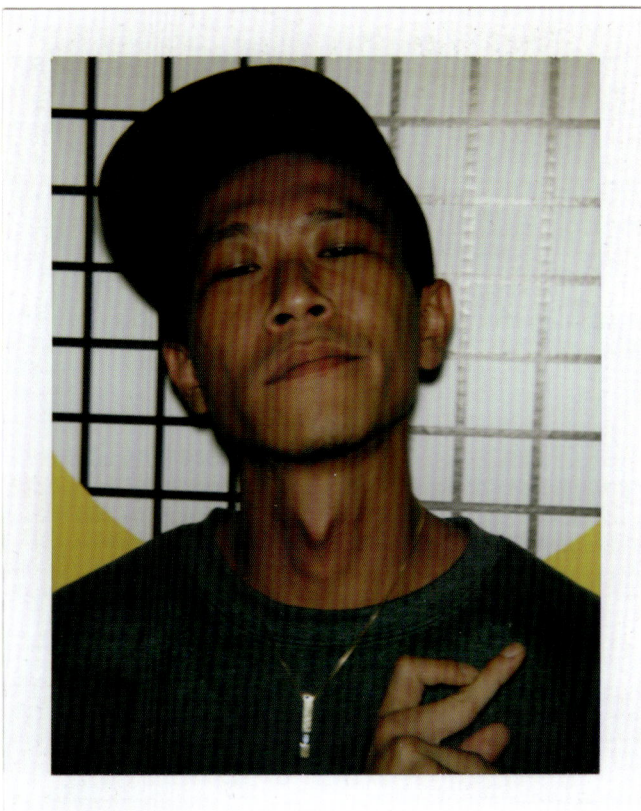

OG FELIX - RADIKAL FORZE

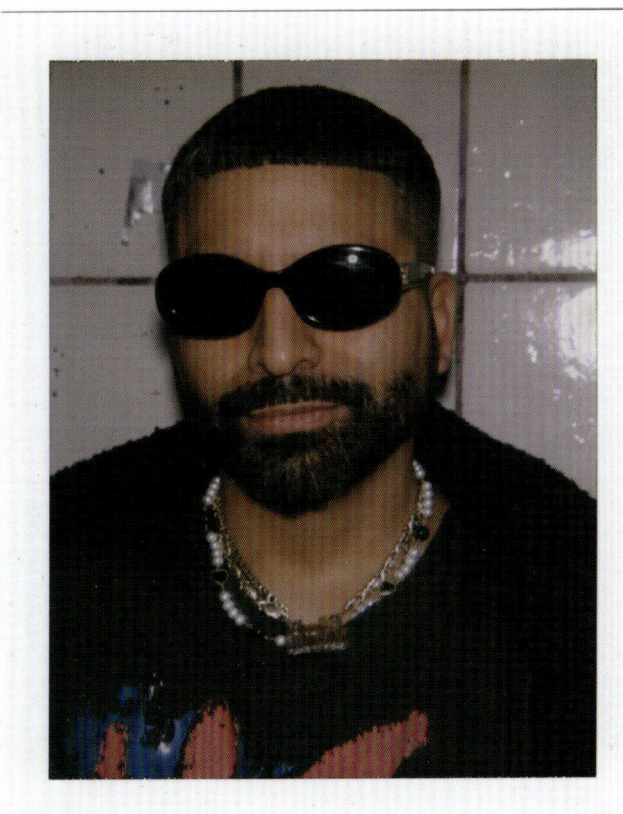

ANGELO BAQUE

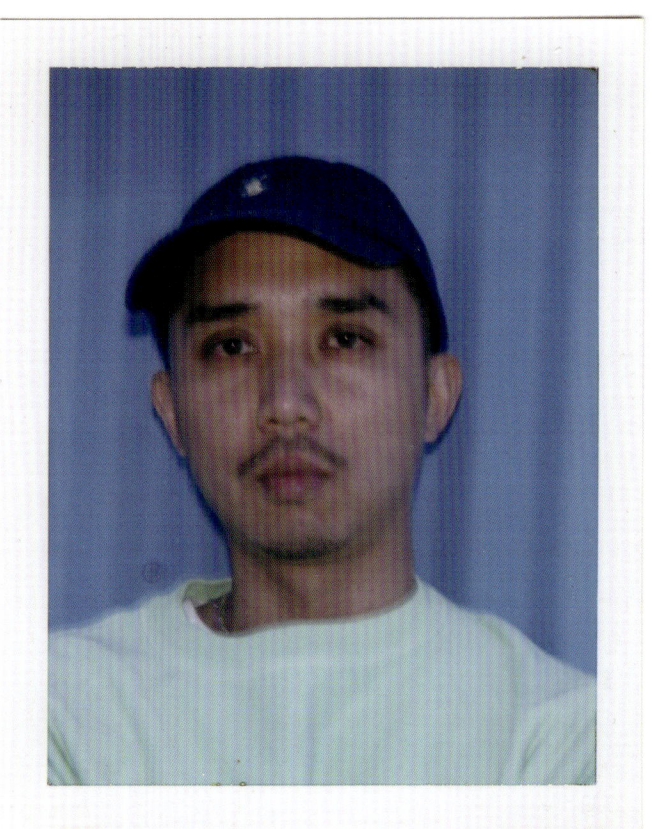

MICK MORENO

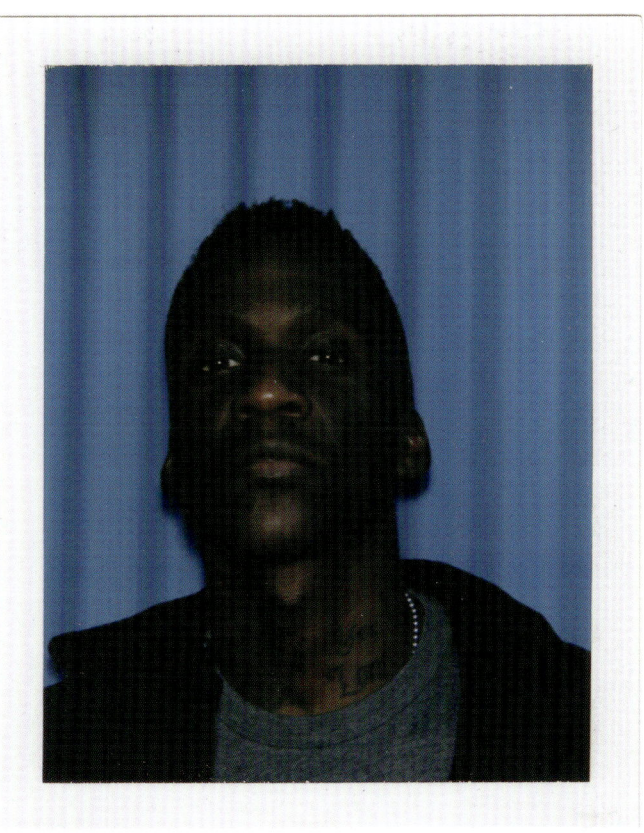

GENE THORNTON AKA NO MALICE

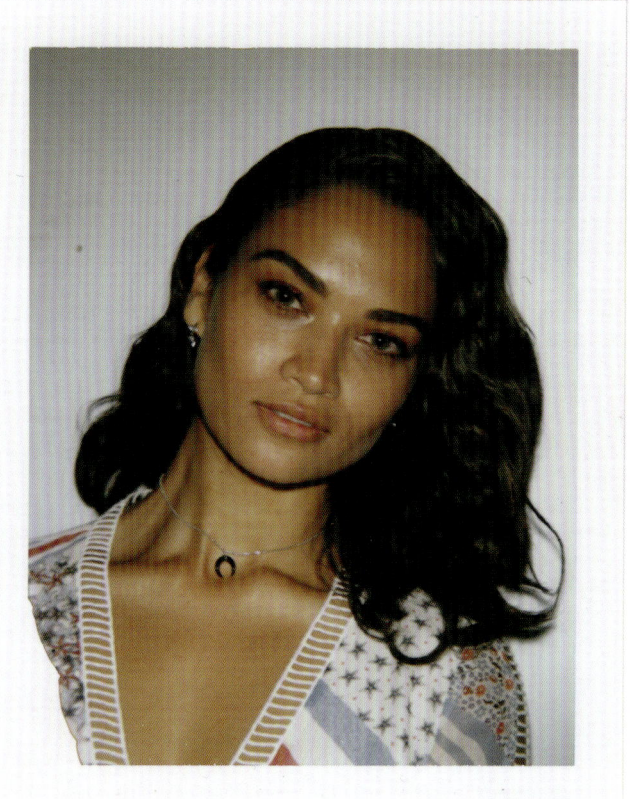

SHANINA SHAIK

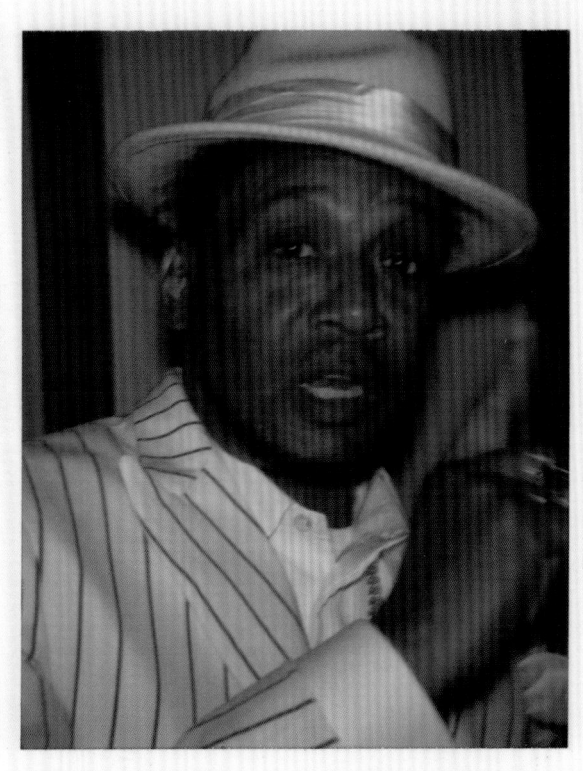

SUPER CAT

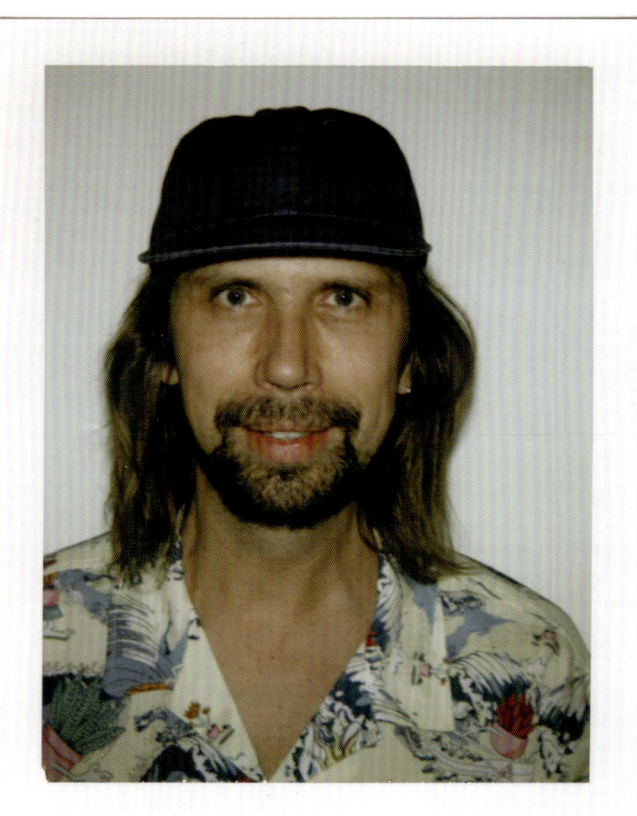

PEDRO WINTER AKA BUSY P - ED BANGER

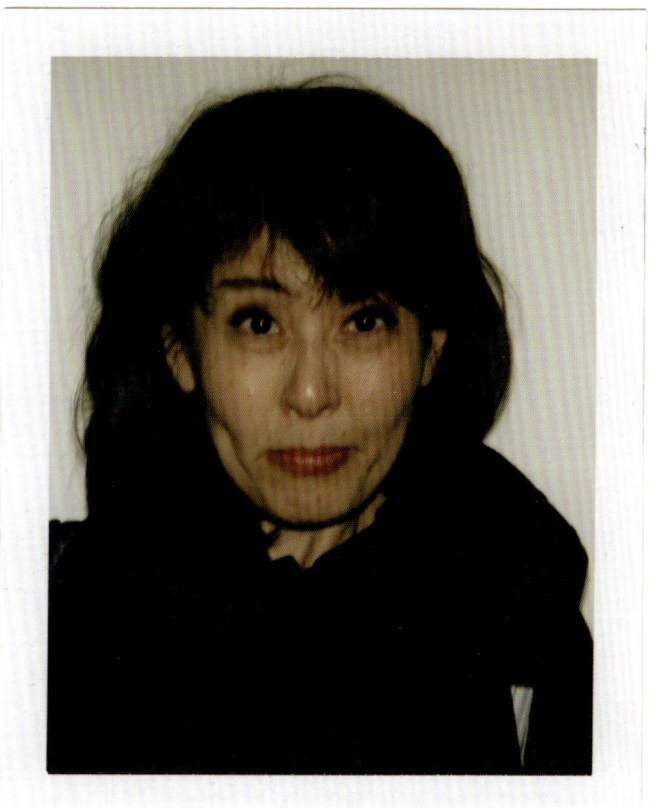

YURIA SHIO

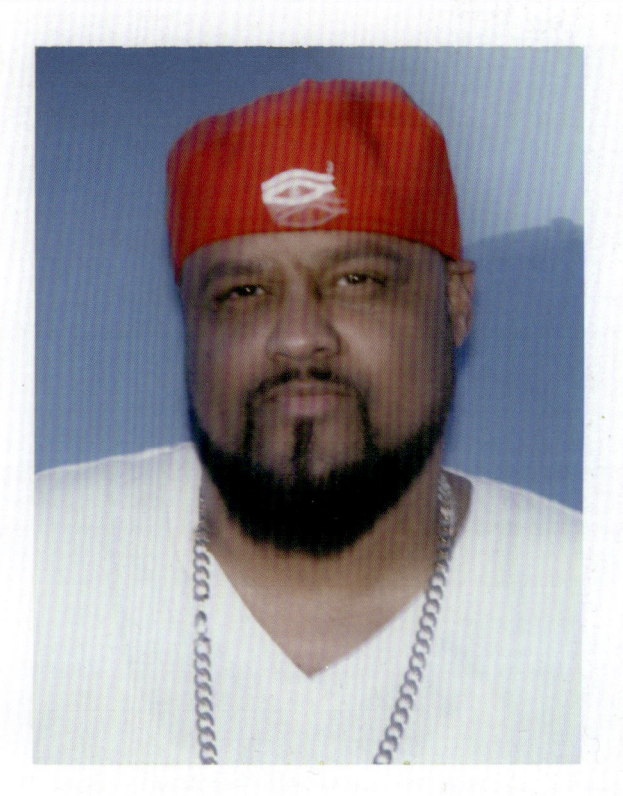

PRESIDENT PUNCH - TDE

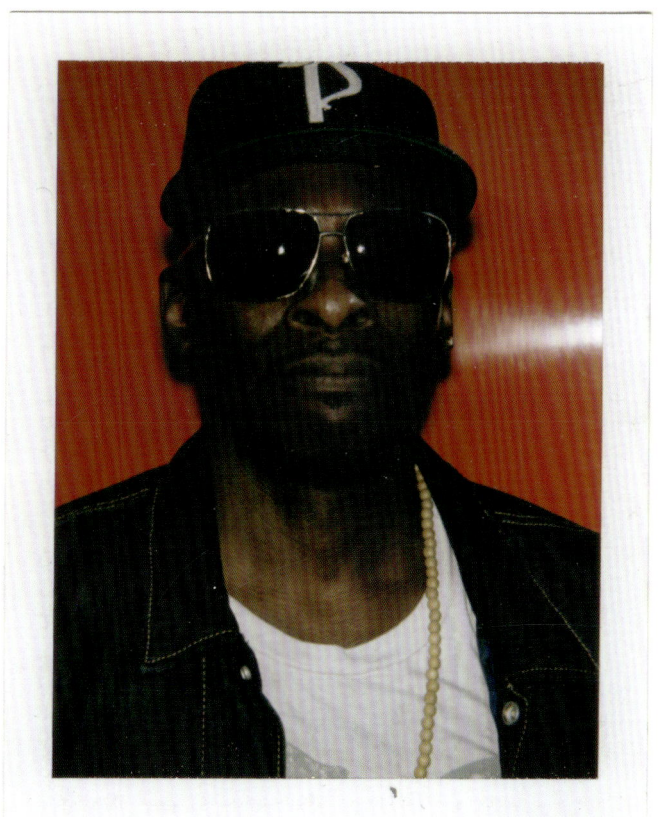

PETE ROCK

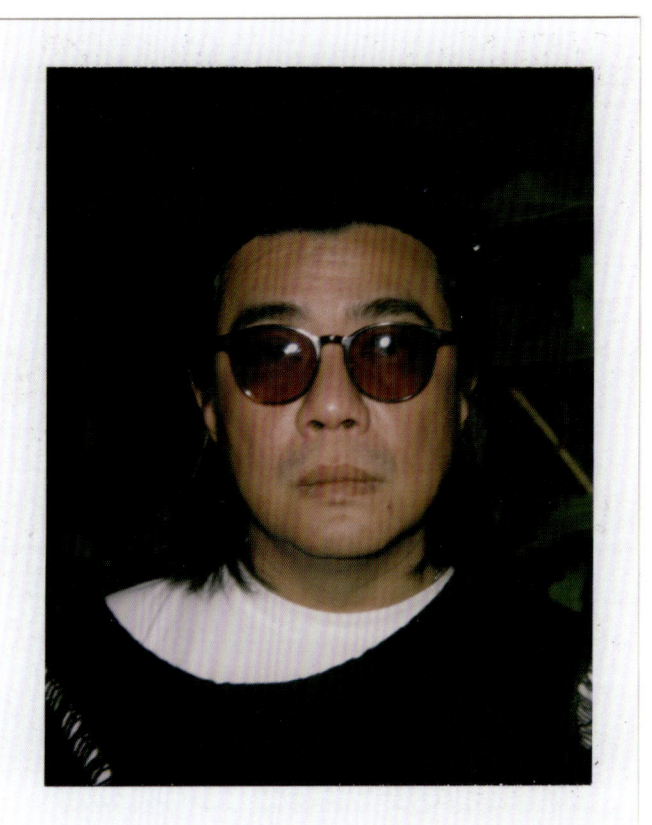

EARN CHEN

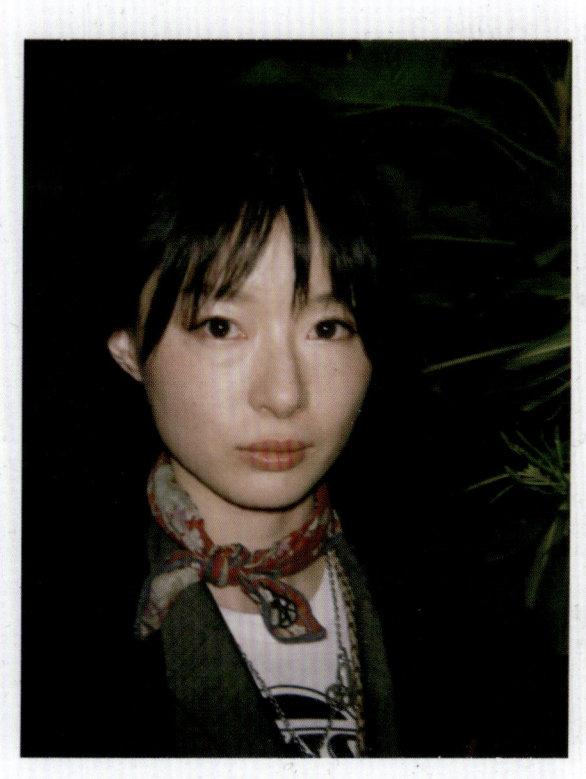

NICOLETTE

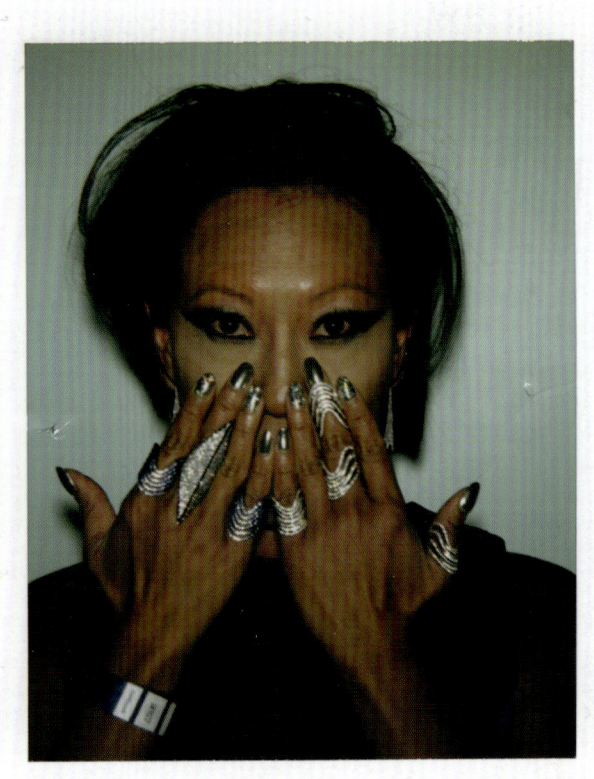

LYNN BAN

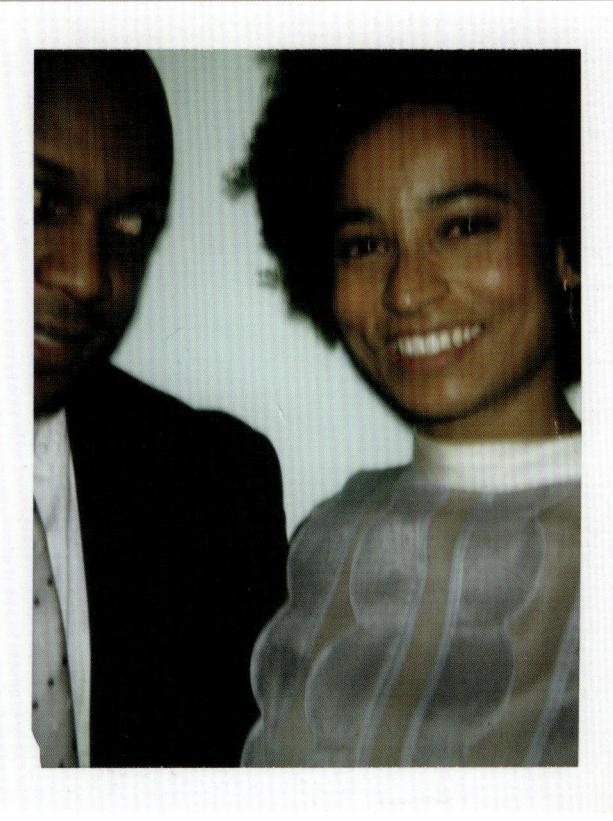

HANK WILLIS THOMAS & RUJEKO HOCKLEY

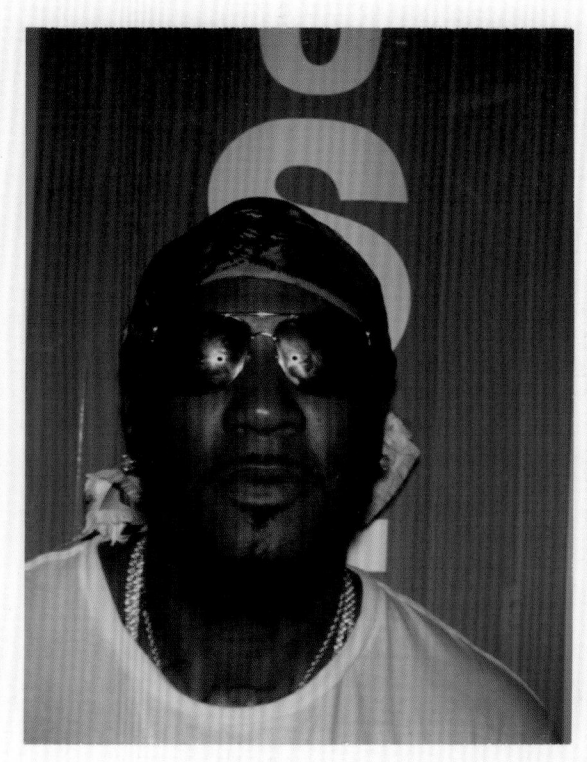

JEEZY

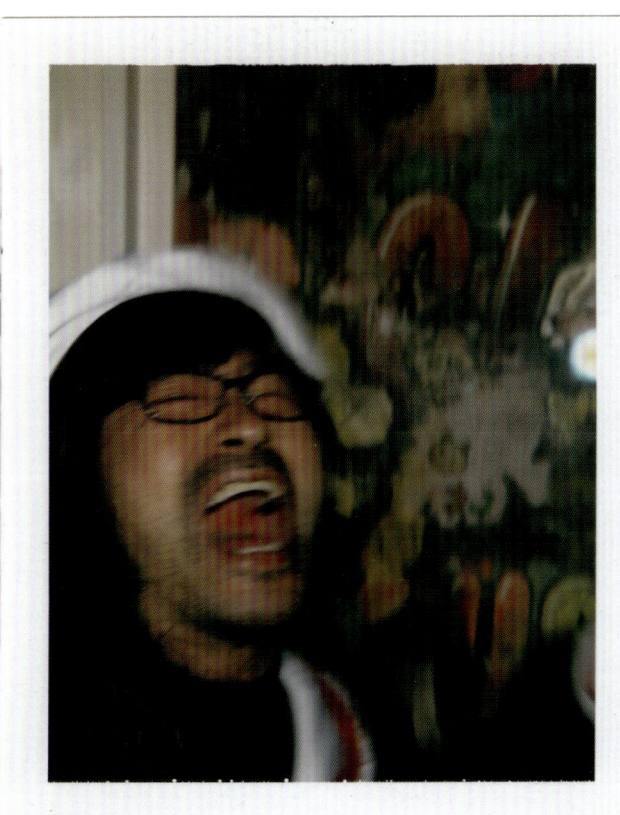

MR. YANEN

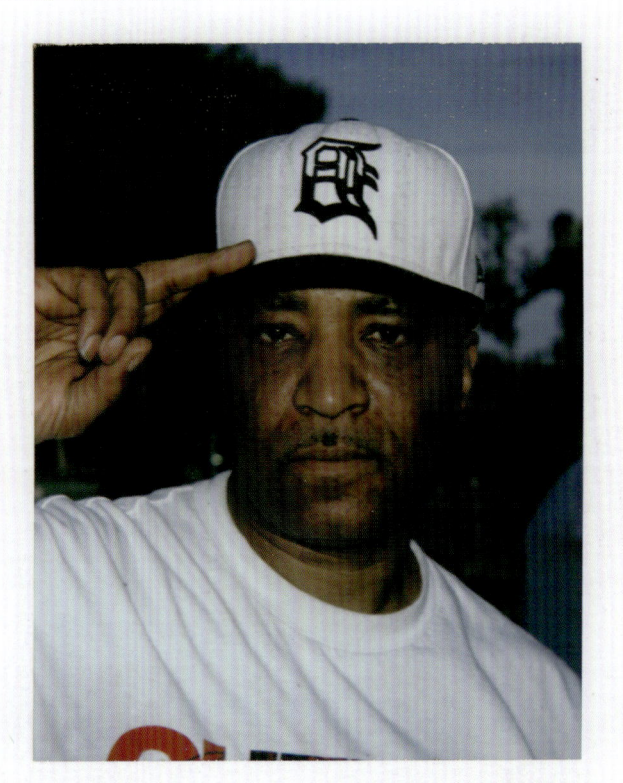

MARLEY MARL

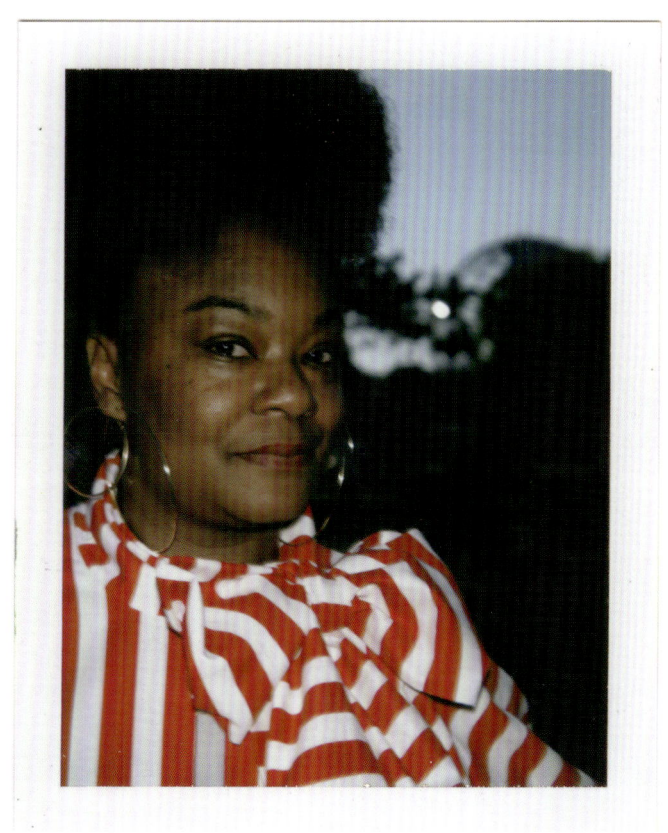

ROXANNE SHANTÉ

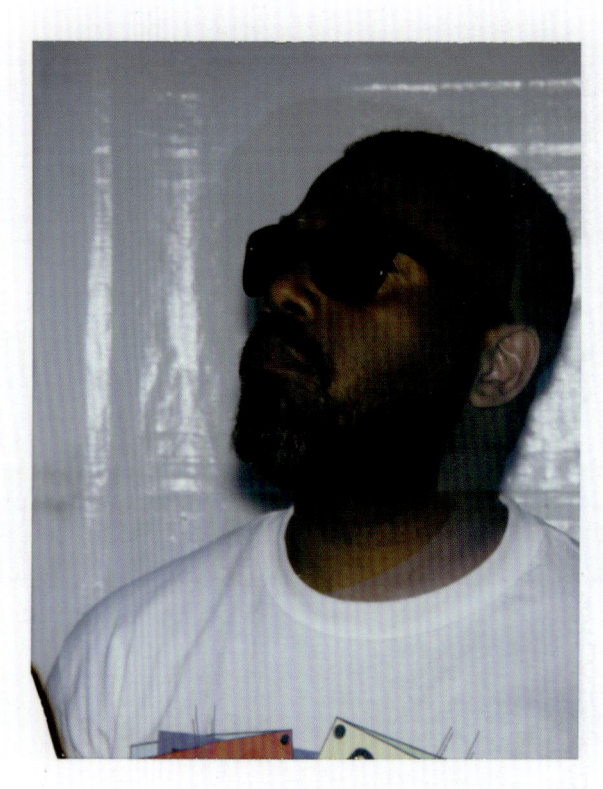

RASHAD SMITH

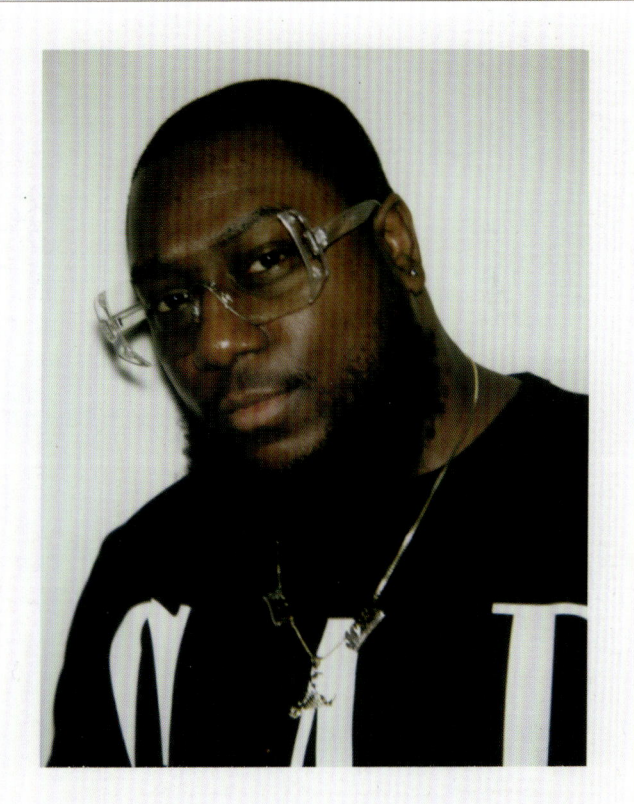

JASON SCOTT HENDERSON

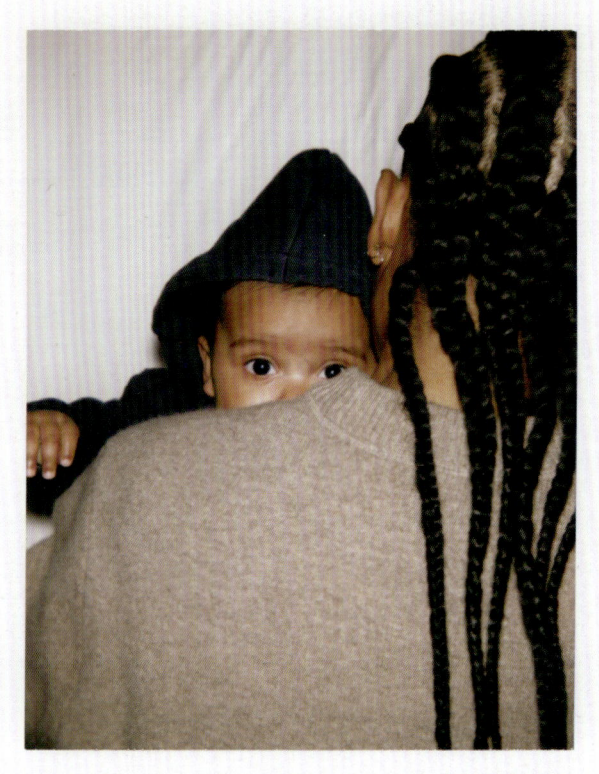

RHODES & JACKIE HOLLAND

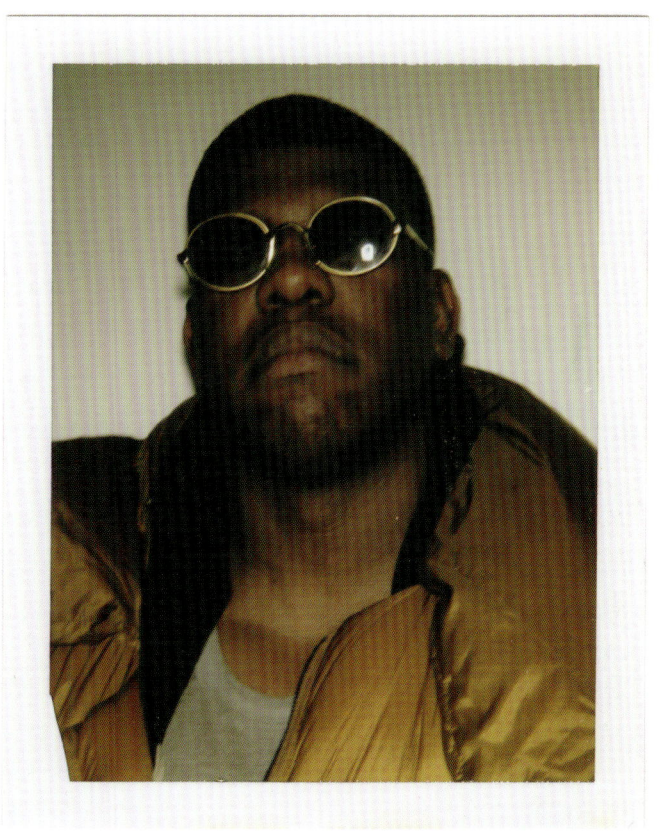

JOHN GRAY - GHETTO GASTRO

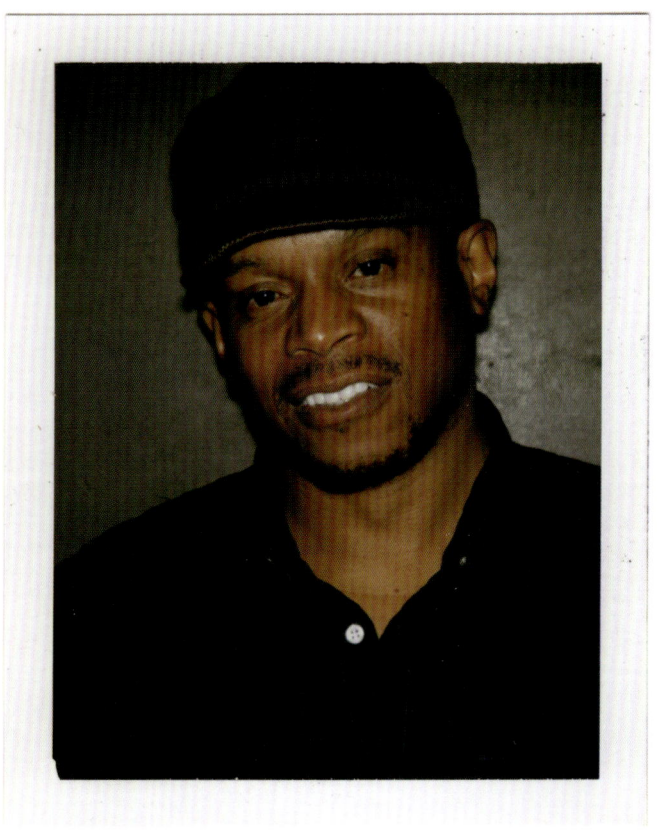

SWAY

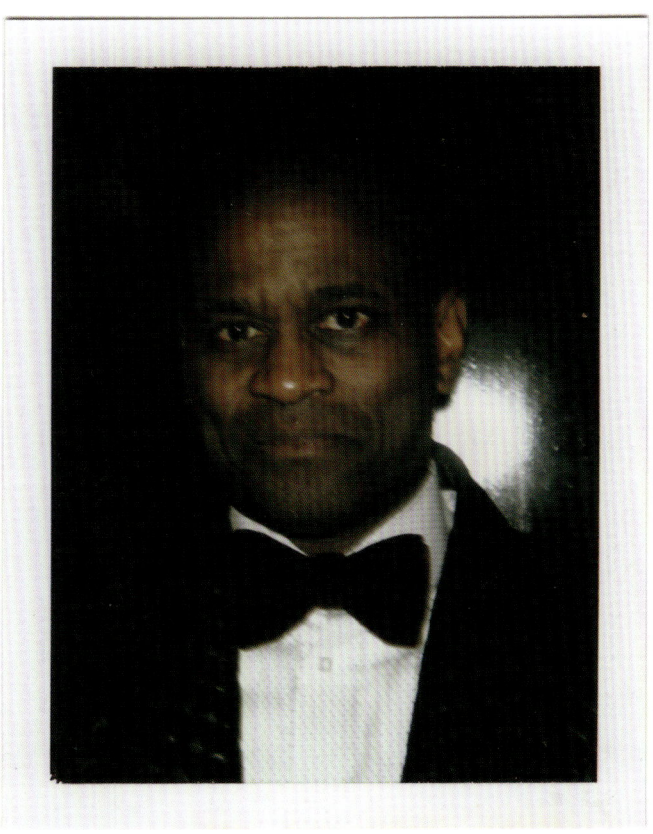

CHAKA WILSON

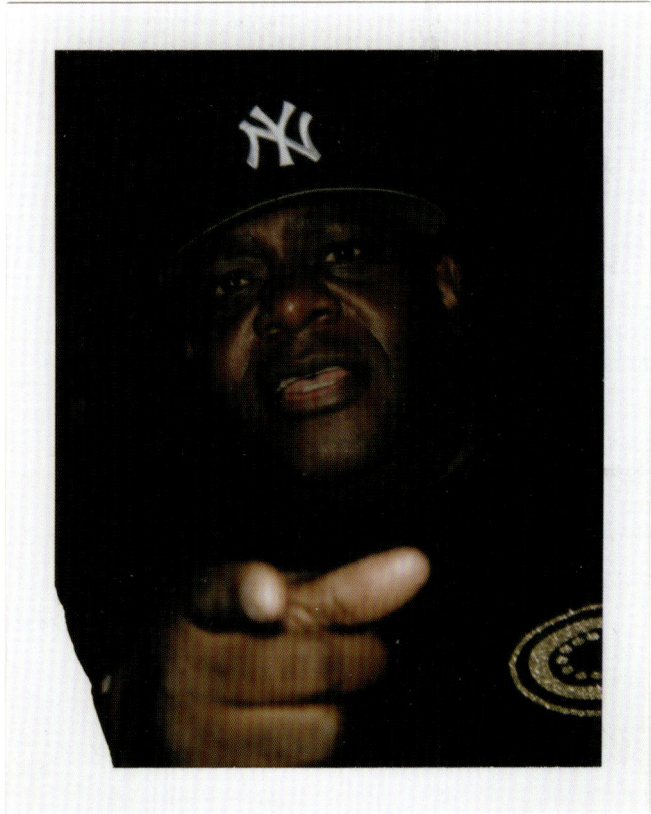

CHUCK CHILLOUT

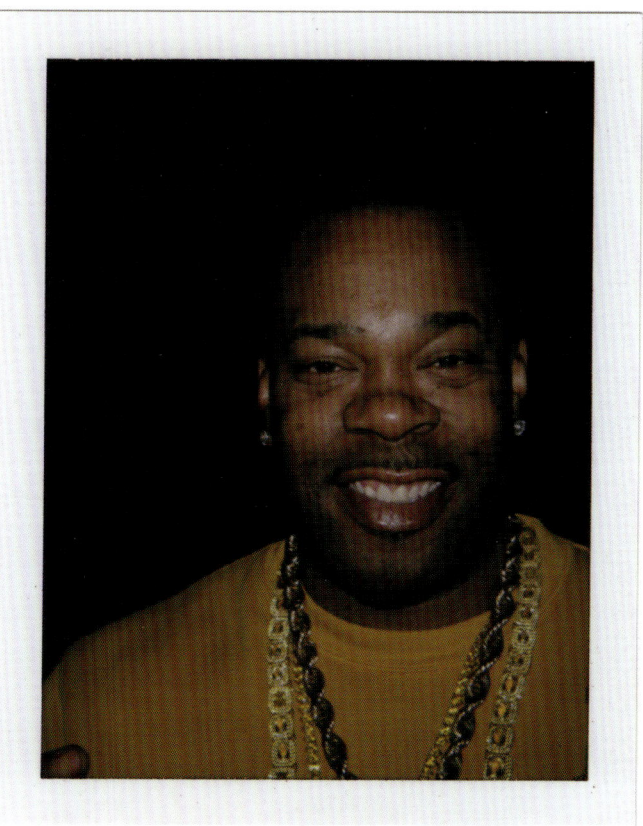

BUSTA RHYMES

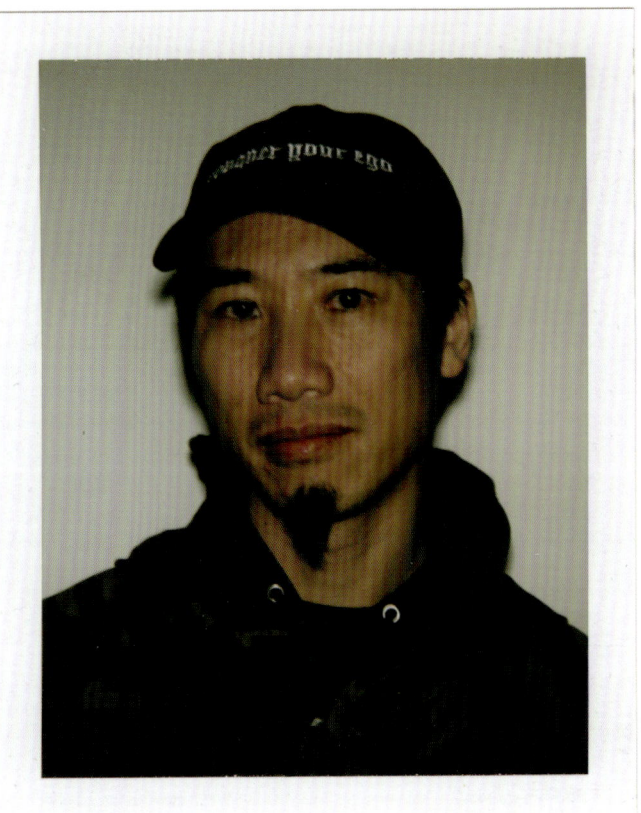

JULIAN WENG

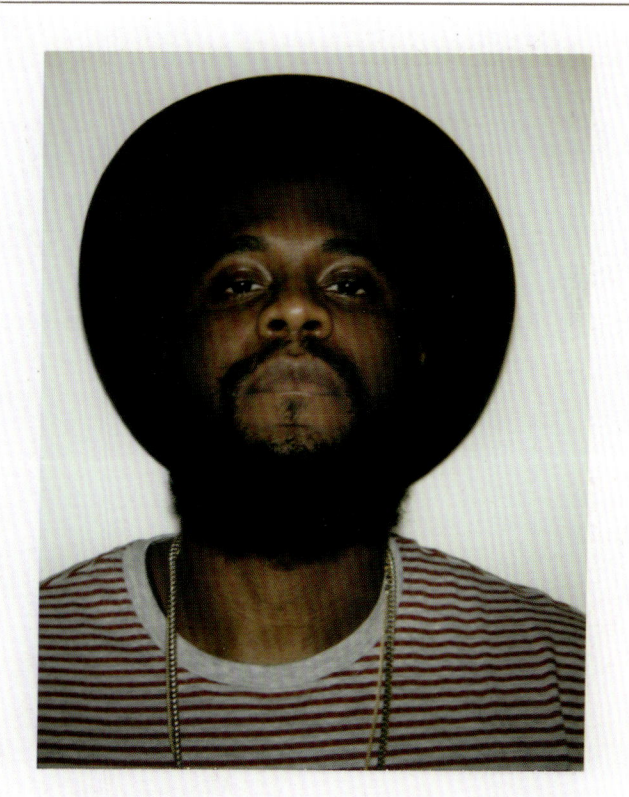

BIG KRIT

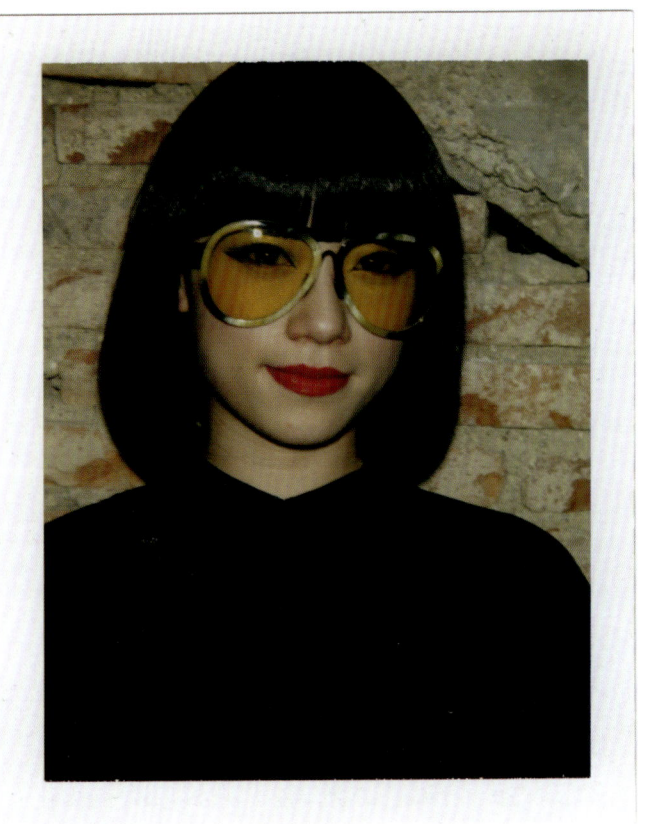

SUKI WONG

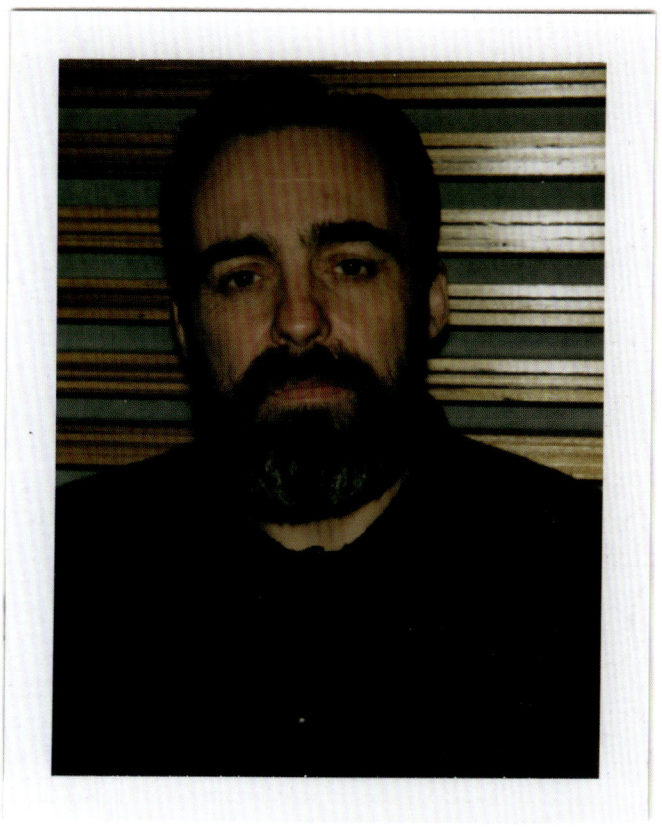

DAN DOYLE

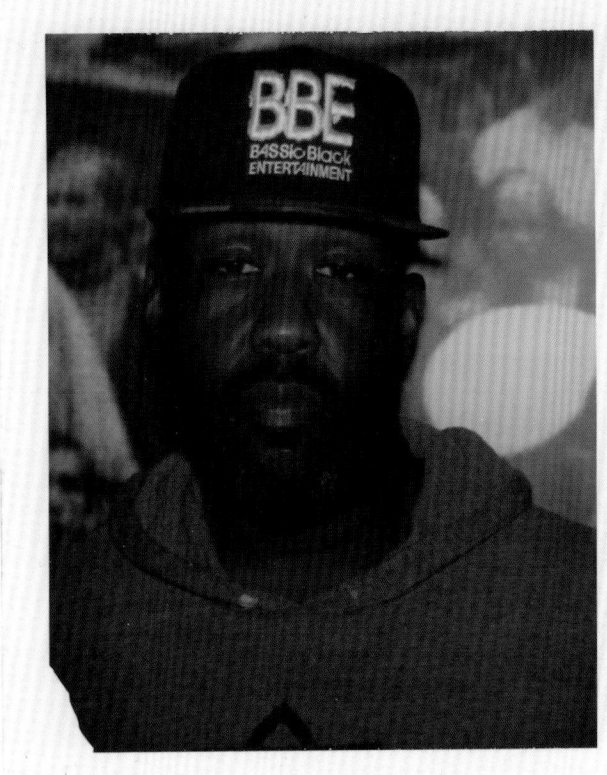

ADAM BLACKSTONE

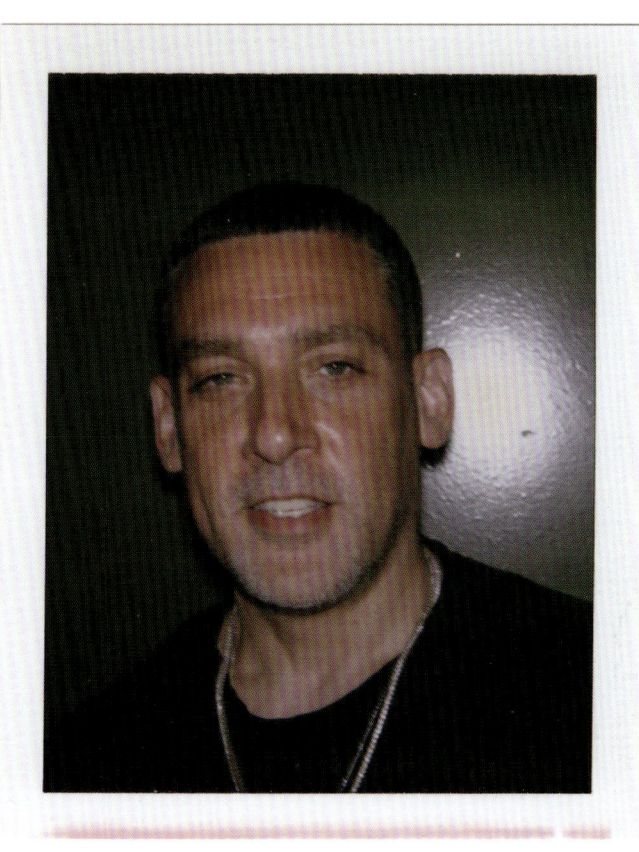

SCRAM JONES

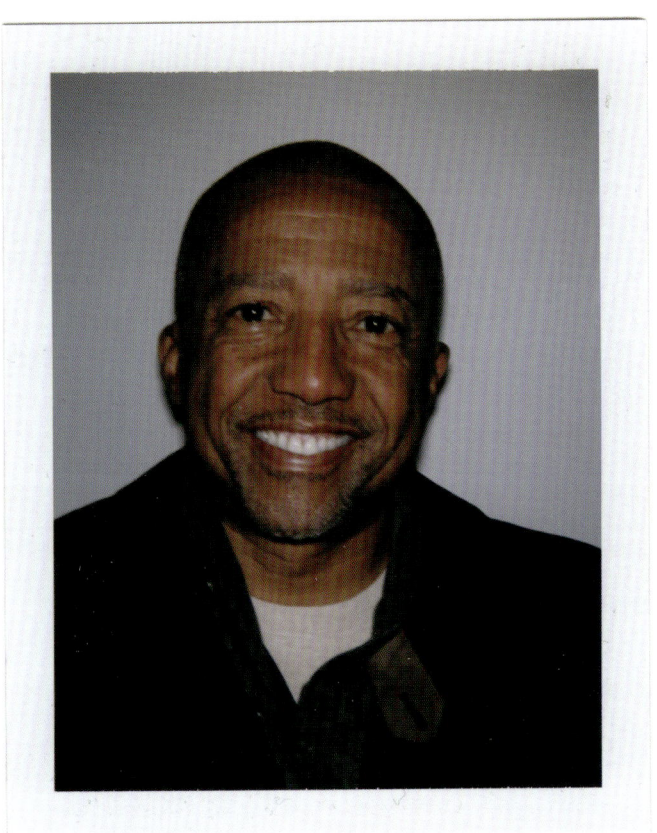

KEVIN LILES

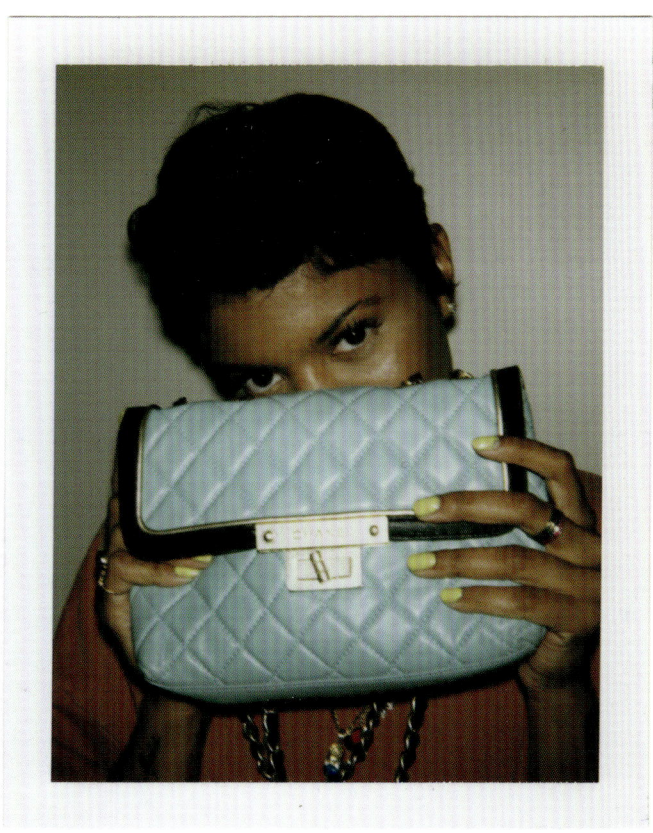

RENELL MEDRANO

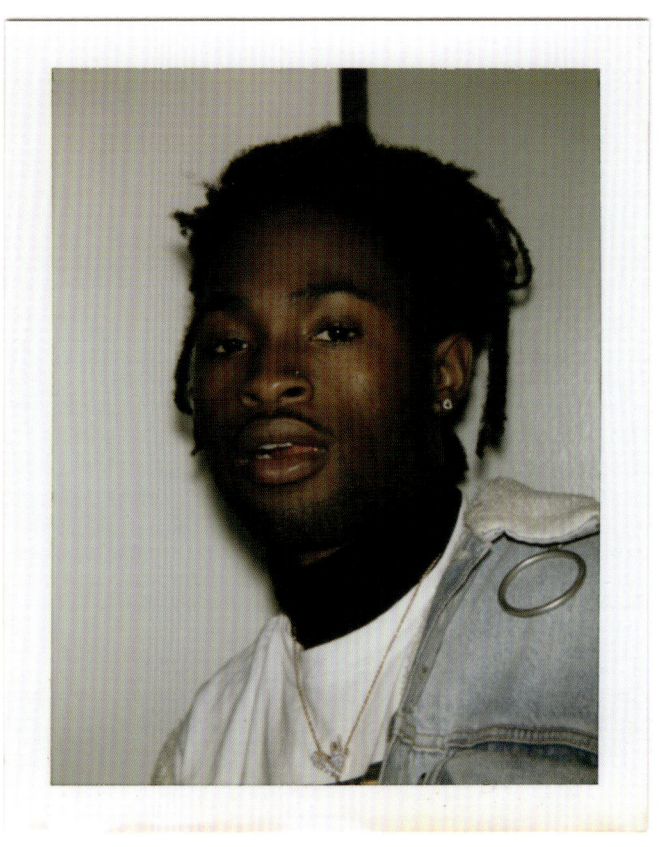

JUSTICE BAIDEN

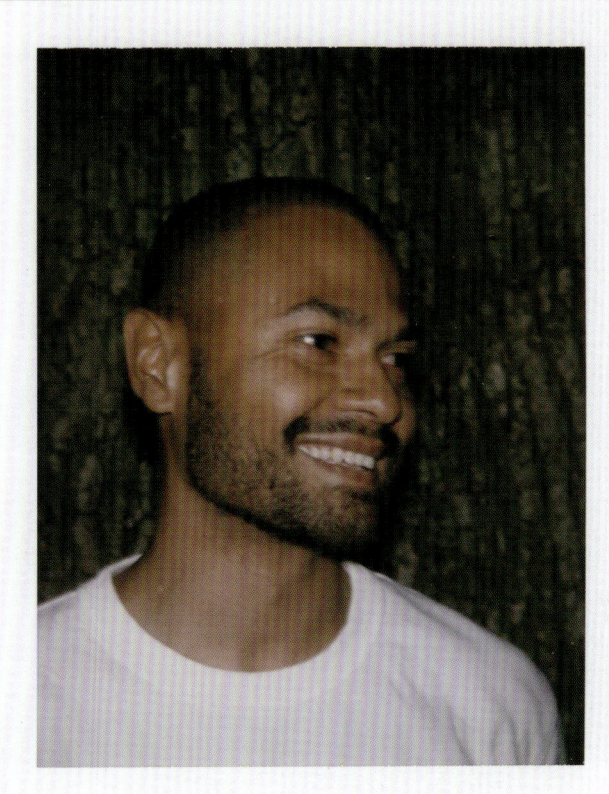

BRANDYNE LACKLAND

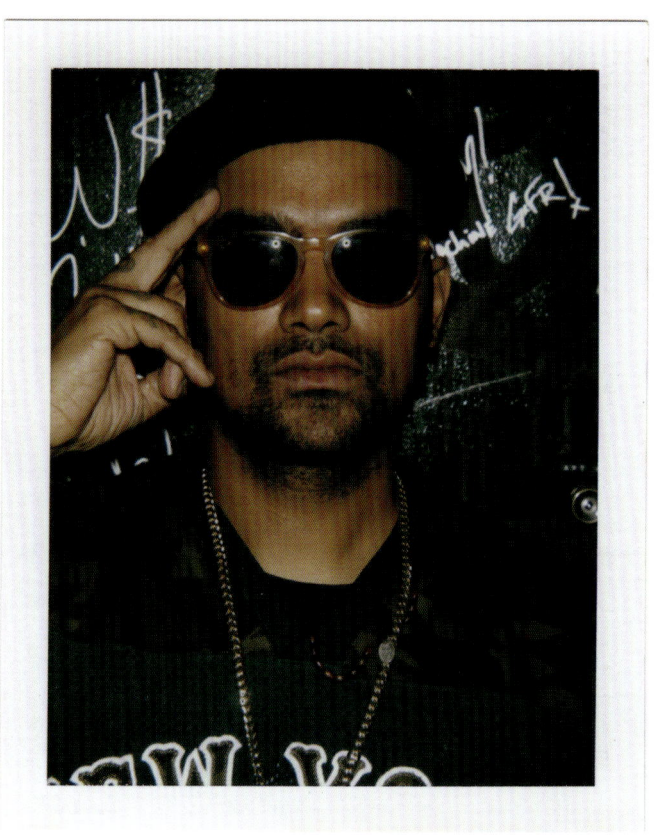

MOON MORONTA - APT. 4B

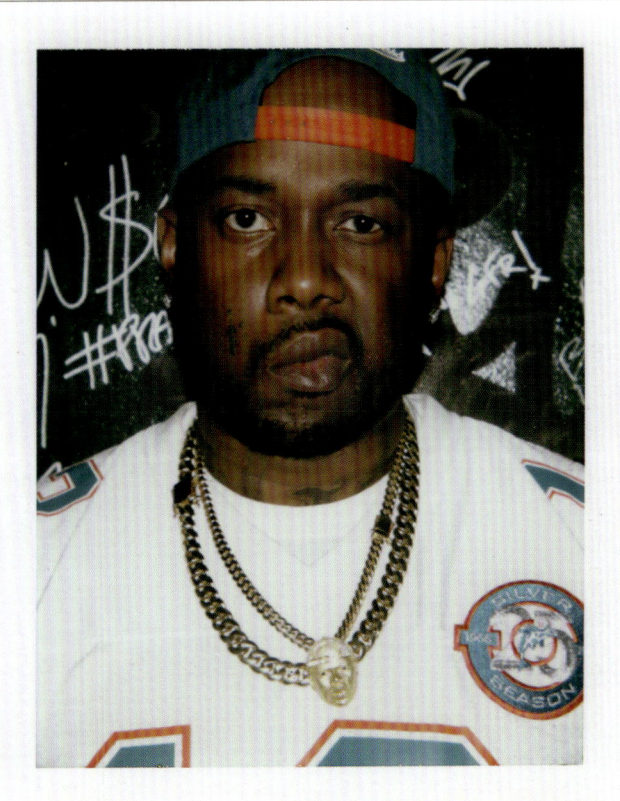

CONWAY THE MACHINE

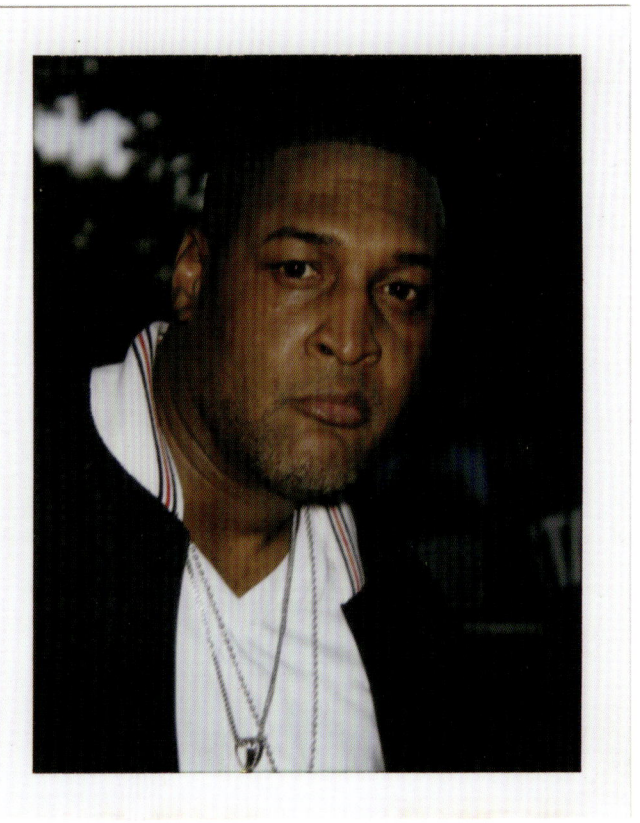

NEEK THE EXOTIC

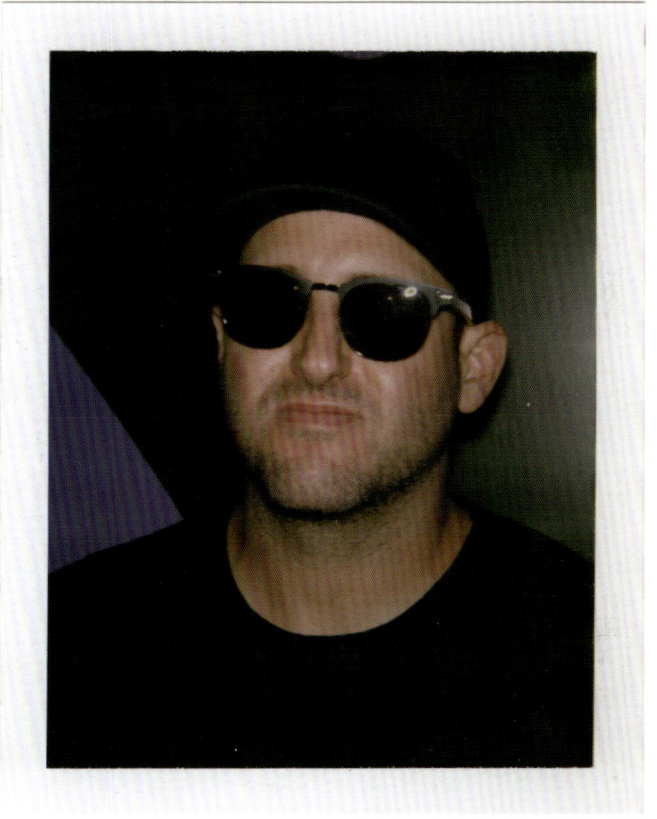

AARON LEVANT

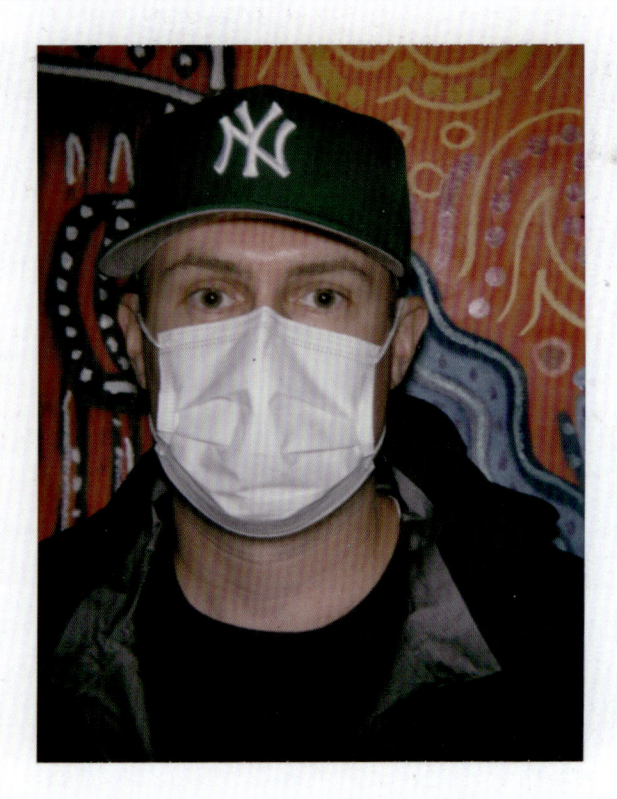

SNOEMAN

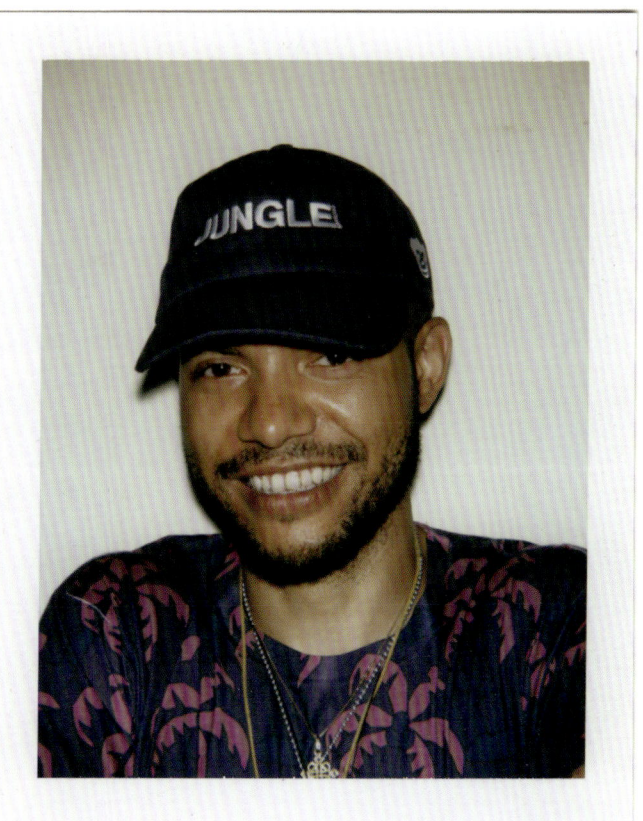

MONSIEUR MIKEY

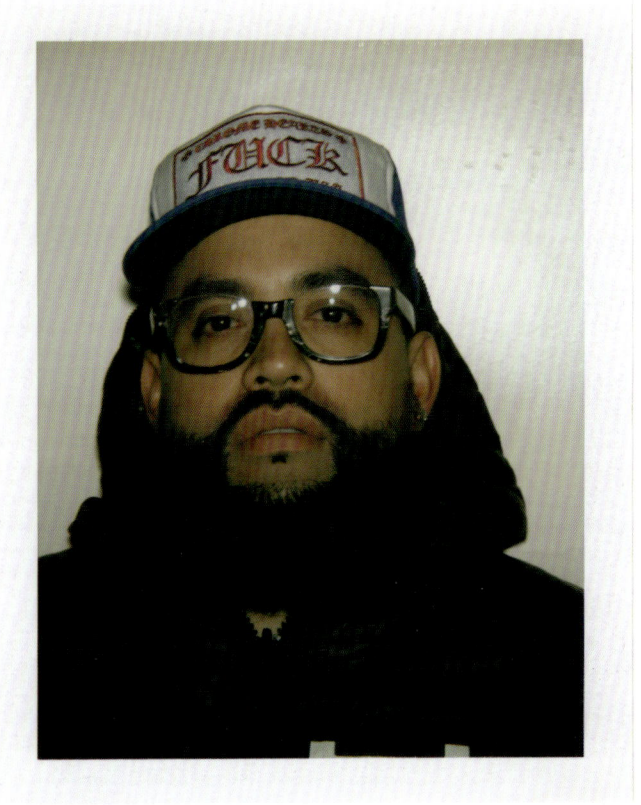

DIEGO

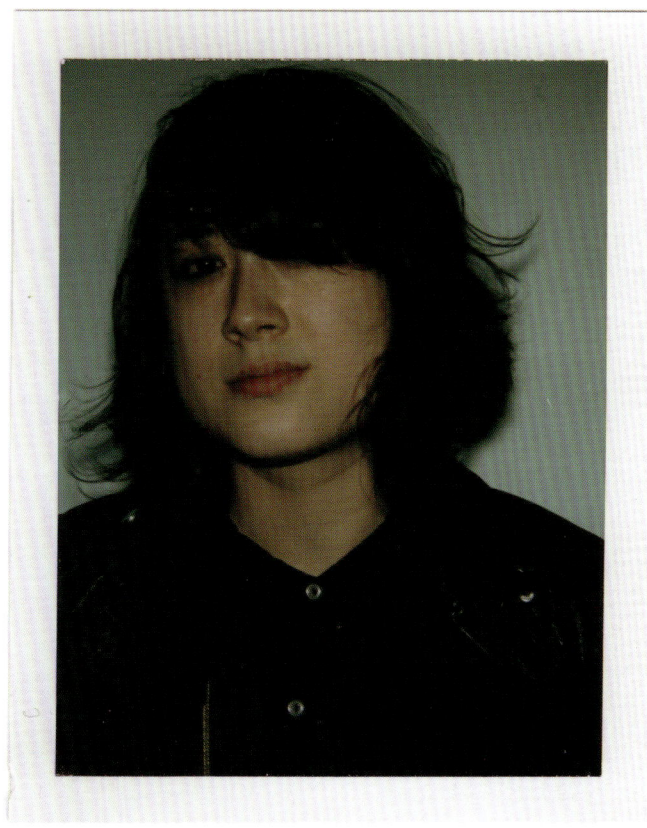

KIMI

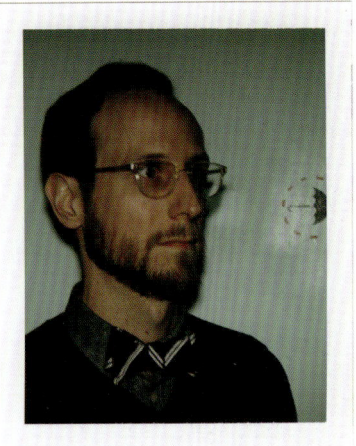

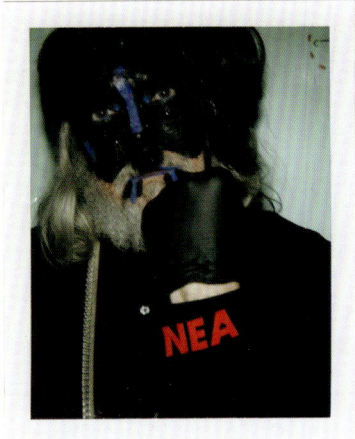

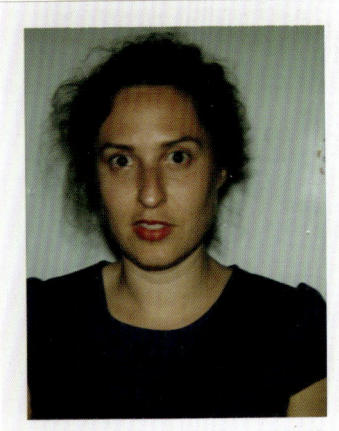

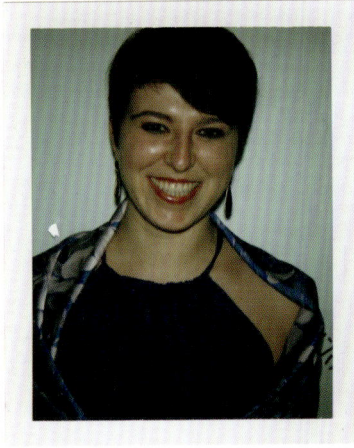

ADAM TOMIAK   ???

JULIA ROTHMAN   RUTHIE MACMANY

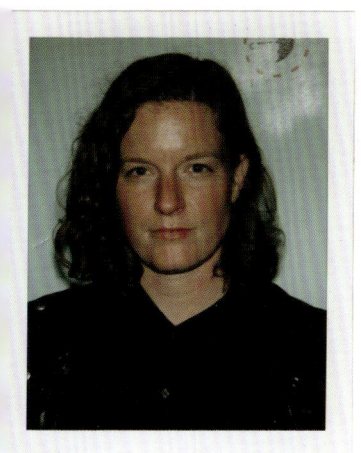

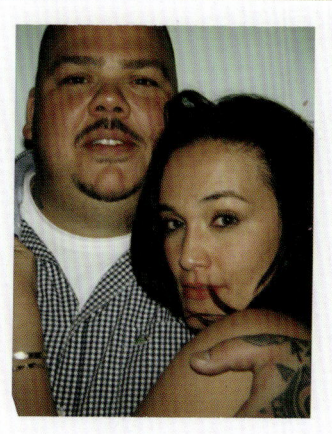

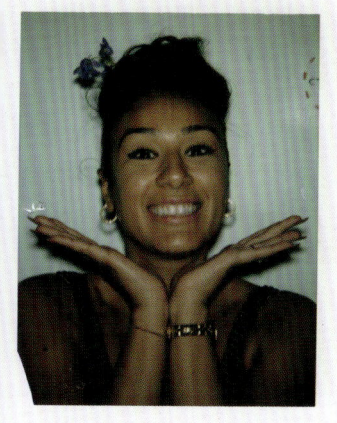

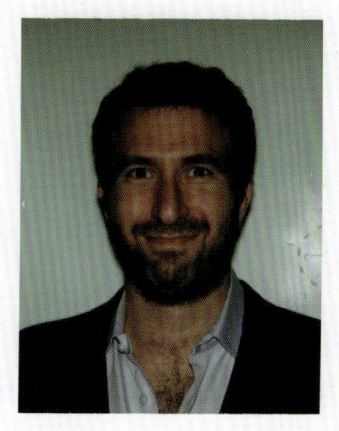

LANE SANDERS

AHLAM JAOUI

BERT & TARA KRAK

NATHANIEL HOCHMAN

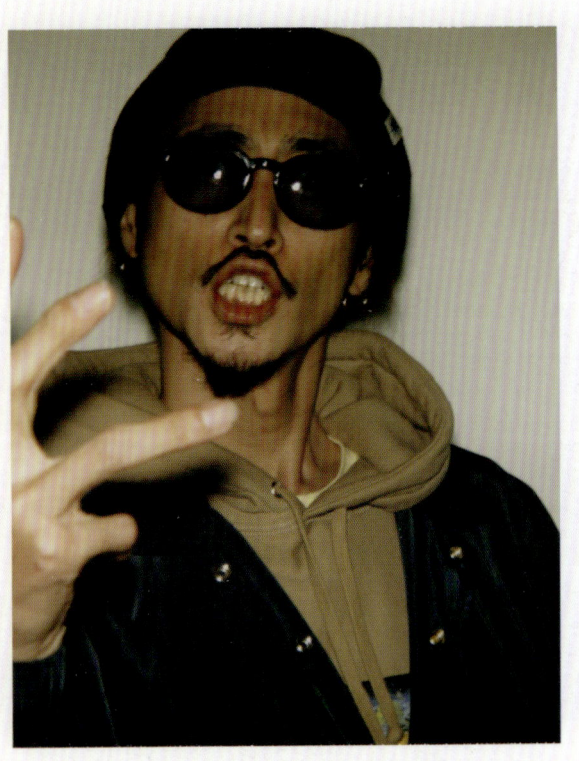

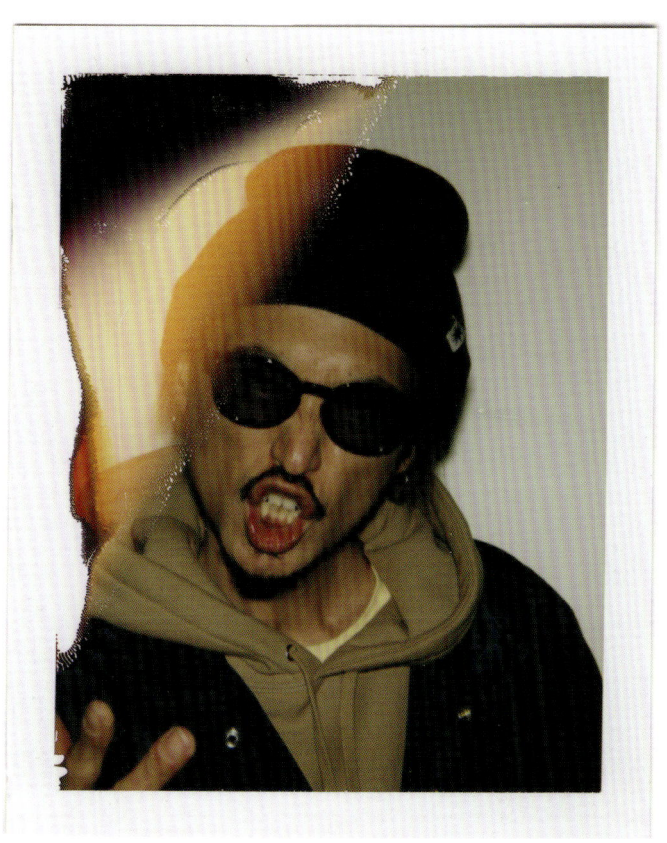

YOSUKE KUBOZUKA

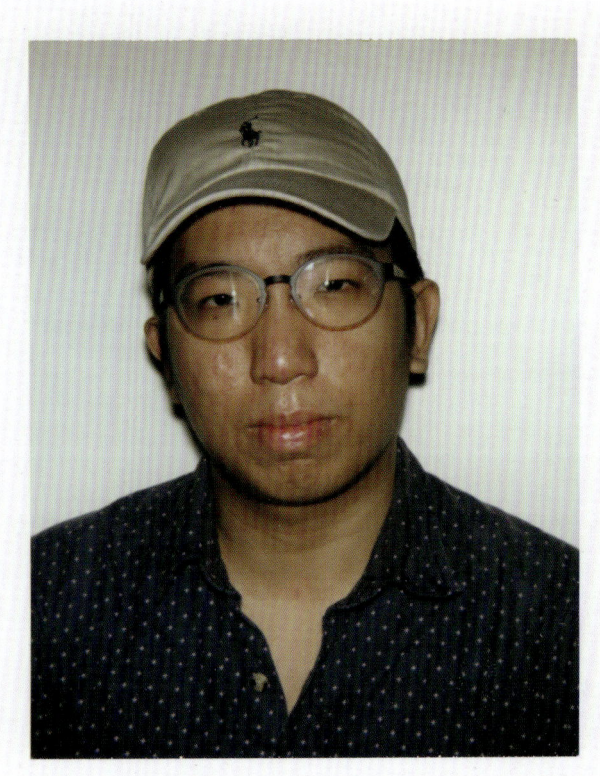

IAN LIM

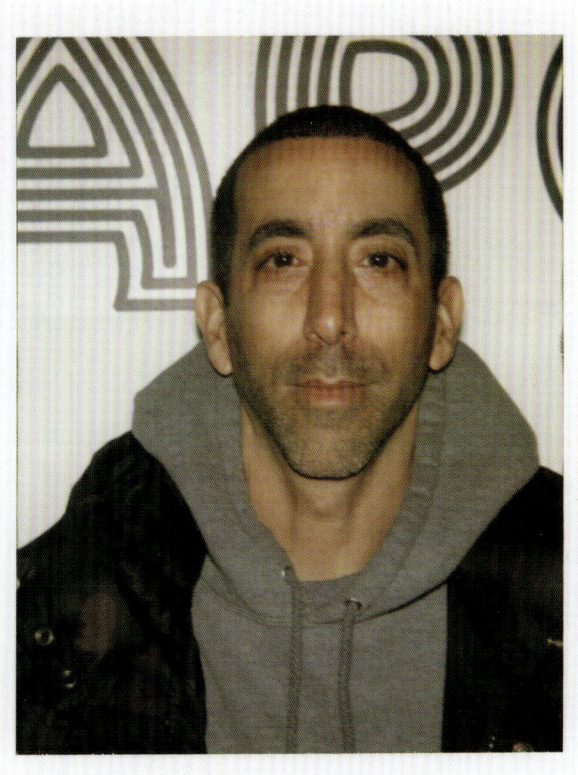

DRU HA

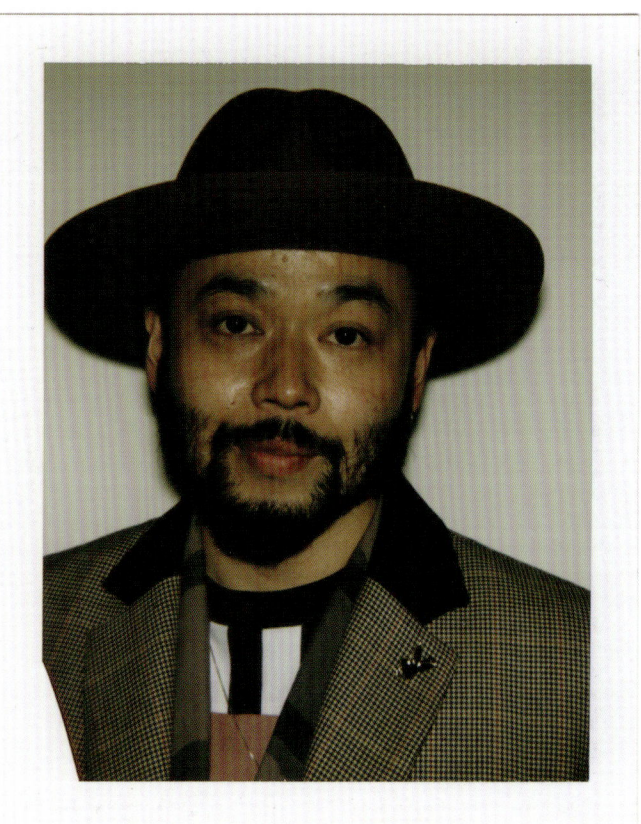

POGGY THE MAN

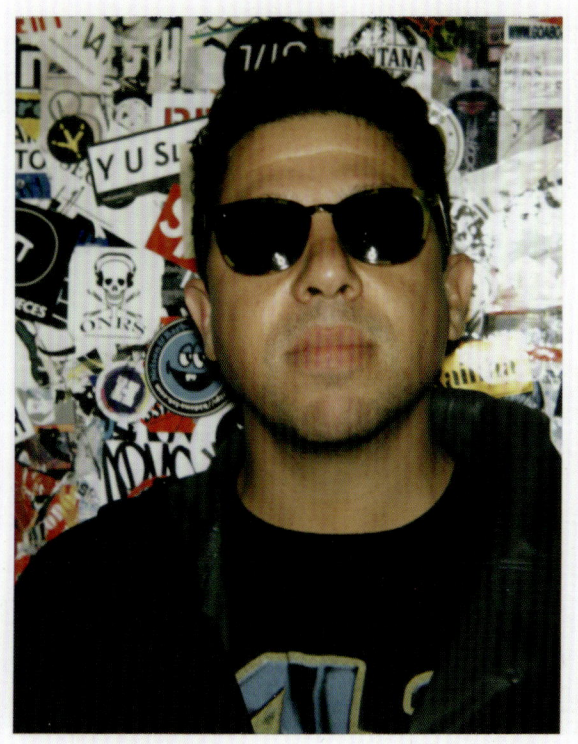

COSMO BAKER

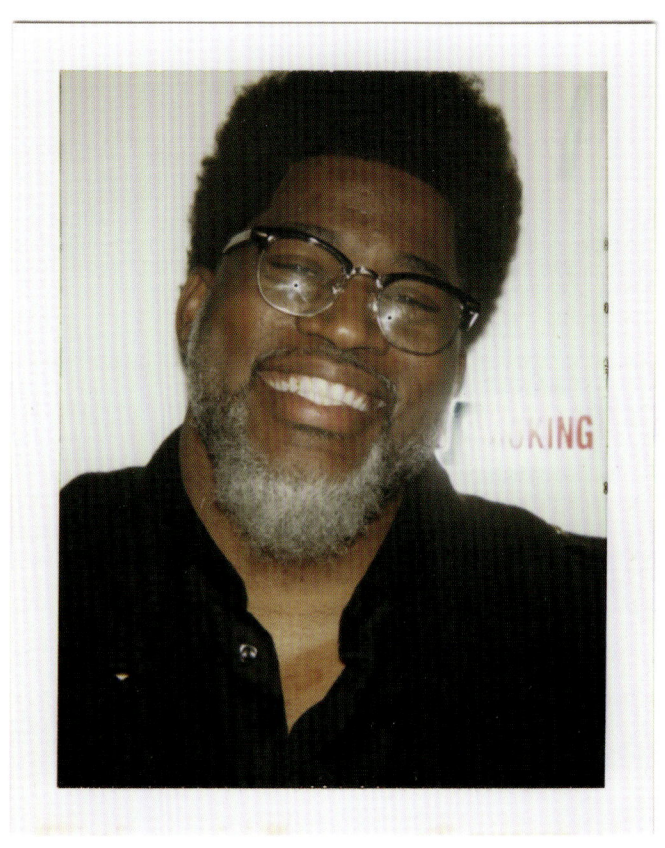

DAVID BANNER

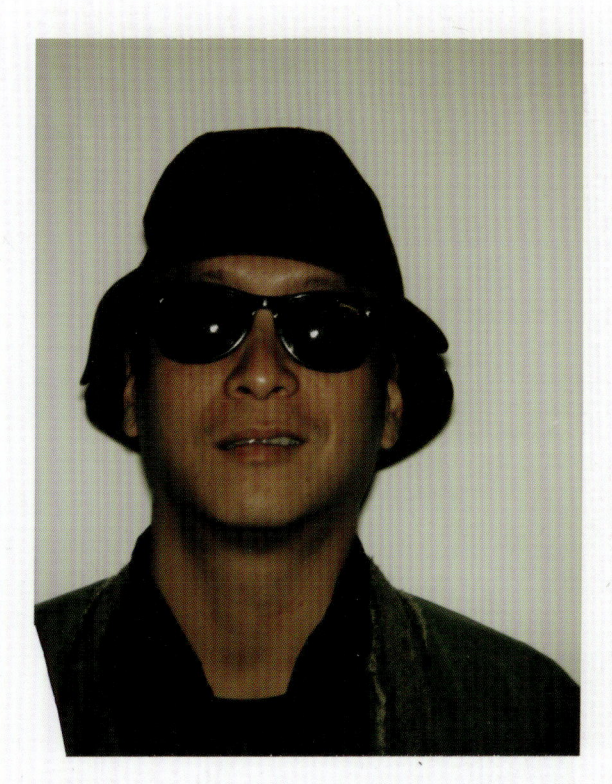

DAVID LIN

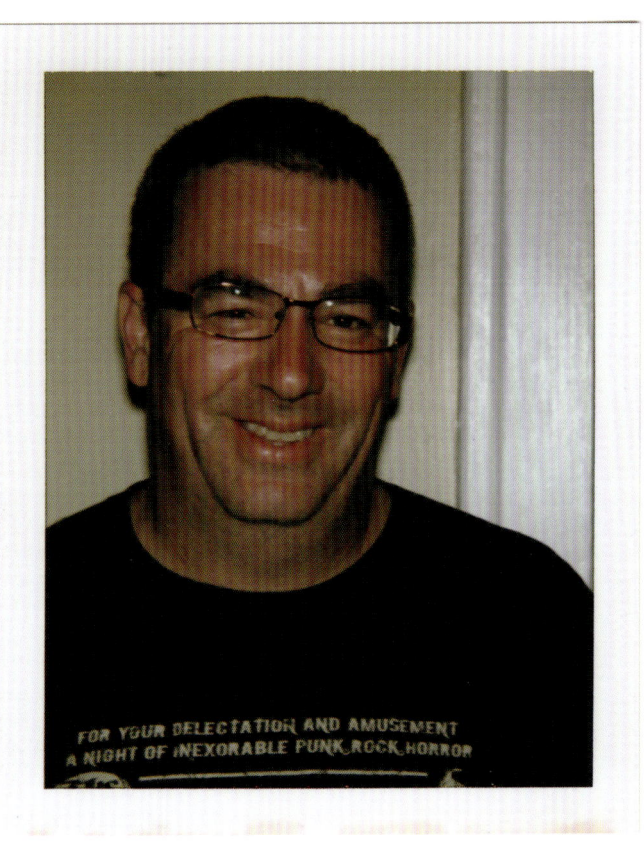

ROGER CLARK

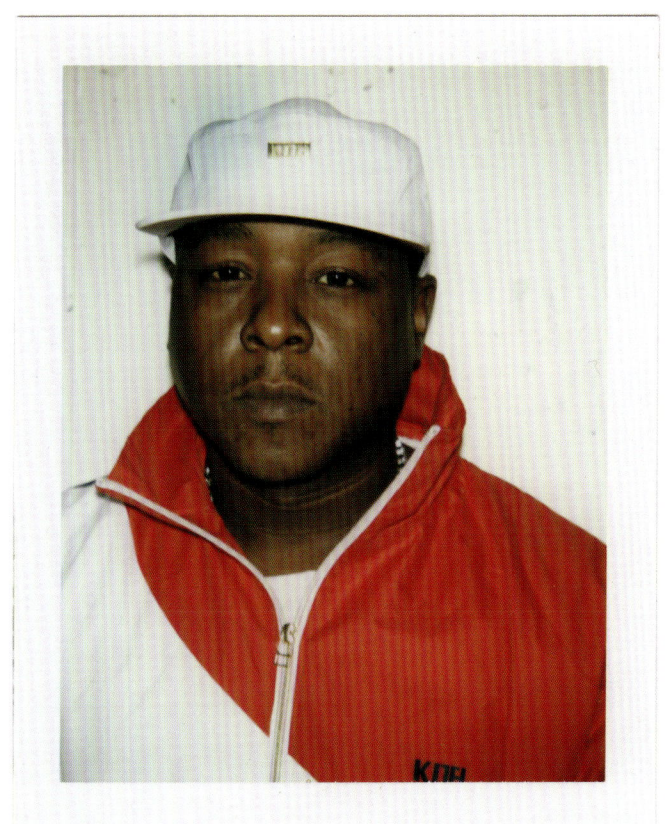

JADAKISS

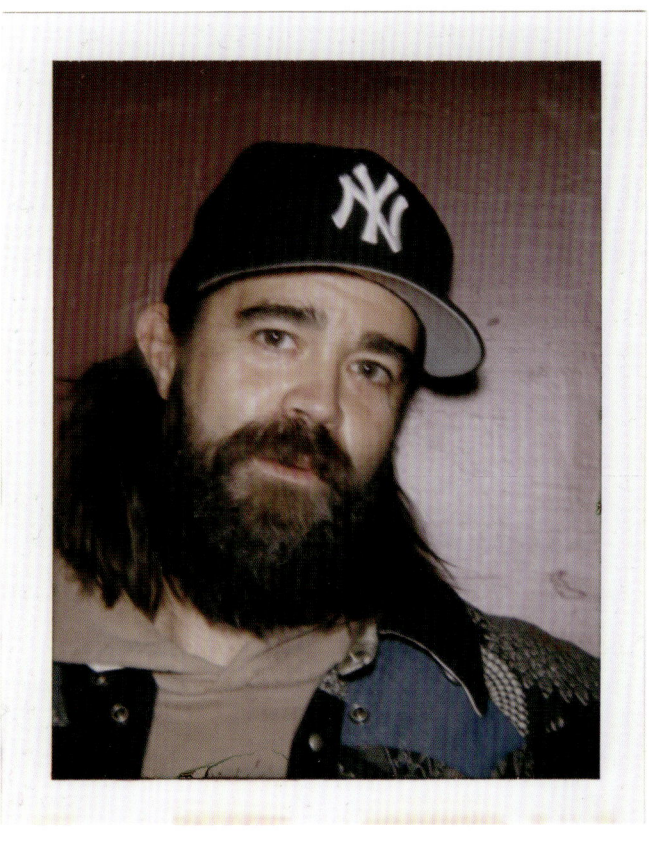

BROCK KORSAN AKA BROCKY MARCIANO

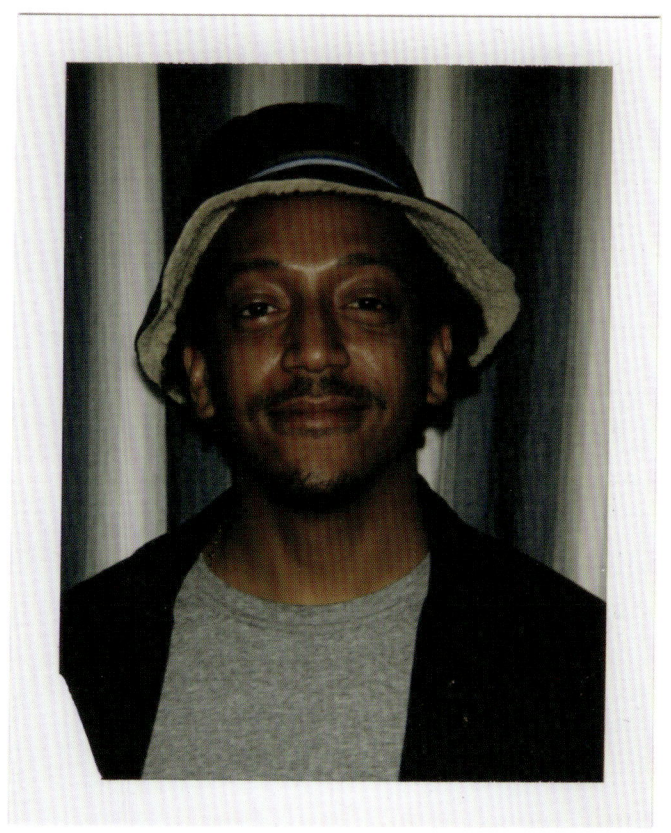

DAVE JULY

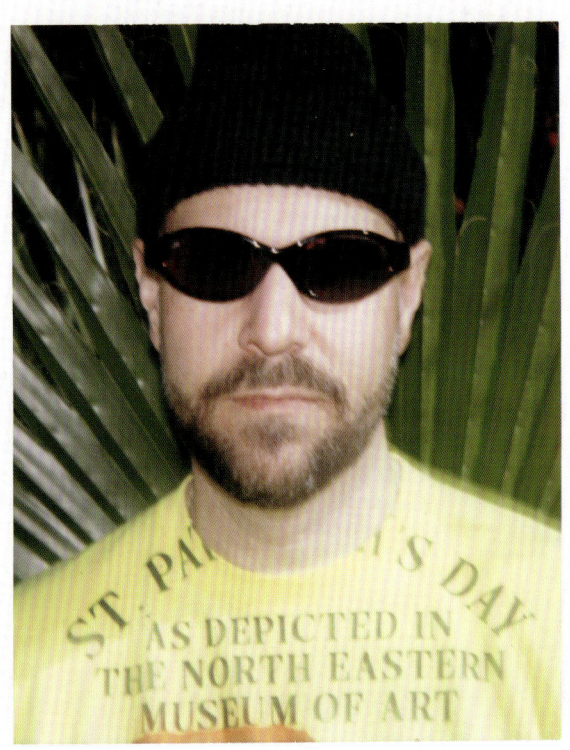

ALEX JAMES

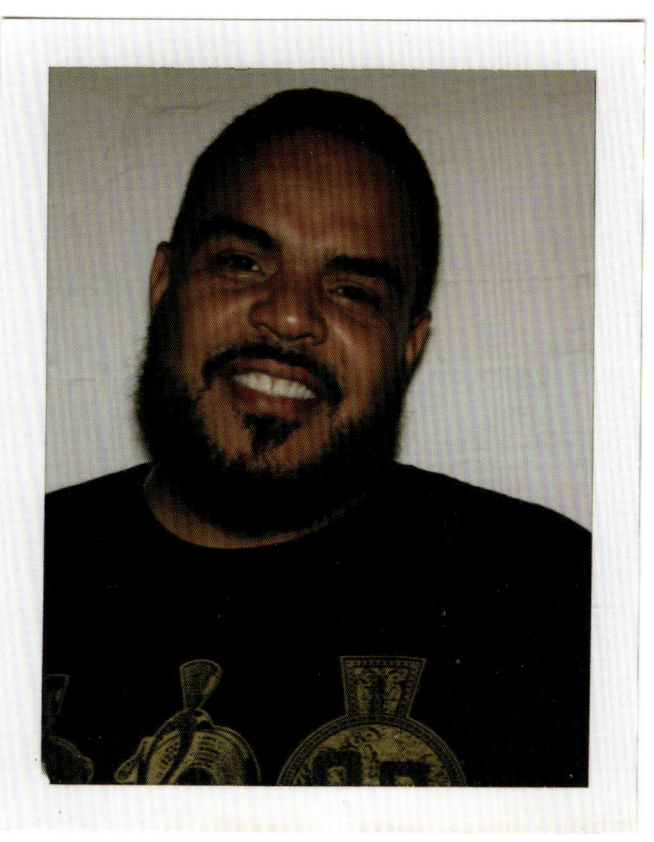

DJ ENUFF

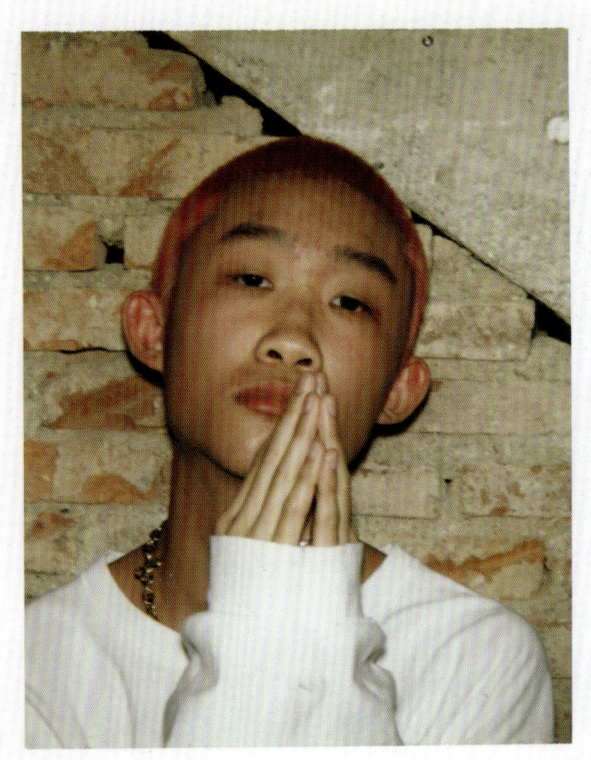

JERRY

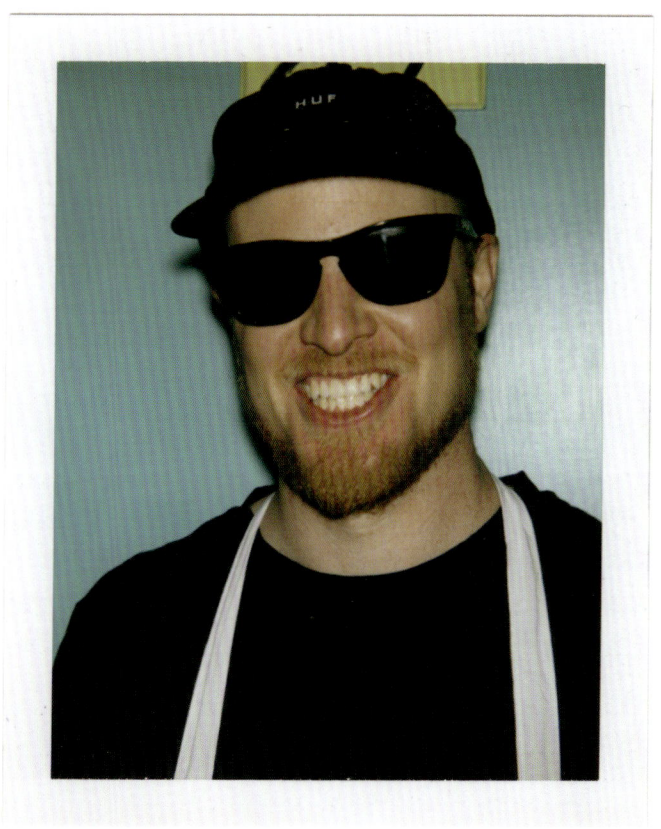

SKRATCH BASTID

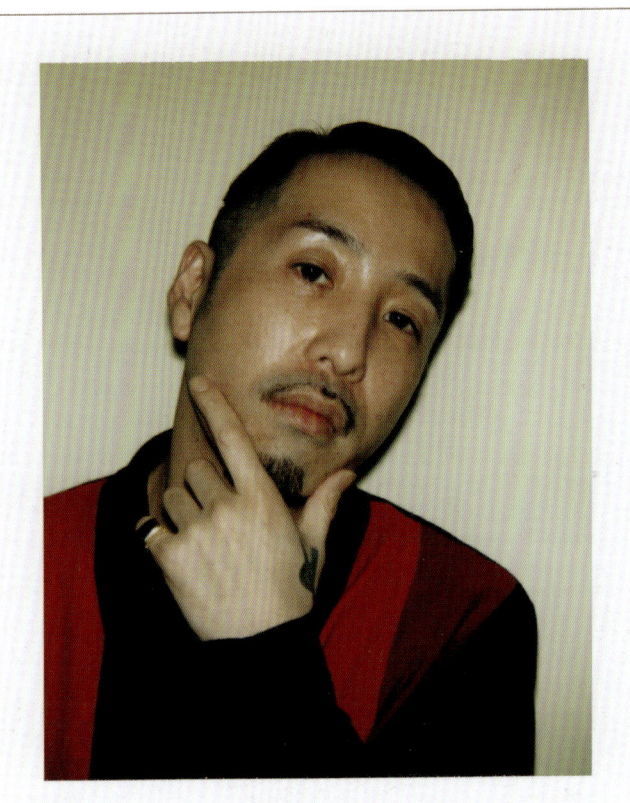

RYUZO

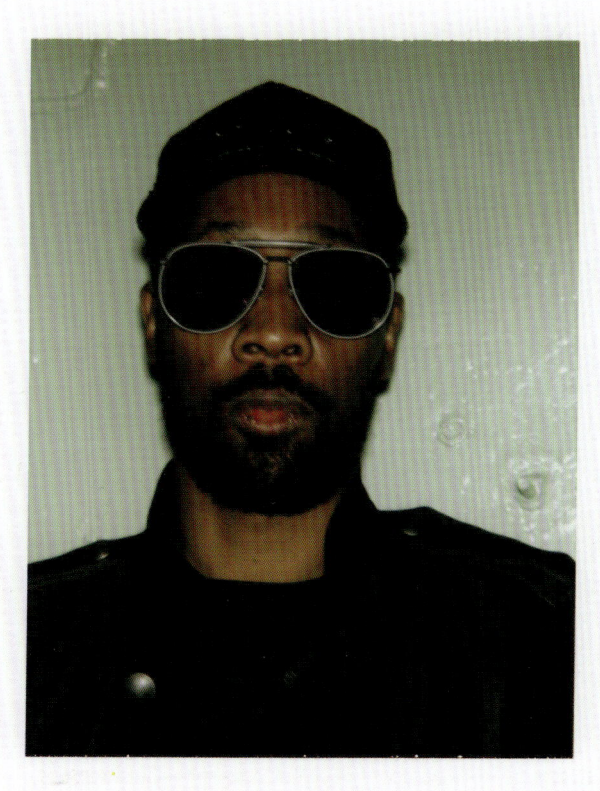

RZA

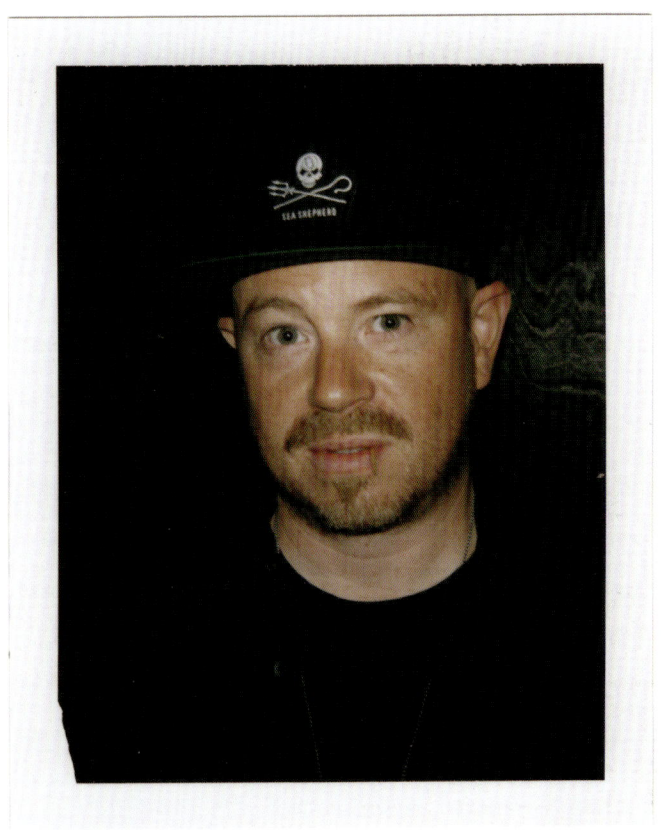

CRAIG WETHERBY

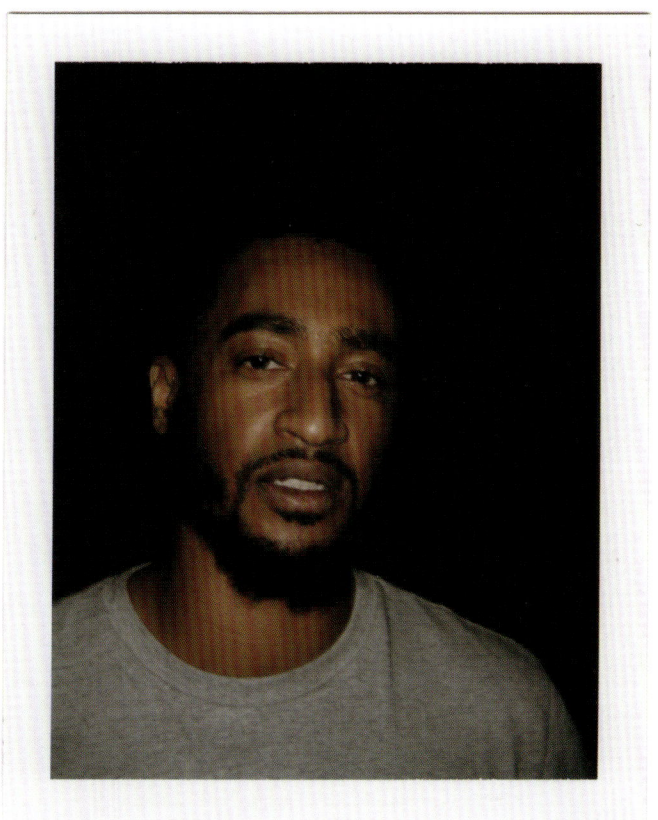

DJ RICK GEEZ

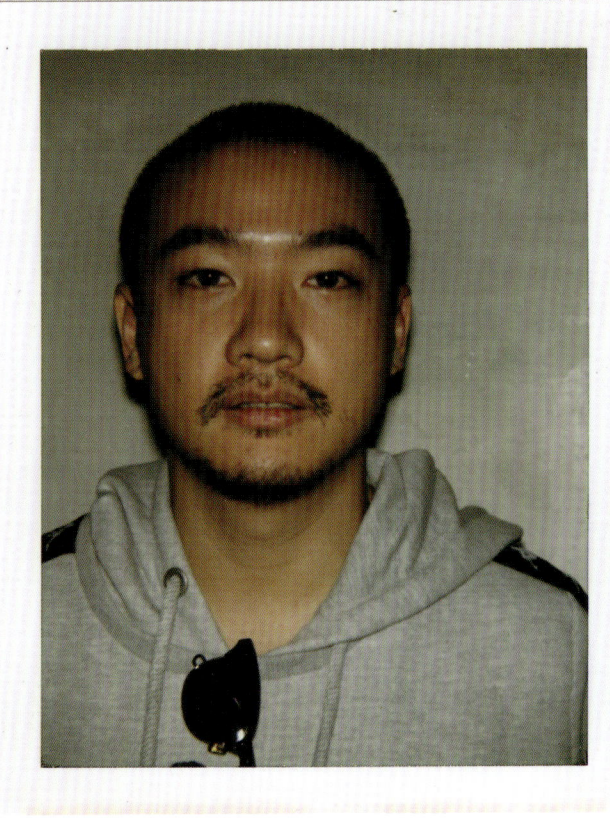

BAROM "TAY" BHICHARNCHITR

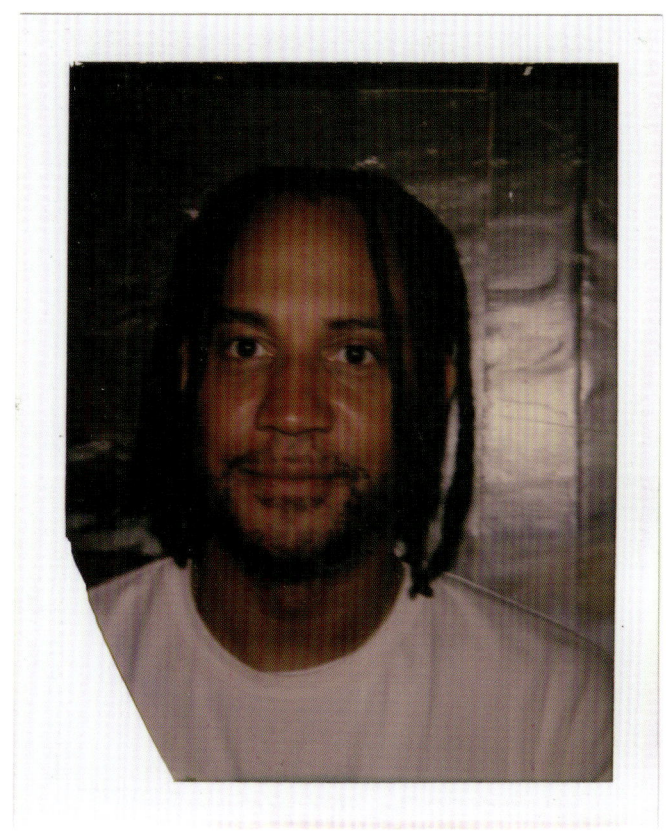

JUST C

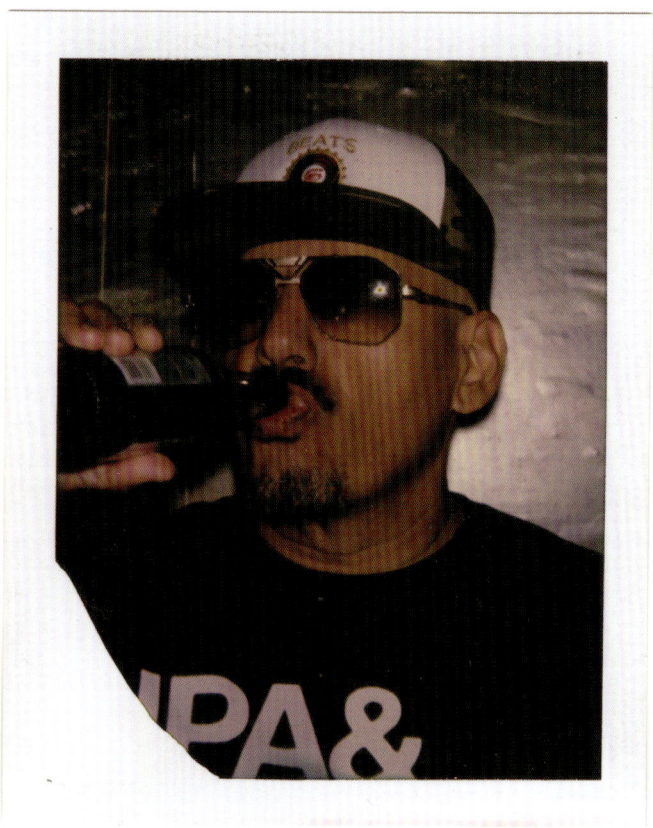

PSYCHO LES

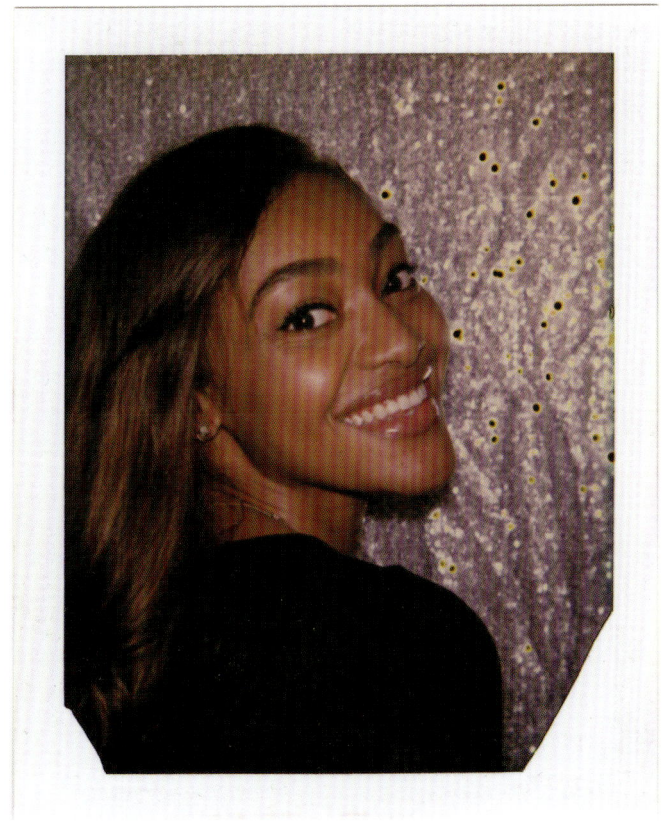

GABRIELLE DJENNÉ

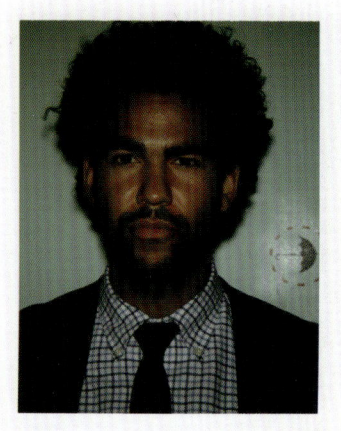

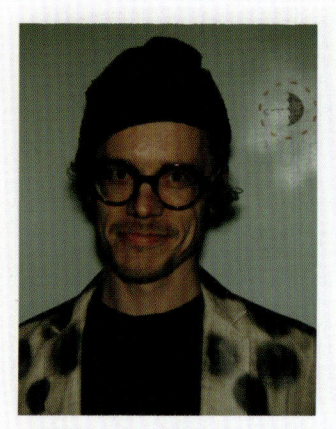

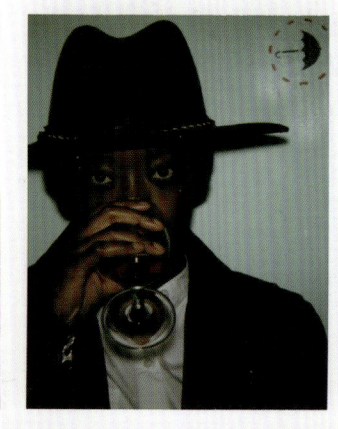

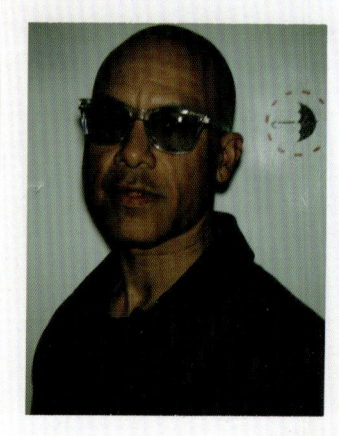

MAX MARKHAM

MARSHALL LaCOUNT

NINA CHANEL ABNEY

NOBLE

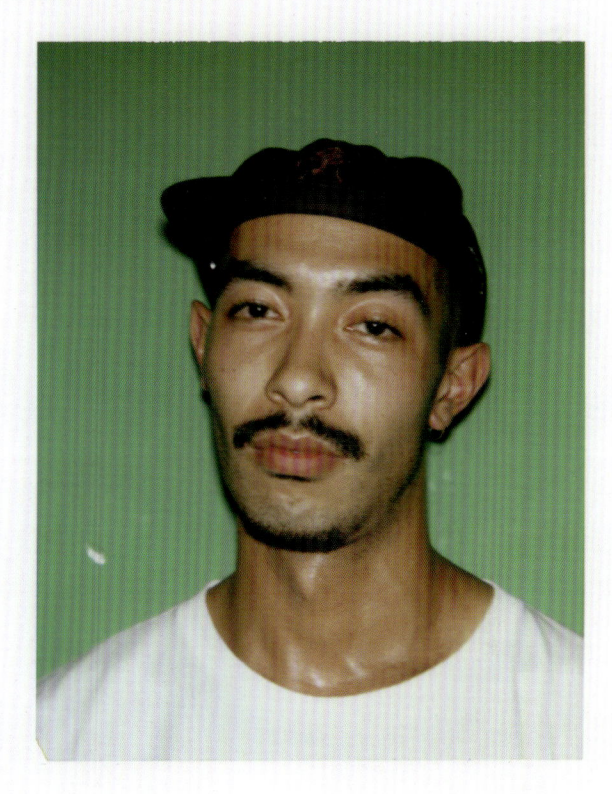

LONO BRAZIL III

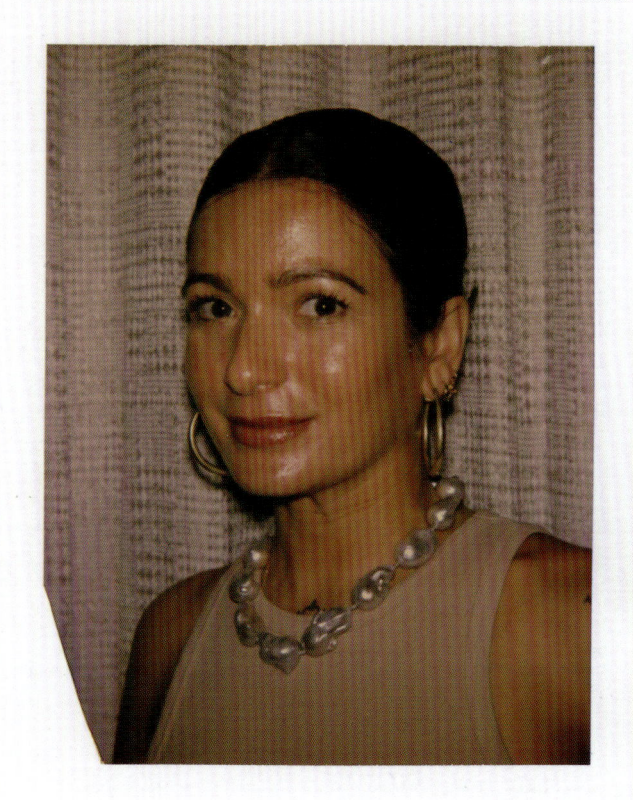

CORALIE BLAMO ROSE

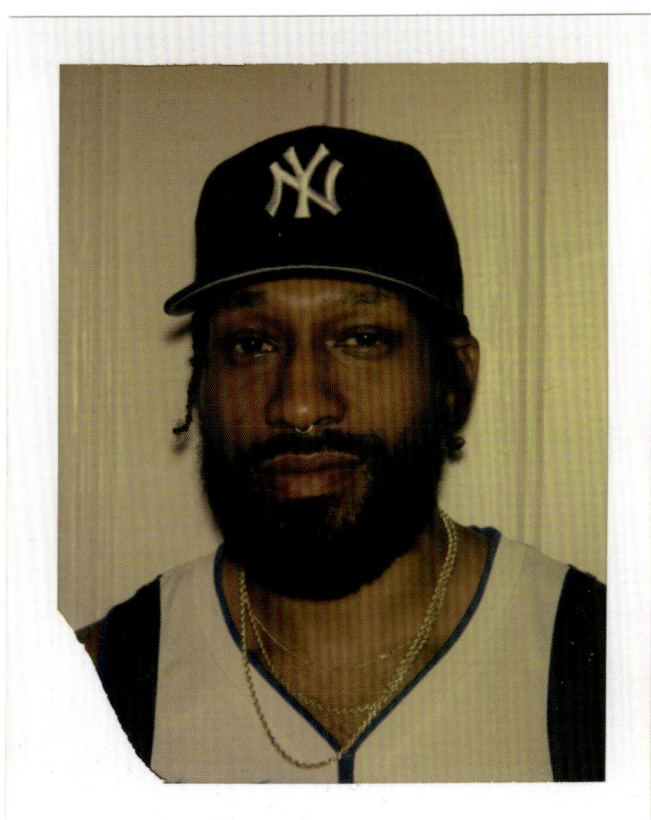

ISSAC CAMPBELL AKA MORESOUPPLEASE

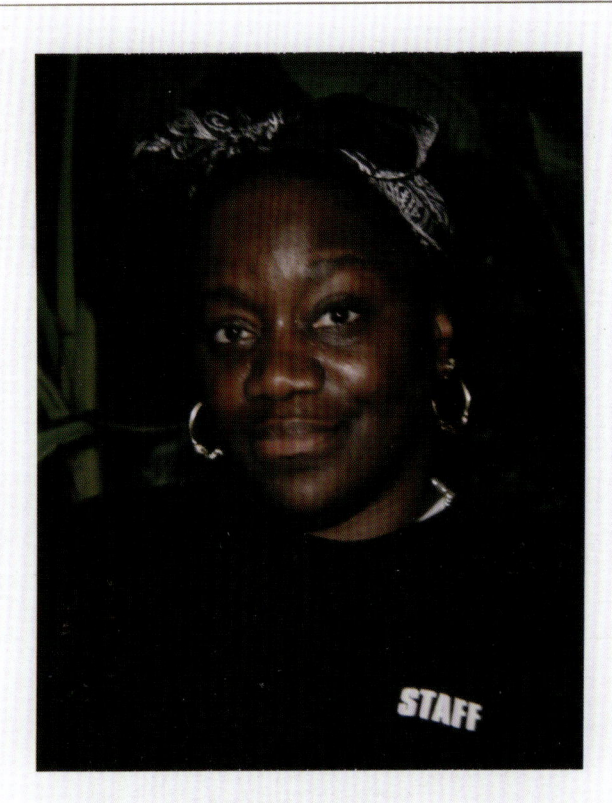

SHANIQWA JARVIS

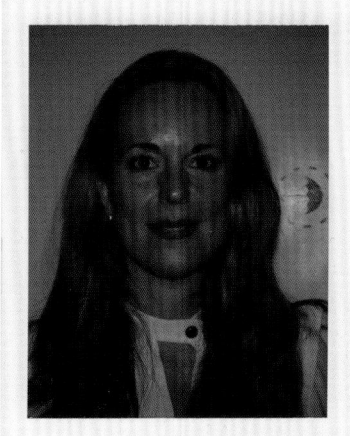
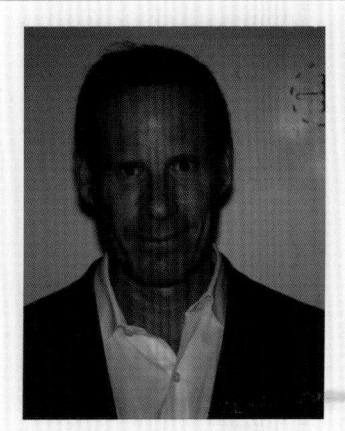
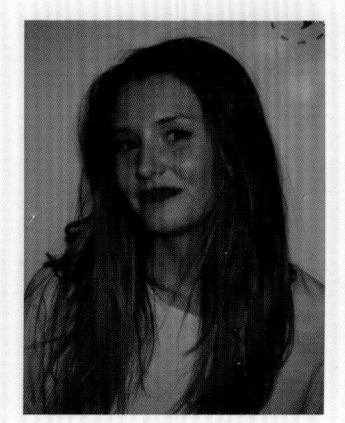
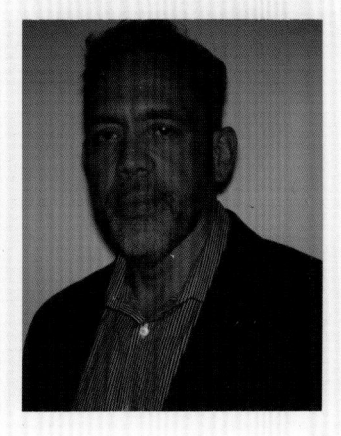

MEGAN WATSON-DONALD   MIKE WEHRMAN

PAIGE SCHAEFER   MARK IRIZARRY

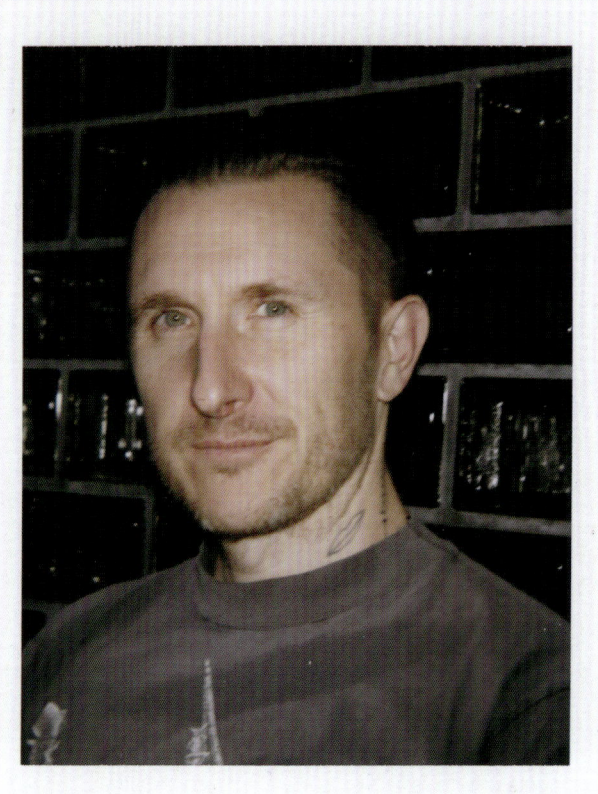

SCOTT CAMPBELL

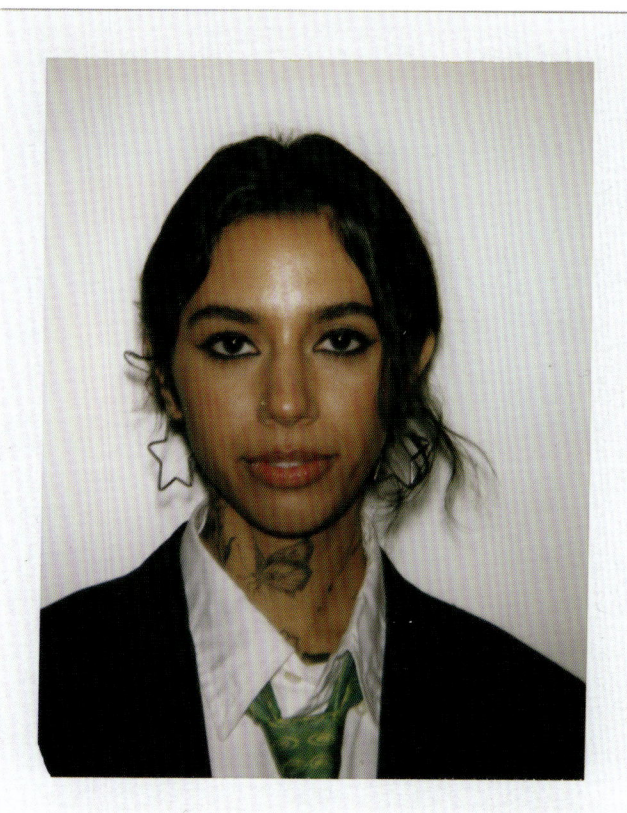

NATI

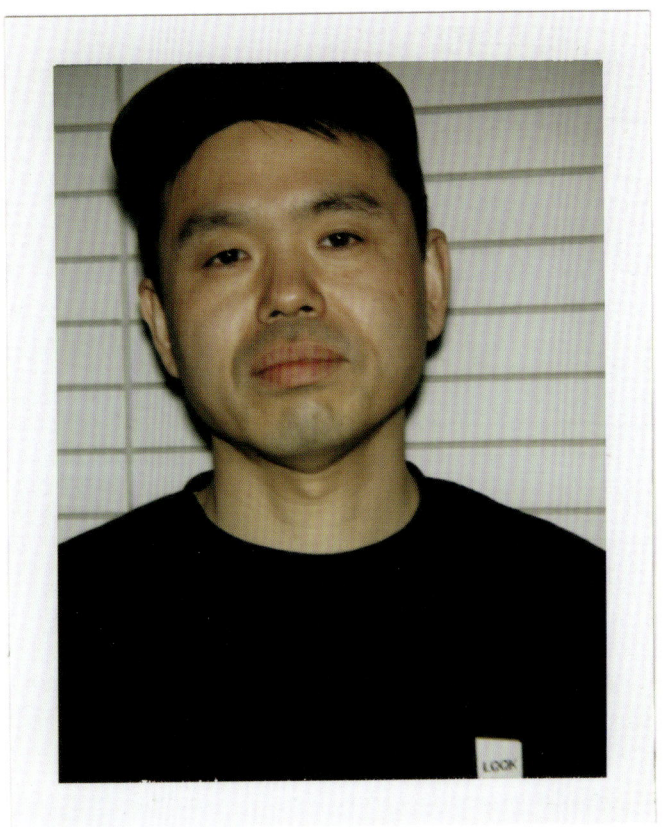

SATO

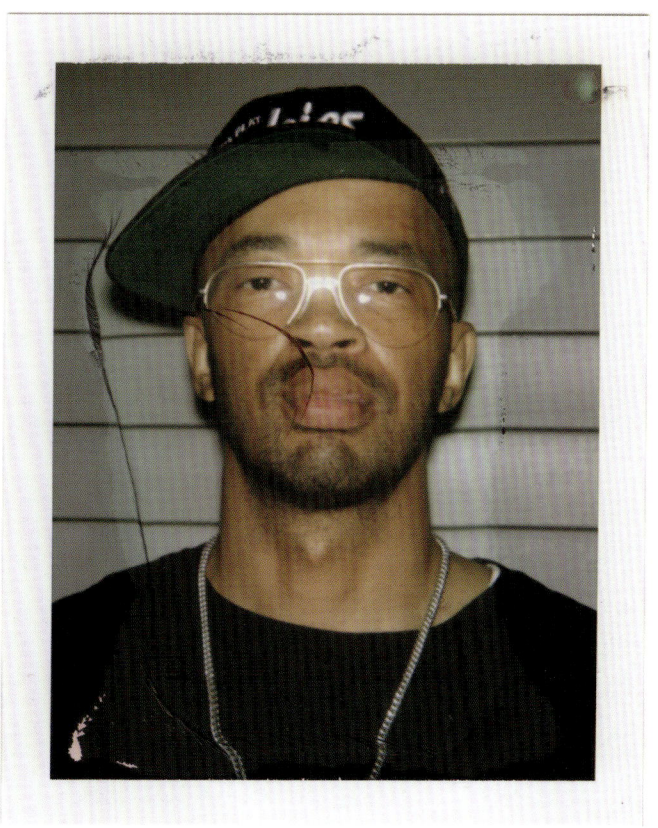

RICH MEDINA

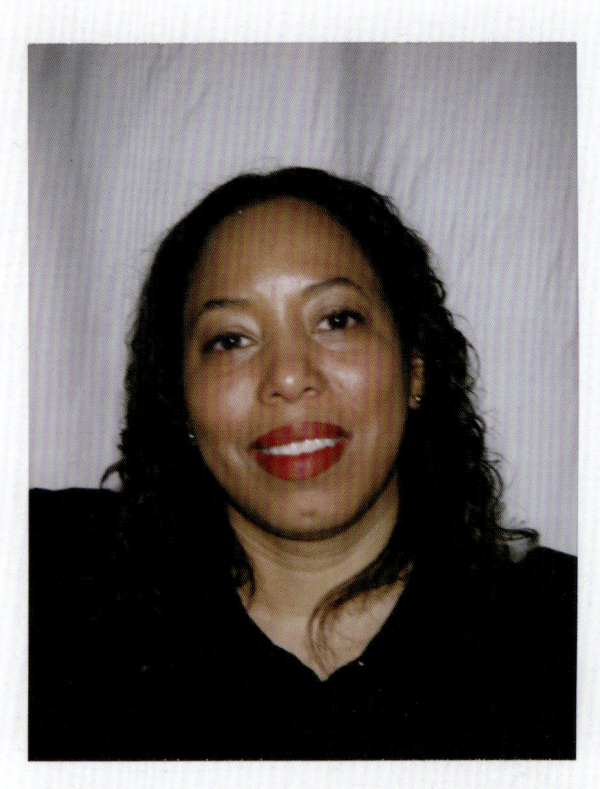

LENISE LOGAN

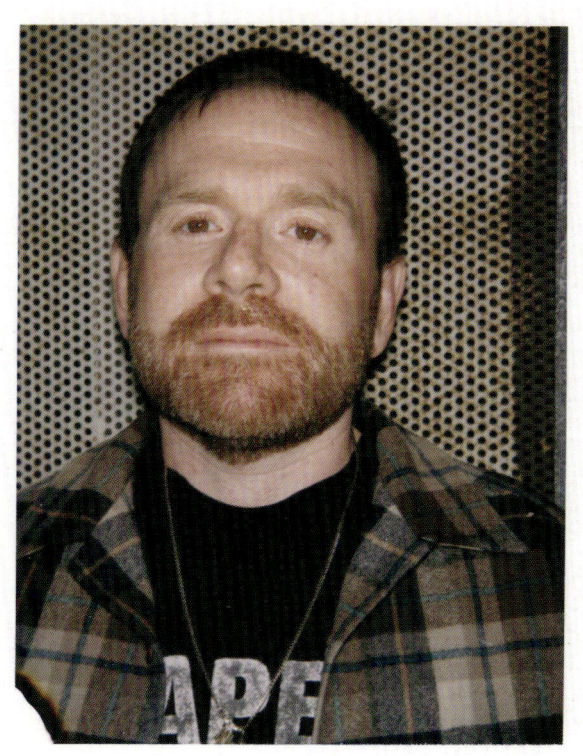

SPICY MIKE

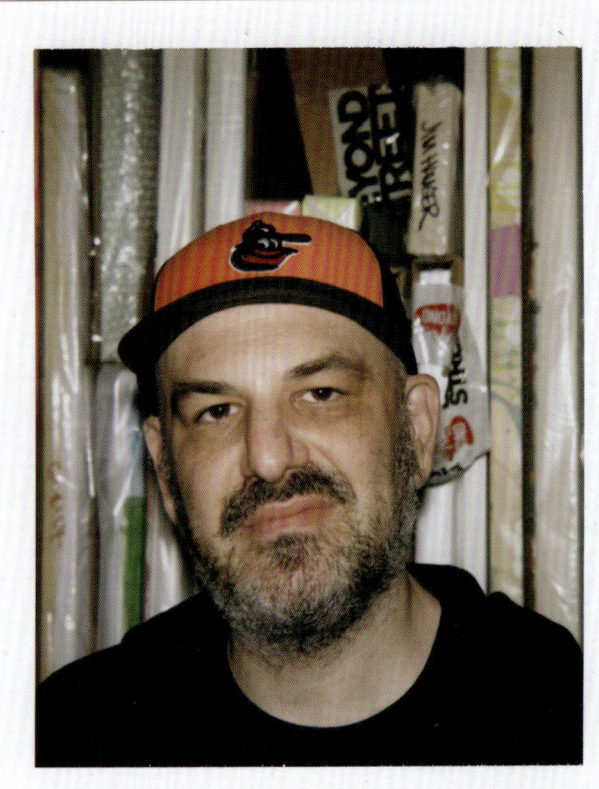

ROGER GASTMAN

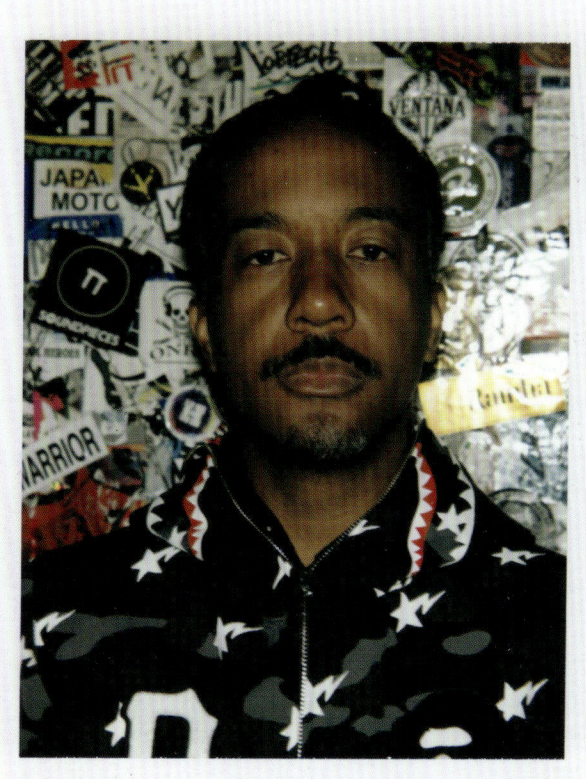

APEXER

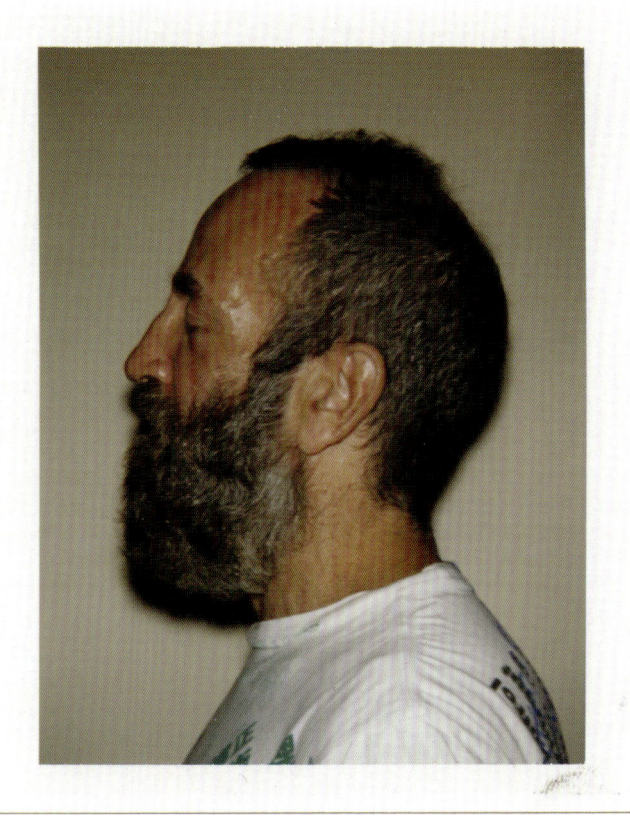

KENNY SCHARF

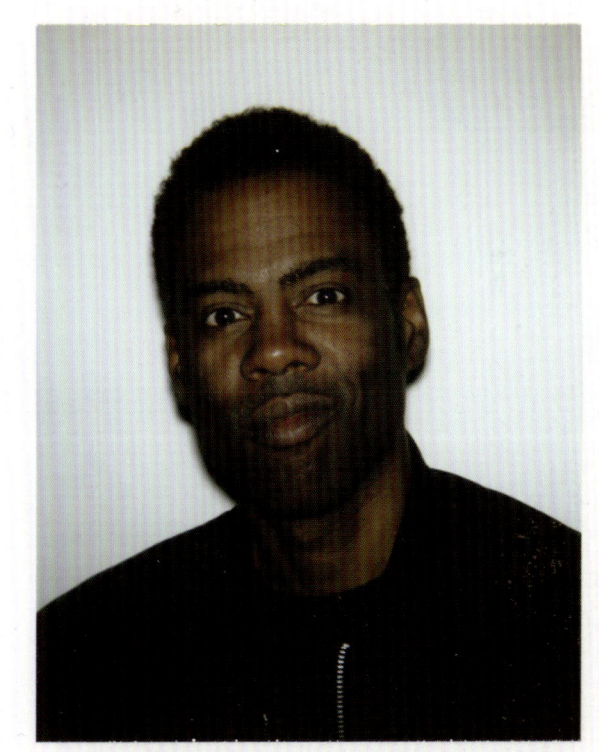

CHRIS ROCK

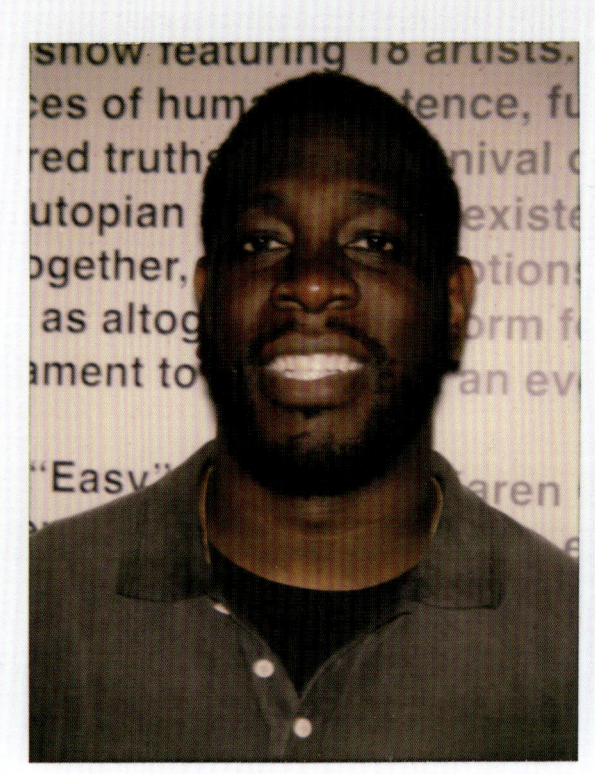

EASY OTABOR

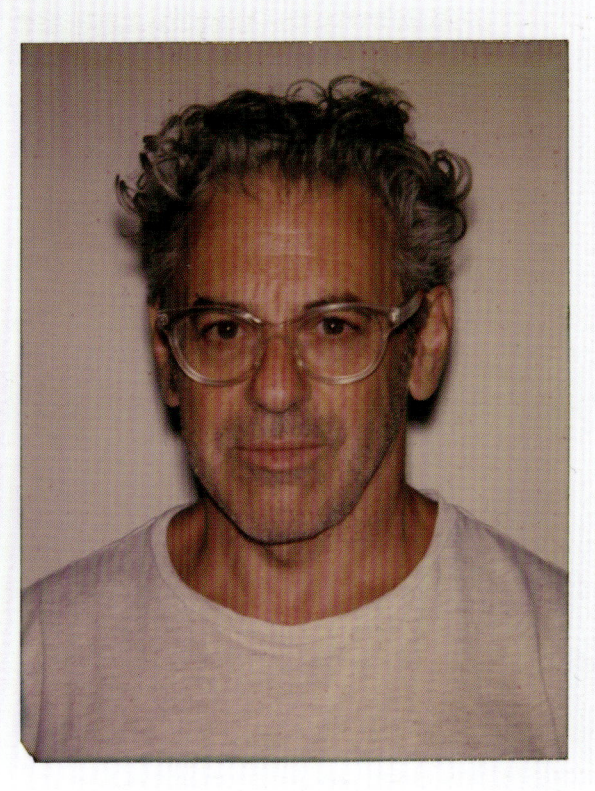

TOM SACHS

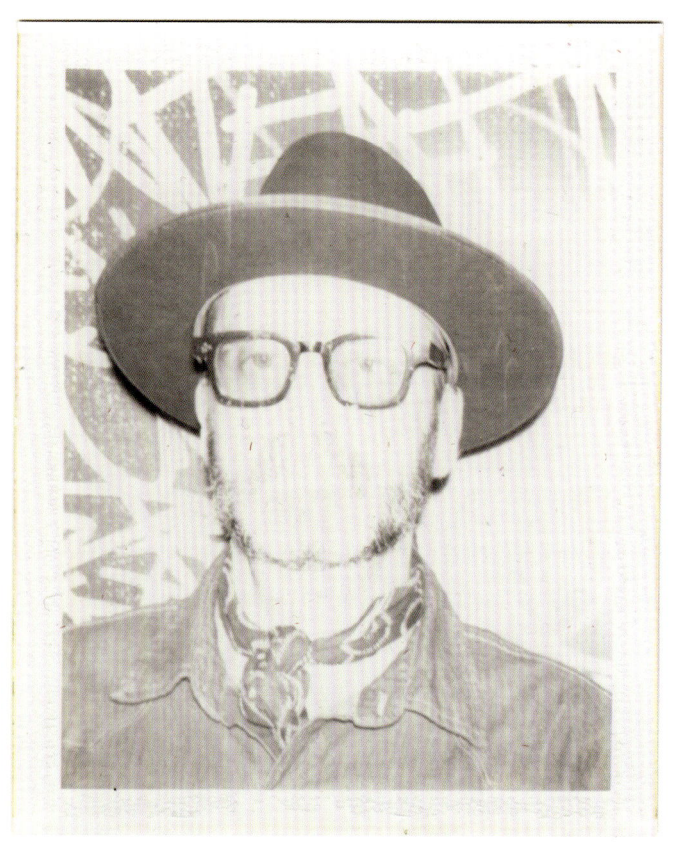

KAVES

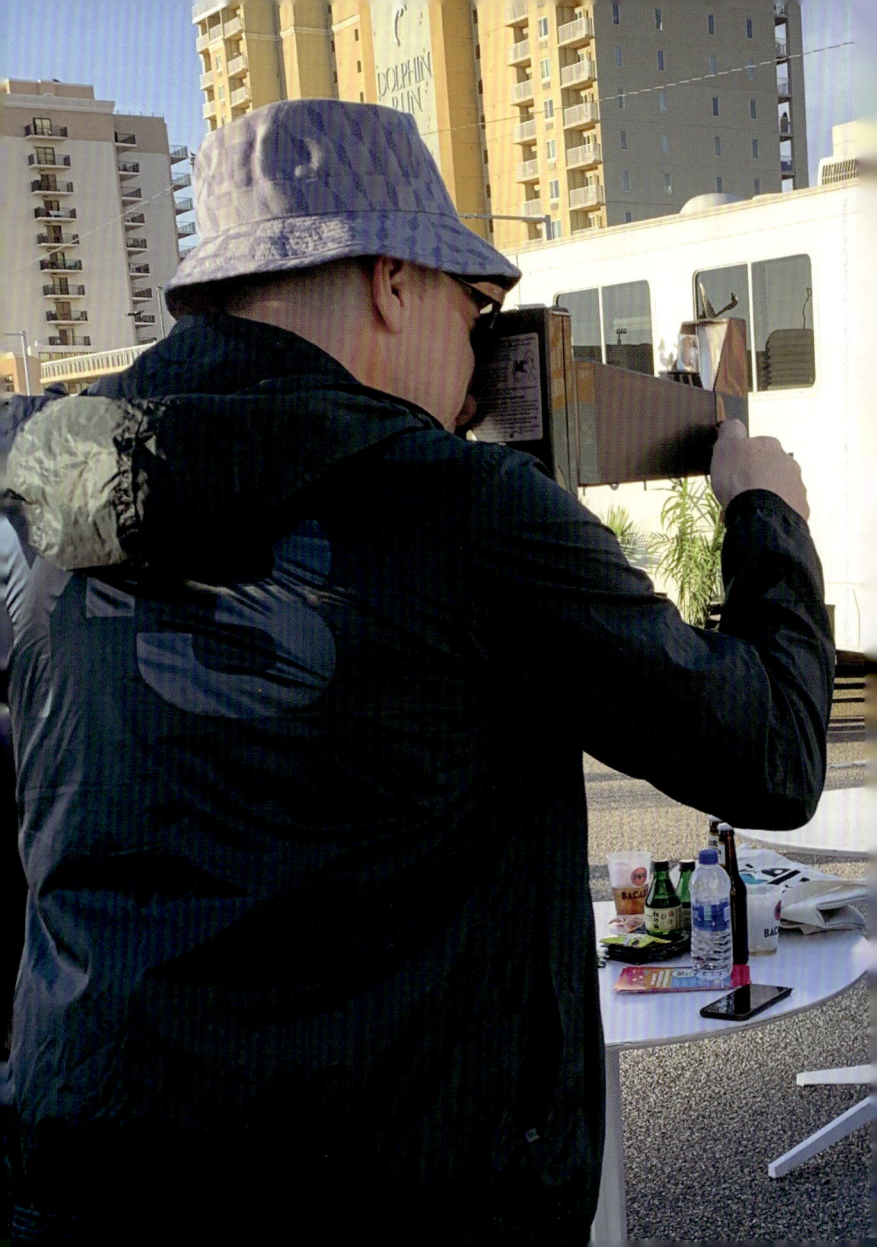

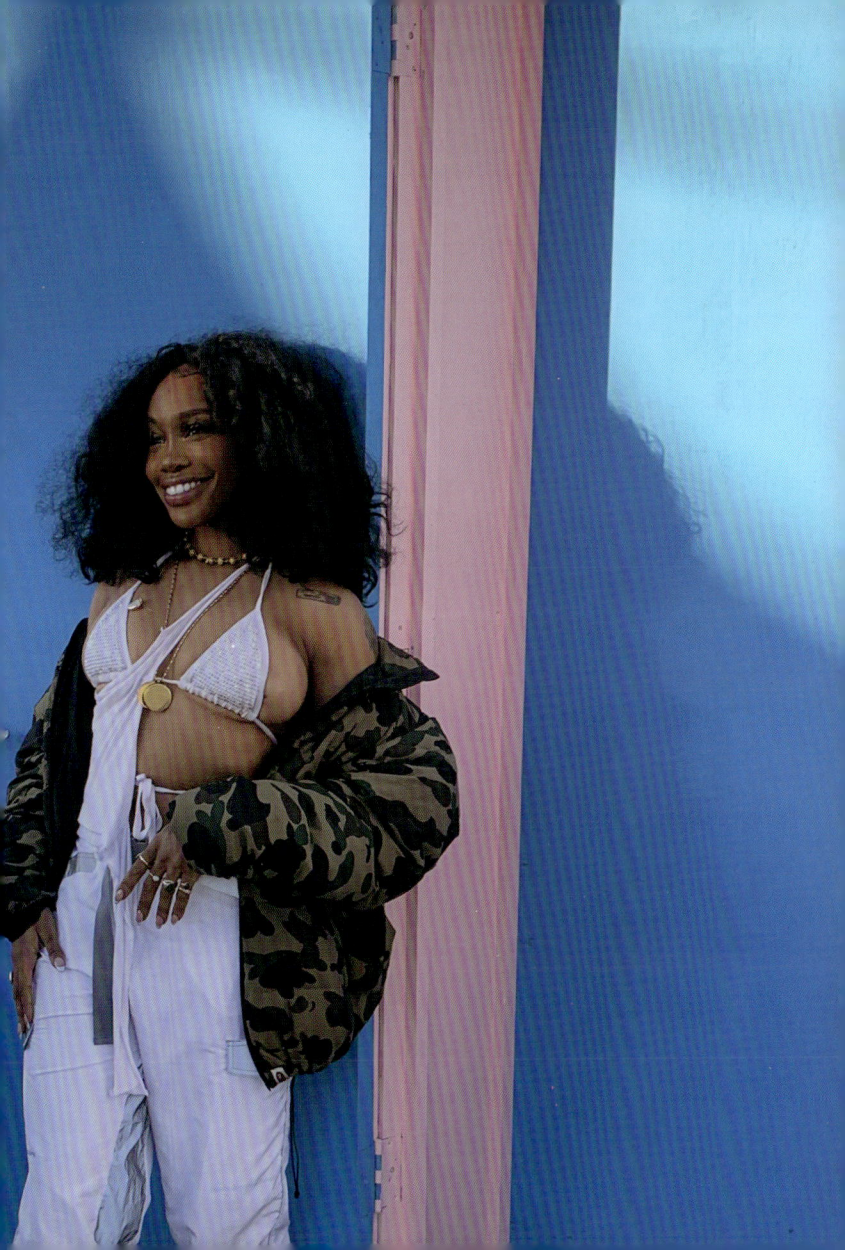

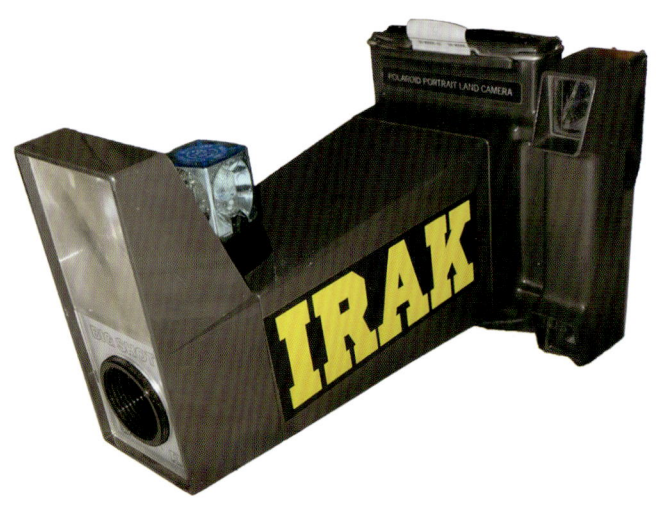

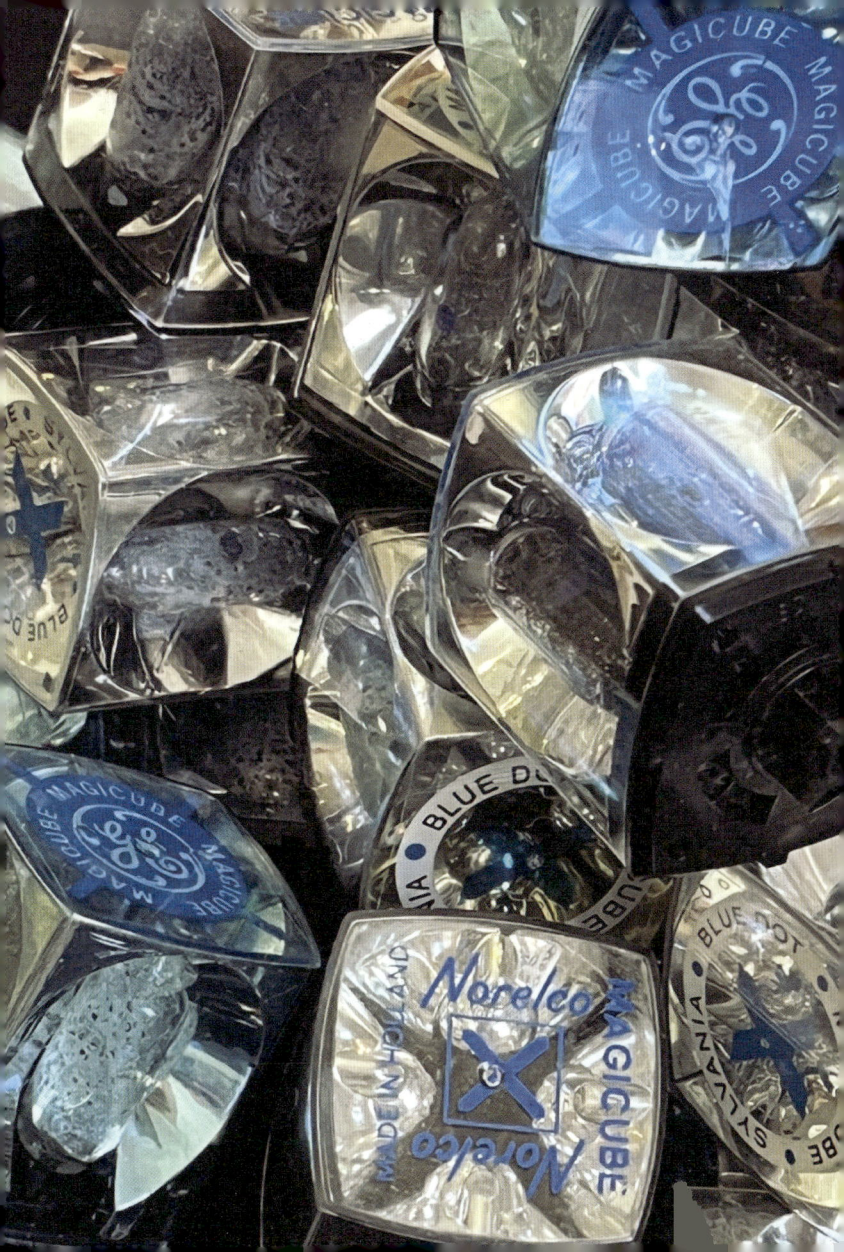